# Dreams of Adventure,

# Deeds of Empire

# DREAMS OF ADVENTURE, DEEDS OF EMPIRE

## MARTIN GREEN

*Basic Books, Inc., Publishers*

NEW YORK

FERNALD LIBRARY
COLBY-SAWYER COLLEGE
NEW LONDON, N. H. 03257

PN
3448
A3
G7

4/80 10.70

78731

Library of Congress Cataloging in Publication Data

Green, Martin Burgess, 1927–
  Dreams of adventure, deeds of empire.

  Bibliography:  p. 405
  Includes index.
    1.  Adventure stories—History and criticism.
2.  Imperialism in literature.  3.  Literature and
society—Great Britain.  4.  Great Britain—Intellectual
life.  I.  Title.
PN3448.A3G7      823'.087      78–73766
ISBN 0–465–01718–5

Copyright © 1979 by Martin Green
Printed in the United States of America
DESIGNED BY VINCENT TORRE
10 9 8 7 6 5 4 3 2 1

FOR

*Linda Bamber, Patsy Vigderman, Rich Moran,*
*and other friends I first met*
*as graduate students at Tufts*

# Contents

# Contents

Contents

# *Prefatory Notes*

(1) Perhaps some readers, standing on the steps of a fairly massive structure, may be encouraged by being given a floor plan. The first two chapters of this book are preparatory, Chapter I in matters of history, Chapter II in matters of literature. They define the concepts of the argument to follow, and describe usefully similar cases. Adventure, it is argued, is the energizing myth of empire; and empire is to be found everywhere in the modern world, disguised as development or improvement. The third and fourth chapters discuss two authors, perhaps the most important in the history of the adventure novel in English. Each one's work is characterized, and also the relation between the two in matters of form—the transformation undergone by Defoe's motifs when taken over by Scott. The third pair of chapters moves the discussion out away from England, to first America and then Russia. We see how the American and the Russian adventure novels, which derive from *those* cultural matrices, are like and unlike the English version. Chapter VII returns the reader to nineteenth-century England, but to the popular and the children's literature of the time, to study cultural images related to adventure. The next three chapters discuss individual authors again. One is English, one American, and one Polish, so they follow an already established pattern. (A master pattern is of course chronological; each writer is simply related to those before and after him in the nearly three hundred years from Defoe's birth to Kipling's death.) And Chapter XI presents contemporary cultural images.

(2) This book is about a big subject; not only the adventure novels of nearly three hundred years, but the imperialist history of that time (in more than one country) and moreover the relation between the two. But I have addressed my argument, as always, to the general reader. (I keep hoping he exists, or can be conjured into existence by the sound of a voice.) That means that my argument is

simplified; I have cut out many cases, qualifications, and general considerations, in order to make a readable book. But if the general reader does exist, I know he won't open his mouth—won't make any response to my argument. It is the specialists who will be scrutinizing and judging me. So I have relegated a lot of the material I cut to the back of the book, as notes. These are sizable paragraphs, in some cases miniature essays. The Defoe, Scott, and Kipling chapters, in particular, have each a kind of appendix on other books by that author—those three being the peaks in the mountain chain of adventure. In the main text I discuss only one or two books by each of them, so it behooved me to show that I knew some others.

(3) This is the second of three volumes of a series to be called *The Lust for Power*. In the first I talk about Gandhi and Tolstoy. In this one I try to apply their teachings to literature and history. I try to find something to do, within my own field of activity, which will not betray the idea, the insight into the human situation, they entrusted to us. So this is a study of imperialism, shaped to satisfy the criteria of scholarly objectivity and free speculation, but also shaped to suit a practical purpose, to fit a social situation which I see as a moral and spiritual crisis. Its immediate reference is to England, but the argument applies to all the Western countries.

When I went to school, a striking feature of maps was still the large areas colored red; geography and history were taught in implicit relation to England's imperial career. The world was ours, so it seemed. In reality, it wasn't, any longer; but the walls of the schoolroom screened out a lot of news. Correspondingly, in ways that were only half-conscious, I learned that a margin of privilege surrounded England, a reserve on which I personally could draw at any moment I chose to leave the island. For instance, other nations needed to learn English, and would pay me for what I had got free. That map and that margin are no longer there, and the Empire manifests itself now in somewhat reverse manner. Instead of being a frontier, a free space outside England, waiting for use, it has moved inside, in the form of immigrants, who are instead an impediment on our freedom of movement. Within the island we feel cramped, limited, our margins shrunk; and abroad we wear only the tattered insignia of our former privileges. (The English accent begins to have a tawdry sound, like tattered lace, now that American is standard.)

We have lost our power; that's what it feels like to us; but in fact, we have still far more than other people. For us, as for all the nations of the West, the big question of the day involves not recouping but renouncing. Will we find a way to give up what we have taken, over the last three hundred years; to give back to the others what we took from them? We took a lion's share, and developed a lion's nature, and unless we can renounce both, we shall ruin ourselves and the world. For instance the per capita rate at which the United States consumes energy is two hundred and fifty times the per capita rate of Nigeria, and England's rate is half America's; the absolute figure for the U.S. is twice the combined total for Africa, the rest of the Americas, and Asia apart from Japan; and the United States and the USSR together account for 60 percent of the $3 billion a year that the world wastes on weapons. Can we renounce our nature as predators? As a speculative question, that is nugatory. As a practical problem, and for students of the humanities, it involves a paradox. For the way to do it is to move into and through that nature, toward and beyond our imperialist fathers, understanding what they did and what they thought they were doing, their dreams of adventure and deeds of empire. The more obvious strategy, to turn one's back on the problem and push away from imperialism, has been tried—as we shall see. Now is the time for a new effort. At least in England, where the nerve of conquest has so suddenly gone slack, it might be possible to influence action through reflection. But only if we imagine the power we once had generously, imagine not only how we lost it but how we won it, without resentment.

The London of today is radically different from the one I grew up in—and much more different from my father's London. I was taught that Trafalgar Square was the Hub of the Empire, and I saw it as such —even if it was the revolving neon ads which really made me think of a wheel. Now I see an imperial city in decay, a Rome peacefully barbarized, unprotestingly ravished and barely aware of her fall. It is a city organized to service foreigners richer than ourselves, a tourists' city, culturally a colonial city. Prominent buildings are sign-posted in Arabic; prominent companies are run by Americans; and our houses are too big for their occupants—modern lives clutter and clatter loosely inside buildings that fitted their forebears snugly. And so it is across the country; the cities are full of ghettos, and are troubled by clashes of race instead of class; imperialism has come home to roost, the anthropoemia has reversed itself. We are often told that the English are glad to be relieved of their size, and the responsibilities and privileges that went with it; and undeniably they have been liberated from manifold tensions, social, sexual, political; they feel free, supple, simple, light. But when they think about large issues, they feel diminished.

Such a situation calls for a radical change in culture, if we are to escape resentment, deep down. It calls indeed for many changes, but the one I am thinking of is in our high culture, our system of value-bearing ideas, and art objects as things to study. There too we need to start again, to go in new directions. In literature, for instance, it would be well to concentrate on new books, which we can come to freshly, and to study them in new ways. And it seems to me that these should be the adventure novels I have been discussing. These are the books that explain how England came to acquire an empire, and so how our immigrant population comes to be English. More exactly, these books ask for a critical commentary which leads into that explanation. In themselves, they are romances, so have some character of personal fantasy, some of social myth; they explain how empire building felt to the men who set out to explore and exploit and acquire, and to their friends and relations at home. But there are other sources—and the classrooms of England now supply them—to tell us how it felt to the native populations they adventured among.

The teaching situation now seems to me very like that which prevailed at the end of the last century and the beginning of this, especially in adult education, when people studying literature found in the great eighteenth- and nineteenth-century novels moral discriminations and literary achievements that invited explanation in terms of the class system and the Industrial Revolution. Those novels told the story of the sisters and their courtship. But critics and scholars who were concerned about the political and social condition of the country found a way to give them a commentary which led naturally into political truths, without ceasing to be literary criticism. Those were the great days of the Workers Educational Association classes, where the classics of English literature were set before the working-class reader, and both books and readers were tested and extended, each by the challenge of the other. To those teachers and critics, I think, the working-class readers felt like the true People of England, disinherited of the treasures of their own culture, defrauded by an upper class—sometimes called Bloomsbury—which trivialized those treasures as it appropriated them. Nowadays, I think the innocent and disinherited readers are not working class but immigrant. *They* are the People of England; theirs are the hands we see reaching up in the public libraries for the big volumes so strange to them, so familiar to us.

It was the Great Tradition novels which could be explained in terms of class conflict and industrialization. It is the adventure novels which could be explained in terms of empire; and which could, in the explanation, bring together native population and immigrants, if they were properly studied. That would not mean studied with an overbearing condemnation of the spirit of adventure—the books were written to be enjoyed, and that pleasantness is one of their strengths in the educational situation—but the readers should identify with the adventurer with a complementary sense of how he looked to his adversaries and subordinates—how Crusoe looked to Friday. It would not be easy, but it should be possible, to create the sort of stasis of interest within which all the people in the English classroom, however various their heritages and their politics, could come to understand each other and themselves better. And if that understanding cuts sharp enough, deep enough, out of it might grow a new mood, ready for seriousness, ready even for renunciation.

*Dreams of Adventure,*

*Deeds of Empire*

# I

# Modern Empire, Caste, and Adventure

MY argument will be that the adventure tales that formed the light reading of Englishmen for two hundred years and more after *Robinson Crusoe* were, in fact, the energizing myth of English imperialism. They were, collectively, the story England told itself as it went to sleep at night; and, in the form of its dreams, they charged England's will with the energy to go out into the world and explore, conquer, and rule.

I shall describe some of the best known of those tales, in terms of both their forms and their themes, and trace the tradition of their development which connects them to each other across the decades. I shall discuss their authors, defining their place in literary history, and the relation of each to the "serious" writing of his times. (What I mean by serious will emerge; the books I discuss are to be taken seriously, and according to literary criteria of seriousness, but the criteria are unconventional.) And I shall put the tales into the appropriate imaginative contexts, from the history of imperialism; especially important being the historical heroes of empire, who were both like and unlike the heroes of adventure fiction.

By empire I mean primarily a country possessing colonies; but

3

the word is also appropriate to some other political systems, in which one group is dominant over others whom it regards as alien and inferior. And in such systems—which are to be found in all large states—the arts, science, and ideas, become charged with the same energies as the politics, and can be called in some sense imperial. This is true even of that serious literature which, implicitly if not explicitly, resisted the cult of empire, and is all the truer of the adventure tale.

To go back to the primary meaning, empire is surely the most exciting kind of politics, and in morally noble as wéll as merely appetitive senses of the word exciting. As J. A. Froude said in *Oceana* (p. 355), "A man who is a citizen of an imperial power expands to the scope and fullness of the larger organism. . . . His thoughts are wider, his interests less selfish, his ambition ampler and nobler. . . ." Thus empires are analogous to large spiritual institutions, like churches or religious orders. Froude continues, "Individual Jesuits are no more than other mortals. The Jesuits as a society are not mortal at all and rule the Catholic world." But except from an ecclesiastical point of view, even the Roman Catholic Church is only an analogy. The great type, the archetype, is empire, and the great example of this excitement, at least in English history, is to be associated with the Imperialism of the end of the nineteenth century—of which Froude's *Oceana* was one of the trumpetings, and Kipling's stories the great fictional expression.

This excitement is often said to begin with Disraeli's speech of 1872, in which he asked England, "Will you be a great country, an Imperial country, a country where your sons, when they rise, rise to permanent positions, and obtain not merely the esteem of their countrymen but the respect of the world?" But Disraeli was merely introducing into the language of official politics what had been gathering force for centuries, as an idea and even more as a feeling. From 1688 on England had been expanding, and the pride of Englishness had been swelling, particularly with reference to the country's overseas possessions. This had been noted even by non-Englishmen, like Emerson. "In the island they never let out all the length of the reins, there is no Berserkir rage, no abandonment or ecstasy of will or intellect . . . [But they have been] pouring out now for two hundred years from the British islands

. . . carrying the Saxon seed . . . to the conquest of the globe."*

This profound excitement (felt not just by Englishmen or Americans about England, but by other Europeans about their empires, in their degree) has been a major motive force in world history for the last four hundred years. It has found innumerable forms of expression, in politics, in economics, in literature, in philosophy, in science and technology; forms of expression that were also the food of further pride and the tools of further conquest. Indeed, if we take empire to refer generally to Europe's power over the rest of the world, we will find it difficult to name any form of European life above the folk level that was not influenced to some degree.

Even the expressions of passionate dissent and organized resistance to that excitement partook of it. Only the work of Tolstoy and Gandhi, and the pacifist-anarchist traditions of thought and action which they subsumed, seem to me really opposite in tendency, and really powerful. But Tolstoy and Gandhi belong to another book. In this one I want to study the way this excitement showed itself and reinforced itself in one literary genre, the adventure tale; and the way that genre related to serious literature, and to the larger culture.

What date shall we take as a starting point? Some of the things we group together under the title of "the British Empire" were to be found in the England of Elizabeth I; most notably, the feeling of excitement just discussed, and the expression of that feeling in literature; Shakespeare can reasonably be called a literary spokesman for that imperialism. Nevertheless, historians tell us that there are reasons for dating the British empire's rise at the end of the seventeenth century, in fact at the Union of England with Scotland, in 1707; which is to say, at the very historical moment when the adventure tale began to be written, since *Robinson Crusoe* appeared in 1719. Defoe was one of the English government's agents in negotiating that union. And Defoe, rather than Shakespeare, is my candidate for the prototype of literary imperialism.[1]

In his history of the word "empire," Richard Koebner points out that Henry VIII officially claimed to wear "an imperial crown," but that in uses of that kind "imperial" was, as it were, a qualitative adjective. It referred to the king's "imperium," his abstract power,

*English Traits*, Boston, 1856.

5

not to the concrete territory he possessed. And territorially it was felt improper to use the term for anything less than the whole British Isles. England had conquered Wales in the Middle Ages, and Ireland in Elizabethan and Cromwellian times; but it could not call itself imperial until it ruled Scotland also. James I, being king of England and of Scotland, spoke of his imperial monarchy, but even this use was felt to be rhetorical rather than literal, because the two kingdoms were separate, even though James was king of both. There had to be an administrative union of the two before Englishmen, or Britons, could speak of Britannia, and His Britannic Majesty. Cromwell much desired that Union, William III worked for it, it was achieved under Anne—and one of her ministers' main agents in Edinburgh was Daniel Defoe.

Most of us don't nowadays think that the United Kingdom was or is an empire; though Scots and Welsh nationalists do, and the rise of their nationalism is the mark of an epoch ending. What we nowadays think of as the empire seemed then rather a string of trading stations and plantations; but they too of course caused a growing excitement of possession in Englishmen, an excitement which had one of its climaxes at roughly the same time, about 1700. John Bowle, in *The Imperial Achievement*, says that the empire's period of reconnaissance and early settlement lasted from 1500 to 1650, ending with the Navigation Acts of Cromwell's government in 1650–1651 and in 1657. By these acts, Cromwell's government won for English shipping the monopoly of the Atlantic trade, and ordered other countries' ships to bring to English ports only the produce of their home countries. England also seized Jamaica, and launched the Western Design against Spain in the Caribbean. The age of empire proper began. And Koebner says that it was around 1688 that England acquired, one by one, the attributes of a model kingdom, according to the ideas of the modern world system; its liberties, its navy, its power in Europe, and finally, its Union.

And in those years the other countries in that system, like France, acknowledged the same criteria for a model kingdom, and so admired and envied England. Over the next fifty years, many famous symbols of imperialism (or mercantile patriotism) were gradually introduced into English culture. (And earlier symbols, like Parliament itself, took on their modern meaning.) In 1717, the mint introduced the golden guinea into the coinage. (Both "gold" and "guinea" are terms charged with imperialist meaning, as we shall see.) In 1736 came Thomson's ode to "Liberty," and in 1740 his masque "Alfred," which culminated in the song "Rule Britannia." (A giant figure of Britannia stood on the roof of the East India Company building in the City.) In 1745 "God Save the King" was popularized. And there was Young's ode, "The Merchant," Lillo's play, *The London Merchant,* and Glover's epic, *London: The Progress of Commerce.*

From 1688 on, therefore, English culture spoke in a triumphal mood, with which we are all familiar, which persisted throughout the eighteenth and nineteenth centuries, and into this one, and which was clearly related to a complacency about England's possessing an empire. And no one has ever doubted that Defoe (born in 1660) was a very representative spokesman for that mood, so to connect him with imperialism will occasion no surprise. But I want to claim, beyond the general connection, that *Robinson Crusoe* is the myth of that imperialism in specific ways, which throw light in both directions, both on empire and on the novels. That novel's silence about the actual empire of Defoe's day, for instance, illustrates certain complexities within the English idea of possessing an empire.[2]

First of all, it must be established that their empire did not always call itself empire. In fact, even in the late nineteenth century, the overt imperialism of Disraeli and Froude had to struggle for some time against the moral and political habit of ignoring the colonies, a deliberate habit of serious England. And in the historical case I will be first considering, England in the early eighteenth century, imperialism usually called itself patriotism or protestantism or freedom of trade, and used the term empire for its enemies, whether Spain or Louis XIV; just as, later, England saw Napoleon, the Tsar, and the Kaiser, as emperors greedy to swallow their peaceful little community of traders. What we now see to have been the English Empire—what was occasionally admitted to be that then, but humorously, or sentimentally, or poetically—was more seriously thought to be England's part in the modern world system.

That is the phrase that a modern historian, Immanuel Wallerstein, has found for the phenomenon, and since he sees it not too differently from the way seventeenth- and eighteenth-century Englishmen felt it, we must not dismiss their self-image too quickly. Let us recapitulate Wallerstein's theory, which he has worked out with reference to the fifteenth and sixteenth centuries, 1450–1650, when the system first developed.

## The Modern World System

Charles V, coming to the joint throne of Spain and the Holy Roman Empire in 1519, ruled a territory comparable in extent with that of his contemporaries, Suleiman the Magnificent and Ivan the Terrible. And *his* territory consisted of the heartland of all Europe, plus the vague enormousness of the New World. Thus it seemed that a world age of empires was beginning, and Vienna and Madrid were charged with the excitement of conscious imperialism. But in 1556 Charles abdicated from his joint throne, and the Habsburg possessions split into two halves, never to be reunited. The idea of empire was discredited.

There followed eighty years of fighting in the Netherlands, which rebelled against Spanish rule. This led to the ruin of the great Habsburg port, Antwerp, the flight of Flemish capitalists and artisans to England, and the rise to commercial predominance of Amsterdam and London. But it was not a new age of city states that was beginning, any more than of empires. The Italian cities fell into a long decay, displaced by the republic of Holland and the kingdom of England, and the economic system directed from that joint center.

Thus the modern world system began, as the unacknowledged structure by means of which these territorial states of northwest Europe wielded power over the rest of Europe increasingly after 1550, and over the rest of the world after 1650; an unacknowledged empire, which was not politically unified, as the old, self-acknowledged empires were, nor administered by a tax-gathering bureaucracy. This system worked by the means of indirect domination politically, of capitalism economically, of protestantism religiously, of rationalism philosophically; and its military and industrial powers were energized by a new science and technology.

The core countries of the system at its beginning—up to and including Defoe's time, let us say—were Holland and England. They exerted power over a semiperiphery to the system, the countries of southern Europe, and a periphery, eastern Europe. One effect of this system was that England and Holland grew stable and unified politically, and economically they freed their artisans and yeomen from feudal bondage, in proportion as in the other countries the political structure grew feeble or brittle, and the workers entered bondage. The former happened in eighteenth-century Spain and Italy, the latter on the huge agricultural domains of Poland, Hungary, and Russia. We shall see the effects of this on the worlds of literature and thought when we come to Tolstoy and Conrad.

Socially, the core countries were dominated by merchants rather than nobles. The degree of this dominance corresponded to the centrality of that country within the system. Thus in England the merchants married with and merged with the nobility, and so became politically stronger than their equivalents in, say, France. The city of London and the new class, "the gentry," became dominant in the seventeenth century. England became a mercantile state, and a mercantile world power. In the 1690s, the state made itself the source of financial credit, instead of private houses, and the administration was generally modernized. This it did in imitation of Holland, and Holland, even more a merchant oligarchy, was England's great model. She was also the great rival, in trade and colonization. Thus the core states intertwined with each other, in political and military mimicry, competing against each other for the profits to be derived from exploiting the periphery and trading with the arena surrounding the system. As the system waxed strong, its perimeter moved out, and more and more of the arena became periphery. And unconsciously or indifferently the core countries weakened the state machinery and cultural life they encountered out there, reducing these states to dependencies if not to colonies.

Colonies, in one form or another, were essential to the system. As it came into existence, Wallerstein says, it needed three things in order to survive: politically strong core states, new labor controls (to facilitate a new diversification of work), and geographical expansion. At its very beginning, the European system had covered the Mediterranean (commercially organized by the Italian cities) plus the Flanders-Hanse network. The conquest of the New World by Spain meant an increase in territory from three to seven million square kilometers. The ratio of land to labor within the system increased enormously, prices rose, and wages fell. Where labor was so strongly

9

organized that wages were maintained anyway, as in north Italy, commerce declined.

The outer arena—notably China, India, Turkey—supplied the system with precious goods, luxury items, exotica. The periphery supplied the lower-ranking, less-rewarded staples. And the labor systems diversified correspondingly. Mines and the sugar industry employed slaves; the large agricultural domains (in East Europe and in South America) employed serfs. Meanwhile in the core states, farming was done by yeomen and skilled work by artisans, new industries were born, ever new skills had to be learned, work became specialized and differentiated. At the semiperiphery the farming work was done by coerced sharecroppers; while at the periphery, for instance in Russia even in the sixteenth century, serfdom was introduced.

The political and moral ideology of this development are easy to trace right up to our own times, in the connotations of phrases like "East of Suez," "South American politics," or "Balkanization." They mean that once you're far from the core countries geographically, anything goes, morally and politically. To take a random example, in *The Political Economy of the War*, F. W. Hirst says, "It would be naive to imagine that the standards of business ethics in the Balkans and in South America in the '70s and '80s were the standards of Whitehall or the Bank of England. Bribery was not accidental or occasional, but essential and systematic in every field of commerce." And we shall come across many such manifestations of the centrifugal cultural field set up by the modern system.

The system developed an ideology in which freedom and morality were the main values; freedom and morality in religion meaning protestantism; in commerce meaning capitalist enterprise; in politics meaning a gentry republic or constitutional monarchy. This ideology was anti-imperialist; the system worked by means unlike those of the old military, centralized, tax-gathering empires, their towering structures crowned by some divinized emperor who blazed forth glory. The new empire was, or felt like, a community of freely competing equals, and called itself a nonempire to draw attention to that difference. Its means and values flourished in the core states, and their gospel was taken to the periphery and beyond, in all confidence that they could take root there, by an act of will. When they did not take root, that was attributed to a failure of will.

Defoe's writings, fictional and nonfictional, are animated by that ideology. It supplies their moral structure, and supplants the imperialism that is not named. I mean that Defoe seems morally unwilling to outright glory in England's power and wealth, its empire, so puts his stress on England's core qualities, its moral *solidity*. [3] (This is an example of what made foreigners call Englishmen hypocritical.) The great value of Wallerstein's theory is to help us to understand why and how Defoe (and the other writers who were in the spirit of the modern system) had to make such substitutions, had to be covert in their fables of imperialism. We must not expect to find in the adventure novels outright celebrations of empire; we must not expect to find outright imperial topics tackled; and we must expect to detect political meanings by interpretation.

We must also expect to find only hints of the more sordid aspects of the trading expeditions that *are* represented in adventure tales, and the more appalling aspects of the technology that the traders employed. It will be necessary to keep in mind some of the basic history of industry and war.

In the sixteenth century, the industrial history of the different countries of Europe diverged. (This is according to John U. Nef in *War and Human Progress*, whose account coincides with Wallerstein's.) In Spain and the Holy Roman Empire, there was less industrial enterprise and more agriculture than there had been before, but less output on the whole; there was even a fall in population. Spain was much less populous in 1660 than it had been in 1550, while Joachimsthal, the mining capital of the empire, had a population of only eight hundred in the 1630s, in place of 200,000 in the 1530s. (The wars were the immediate cause.) In the same period, in France, Italy, and Switzerland, there was a slight increase in heavy industry, and a large increase in the luxury and art trades; France, in particular, developed technical and administrative aptitudes in those trades, modeled on Renaissance Italy. But in England, Holland, and Sweden, the Protestant powers of the northwest, there was a great growth of heavy industry.[4] Between 1564 and 1634 the shipments of coal from the Tyne to the south of England increased by a factor of fourteen, and the use of iron in the country as a whole increased by a factor of between five and six between 1540 and 1620. In Sweden, iron and copper metallurgy developed under the guidance of the great Calvinist capitalist, Louis de Geer, whose headquarters were in Amsterdam; which shows the manifold interconnections of the Protestant states. De Geer had great influence over Gustavus Adolphus, king of Sweden and military hero of Protestant Europe (one of Defoe's heroes, for instance). He who produced iron, or rather he who controlled its production, dominated the scene. Iron is the emblematic metal of the system, and symbolic play upon it runs through the literature of these two hundred years.[5]

Lewis Mumford points out, in *Technics and Civilization*, that mining and metals in general has always been specially linked to capitalism (which is to say, to the modern system) and to militarism.[6] It is linked to the first because mine work broke away from the labor controls of the guild system very early in the history of capitalism; and because mining produced the silver on which the Fuggers' fortune was based, and the Fuggers financed Spanish imperialism. It is linked to militarism because the mines produced the metals used in weapons and armor, and used the gunpowder also used in petards and guns.

Mining was also a great source of industrial mechanization because of its connection with smelting, refining, smithing, and casting. Half the skills needed to mechanize other processes of production and distribution derive from it. And in its social and ecological effects it has always been destructive, opportunistic, and exploitive. In most cultures, the mine is associated with Hell, and in its moral and political character as well as its physical. It employed slave labor even in Europe until the late Middle Ages, and in Scotland serfs worked in mines long after their equivalents in agriculture had been freed. The work was done in darkness and danger, and required power tools and high temperatures, and it created around the mines the inorganic environment of slag heaps. For all these reasons, it was deeply shameful to the modern system, and to its humanism; so was hidden or exiled to a geographical periphery as much as possible.

But it was also vital to the modern system. For instance, in matters of war, metal gradually displaced wood and stone. Besides guns themselves, bayonets began to be attached to guns about 1660 and, like many military innovations, seemed particularly devilish at the time. Voltaire called them the demon of war. The Swedes used them only against the Russians, and the Austrians only against the Turks; that is, against enemies on the periphery or outside the system, and so not fully human.

And the importance of metal was matched by that of gunpowder, which was culturally of a very similar character. About 1660, Robert

Boyle observed that gunpowder had quite altered "the conduct of martial affairs, by sea and land." The invention of the gun had been attributed by folk legend (and also by scholars like Polydore Vergil, in 1499) to a sinister monk called Schwartz; and it was generally considered to be the devil's work. This was partly because of the origin of gunpowder, and more particularly of saltpeter, an essential ingredient.[7] One way to obtain this ingredient was from excrement —even human excrement—and men were commissioned to collect this for royal authorities. Partly for reasons of safety, it was prepared in small installations, and in lonely parts of the country, for fear an enemy might capture the deadly powder. Several aspects of the trade, therefore, made it abhorrent; another instance is its association with forced labor. Coal mines, salt works, and alum works, which also used excrement, were among the first factories. Sulphur, that other ingredient of gunpowder, was also associated with the devil and excrement and danger. When Cortes invaded Mexico, one of his men was lowered four hundred feet into a volcano to scrape sulphur off the walls, to make gunpowder. And Cortes' guns were of crucial importance in his conquest of Mexico. So the metals, mines, and explosions we meet all the time in adventure settings have political resonances we must not miss.

Guns and explosives have had a world character of being especially European and modern system products. China first developed gunpowder, but used it for fireworks and not for artillery. It was not China but England, therefore, that exported one thousand barrels of powder to India in 1629. European gunners sold their services outside the modern system. In India, for instance, the Moghuls employed European gunners until 1707, and the Muslims, who replaced them after that, were considered much inferior. Gunnery was a white man's art. For different reasons, but with a similar effect, in the English armies the sepoys or Africans were not given access to the artillery or to the Gatlings.

But probably even more important than the modern system's introduction of new weapons was its imposition of drill and organization. That is what made the European soldiers superior to, for instance, the Indian armies they fought. And Michael Howard in *War in European History* tells us of the nadir of brutality and near-anarchy which the Thirty Years' War reached at the end of the feudal period, when the old empires were dying. Warfare escaped rational control and became purposeless violence, except in the United Provinces, where the modern system was established. There armies were regularly supplied and paid, and fighting made political and social sense. The Dutch made their soldiers work, at digging and drilling. And later the Swedes introduced the further rationality of uniforms and mechanical maneuvers. (This is another example of the connections between the Protestant countries.) Prince Maurice of the United Provinces taught Delagardie, who later became military tutor to Gustavus Adolphus. It was the latter, Howard says, who provided the rest of the world with the modern blueprint for getting an army under the control of a single will. He showed how "the violent element which permeated European society could be canalized and put to the purposive, legitimized uses of the developing state machine . . ." (p. 60). It was the Bourbon kings of Catholic France who applied that blueprint; by 1680 the French forces were 300,000 strong; the wonder of Europe. And the Hohenzollerns imitated the Bourbons, and the Romanovs the Hohenzollerns.

Thus the Dutch model was gradually followed all over Europe in what Howard calls "The Wars of the Professionals," in the eighteenth century. Long before 1800 all the core countries had the state machinery to pay, feed, arm, and clothe a full-time force on foot, in war and peace. This was the militarism of the modern system, though developed furthest by the Bourbons and the Hohenzollerns. Those dynasties and their regimes were not as *typical* of the modern system as English merchants—at least if one is contrasting that system with the feudal—but they were not wholly atypical. That system still had its military castes, though they were "officially" subordinate to the merchants. England's style in war was superficially different, because she relied mainly on her navy. She was in some sense a nonmilitary nation. But Cromwell's Roundheads and the Ironsides will remind us that England too had an army, and of the modern kind.

Thus the English empire (and the modern system of which it was a part) grew by a great variety of means, some of which, like mining and militarism, were obscured by the system's ideology. We need to remind ourselves therefore of those hidden means; but our principal concern will be with that ideology, and the special character of its energizing myth, adventure. The modern system's kind of adventure —exemplified in the fiction of Defoe—differs from other kinds because of the merchant caste's dominant position.

## Caste

Caste is a concept I shall use often, and throughout the book, to explain the imaginative characteristics of the modern system and its literature. By caste, I mean the social character men derive from their profession or vocation, or from their parents' vocation, for these traits are often acquired in childhood. These traits, friends and enemies alike agree, are independent of the caste members' individualities. They manifest themselves primarily but not exclusively in matters connected with that profession. But play habits can be as important as work habits; thus the military caste habitually, in all countries, hunts; an activity that clearly relates to their profession, and prepares them for war even in times of peace, but which also characterizes them in other ways, social, political, economic, not directly connected with war. (Think how important hunting is in the country squire's life described by Tolstoy.) Thus a caste is not formally organized as such, and its members do not necessarily constitute an active group. It is often a tendency rather than an action which the term points to. On the other hand, to speak of "caste" is appropriate only if that tendency and those traits amount to an important characterization of an important number of people.

It seems to be true also that—within the modern system—the term applies best to the members of one profession; the one that has no cultural function proper in the system. I mean the military caste, whose members, judged by that system's work ethic, function only degradedly in times of peace, as fighters and consumers, unproductive, essentially idle, overprivileged. Times of war are very abnormal, according to modernist ideology, so normally speaking the military caste have status rather than function—that is why they are defined as a caste. (Of course they were seen very differently while they were the dominant caste, in the feudal system that organized society in premodern times.) By analogy with them, moreover, it seems possible to talk of a merchant caste, as being the dominant one culturally, in seventeenth- and eighteenth-century England. And there was also a group we can call a Brahmin caste, mostly scholars and clergymen, the society's "writers," who had in their keeping its conscience and to some degree its imagination.[8]

Caste is an awkward term. It is an acceptable category according to a feudal ideology, but in a modern system—which was antifeudal in origin and feeling—its terms are always prejudicial. We are not supposed to be caste members ourselves or caste conscious about others. Caste thinking is the prototype of class- and race-thinking—something dangerous and disgraceful, although we all do it. It ties status to vocation. We are supposed—especially in America, the most modern of modern system countries—to take everyone on his merits, and accord him the status appropriate to them.

The prejudicial status of the concept caste is however deceptive. Like class (and race) caste lives a powerful subterranean life, which is independent of economic or social-scientific fact. Caste exists, as an inhibition and an inspiration, wherever people think it does; and they *like* to think it does; it is one of the games people play. Society therefore always has lively ideas in circulation of what constitutes a typical house or a typical child, or a typical marriage, for each caste. The range of human possibility is divided up between them, and to some extent each caste has its own set of typical stories, its own myth. But the whole society enjoys all these stories, barely acknowledging their caste connections. One difference between those sets, which bears on the history of the novel, is that erotic idealism attaches itself more easily to the military than to the merchant or the Brahmin castes; the young officer is a more romantic figure than the young shopkeeper or the young curate; and this feeling is felt by the society at large. Crusoe is not a romantic figure, but Waverley is, because Scott wrote for the military caste, Defoe for the mercantile.

Then certain kinds and degrees of political participation have seemed appropriate to certain castes also. For instance, in *The Complete English Tradesman,* Defoe tells us of an upholsterer who became so concerned for the liberties of his country that he fell into debt, and was thrown into jail. Defoe's moral is, tradesmen should mix with tradesmen, not with gentlemen, and should stick to tradesmen's interests. That man should have shut up shop and bought himself a commission in the army, if politics was his main concern. And there is even a certain stylistic affiliation to be discerned for each caste, as Defoe indicates in the same book. "As plainness and a free unconstrained way of expression is the beauty and excellence of speech, so an easy concise way of writing is the best style for a tradesman" (p. 11).[9]

Caste, moreover, has more important effects than are officially (in a modern system) admitted, because it creates alliances and relations of trust between people in power. It is, for instance, a vital part of how establishments function. The group within which it works is often small, and the members often deny—some quite sincerely—that caste affects their relations with each other; but outsiders see its effects. Thus its signs are particularly to be looked for in symbolic figures and symbolic anecdotes, though not of the most official kind —in other words, in art.

It has also some importance in the workings of large groups, where it is habitually called "class." The difference between caste and class can perhaps be usefully discussed in relation to Defoe. Defoe was much concerned with class, and with claiming membership of the one he preferred, though he didn't speak of upper and lower. For him —as for most people in the period we are studying—the key term was "gentleman." Defoe suffered a good deal under the imputation that he was not a gentleman. This is really a caste idea, though applied within a class system.

He argued (in *The Complete English Gentleman*, for instance) that according to the true idea of a gentleman, status is not conferred by the current false criteria of a man's pedigree, or his classical learning, or his title, or his not working for a living; "gentleman" should mean (of course) the virtues and the graces. However, it is noticeable, in both Defoe's behavior and his imagination (as displayed in his novels) that, in fact, he hankered after the current false criteria, the trivial fripperies of gentility. To be De Foe, to have a coat of arms (which he achieved in 1695) and a motto (which he acquired in 1706), to challenge opponents to a duel, to be acknowledged by others as a gentleman, and (as Moll Flanders) to know how to talk genteelly, to sing, dance, and speak French, and to have a gentleman for a husband, or (as Colonel Jack) to have a genteel wife with "the fine hand of a lady."

Defoe wanted it both ways; both to disprove the criteria of the old feudal idea of a gentleman (substituting a reformed Protestant version) and at the same time to satisfy those criteria and rejoice in those gaudy privileges. Much the same could be said of later writers like Scott and Dickens, and of earlier ones like Shakespeare, and indeed of nonwriters. Success in England has always meant to join the gentleman caste. I want to suggest that this was not mere weakness of mind.

Clearly the fine hand of Colonel Jack's first wife, and the dashing demeanor of Moll Flanders' favorite husband, make no sense morally by Defoe's theory. This is not "true gentility." But then they make no sense immorally either—they bring no practical advantages. They show, I want to suggest, a disguised sense of caste at work, which looks meaningless because—using the language of class—it denies its own values as it operates. As a status system, class is overtly moral, covertly economic in its criteria. Caste, on the contrary, is hereditary —the thing a man must do is the thing he was born to. And it is amoral; or its morality is aesthetic and romantic; it values certain *styles* of being, and judges them by their graces as much as by their virtues. And as the merchants settled into power, they became sympathetic to such aesthetic views—only not bare-facedly.

Hence arose a good deal of confusion. But originally the denial of caste was a maneuver in the conflict between the feudal and the modern systems, a maneuver directed by the dominant merchants against the knights they were displacing.[10] The latter were especially associated with caste and status, and the former, as they rose to power, set up a new system of classification. According to this, nobility had nothing to do with vocation; the gentry were not the warrior class, but the privileged class; the aristomilitary caste was demilitarized.

By vocation, the nobility and the gentry had always borne arms, in both senses. But henceforth they would not carry weapons, and they would not—by birth—even have armorial bearings. They were to be recruited—the gentry directly, the nobility more indirectly— from the rich merchants. They would be those who deserved a high status in the community. This was a phenomenon Defoe was never tired of pointing to, with pride, as proving the power and dominance of the merchants in England. But that recruitment did not mean that caste had ceased to exist.

Probably caste is a universal phenomenon, and persists residually even under systems determined to eradicate it. In seventeenth-century England, at least, the concepts gentry and gentility smuggled caste feeling back into the class system. The characterizing marks of the knights did not simply disappear; after being gentry for a generation, rich merchant families tended to assume the character of the aristocracy and to slough off their old character. But this both offended against the new classification and seemed like the grossest snobbery and failure in seriousness. For it was the merchant caste that was dominant in terms of the country's serious cultural values —that was, as it were, in official alliance with the Brahmins. The military caste was held at a distance from official values. It was supposed to be at best decorative in peace time, not part of the government of the country. (Though one had only to look at France, Germany, or Russia, to see immediately and clearly what was hazy and muted in England, the functional connection between all aristocracy and the army and diplomacy and government.)

This helps account for that curious English snobbery, in life and in literature, which has so puzzled foreigners and plagued natives. Everyone wanted to be genteel—the word soon became embarrassing, but the appetite persisted—and genteel meant bearing the marks of the aristomilitary caste. But they were external marks, cut off from all social and personal function, and used for adornment, like cut flowers withering on a ball dress.

This paradox continued over centuries, as long as the modernist ideology flourished. It can be seen in the heroes of novels, or at least in the men the heroines marry—the men considered worthy to reward them; who were so often aristocrats even while the novels were teaching the superiority of the middle class. This was independent of the individual author's sympathies. There is more mere decorativeness in Scott's gentlemanly heroes and heroines than in Defoe's, despite Scott's self-proclaimed love of feudalism, chivalry, aristocracy. Scott didn't really *believe* that chivalric values could be valid again; he *believed* in modern system values, according to which the military caste had no cultural function. He had no faith in what he loved. So the use he—and his successors—made of such values was largely sentimental and snobbish. It is only when a reader meets people who did live by those values, like Richard Burton in the nineteenth century, and Isak Dinesen in the twentieth, that caste traits cease looking like genteel adornments, because one sees that they are rooted in a serious identity.

The modern novel has been largely about the conflict between castes and caste values, but in a covert and obscured way. The caste dialectic was muffled and disguised everywhere in the modern system

19

by the dominant work ethic, which stripped the aristocrat of his vocational dignity. And in England the situation was especially confused by the greater power of its merchant caste, so anxious to dub itself gentlemanly—that is, aristocratic but not military. The English novel of adventure reflected that confusion, and imposed class terms upon it. For the purposes of this book, however, it is necessary to avoid the word class, and to sort out the caste confusion behind it.

For instance, Robinson Crusoe's character as an adventure hero, so inventive, so busy, so unerotic, and the character of his adventures, both derive from his serving—as imaginative representative—the merchant caste. Scott's heroes are different because they serve also (rather than instead) the military caste. Crusoe was prudent, Ivanhoe is chivalrous; because by 1800 England's participation in the modern system was beginning to turn into straight imperialism, and the merchant caste was almost openly allied to the military. By 1900 Kipling's heroes have very little of the merchant in them, and their chivalry is modified instead by the primitivism of saga and epic; because by then the empire felt dangerously great, and the aristomilitary caste felt in need of the crudest energies of self-assertion. Thus the caste character of the ideology, manifested in the adventure hero, changed as the empire changed.

## Capitalist Adventure

The change over time in the caste character of the adventure tale could be considered not a change so much as an acknowledgment of what had been hidden—of the dependence of the merchant on the soldier. Similarly, there was a change in the character of the economy, as imagined in fiction, from the export of stout English textiles to the exchange of intoxicants and explosives (from Defoe to, let us say, Waugh and Greene). And that change also can be considered to be more properly an acknowledgment of something present from the beginning but hidden.

For instance, a major export of the modern world system was alcohol, the manufacture of which was established in the sixteenth century, consolidated in the seventeenth, and popularized in the eighteenth, according to Braudel. It soon became the practice to give it to soldiers before battle, and to "natives" with whom one traded. It was Europe's poisoned gift to America and Africa. After 1600 the Spanish state revenue in Mexico from pulque was half that from the silver mines. The Far East, with its highly developed civilizations, alcohol did not conquer. But it was an essential feature of colonization and imperialism elsewhere.

The corresponding import was spices—pepper, cinnamon, cloves, nutmeg, ginger—as dear as pepper, was a common saying in the fifteenth century, and it was in search of such cargoes that it was worth making perilous voyages. This, indeed, had been a passion of the Middle Ages; it was in full swing by the twelfth century, Braudel tells us, in *Capitalism and Material Life.* The craze passed away in the early eighteenth century, when the more characteristically modern tastes for coffee, tea, chocolate, and tobacco took its place.

Werner Sombart derived the growth of capitalism as a whole from the spread of luxury. He said that when, in the sixteenth and seventeenth centuries, men studied the growth of cities, they always attributed them to a coming-together of nobles and princes, and to the luxury trades that followed them. In the cities, the sculptors, architects, silk-weavers built around the nobles a world of fantasy—that is, a world declaring itself unlike the reality of workers' lives. He makes an important event out of the entry of the courtesan into society. "All personal luxury springs from purely sensuous pleasure. . . . In the last analysis, it is our sexual life that lies at the root of the desire to refine and multiply the means of stimulating our senses. . . . For this reason we find luxury in the ascendancy wherever wealth begins to accumulate and the sexuality of a nation is freely expressed." (p. 60) He points to the elaborate and gold-spangled costumes, feasts, galas, gifts, coaches, servants, and liveries, which marked the growth of prosperity in the seventeenth century.

This was also marked by the consumption of new commodities, like sugar and tea. Sombart gives the figures for the latter as being 100 lb. imported into England in 1668, but 26,000 cwt. in 1761, and 86,000 cwt. in 1784. Assuming that half the quantity imported was consumed in England, that means a per capita consumption of 0.01 lb. in 1700, 0.5 lb. in 1784, and 6.51 lb. in 1901. While sugar consumption in Europe as a whole is given as 4.5 million cwt. in 1800, or 0.75 lb. per head; in 1913 it was 38 lb. per head in Germany.

Many scholars agree that it was these luxury trades that drove the engine of capitalism and imperialism, to begin with, and unified European culture. As Braudel says, luxury may not be a good way of supporting an economy, but it is a good way of holding a society together, because of the fascination which the haves exert over the have-nots. The mass-production and exchange of staple goods came later. Sombart points out that before the eighteenth century only colonies and armies took bulk sales of composite goods. Of course, as time went by, and methods of bulk transport improved, the modern system began to move staples too, but it was the lure of luxury that set the system going.

As we shall see, the modern system (insofar as represented by Defoe) officially disapproved of luxury. England identified luxury with frippery, and saw its own products as, on the contrary, stout and sturdy and plain. And in the adventure novel objects of use were exalted, objects of luxury degraded. Iron was exalted, gold—though ambivalently—was degraded. Crusoe values "that very useful thing called a grindstone," not the gold he finds on the ship.

But this myth (to some degree representing actual feeling and even practice) came to imaginative life only as a part of the general drive *toward* luxury—it could be called the moral luxury of the luxury trade. It was an attitude in economics parallel to the attitude in politics that opposed empire, and to the attitude in adventure fiction that opposed romance. (In fiction, the posture of Robinson Crusoe was antithetical to that of Amadis de Gaul.) In all three cases, that posture, though meaningful and of course sincere, must not be allowed to obscure the underlying truth. British textiles were a form of luxury, just as the modern system was a form of empire, and the adventure tale was a form of romance. In fact they were *the* forms, for the nearly three hundred years from the birth of Defoe, in 1660, to the death of Kipling in 1936.

The paradox here is related to the old paradox of worldly Puritanism, which Max Weber explained, and which in a sense everyone had always understood. The Puritans and Protestants who dedicated their lives to religious values learned a disciplined energy which led them to greater worldly power than anyone else. They became more worldly than anyone else—modern-worldly. They knew this. Defoe at least was perfectly aware of the importance of his own class and sect as agents of modernization—as was Burke from an opposite vantage point—and the Dissenters themselves in the eighteenth cen-

tury acknowledged their relation to the bourgeoisie they led. What I called the excitement of empire was in modern times quite largely the self-congratulation of that worldly Puritanism.

But Puritans could never associate themselves overtly with empire. It was only the military caste that could exult in outright imperialism. So we must learn to recognize caste alliances that lie hidden beneath apparent hostilities, or beneath terms that have become too familiar to us. Underneath the term Puritanism lies a powerful alliance between the merchant caste and the Brahmins. The writers of modern England devised an ideology and a myth which served the purposes of her merchants. That myth is to be our primary object of study here.

Let us begin with an attempt to define adventure, first in general, and then in the modernist meaning appropriate to Defoe and his successors. I am thinking, as will be obvious, primarily of adventures in books, but the definition has its applications to real life too. In general, adventure seems to mean a series of events, partly but not wholly accidental, in settings remote from the domestic and probably from the civilized (at least in the psychological sense of remote), which constitute a challenge to the central character. In meeting this challenge, he/she performs a series of exploits which make him/her a hero, eminent in virtues such as courage, fortitude, cunning, strength, leadership, and persistence.[11] That seems to cover most kinds of literary adventure, down to girl detectives battling opium fiends in San Francisco's Chinatown. (Of course, it doesn't cover, for instance, commercial or financial adventure, which are quite important to consider in connection to Defoe; associated meanings like that will have to be specially introduced whenever relevant.)[12]

In the modernist adventure, that kind especially representative of the modern system and its imagination, the adventurer defeats the challenges he meets by means of the tools and techniques of the modern world system. By tools I mean guns or compasses, and scientific knowledge, such as of when an eclipse is due, and so on. By techniques I mean things like keeping a diary and keeping accounts and the Puritan examination of conscience and the conviction of righteousness; but also any rationalized and systematized and demystified habits of thought (Twain's *Connecticut Yankee* provides some good examples).

This definition, however, needs to be qualified by other ideas, equally important and partly contradictory. In later adventure writers, in fact from Scott on, the adventurer himself is not simply identified with such tools and techniques. (Because, as I have pointed out, Scott's heroes are part-chivalric, and not all-mercantile.) In Scott, the character of the modern world, and its contrast and conflict with another ancient or exotic world, is often emphasized by other, sometimes subtler, means. Waverley, for instance, has no tools; he *observes* the ancient and exotic world of the Highlands with the eyes of modern (Hanoverian) England. Sometimes, notably in Cooper, the adventurer contains within himself the conflict between modernist tools and those of that other world—Natty Bumppo embodies the Indian world too; he is both white and Indian. So the definition of modernist adventure is not absolutely simple to apply; but it will enable us to distinguish the adventures we are concerned with from *Amadis de Gaul* and the romantic adventures of chivalry. Amadis makes no use of modern tools or techniques, and does not represent the modern world in any way. (It will also help us to distinguish between the romances and the adventures amongst our own books: using romance for the Scott and Scott-type books, adventure for Defoe and his affiliates.)

But between the individual hero, like Robinson Crusoe, and the British Empire, there stretches an incommensurability. To fill in that blank space, it is necessary to describe some real-life adventurers of empire, and to relate them to the heroes of fiction. (In many ways, this book will be a history of the WASP hero.*)

What has been said so far is true of the adventurer of fiction (and those real-life figures who resembled him) while there are various differences between him and the adventurer of history; using that phrase for the military conquerors on whom historians spend a lot of their time. (In action, as I have indicated, the modern system has been quite largely military, though in ideology it has been mercantile and anti-militarist.) I am not talking about a difference between reality and imagination, but between two embodiments of imagination. Studying that difference will, I think, bring out a hidden structure, a cultural character, to the "literary" form of imagination.

Let me describe three of the great historical adventurers of empire. None of the three has a close connection with any of the fictional

_____

*The White Anglo-Saxon Protestant concept is a facet of the modern system ideology, and I shall use the acronym often.

heroes I shall be concerned with. That distance between the two groups is a part of my point. But they and their stories powerfully excited and stimulated the West's imagination of itself and its opponents, and of human possibilities generally. Embodying individual and small-group struggle, but also large-scale achievement and power, they created our idea of the hero quite as effectively as our fictional heroes did. Indeed the narratives of the historians have been more important than those of fiction in shaping the image of the culture heroes of empire. We must contrast them with the adventure heroes, to see what the novelists don't mention.[13]

The three are Cortes, Clive, and Napoleon. I shall have much more to say about Cortes than about Clive, and very little about Napoleon. That distribution of attention derives from my particular focus on English fiction. If I were dealing with French literature, or for that matter most other European literatures, I should say a great deal about Napoleon—for instance, about how much he meant to Tolstoy alone. But except for Byron, English writers treated Napoleon simply as a moral scandal, up to the very end of the nineteenth century. Conrad was clearly fascinated by that figure, Kipling and Conan Doyle, too, but the 1914 war put an end to that nascent development of fictional interest.

Cortes had no more direct influence on English literature than Napoleon, but his connection with the Spanish romances so interestingly parallels and contrasts the connection between the English voyagers and the English adventure tale that it is instructive to consider him at some length. As before, the literary question is inseparable from the political and the economic. The English adventure tale differs from the Spanish romance in the same way as the English empire differed from the Spanish. The fiction that Defoe made out of the English facts, is, like those facts themselves, in the purest spirit of the modern system; it is a story of individual enterprise, Protestant piety, hard work, and self-help. While what we meet in the story of Cortes and the conquest of Mexico is the spirit of chivalry's archaizing romance and glory, and conscious flamboyant imperialism. (Cortes addressed his Emperor as Caesar in his despatches, and played the Roman general himself. Indeed, his Emperor dreamed of chivalric deeds himself, and in 1536 challenged his political enemy, François I of France, to single combat.) Spain, and the phase of the world system it dominated, was never modernist in spirit, which was one reason it soon lost power. The supplanting of Seville by Amsterdam and London, in the realm of finance, exactly paralleled the supplanting of *Amadis de Gaul* by *Robinson Crusoe* in the realm of fiction.

In Defoe (and Richardson and others) our literature made an alliance with the mercantile caste. That is why we have a large difference to note between Cortes, the Spanish hero, and Crusoe, the English hero, representing military and commercial castes respectively. And the mercantile hero continued to be dominant in English adventure tales right through to the days of John Buchan. But of course since England *had* a military caste, Defoe's triumph was only partial and passing; concurrently the military caste made its claims felt, in the form of a demand for romance, from Scott's time on; and if military heroes are rarely to be found in novels, there are often adventures which turn the merchant into a temporary soldier. While in Kipling's time, at the end of our period, the hidden heroism of the soldier was revealed, and he triumphed over the merchants and their allies among the children of light.

That is another reason why it is important to examine the historical heroes of adventure. Their stories, even if written by historians and not novelists, powerfully expressed the imagination of the military caste, and therewith the claims of that caste also to represent or lead the imagination of the whole society. Those stories can be felt as a pressure on the writer, when reading, say, Scott; though most serious writers resisted that pressure, which they thought morally unserious. Those stories are full of the value of warfare, and empire, and aristocracy.

For instance, our three adventurers belonged to old and honorable but impoverished families. And they used the rewards of their success to reestablish their families as noble. Through them and men like them, the riches of the empire and frontier strengthened the aristocracy. Hannah Arendt has shown that this link is what made imperialism attractive to the ruling classes of most European countries, even when the governments were opposed to it.

Thus John Strachey tells us, in *The End of Empire,* that the first Sir Henry Strachey, who was Clive's secretary, was helped by him to redeem his family estate in Somerset. That is where the plunder of Bengal was spent, rebuilding the fortunes of the English gentry. And Warren Hastings grew up in Daylesford, a village whose manor had belonged to his family for hundreds of years, but had been lost to them. At the age of seven he took a vow to redeem those acres, and achieved his vow by means of the wealth he took from India. Cortes became a great nobleman of Spain with his American wealth, and Napoleon, of course, set his brothers and sisters upon half the thrones of Europe. This is an imaginatively potent idea, but not one to be approved by modernist ideology.

In England, modernist ideology (compounded of half-truths, like other ideologies) developed an energizing myth of adventure, with heroes who represented mercantile capitalism. But England lived by other myths also, notably militarist ones, though they were told by historians rather than novelists. So in responding to the adventure tales and their heroes, we have to glance at the historical heroes also, that shadowy company behind and between the men the novelists paint.

## Cortes, Clive, and Napoleon

Since I am concerned with what these heroes meant to those who heard about them, I shall consider Cortes and Clive via a famous historian's account of each—in Cortes's case, W. H. Prescott's *Conquest of Mexico* (1843); and shall refer to a more modern account —J. M. White's *Cortes and the Fall of the Aztec Empire* (1971)— to allow for the biases of the first.

The way Prescott saw Cortes was directly borrowed from his Spanish sources. In his diary he spoke of the Spanish chronicles of the Conquest as being sprinkled with the gold dust of imagination; but his use of that gold dust himself testifies to his own similar excitement by the story—though of course to some degree he distanced and ironized Cortes's achievement and his adventure. The latter is not presented as a model in the way that Crusoe's is. Prescott's hero-worship is "romantic"—that is, aesthetic, not quite serious.[14]

The essence of the Cortes story is that he landed in Mexico on Good Friday, 1519, met the Aztec emperor Montezuma on November 8 of that year, and by 1521 the whole Aztec empire had capitulated to him; he could have become its king, merely for the asking. He arrived with only eleven ships, five hundred soldiers, sixteen horses, ten bronze guns, four falconets, and thirteen muskets. Some of those men he had to send away, as dissidents, so only four hundred reached Mexico City. But he acquired 200,000 allies along the way, mostly Tlascalans, who constructed thirteen ships, to Spanish design, and transported them in parts to Mexico Lake, assembled them there, and made him master of the water, so that he could defeat Aztec forces enormously greater than his own. He took over the kingdom.[15]

The story of the other great conquistador, Pizarro, is in its disproportions even more extraordinary; he left Panama for Peru with only one ship, a hundred and eighty men, and thirty-seven horses. The chief Inca, Atahualpa, had thirty thousand men in his army; but Pizarro brought three or four thousand to a meeting with him, seized him, had him strangled, and took over the kingdom.

These stories have a profound effect, stimulating pride in those who can identify with the winning side, fear in those who can't—of an intensity which only myth can express; and Europe's self-image in the eighteenth and nineteenth centuries derived from many such acts of mythic self-identification. No doubt her men of conscience always or often repudiated such identification; but the consequent split between conscience and imagination has not been entirely to the culture's advantage. The pride was there, whatever the guilt. One crude manifestation of that pride is the nationalist slogan: Shakespeare's Henry V said that one Englishman was worth three Frenchmen; but Columbus said, with a magnification suitable to the greater cultural gap, that a thousand Indians would not stand before three Spaniards.[16] Crude as such formulas are, and the emotions behind them, they are better indications of the sources of world-system psychology than more sophisticated ideas.

Prescott treated the Cortes story as romance, explicitly; and in fact it reminds us of romance—adventure in fiction—I mean the stories of Scott and Rider Haggard, not those of Defoe. It is suited to the military-caste imagination, not the mercantile. At the beginning of his book, in Volume I, on page 3, Prescott says, "The subversion of a great empire by a handful of adventurers, taken with all its strange and picturesque accompaniments, has the air of romance rather than of sober history." And in Volume I, on page 7, it was "as adventurous and romantic as any legend devised by Norman or Italian bard of chivalry."

He gives Cortes a romantic character, speaking of "the amorous propensities which belong to the sunny clime where he was born," and how he was often involved in affairs of honor. (Sexual glamour is more appropriate to the aristomilitary caste than to the merchant.) When Cortes arrived in Hispaniola, he was offered land to work, but said, "But I came to get gold, not to till the soil like a peasant." In Mexico he saw himself as a Roman general, leading Roman legionaries. He told his soldiers that he would lead them to countries more vast and opulent than any yet visited by Europeans. "I hold out to you a glorious prize." But it was also for him a holy war. In all these traits he stands far from Robinson Crusoe, of course.

When Prescott's story reaches Mexico, it involves an extraordinary concatenation of the motifs of the adventure tale to come; notably the treasure, the exotic landscape, and the love of a native princess. Treasure, in the form of gold, jewels, carvings (packed in chests, often) is much stressed. Cortes wrote to the emperor that "the land teems with gold as abundantly as that whence Solomon drew the same precious metal for his temple." The precious metal spills over into Prescott's metaphors, too, so that we hear of golden reasons and golden arguments.

On page 244 of Volume I, he describes the valley of Mexico City, "the land where the fruits and the flowers chase one another in unbroken circle throughout the year; where the gales are loaded with perfumes till the senses ache at their sweetness; and the groves are filled with many-colored birds, and insects whose enamelled wings glisten like diamonds in the bright sun of the tropics." And a little later, a land "of exuberant fertility, almost impervious from thickets of aromatic shrubs and wild flowers, in the midst of which tower up trees of that magnificent growth which is found only within the tropics." This is the landscape which romance-novelists were using as late as Conrad.

And then there is the story of Malintze, or Marina, given Cortes as a slave by a Tabascan chief; apparently she was of noble birth, but sold into slavery by her mother, in order to secure to her half-brother the inheritance which should have been hers. She served Cortes as an invaluable interpreter and spy, became his mistress, and bore him a child. It was because of her persuasions that Montezuma yielded himself to the protection of the Spaniards, which event broke the back of any possible Aztec resistance. Thus Cortes seduced and mastered the whole of Mexico in the person of Malintze, at once sexually and militarily triumphant.[17]

The figure of Montezuma himself is of the greatest importance in the romance-adventure landscape, combining as it does the exotic, the imperial, and the horrifying, plus a feminine unresistant succumbing to the conquistadors. We first hear of him that he lived in barbaric and oriental pomp, and was an arrogant and sacerdotal prince. When he finally appears on the page, however, to meet Cortes, he is slim, melancholy, long-haired, timid; borne to the meeting in a royal palanquin blazing with burnished gold, he then came forward on foot, leaning on the arms of two powerful vassals. Meanwhile Cortes dismounts from his horse, throws his reins to a page and advances to meet him—all virility (Vol. I, p. 341). In the palace, "Clouds of incense rolled upwards from censers, and diffused intoxicating odours through the apartment. The Spaniards might well have fancied themselves in the voluptuous precincts of an Eastern harem, instead of treading the halls of a wild barbaric chief in the Western world" (Vol. I, p. 347). And on page 350, "In the pompous and burdensome ceremonial of the court, he saw that nice system of subordination and profound reverence for the monarch which characterize the semi-civilized empires of Asia." The conquistadors are often called men of iron, of stern visage, etc., to compare with the gold of the Aztecs. In Book V, Chapter I, Montezuma was dangerously wounded, when he addressed his people on Cortes's behalf, and they shouted at him, "Base Aztec, woman, coward, the white men have made you a woman—fit only to weave and spin," and threw stones at him. Prescott tells us that Montezuma was gentle even to effeminacy in his deportment, and constant in his affections.

Prescott's reader is implicitly called on to identify with Cortes, and to rejoice in his victories—because, for the time being, for the sixteenth century, and in this confrontation, Spain is the modern system. The Spaniards of this period were in fact habitually described by nineteenth-century WASP historians as Visigoths, and as thus full of barbaric vigor. (The Spaniards of later generations were not allowed any Gothic heritage.) Thus on page 407, "Cortes had triumphed over all his enemies. He had set his foot on the neck of princes; and the great chief of the Aztec empire was but a convenient tool in his hands for accomplishing his purposes." And at the end he is summed up, "He was a knight-errant, in the literal sense of the word. Of the band of adventurous cavaliers, whom Spain, in the 16th century, sent forth on the career of discovery and conquest, there was none more deeply filled with the spirit of romantic enterprise than Hernando Cortes."[18]

The conquest of Mexico is the other side of the coin to the cultivation of his island by Crusoe. If we consider them both as stories, Prescott's book and Defoe's are, respectively, the military caste's and the merchant caste's responses to the fact of empire. Though each is the antithesis of the other, they belong together, and each needs the other, to be fully understood. *Crusoe* is so attractive to the mercantile and Puritan mind just because it puts the best face on a complex operation of which another face is military conquest. The Cortes story is attractive to the military imagination because it puts the most romantic face upon an operation that was also sordidly economic.

Turning to England's conquest of India in the eighteenth century, the essence of the Clive legend can be given in Macaulay's words: "A handful of [our] countrymen, separated from their home by an immense ocean, subjugated, in the course of a few years, one of the greatest empires in the world."* Macaulay makes use of the Cortes legend to define Clive's achievement, and to make it demonstrably the larger of the two. Under Clive's leadership, he says, the English defeated a nation who were as highly civilized as the Spanish who had defeated Mexico. This inversion of the Cortes story, with the Spanish now in the role of the Mexicans, was a standard device of nineteenth-century history. It ingeniously intensifies the modern system pride of consciousness. Traces of it can be found in Prescott himself; it is full blown in Motley's *Rise of the Dutch Republic,* and in Kingsley's *Westward Ho!;* and it goes back as far as Defoe and Hakluyt.

In psychology as well as achievement, Clive was a military caste hero; as a child, he was a "good bad boy," as the nineteenth-century called that type, or hyperactive to use our term; he organized the idle lads of his native town to blackmail shopkeepers. As John Strachey says, Clive really was, "as we all learned at school, a boys' storybook sort of hero, if ever there was one" (*The End of Empire,* p. 23). Even when he got out to India, he was insubordinate and rude to his superiors; indeed, unhappy; he twice attempted suicide before he

---

*"Lord Clive," *Edinburgh Review,* January, 1840.

found his vocation, in war. Then, at the age of twenty-five, he led two hundred English and three hundred sepoys to the capture of Arcot, its defense for fifty days of siege, and the eventual defeat of a besieging force of 10,000. The garrison lost five or six men, the enemy four hundred. And soon after he drilled into an effective army two hundred newly landed recruits, and five hundred newly levied sepoys. His men, English and native, came to adore him.

When Surajah Dowlah locked up some English prisoners in the Black Hole of Calcutta, from which they never emerged alive, Clive led an army against him, and defeated him at the battle of Plassey, although enormously outnumbered. Macaulay tells these stories with the greatest indignation and triumph. Surajah Dowlah is made a more villainous Montezuma, feeble and luxurious; ruling of course an oriental despotism, which glitters with treasures like the Peacock Throne and the Mountain of Light. The idyllic aspect of the Cortes-Montezuma relationship was not echoed with Surajah Dowlah, but it was with Mir Jaffir, the prince Clive set on the other's throne. After things had gone wrong in India, and Clive had to defend himself in the House of Commons, he told his fellow Members, "If ever a Mussulman loved a Christian, Mir Jaffir loved me."

When a historian like Macaulay, whose prime loyalties are to mercantile values, has to comment on heroes like Clive, he, like Prescott, relies rather heavily on the amoral categories of romance and the exotic; which is yet another testimony to the way the military caste was linked with the romance genre, even in the nineteenth century.

In Macaulay's story, Hindu religion is presented as all cruelty and superstition, Hindu character as at best feminine. Macaulay's characterology is a direct reflection of the core-periphery-arena structure which Wallerstein describes. At the core one finds firmness, vigor, virility; but the farther you go from the core, the less virile you find men to be. Thus he says of the Brahmin Nuncomar, in his essay on Warren Hastings,* "What the Italian is to the Englishman, what the Hindoo is to the Italian, what the Bengalee is to other Hindoos, that was Nuncomar to other Bengalees. The physical organization of the Bengalee is feeble even to effeminacy. . . ." (p. 562). and a long passage develops the idea. While the stuff Englishmen were made of

---

*In *Edinburgh Review,* October, 1841.

could be seen at Plassey: "With the loss of twenty-two soldiers killed and fifty wounded, Clive had scattered an army of near 60,000 men, and subdued an empire larger and more populous than Great Britain" (*Essays*, p. 514).

Clearly the reader feels there a very powerful personification of the British empire—even though the explicit idea "empire" is attributed to the enemy. Indeed Macaulay is almost overt about his propagandist intention. He begins his essay, "We have always thought it strange that, while the history of the Spanish empire in America is familiarly known to all the nations of Europe, the great actions of our countrymen in the East should, even among ourselves, excite little interest."[19] And Macaulay's lead was followed up by, for instance, G. A. Henty, who wrote a *With Clive in India* among his nearly eighty very popular adventure tales for boys.

Looking for a cooler, in some sense postimperial version of the same story, we can take Philip Mason's *A Matter of Honour*, 1974, about the history of the Indian army. Mason's account is that by 1750, all India had discovered that the Europeans, and the English even more than the French, possessed a military secret, which enabled them to defeat much larger forces. This, Mason says, was not so much their firearms as their drill and training and organization, and the permanent and continuous policy of the English leaders. (These were, I have argued, another expression of the modern world system.) Indian armies, by contrast, were improvised for the occasion, and their commanders disappeared after a campaign. The soldiers were only paid eight months in the year, and pay was often in arrears. The organization was feudal, and many of the vassals' troops (which accounted for the enormous numbers cited) were not to be relied on; treachery was expected and accepted. The Indian social system was religious in its sources and sanctions; politically it was largely chaotic.

By contrast the English social system, as reflected in the army, was much more solid, and the links between officer and man much more vigorous. The victories in India were to be attributed to Stringer Lawrence as well as to Clive, for the former built up the organization of the army, gave the sepoys regular pay (which could be advanced before a campaign), pensions, uniforms, regular rules for promotion, court-martial, and so on. Sepoys took an impressive oath of loyalty, and their regimental colors became objects of veneration—became the emblems of their craft, comparable with the emblems every craft

BERNALD LIBRARY
COLBY-SAWYER COLLEGA
NEW LONDON, N. H. 03257

in India venerates. This disciplined infantry was what defeated the
Indian hordes, with their armored elephants and their cavalry, which
was much flashier than ours. The Indian horsemen were trained to
develop steely arm and hand muscles, and to pick up pistols from the
ground, and to ride in gambade against the enemy, but they broke
on the rock-like British infantry. The English triumph was thus a
triumph of infantry over cavalry, in a sense a triumph of the merchant
caste over the aristocracy; which was the pattern the English associated with all their victories. Cavalry, even within the British
army, had the traditions of gentlemanly swagger, sartorial elegance,
aristocratic extravagance; but the military tune every Englishman
knew was "The British Grenadiers." The English were—or believed
themselves to be—*yeoman* soldiers.[20]

John Strachey tells the same story in *The End of Empire*,[21] and
says that Clive's victory was crucial to the history of the British
empire. The decision to attack Calcutta in 1757, he says, "marked
the moment in history when a daemonic will to conquer and to rule
seized the British . . . and possessed them for two hundred years" (p.
31). It was also a crucial moment in the history of England. "For us
in Britain," he says on page 13, "this 18th century event lives in a
way that none of the other conquests of world imperialism can do.
The Black Hole . . . etc. . . . are part of our national folklore. Countless
British families, exalted and obscure, have served—as mine did—
generation by generation in India; their children still see hanging on
the walls of their homes this or that memento of the conquest." The
first Sir Henry Strachey was Clive's secretary, and the historian's
family has private anecdotes about him, handed down through the
generations.

Thus Strachey has special reasons for responding imaginatively to
the story of Clive, and he talks of ". . . the still mysterious event of
the conquest of a vast empire by an only moderately successful trading company, intermittently supported by the government of a European state of the second rank, itself inhabited by less than 6 million
people." Which is not to say that the historian's attitude is uncritical,
either politically—his orientation is Marxist—or morally—he suggests that Clive's hysterical tears when he left India may have come
from his knowledge of what he had done to Bengal. But however
critical he or anyone may be, the story of Clive, like that of Cortes,
is one of those great imaginative moments which changed the history

of the world, and changed it for European and native alike. As Braudel says, Plassey began a new era for the world, because it marked the triumph of Europe over India. Every European afterward felt himself bigger.

But the novelists had to find indirect ways to express that feeling. Only historians, licensed by fact, were allowed to create images of imperial glory, of military conquest, and of triumphant domination. Fiction had to obey moral restraints, to celebrate mercantile virtues, and consequently to approach the facts of imperialism—individual and political—very obliquely.

The case of Napoleon can be dealt with more briefly. The poor young man who started with no advantages and raised himself by his own efforts to the heights of his profession, and then seized supreme power in France, rewrote its laws and education system and everything else, became emperor, and finally ruled Europe and dominated the world—this is a classic story of modern system qualities triumphing. Here we see the modern system and the military caste perfectly fused. Napoleon's enemies were old established systems of privilege and sentiment, feudalism, tradition, corrupt empires. He conquered Egypt—sustained the gaze of forty centuries looking down upon him—and thought of conquering India. That story energized the literature of nineteenth-century France, notably in the case of Stendahl and Balzac, for instance. It aroused young imaginations in Germany, Poland, Russia, India, all through the nineteenth century.

This had its effects in politics, of course. Alexander Herzen wrote to Turgenev in 1862, about the legacy of Napoleonic militarism in France. "Yes, if the army could be reduced to the defenders of property, the bodyguard of capital, everything would quickly reach its stable, final order. But . . . the hereditary knightly element keeps up the ferment and prevents bubbling life from settling down. . . . What is to be done with the great people who boasts of being a military people, which is all made up of Zouaves, pioupious, and Frenchmen, who are also soldiers?" Herzen saw this Napoleonic militarism as the main threat to the success of the modern system; in which "The bright image of the shopkeeper—the knight and the priest for the middle class—hovers before the eyes of the casual labourer, until his tired, horny hands drop on his sunken chest. . . ."*

*The Memoirs of Alexander Herzen, pp. 1736, 1688.

From our point of view, however, the meaning of Napoleon blends into that of the modern system. Both were aspects of the modernist imperialism. The story of Napoleon was one of the great means by which the imagination of Europe was charged with the deep and heart-pumping excitements of empire. But in England, and somewhat less in America, that story was not available to writers, except very indirectly, because British sentiment had been powerfully organized against Napoleon—depicting him as an emperor and despot, against whom Britain struggled in the name of freedom and the modern world system. Scott, the great romancer, wrote the standard British biography of Napoleon, which insulated the British imagination against him. The stimulus to the world imagination was enormous. The response, in English literature, is missing. That in itself interestingly suggests the laws and limits of literature's function within the general cultural imagination, a function which is to be a main object of this study.

These three adventurers may be taken to represent thousands of others, some only locally known, who altogether amounted to a great energizing force—an inspiration to young men particularly to achieve something similar. They are the equivalents in the Western world for the legends of Genghis Khan, Tamburlaine, Attila, and so on, among their peoples. But the Western world has been a modern world system, and not an empire. (I do not forget that this formula is profoundly false. Nevertheless it is also true. Both sides of the coin must be felt at the same time.) Therefore the high culture at its most conscientious has disapproved of adventurers of this kind, and has often averted its gaze from them, or subsumed them under other headings, *interpreted* them. The stories the most serious writers told were not adventures at all, and the less serious wrote adventures suited to the mercantile imagination.

# II

# Narrative, Other Forms,

# and

# Literature-As-A-System

IN this chapter I want to tackle "literature"; to bring that complex phenomenon, and the high culture it is part of, into relation with "empire." The most important relation imaginative writers found, as I have suggested, was adventure. To celebrate adventure was to celebrate empire, and vice versa. But not all writers could sincerely adopt a celebratory attitude to empire. In fact, the morally serious were more ready to condemn it, or purposefully to ignore it. But that equation holds good, nevertheless, and relates the form to the ideology, for writers as a whole.

Some writers (like Defoe) understood the empire to be a place where adventures took place, and men became heroes. Some (like Swift) refused to understand empire in any such favorable terms. Some (most serious novelists) refused to understand it at all as a subject for fiction. All of them took the adventure narrative to be the generic counterpart in literature to empire in politics. And by writing such narratives, the first group of writers prepared the young men of England to go out to the colonies, to rule, and their families to rejoice in their fates out there. While the others turned away from adventure, to write serious fiction—or essays and poems—which implicitly advocated a quite different career.

But before getting to full-length narratives, it is worth considering other forms, and other, more fragmentary, aspects of literature. It is worth asking what, for instance, poetry in English owed to empire; what the poets took from the voyagers and empire-builders who wrote out their exploits, or were written about.

The news of the New World stimulated the imagination of writers, like everybody else; but the effects are hard to summarize, because the evidence is contradictory. Columbus's first letter describing the New World was printed and published nine times in 1493, and by 1500 had had twenty editions. So he and America were soon notorious. And the stories of New World voyages began to appear in print soon after 1500. Francanzano Montalbodo's collection, *Paesi Novamente Retrovati*, came out in Venice in 1507, and had fifteen editions; and Ramusio's collection (these set the precedent for Hakluyt in England) followed at mid-century.

On the other hand, Charles V never mentioned America in his memoirs, and up to 1600 geographies regularly described the world as if the discovery had never taken place. In sixteenth-century France, twice as many books were published about the Muslim threat as about the American promise. The facts were undeniable, and exciting; but they were hard to assimilate, at the serious levels of the imagination; and so in a sense they *were* denied. Only after 1650 did Europe's mental horizons expand in rebellion against antiquity's authority.*

We can take an example of this that relates to Columbus himself. His first account of the Caribs he met was friendly, vivid, and moderate; he noted with appreciation their handsome bodies and good faces, their neat and clean houses, their ingenious nets and hooks, etc. He was in this first letter the most realistic ethnographer since Herodotus;† but his later accounts were quite fantastic. As the habits of European culture reasserted themselves in his mind, he ceased to see the non-Europeans clearly. His first account was less medieval-

*J. H. Elliott, *The Old World and the New, 1492–1650.*
†Margaret T. Hodgson, *Early Anthropology in the 16th and 17th Centuries.*

fantastic than Walter Raleigh's was to be, of the same people, a century later; even though Raleigh was an intellectual. And this pattern was to prove typical; the European mind, even at its most adventurous and ambitious, did not absorb the new facts easily, and often retreated before them, into fantasy.

Notably the men of letters, the men of the arts in general, were not seriously curious about the news. Dürer noted having seen works of art sent from the New World, but neglected to record or speculate about what he saw. Rabelais used the New World news for purely playful, satiric, or fabulous purposes. In some ways, the high-culture imagination of Europe remained medieval in the sixteenth and seventeenth centuries. In medieval times, curiosity, *turpa curiositas,* was not given high status as an intellectual motive; new information, at least of a geographical kind, was not intellectually important. After the discoveries, that status changed, but gradually and slowly. The high culture and the serious mind of Europe lagged far behind the work of her sailors and adventurers. Among even Augustan men of letters, it was only Defoe—who was only marginally a man of letters —who participated fully in the new interests.

Defoe was a geographer, and geographical exploration is the most empirical form of inquiry, the most destructive of a priori reasoning. Like medicine and war, navigation and cartography were comparatively free from classical precedent. But for men of letters that precedent was not a merely inert pressure; it actively denied the new ideas —deriving energy from the denial; and humanist culture has gone on doing that these two hundred and fifty years. Humanism is essentially conservative, in both good and bad senses.

Education gradually accepted the knowledge, especially the education of the Dissenters. For instance, Defoe (like Locke) particularly recommended geography for a gentleman's education, and in history put a stress on the modern. He wanted boys to know the stories of Cortes and Pizarro. And in Germany we find J. H. Campe's *Discovery of America, for the Use of Children and Young Persons,* translated into English in 1759. (Campe also wrote *Robinson der Jüngere,* a hugely successful adaptation of Defoe's book.) In these ways education gradually made use of the new knowledge, in the course of the eighteenth century. But that knowledge did not replace the classics, especially in the education of the ruling class. And literature was even slower to respond to it.

Of course the excitement of new wealth (of windfall, to use W. J. Webb's phrase) can be felt in such early and important works as *Doctor Faustus* (1588) in lines like,

> I'll have them fly to India for gold
> Ransack the ocean for Orient pearl.

And again in *Paradise Lost,* a century later:

> High on a throne of royal state, which far
> Outshone the wealth of Ormus and of Ind,
> Or where the gorgeous East with richest hand
> Showers on her kings barbaric pearl and gold,
> Satan exalted sat. . . .

But such uses imply deep uneasiness as well as excitement.

The Milton passage is thought to derive from Sir Thomas Roe's description of Jahangir, the Mogul emperor to whom he was sent as ambassador. Its being used to evoke Satanic rather than Divine state is typical of the imaginative geography the modern system developed. The same flavor of excess, of the forbidden, is after all implicit in the Marlowe passage. The new lands were sometimes described as Paradise, sometimes as Inferno; and judgments as to whether they were Heaven or Hell sometimes varied within a single account. They seemed to combine characteristics of both. But the diabolic element (often personified in "savages") counted for more in the reflections of morally realistic writers. There was a resistance in the moral mind, a reluctance in the literary imagination, facing those lands.[1]

Empire was also discredited by the opposite element, the childlike innocence of the natives—or more exactly by the cruelty and deceit of the European traders who took advantage of that innocence. The cruelty of the Spaniards to their Indian subjects was a constant theme of Protestant moralists everywhere. And it was linked to their wealth. If America and India were seen as treasure houses of gold, gold had always had sinister connotations, for moralists.

Columbus himself began the stories that so appealed to the European mind, of Indians childishly trading gold, *pure* gold, *solid* gold, for trifles like beads, mirrors, knives, and so on. Peter Martyr's *De Novo Orbe* (1500–01) exaggerated Columbus's account; he spoke of golden trees and fishooks, golden cannon, and kitchenware. Hakluyt described natives dancing with eagles of gold hanging on their breasts, and pearls in their ears. The implicit message to the reader was plunder. England saw America as a fountain of gold and gems, says R. R. Cawley, in *The Voyagers and Elizabethan Drama*. Also as an earthly paradise; Raleigh said the Indies lived in a perpetual spring, and in Mexico the wheat grew high as trees. But that paradise was purely material, and associated with moral failure. Thus in 1658 Davenant had natives appear on the London stage carrying baskets full of ingots of gold and wedges of silver; but the title of his play was *The Cruelty of the Spaniards in Peru*.

Of course, many Elizabethan writers wrote enthusiastically about the new lands, and the English colonies on them. J. H. Parry says that propaganda was a vital part of English and Dutch imperialism (as distinct from Spanish) because those two countries needed capital investment by city merchants. The enterprise depended on persuading the latter to put their money down—men like Sir Thomas Smythe, who contributed to the Muscovy Company, the East India Company, and the Virginia Company, in turn. The English crown paid for much less of the total costs of empire than the Spanish crown; hence English propaganda was mercantile in character; and hence it was England that had a Hakluyt and later a Defoe.

It was from the persuasive propaganda of the Hakluyts that the creative writers took off; Spenser, Bacon, Drayton—whose ode "To the Virginian Voyage" draws directly on the Hakluyts; and later Middleton, Fulke Greville, in his 1633 *Life of Sidney*, and finally Defoe. But by definition, propaganda is repugnant to the literary conscience. Literature-as-a-system relegates such writing to exile, far from its value center.

Of course, the subject of the relegated writing may flourish in literary exile. As a cultural image, it may root itself in every imagination, even if rejected by literature—and may return to haunt writers at a later date. Thus one of the most famous imperial projects of Elizabethan times was to colonize Guinea/Guiana; a project to be associated with Raleigh, both as colonizer and as propagandist. (And Defoe, a great admirer of Raleigh, took the scheme up later.) The scheme was given literary praise by Marston, and by Chapman in his "De Guiana Carmen Epicum," which begins, "Riches and Conquest and Renown I sing." Its tone can be gathered from lines like these:

> Guiana, whose rich feet are mines of gold,
> Whose forehead knocks against the roof of stars,

> Stands on her tip-toes at fair England looking
> Kissing her hand, bowing her mighty breast.

This shows us literature in subservient alliance with imperialism.

But we can take Raleigh's scheme to be typical, not only because of its imaginative glitter at the time—Guinea was the land of the El Dorado legend—but also because of the many forms in which it returned to haunt the literary imagination. Though Raleigh's project failed completely, the Pilgrim Fathers considered Guinea a possible site for their colony, as late as 1619; another Guinea Company was founded in 1627; and Defoe promoted its colonization a century later. While El Dorado recurred as a motif of the most serious literary meaning, as late as Conrad's *Nostromo,* and Naipaul's *Loss of El Dorado.* (By the twentieth century, a Pole and a Trinidad Hindu, both writing in English, were involved in the myths of West European imperialism.)

So clearly men of letters were excited about empire, from the sixteenth century on; it contained much to simply delight their fancy. But it was not so simple to integrate that excitement with the serious moral imagination and its literary forms. That problem has been in some sense unending and insoluble. As we see in the case of space exploration today, serious literature generally is reactionary, and will not or cannot ally itself to contemporary excitements. Insofar as the problem did find a solution, it was in the adventure tale, but that was no solution for serious writers.

## Other Literary Models of Empire and Adventure

The English adventure tale will be discussed in the next chapter and those that follow. But it is useful to bring to that discussion a sense of the alternatives—the like-but-unlike precedents for the incorporation of empire-excitement into large literary forms.

The first of these precedents is Virgil, and his relation to the Roman empire forms an interesting contrast (sometimes not a total contrast) to the relation of some of our authors to the British empire. The aspects of empire treated in the *Aeneid* show the moral responsibility that goes with conquest and domination, not the windfall and boom aspects dominant for the Elizabethan writers. But the two are connected, and later English writers faced the same problem as Virgil. Indeed, if we think of England's empire as the United Kingdom rather than the colonies, we shall see a similarity to Rome even in the earlier period. The establishment of the Tudor dynasty was for Shakespeare a political and moral event of the highest significance, just as the establishment of the Caesars was for Virgil.

As John Bowle puts it, the Roman empire determined the political and cultural future of Europe; while the British spread over the rest of the world; so the two demand to be put side by side. Politically speaking, however, the Roman empire was more purely a military phenomenon than the English. It was not merchant-dominated, like the modern world system. Economically speaking, the significant contrast, according to Paul Petit in *Pax Romana,* is that while Rome's commerce was highly organized, its production was run along cottage industry lines. Roman commerce had no mass production or assembly-line methods, no machines to speak of, no standardization, and only low-level technology.

On the other hand, there were great capitalists, especially in industries like pottery, tiles, and bricks; there were great financiers; and there were agricultural capitalists, working the enormous latifundia. But the important similarity for us was the predominance of the home country over the rest of the Roman empire, which must remind us of the position of England within her empire.

Petit says, on page 195, "Italy, from Sicily to the Alpine border, was the centre of political and intellectual life, the country of the master race, wholly unified in itself since all its citizens had received citizen-rights. Basking in the glory of its history and in the presence of the imperial government, it possessed over those provinces which until a few years before had been merely exploited, a superior and privileged place which guaranteed a solid prosperity in the first century of our era." The empire was of course the successor to and the inheritor from the great Roman republic. If we take the British empire's history to stretch from 1688 to 1930, then the period corresponding to that first century A.D. might be 1870–1930; in which case it would be appropriate to compare Roman authors like Virgil and Horace with English writers like Conrad and Kipling.

Petit says it was the work of Augustus, the first emperor, to repair the ravages of the civil wars (which lasted from 50 B.C., when Caesar crossed the Rubicon, to the battle of Actium in 31 B.C.), but also to ensure that predominance of Italy. Between the battle of Actium and the rise to power of the Severans, in A.D. 193, the area directly administered by Rome doubled in size, her frontiers advancing in all directions away from the Mediterranean. Augustus' great enterprise was to romanize western Europe, and the profits of that enterprise drained back from the colonized countries to Rome, just as the profits of the British empire drained back to England in Kipling's time.

The concept of Empire was as new to Romans in Virgil's time as it was to Englishmen in Kipling's time. Koebner tells us that it was first in 184 B.C. that Scipio Africanus referred to the imperium of the Roman people as territory, and that usage continued to be rare. Cicero always used the word to mean the state's power to enforce the law. The territorial meaning was invoked only on monuments to successful generals. But in 38 B.C. Octavian made his position paramount, and claimed he inherited from Julius Caesar the title "imperator." In 27 B.C., the Senate granted him a proconsular imperium, and four years later that was declared permanent.

Once emperor, Augustus wanted to make his new powers seem old, to legitimize them. His "argument" was that the republican aristocracy having been ruined in the civil war, Rome's ancestral tradition should now be renewed under the guidance of the princeps (himself). He needed the support of ideas and of literature, just as British imperialism was to, and the support was lavishly given. He and his minister, Maecenas, induced Horace, Virgil, and Livy to sing the imperium romanum—in Horace's *Carmina,* in the *Aeneid,* and in the *Ab Urbe Condita.* Virgil and Maecenas are said to have taken turns reading the former's poetry aloud to Augustus. Virgil and Horace, who both lost their patrimonies in the civil war, both admired Augustus, and welcomed the peace which empire promised. They wanted to see the land resettled and the cities diminished. (This dark background of civil war was not there for the British empire Kipling and Conrad knew; it *was* there earlier—in much diminished degree —for Shakespeare and Defoe; and it inspired stresses in their work recognizably similar to Virgil's.)

As W. R. Johnson says, in *Darkness Visible,* "Virgil lived in an age when the shared metaphors which any society requires in order to exist were disintegrating. . . ." The poet was not twenty years old when war broke out between Caesar's men and Pompey's; twenty-six when Caesar was murdered, and when Cicero was trying to sum up, in *De Officiis,* what the republic had tried to be. It is not surprising that his foundation epic, the *Aeneid,* celebrates Augustus' empire as the creator of order, a boon worth any price.

Virgil was essentially an Empire poet, the spokesman for a large state, more civilized than its rivals or its own antecedents. That comes out in the ways he is praised when he is compared and contrasted with Homer. Arnold and Nietzsche preferred the Greek poet. But T. S. Eliot and C. S. Lewis (themselves citizens of a great imperial metropolis) acclaimed Virgil as *the* poet of civilization. Lewis says that Achilles was a boy, Aeneas a man; and that in the *Aeneid* European literature "grew up." And indeed Aeneas can be seen as a Stoic hero, a hero of maturity, struggling away from the primitive codes of a tribal society, toward the civilized values of *humanitas, pietas, ratio,* and *salus.* He is less single-minded than Achilles, because in Virgil's time the themes of national destiny, the birth and death of nations, and the costs of civilization, were problematical. Intellectually, Virgil is clear in his resolution of those problems; Aeneas is not to be considered an interloper in Italy; he is the instrument of fate, the agent of civilization, the agent of empire. But emotionally, Virgil's story remains ambivalent.[2]

The poem is about the problem of containing the violence of history. In Book I, line 257, Jupiter begins a speech foretelling the glory of Rome and the enchainment of Frenzy. Rome's enemies are in a sense crazy; Turnus is infected with madness by Allecto in Book VII (as is Amata, Lavinia's mother, another of Aeneas' enemies); and Dido is infected by Cupid, in the form of Aeneas' son. (Dido is the foreign queen who loves Aeneas and is deserted by him; Turnus is the native prince whose kingdom Aeneas conquers and whose bride Lavinia he marries; both figures have important parallels in our own imperial myth.)

But it is clear that Dido and Turnus are not merely crazy, and that the violence is not all on their side. Virgil gives us a strong sense that "inexcusable" violence is being employed by Rome itself, and that Aeneas' virtue, his famous *pietas,* is "inauthentic"; that is, the balance between good and evil in his conduct is palatable only when he is considered as a representative of civilization and Empire, not when he is considered as an individual. He is first called "pius Aeneas" in Book IV, line 393, immediately after Dido denounces him as a

**45**

faithless lover. His piety compensates those who identify with him for his infidelity. Hunt's chapter on Dido and Turnus is headed "The Realm of Tragic Guilt," and clearly the guilt is not all theirs. Both those characters arouse a strong emotional response in the reader, which is in part sympathetic identification.

Dido is a heroine out of Greek tragedy, and Turnus is brave, handsome, passionate, patriotic. Both represent old cultural values which are going to be diminished as Roman civilization is established. In Book XI Turnus tries to awaken the ancient heroism of his people, the Latins, with the speech beginning line 415, "O si solitae quicquam virtutis adesset."

Turnus is a figure of feeling, attracting all our sympathy. He was described, when first introduced in Book VII, as the bravest of men, but the most passionate. (The comparable figures in the English foundation epics are Shakespeare's Hotspur and Scott's Fergus Mac-Ivor.) Aeneas is a less passionate lover, and his marriage is externally arranged by fate—as it were, given to him from outside. Yet the reader is not in any doubt that Aeneas and not Turnus deserves to marry Lavinia; but the reader *is* led to question the concept of "deserves." Just so Carthage is depicted as luxurious and epicurean, and Dido is associated, by means of literary allusions to the *Argonautica*, with Medea, the murderous witch of Lemnos. So we know it is right for Aeneas to desert her; but we are led to question the concept of "right." This is how the *Aeneid* renders empire into poetry, and it offers useful points of reference for a theory of the imperialism in English literature, despite the differences in both literary form and political structure. In Scott's *Waverley*, Flora Mac-Ivor is a Dido figure; in Shakespeare's *Antony*, Cleopatra is; while Waverley and Octavian have the same function as Aeneas. All three writers show what is gained and what is lost when peace is established and a great civilization founded. If neither Virgil nor Shakespeare makes much of adventure, the reasons for that will become apparent, and are equally interesting from our point of view.

As I have indicated, the foundation epic of the British empire was told by Shakespeare in his history plays, and by Scott in his historical novels. Scott we shall come to in Chapter IV of this study, but Shakespeare did not write adventure tales, nor narrative in any strict sense, so I have nothing to say about him except a preliminary word here. It will perhaps be enough to quote the famous speech from Act

II, Scene I, of *Richard II,* to show Shakespeare as an imperial writer of the ornamental or propagandist kind.

> This royal throne of kings, this scepter'd isle,
> This earth of majesty, this seat of Mars,
> This other Eden, demi-Paradise,
> This fortress built by Nature for herself
> Against infection and the hand of war,
> This happy breed of men, this little world,
> This precious stone set in a silver sea,
> Which serves it in the office of a wall
> Or as a moat defensive to a house,
> Against the envy of less happier lands . . .

What is specifically imperialist there is the precious metal and precious stone images (I would suggest that the mythological allusions are subsumed in these) combined with the stress on defensiveness. The language makes England into a treasure—something that needs to be defended against both predators and barbarians. (We shall see the same thing going on in *Robinson Crusoe,* to define our feeling about Crusoe's kingdom, but Defoe's imaginative style is much more modernist.)

The history plays were of course part of the Tudors' propaganda to legitimize themselves and their idea of England; an idea which by Elizabeth's time partook of the excitements of Empire also. Shakespeare took the task over from earlier propagandists. In *English History in the 16th Century* Lily B. Campbell tells how Henry VII set Polydor Vergil and Bernard Audre to writing histories that would serve Tudor purposes. While Henry VIII set John Leland to recover the antiquities of England, and in a report of 1546, Leland promised "to establish the antiquity and originality of the English church, the claims of Englishmen throughout the ages, the historical greatness of England, shire by shire, and the true relation of England to Ancient Rome" (*Shakespeare's Histories,* Eugene M. Waith (Ed.), p. 20). Polydore Vergil's book (published in Latin in 1534, in English only later), influenced Hall, whose *Union of the Two Noble and Illustrious Families of York and Lancaster* Shakespeare used.

Hall's chronicle, which appeared in 1548, promised to prove Henry VIII "the indubitable flower and very heir of both the sayd lineages," and pageants of the York-Lancaster union were presented to Elizabeth on her coronation procession. The Wars of the Roses were for

Shakespeare and the Tudors what the civil war in Rome was for Virgil and Augustus; a period of devastation from which the country was grateful to be delivered. (An equally strong feeling can be detected in Defoe against the civil war in England in the seventeenth century.) Hall's chronicle covered exactly the period of Shakespeare's two historical tetralogies. Both writers show the sin of deposing Richard II, the punishment that sin received, and its expiation in the death of Richard III and the accession of the Tudors.[3]

Critics have pointed out a connection between these plays and Shakespeare's treatments of Roman history, because both subjects bear on the same theme: empire. Traversi, in *Shakespeare: The Roman Plays*, calls *Antony and Cleopatra* the last and greatest of the English chronicle plays; and he reminds us of the *Aeneid* when he says that *Antony*'s subject is the founding of a universal empire. And Ernest Schauzer, in *The Problem Plays of Shakespeare*, says that the second tetralogy of English history plays "leads up to" *Antony* because they all deal with kingdoms, their greatness, and their costliness (the price to be paid in other values), just as Virgil does.

J. H. Walter even makes specific comparisons between *Henry IV* and the *Aeneid*. "The play gains in epic strength and dignity from Falstaff's death, even as the *Aeneid* gains from Dido's death. . . . both Dido and Falstaff are sacrifices to a larger morality they both ignore." Aeneas and Henry both neglect duty for dalliance; are recalled by divine interposition; and submit. Henry's order to kill the prisoners, at Agincourt, is an act of epic-hero's rage, just like those we see in Books X and XII of the *Aeneid*. And the justification of Aeneas, Book I, lines 504 and 505, applies to Henry also:

> rex erat . . . quo iustior alter
> nec pietate fuit, nec bello maior et armis

Thus Virgil and Shakespeare offer us major models of the literary treatment of empire. Very occasionally I shall be able to make a comparison between those models, in epic and drama, and the adventure narratives, fictional and nonfictional, which the modern world system has predominantly made use of. More generally they are valuable to my argument as a backdrop, a reminder of historical perspectives and alternatives.

One difference between these models and the adventure tale, the difference in literary dignity, is an important clue to the right critical treatment of the latter. Virgil wrote in the grandest literary genre of his time, deliberately aiming at greatness. Shakespeare took advantage of a striking flexibility in the literary system of his time, to rise to the highest levels occasionally within works which were much of the time entertainment. Both addressed the imperial theme directly. The adventure tale has been a low genre; just as—a connected fact —it has not confronted the imperial topic. That does not mean it has not dealt with that theme, or that high powers of intelligence and imagination are not at work within it. It only means that conventional critical methods will not suit the tale, and that an important topic has been neglected by literature for that reason.

The third literary model I want to sketch, that of the Spanish romances of the sixteenth century, bears much more directly on Defoe, and is more similar in literary type. Like the modernist adventure tales, the romances do not confront the imperial topic, and their literary status was never so noble as Virgil's. Like the adventure tales, they express a caste ideology (rather simple-mindedly) but a different caste, and by means of a different mode of expression.[4]

The bulk of these romances were written in Spain, at the rate of about one a year from 1508 to 1550, plus nine more up to 1588— the defeat of the Armada was a defeat for the military class they served, and a check to the imagination they expressed—so only another three appeared after that, up to 1605.[5] This is Henry Thomas's account in *Spanish and Portuguese Romances of Chivalry* (Cambridge, 1920) and he tells us what enormous influence they had, despite that simple-mindedness mentioned before. (It is not the complex works of art—that is, the spiritually rebellious—which have the most social influence. The modernist adventure tale probably was more influential than the serious novel.)

The romances were much translated, and came second in bulk of printed matter to devotional literature only. Statesmen and emperors delighted in them, abroad as well as in Spain. François I had *Amadis de Gaul* translated, and many court ceremonials under Henri II were derived from it; social historians have called it the social breviary of Henri's court, and say that international political ceremonies like the Field of the Cloth of Gold were designed by reference to it. Treasuries of thoughts, on education and courtesy, were compiled from the romances and published separately. Children were named after characters in the romances. It was widely believed that under-

49

neath and in their fantasy was to be found profoundest truth.

*Amadis de Gaul*, the most famous of them, was written over a period of forty years, different parts by different authors, and amounted finally to twenty-one books. It exerted great influence over, strikingly, both St. Ignatius de Loyola and St. Teresa de Avila; and perhaps even more striking testimony to its social power is the official decree against importing it into the Spanish colonies, declared in 1531, because of its excessive popularity. Its imaginative influence runs through the conquistadors' accounts of their conquests, and—there seems every reason to suppose—through their most private ways of seeing and naming their exploits. When they first saw Mexico City, Bernal Diaz says, it seemed to them like something out of *Amadis;* California was named after the Amazonian kingdom described in Book V; and so on.

John J. O'Connor, in *"Amadis de Gaul" and Its Influence on Elizabethan Literature*, analyzes it under four categories that contrast vividly with the sort of adventure tale which Defoe was to tell. It was a book of war; of which the technology was archaic, and the enemies fantastic—monsters, pagans, giants. It was a book of love; part sensual and part ideal love, but always outside marriage, between knights and princesses, and involving swoons and madness and irresistible passion. It was a book of courtesy; including whole educational treatises, based on the value of high birth and the code of honor. And it was a book of marvelous adventures; some of whose most prominent agents were magicians and Fortune. That is enough to indicate the distance between such stories and the kind we are used to. Those are four categories of the military imagination, not the mercantile.[6]

The plot is said to begin not long after the Crucifixion, but the sense of time and place have nothing to do with reality. Amadis is said to be born of a secret union between Perion, king of Gaul, and the princess Elisena. She and her maid, Darioleta, push the baby out to sea in its cradle, and it floats away up to Scotland, where Amadis is taken ashore and grows up in ignorance of his origin. Inspired by love of Oriana, daughter of King Lisuarte, he performs innumerable feats of arms, in none of which is he ever defeated. And so on.

The famous reaction against chivalric romance is of course *Don Quixote*, which appeared in 1605. Generically speaking, that book certainly was an antitype of the chivalric romance, and modernists like Twain have often claimed it as their sponsor. But irony is always a kind of tribute paid to the thing ironized, and it seems plausible to consider *Don Quixote* as the last chivalric romance rather than as the start of something new.

That is Alexander A. Parker's theory, in *Literature and the Delinquent* (Edinburgh, 1967). He says that the true antitype to romance in Spain was a new moral realism in fiction, which began with *Guzman de Alfarache,* in 1599. This was the first of a whole line of picaresque novels throughout Europe, of which the last was Smollett's *Ferdinand, Count Fathom,* 1753. One aspect of Defoe's literary activity, that represented by *Moll Flanders,* is similar to this picaresque fiction, though it seems likely that Defoe's source was that other popular form, the criminal's biography. In any case, this is not the side of Defoe's work that I shall be concerned with. The real start of new adventure narrative in England, I am convinced, was *Robinson Crusoe.*

The connection between the romances and the adventure tales is therefore not at all genetic, either in the intellectual biography or the literary genre sense, but contrastive. The romance did not give birth to the adventure. It is a social-historical contrast I am drawing attention to, between the spirit of the romance and the spirit of the adventure tale. Those "spirits" should be defined in terms of their social-cultural functions. Perhaps I can illustrate the chivalric spirit in a piece of actual history, the Paso Honroso (or exploit) of the knight Suero de Quiñones in 1434. Henry Thomas tells us that this knight and nine comrades tilted against all comers for thirty days, because he wanted to free himself from a vow he had taken to wear an iron chain around his neck every Thursday, in token of servitude to a certain lady. One man was killed and many wounded (including all but one of the ten defenders) before the exploit was stopped by the authorities. This is what the spirit of romance could inspire men to, until it was replaced by the spirit of adventure. As for the latter, the shrewd exploits of the merchant caste can be illustrated from *Robinson Crusoe,* or from William Phips's rise to wealth, as told by Cotton Mather, or from the story of any adventurous apprentice who ended up Lord Mayor of London.[7] But I shall be concerned with the form as much as the spirit of adventure.

## Method of Analysis and Comparison

In order to study the adventure tale form as it develops over the two hundred years and more after *Robinson Crusoe,* I am going to use a vocabulary of critical concepts derived from the structuralists. My understanding of these concepts differs somewhat from theirs, because my interest in literature and society differs. But they are the critics (amongst those I know) who have worked in the area of theory I am concerned with, and they have developed a set of stimulating ideas which have given shape to my own. My interpretation of those ideas is in some ways radically different, but—seen from another point of view—is only an extra twist given to them to make them suit my purpose.

I am interested in narratives that are imaginatively true, and these are histories and biographies as often as fiction; so the opposite to imaginative truth is not nonfiction but imaginative falsity or deadness. Thus, though I agree with the structuralists when they say that their central problem is always "What is literariness?", I mean something different by the question. They mean, it seems, "What is imagination?" while I mean, "What is this kind of imagination?"

What they have to offer me I can suggest first by a passage from Genette's *Figures,* pages 159–160 (quoted in Robert Scholes's *Structuralism and Literature,* p. 8) when he says that structuralist theory applies most obviously "to literatures distant in time or space, infantile or popular literatures, including recent forms like melodrama and the serial novel, which criticism has always neglected . . . structuralist criticism can treat this material anthropologically, studying its large masses and recurrent functions, following the way traced by folklorists. . . ." Whereas to "living literature" hermeneutic criticism seems appropriate. But in fact, Genette goes on, the true distinction is not to be drawn between two kinds of material; we can use structuralist methods whenever the object is "other" to us. This suits my purpose perfectly, for I am concerned with particular books, the products of the highest intelligence, as much as with "large masses."

Then structuralism, says Scholes, establishes a model of the "system of literature" as the external referent for individual works. It seeks to explore the relation between them and it, and also the relation between that system and the culture of which it is a part. System in this sense means a complete, self-regulating entity that adapts to new conditions by transforming its features while retaining its structure. The idea is adapted from linguistics, where the system of a language is called a *langue;* the other of the two key terms is *parole.* (French terms are used because the theory originated with de Saussure.) *Parole* means any particular utterance, and includes poems and novels, but also slang and mere ejaculations. And yet no *parole* can be understood before you understand the *langue* in which it is spoken, while the latter is systematic and theoretical. (Of course it does not have to be learned systematically and theoretically to be used correctly, for children do not learn their native language that way. But from that correct usage a system can be induced—in fact, must be, if a language is to be taught or studied in any way other than the way native-speaking children learn it.) This is the sort of system which structuralism studies in literature, the *paroles* in this case being individual works of art, the *langue* being a genre or perhaps all literature at a given moment. (As that loose alternative suggests, literature is not so much of a system as language. But it has some systematic characteristics.) And this is what I am studying, my *paroles* being primarily adventure tales, my *langue* literature-as-a-system.

Tenn A. van Dijk, in *Some Aspects of Text Grammars,* says that we need transformational grammars of literature, to explain the deep structures that underlie particular literary texts and out of which those texts are generated. Such a grammar would be transformational in the sense that it would allow us to produce and interpret an infinite number of texts in a rule-governed way. If I understand this correctly, a transformational grammar of language gives us the rules for transforming a single affirmative statement into its negative, interrogative, past and future, compound and complex forms. Such a grammar of literature (with perhaps a genre being the equivalent of a language) would explain how a given story could be transformed into another; *Waverley* into *The Pathfinder,* let us say, or *Pamela* into *Jane Eyre.* That, at any rate, is what I shall try to do.

The structuralists say that literary study should concentrate on the motif, which is any irreducible element entering into a number of works of art. I shall define the adventure tale, and mark its development as a genre, primarily in terms of motifs; though I shall use

Lévi-Strauss's term, *mytheme,* when I think of a story as a myth instead of a tale.

But the most important formalist idea for my purposes is that of genre—genre as a mechanism of the system of literature—and here Claudio Guillen's *Literature as a System* is most useful. Guillen says that the genres are mental codes, by means of which a writer comes to terms with his writing. Taken all together, they codify the subjects available to a writer, the styles appropriate to them, and the rewards to be expected from each. There have always, he says, been styles and counterstyles, genres and countergenres; for instance, praise and vituperation, tragedy and comedy, pastoral and picaresque; together these map out the possibilities for a writer. They constitute the code of literature at a given moment.

Robert Scholes usefully extends this idea by pointing out that reading as well as writing is a generic process; we postulate a genre whenever we begin to read, and that genre implies certain expectations, against and with which the writer works. Each specimen is likely to alter slightly the laws of the genus, for this is not taxonomy —this is an artistic, not a scientific process—but they are still laws, exerting pressure on both readers and writers. This idea helps me to understand the relation of the adventure tale to other forms of fiction, notably the morally serious domestic novel. I see the state of literature at any given moment as a system of forces acting upon both writers and readers, persuading them to give "appropriate" depths and strengths of response to literary forms and their subject matters. (Perhaps the best mechanical analogy is the centrifuge, which sorts out the heavier elements from the lighter—but those elements must here be understood to be reader responses as well as the literary forms with which they are paired.)

The genre map of literature, the grid of the system, that shows which forms are dominant, and where the beginning writer may aim at greatness, changes as the larger map of culture changes. In the Renaissance, the epic poem and the tragic drama were dominant. After 1688 in England the novel was born, and gradually displaced those forms. And among the subgenres of fiction, serious literary interest came to focus on what can be called the courtship or domestic novel. The adventure novel was assigned less significance, and matched with more superficial responses. This does not mean that all the writers of adventure were nonserious, or that the thematic material was trivial. But this point I must return to.

The structural anthropologists and folklorists have something to contribute to my method, too. Lévi-Strauss works with not tales but myths, and he defines a myth as a body of materials, mainly narrative, which "deal with" one aspect of a culture. The narrative often obscures the myth, in order to make that aspect of the culture palatable to its members. (As adventure obscures imperialism.) The myth is a coded message from the culture as a whole to the individual members; it can be delivered in a variety of different ways; and it remains valid as long as the culture remains homogeneous. I find this very suggestive when applied to the birth and death of the adventure tale from Defoe to Kipling.

The code of the message, says Lévi-Strauss, can be read only if we rearrange the mythemes (the motifs or units of myth) into a nonnarrative order. (This is of course what criticism does to literature, and what my interpretation will do to adventure.) Thus he breaks the Oedipus myth down into four columns of units, some of which are semantic, not syntagmatic; for instance, the fact that "Oedipus" means "swollen-foot." The culture that developed the Oedipus myth, according to his interpretation, *believed* that man is autochthonous, but *knew* that men are born of man + woman. The myth evoked that puzzle but connected it with another puzzle, involving problems of kinship and incest, which the culture had worked out. By associating the adjustments of social life with the enigmas of religious mystery, the myth made the latter familiar and acceptable.

But the value of Lévi-Strauss to me does not depend upon any particular method of interpreting, such as the column of units, much less any particular interpretation. Some of Edmund Leach's essays are much closer to my purposes and better as models. Lévi-Strauss's value above all lies in his teaching that myths, while sometimes constituting models for their societies—to perpetuate beliefs or practices—sometimes instead expose the mainsprings of their societies, in all their contradictions. A decoded myth is a theme with variations, the theme being some self-contradiction within a morality.

Edmund Leach has applied these ideas to literature, and so has brought them much closer to my own uses. In "The Legitimacy of Solomon" (1966) he shows how the Biblical story of Solomon's family origins mediates a contradiction in Jewish culture: the contradiction between the teaching of endogamy (with the idea that Palestine was a direct gift of God to the Jewish people) and the fact of exogamy (with the knowledge that Palestine was a conquered country, with a racially mixed population). This story was written at a time when religious rules were very important; because of Ezra and Nehemiah, Judah had become a religious community, represented by a high priest instead of a king. The only half-Jewish origin of Solomon, told in the story, admitted the fact of exogamy, but made sense of it in the larger context, related it to the teachings of the Divine fate of Israel.

Another study in the Leach line is even closer. This is Marguerite S. Robinson's "The House of the Mighty Hero or the House of Enough Paddy?." This is about Prince Dutthagamani (161–137 B.C.), the prince who restored the Sinhalese dynasty and Buddhism in Ceylon. It is again an endogamy-exogamy contradiction which lies behind the myth, and it is mediated by an equivocation about exactly how the people who tell the story, the Morapityans, are descended from the Prince. This equivocation makes the contradiction comfortable and acceptable. But the culture also contains a contradiction between priestly and kingly authority, mediated in this story by the combination of the man of peace and the man of war in Dutthagamani. That is what is announced in the title of the essay; the Morapityans have to ask, is it for his might and heroism they celebrate him, or for his skill in producing and providing? Is it not for both, even though the two legends present themselves as mutually exclusive?

At this point we can make an easy transition to the modernist adventure tale, and apply similar methods to it. For there is in Defoe's *Captain Singleton*, and in several later stories of that kind, a comparable figure, whom we can label "the bloody Quaker." This figure (in *Captain Singleton* he is called William) is both a sincere Quaker, devoted to peace, meekness, and self-denial, and at the same time a pirate, an expert in war, and ruthless against his enemies. I will explain later how Defoe, and the other writers, resolve the contradiction. But it's obvious that it arises out of a contradiction in their feelings, aspirations, and values, and in their readers' feelings—a contradiction that works in the culture itself, just as one did in the culture of the Morapityans.

And the association of the explicable with the inexplicable, which Lévi-Strauss points to in myths, is paralleled in the adventure tale by an association of the familiar with the unfamiliar, of the palatable with the unpalatable, which one can see in Kipling's "The Man Who Would be King," for instance. Much of the "theory" of human nature and history which this story implies is deeply disturbing, but it is mixed with much that is familiar and comfortable. (Of course the element of the enigmatic, which Lévi-Struass stresses in myth, is much smaller in art—at least in the serious art of the domestic novel.) The other structuralist concepts will be applied in the chapters to come, and will prove especially fruitful in explaining how a genre develops and how the system of literature relates both inwardly to the adventure tale and outwardly to the system of culture as a whole.

But it is worth describing in advance the one genre of fiction that came into existence at the same moment as the adventure tale, and with roughly the same cultural sponsorship, but which developed into a much more serious literary genre. The domestic or courtship novel, which also took an initial impetus from the hands of Defoe, gradually won a literary status for itself which the adventure novel never equalled, and indeed preempted the prestige of literary seriousness. It won itself a place in the center of the system of literature.

It did so because this form was employed to carry both key values of the ruling mercantile caste, and at the same time a protest against the crudest expansive thrusts of the modern system—including imperialism and adventure. Perhaps "protest" will seem too assertive a word for something that showed itself at first as voluntary ignorance —aversion of interest. But there is spiritual energy in fiction like Richardson's, and the curve of that energy, at least by extrapolation, carries the reader away from the triumphant capitalism and militarism of eighteenth-century England; while in the nineteenth century there was of course demonstrable protest, against industrialism, in the domestic novel. The serious writers, reacting against what they hated in their civilization, could indirectly attack it in the courtship novel, while more clearly asserting the caste values they shared with their audience. They created a literature of largely silent resistance. The adventure novel, on the other hand, did not protest. This is the source of the distinction, serious vs. nonserious: though of course individual writers had to give a literary validity to the distinction, by the imaginative effort they put into the domestic novel.

It is also worth sketching briefly the history of this genre because it is a paradigm of the development of a genre, of both the changes and the continuity in its motifs. Because these books are so well-known, and because great writers have written so often in this tradition, it is easy to demonstrate the development in their case; and then we can use that demonstration in considering the adventure tale. We find there a very different development, all stops and starts, with nothing consummated artistically.

Let us merely name the motifs of the domestic novel, from Defoe and Richardson to Lawrence. There is the group of marriageable girls —as in Jane Austen; the middle-class family life—as in George Eliot; the wild young aristocrat—as in Richardson—who seeks one of the girls; the process of courtship, which is the main action; the young man's conversion (or not); the melodrama of seduction; the married woman who made the wrong choice (particularly frequent in Dickens and Thackeray); and repentance (particularly strong in George Eliot and Tolstoy). These can all be found in Defoe's *Religious Courtship* and *The Family Instructor.*

## The Domestic Novel

The essential subject of this kind of novel is marriage, its essential action the right choice of partner for the heroine. The relations between it and the adventure novel can be described as polar, and that polarity is a major clue to the operation of literature-as-a-system in England. To keep to our previous metaphor, the courtship novel became one of the heaviest elements in the centrifuge, the adventure one of the lightest. To put it more simply, serious fiction writers in England were warned away from the adventure tale, and toward the domestic novel, even though, during this period of 1700 to 1900, the adventure material bore much more directly upon the serious history of England.

To come to Defoe's own contributions, in *Religious Courtship* he tells the story of a middle-class widower's three daughters, whose mother had been devout and had told her daughters never to marry an irreligious man nor one of a different faith. Their father is comparatively worldly, but their mother had said, "A religious life is heaven upon earth," and so each daughter has to work out her own fate between those two options. The interest of the novel derives

from comparison of their fates. The youngest is courted by an aristocrat, but finds him insufficiently serious about religion, and so rejects
him, braving her father's wrath. The young man goes off in high
dudgeon to his country estate, but there converses with William, a
poor but honest peasant, who teaches him religion, after acquiring
which he is accepted. (Two motifs here were of great importance in
later fiction: the *Wakefield/Werther* pastoral, and the idea that the
aristomilitary caste scorn religion.) The oldest and steadiest sister,
confidant of the others' problems, declares she won't marry at all,
because the times are so wicked (though at the end she gets a suitably
unexciting partner). But the middle one, being morally lazy, accepts
a man who turns out to be a crypto-Catholic and keeps a disguised
altar in his closet, and causes her a great deal of grief in the long run.[8]
And at the end of the book, the father too is converted to seriousness
by his daughters' sufferings.

This story is told at considerable length, with dialogue and imagined scenes and settings, though more sketchily than a real novel such
as Richardson was to write. But the plot is of the type that was to
be of great use to Richardson and subsequent novelists, notably Jane
Austen. *Sense and Sensibility, Pride and Prejudice, Mansfield Park,
Persuasion,* are all strikingly similar to this story.

*Conjugal Lewdness* (1727) also contains several anecdotes about
wicked aristocrats marrying sober citizens, and about tyrannical fathers interfering with their children's choice of partners. Max Novak,
in his introduction to the 1967 edition, says that Defoe here was the
first to depict conjugal quarrels in realistic fiction, complete with
feminine irony, masculine defeat, and the sexual implications of
apparently remote differences of opinion.

But I would like to spend more time on *The Family Instructor,*
where the stories are developed at more length.[9] In the Preface,
Defoe says that some have called this a religious play, and he had at
first intended to treat the material in a dramatic poem, which is
perhaps some indication of the seriousness with which he had imagined it. In Part I, "Relating to Fathers and Children," a father and
mother, suddenly aroused to religious consciousness, decide to reform
their family. Though their children are not immodest or dishonest,
the elder daughter, for instance, loves to play cards all night, to go
to the playhouse, to wear patches, to read romances, and to sing idle
songs: ". . . they were bred up with gaiety and gallantry, as being of

good fortune and fashion; but nothing of religion. . . ." (p. 71).

The parents' reform begins with a family rule that the children shall not go to the park after church, and this provokes a big quarrel, the elder daughter and the elder son being bitterly resistant. A younger brother and sister are amenable, having seen the advantages of religion in other houses they have visited. But the older ones, in an ingeniously conceived scene, walk out into the garden back of the house while a family meeting is held, giving the impression they have gone to the park, without risking such outright disobedience in reality, in order to test their parents' reactions. Later they both leave home.

Part 2, "Relating to Masters and Servants," tells quite a different story, of good and bad apprentices. On the whole this story fell into the hands of moralists rather than novelists in later years, so I shall not occupy myself with it.[10] Part 3, "Relating to Husbands and Wives," takes up again the story of the family. The elder daughter, who had been in love with Sir Anthony, an aristocrat and a rake, marries a serious-minded citizen with old-fashioned Protestant principles. He will take her to the playhouse door, but will not go in himself; in fact he institutes family prayers, to her disgust, and teaches the children religion. They quarrel; she repents her malice against him; falls into a fever, and repents her evil ways as she recovers. The elder brother, on the other hand, having joined the army and lost an arm in the wars, comes back to England unrepentant, and so dies rejected by his family.

And Vol. II, Part 1, "Family Breaches," tells the story of two bad wives, married to two pious citizens who are friends. The first wife objects to her husband conducting family worship, on the grounds that he is unworthy—it is clear that she is morally jealous of him. She becomes pathologically angry, falls sick, goes mad, and when she recovers doesn't fully remember what has happened—is diminished. The second wife is born an aristocrat (her brother is called Sir Richard) and so is used to luxury, and to riot and gaming. She mocks her husband when he asks that grace be said at her brother's table. Sir Richard is much struck by her husband's integrity, however, and when she returns to her brother's house in dudgeon, he quarrels with her and is even himself converted to moral seriousness by the spectacle of her dissipation. He takes her back by force to her husband, and there she falls sick and eventually repents.

The motifs of these stories echo through the rest of eighteenth- , nineteenth- , and even twentieth-century serious fiction; in the Brontës' novels, in Dickens, in Thackeray, in George Eliot, in Hardy; they are to be found, somewhat transvalued, in D. H. Lawrence. (Indeed, crudely as they are written, there is evidence elsewhere in Defoe—notably in *Roxana*—that he had a novelistic imagination of no mean order, and could, given other circumstances, have won himself a place in the history of serious fiction.) This is the story of caste psychology and intercaste conflict, of manners taken seriously and marriage taken solemnly, with which we are all familiar because it has been central to our literary culture.

Of course the story develops and changes. One cause is that a talented artist will not simply repeat his predecessor. The sexual assault upon Pamela, by which Richardson demonstrates her virtue, is refined away to practically nothing in *Mansfield Park.* While Richardson's Mr. B. undergoes an enormous development to become Mr. Rochester in Charlotte Brontë's novel. But Pamela, Fanny Price, and Jane Eyre are the same figure, have the same function, to use Propp's term. In the second half of the nineteenth century, a different kind of change occurred in the heroine, which involved a more complex development in the story. In the hands of George Eliot and her successors, the girl becomes more substantial. Physically and morally, Dorothea Brooke and Maggie Tulliver are larger than the girls they stand beside—while their predecessors were smaller than their equivalent contrasts. Hardy and James were more equivocal about physical size, but at least some of their girls can seem large, figures to be admired rather than pitied. The girl's counterplayer, an aristocrat to begin with, is often given foreign blood instead by George Eliot, a proletarian origin by D. H. Lawrence, and East-European or American-radical credentials by Doris Lessing. It is, I think, obvious, what external forces caused these substitutions and displacements. The more striking fact is surely the continuity.

Why was this story taken up by major writers while the adventure tale was not? Of course, there was resistance to this story too, at first, as we see in Fielding's mockery of Richardson. But that resistance did not last long; Fielding's last novel, *Amelia,* is Richardsonian, or one might say, thinking of these books, Defoesque. It seems clear that the difference derives from the close alliance that was forged in the early eighteenth century between literature and the religious-moral-sexual interests of Puritanism. Though Pope and Swift might keep those interests at arm's length, Steele and Addison embraced them in their writing for *The Tatler* and *The Spectator,* which include many short stories comparable with those Defoe told.

Puritanism was a major—many historians would say the major—element in the ideology of the modern world system. Its energies can be found at work everywhere, in religion, in morality, in commerce, in science.[11] Of course it was not unopposed, but its relations with its opponents within the modern system ideology seem to be a good example of the Hegelian triad, in which Puritanism was the thesis. (Puritanism was the merchant caste's form of Christianity, so the dialectic just named was also the dialectic of the castes.) Thus in the case of literature it seems clear that Defoe and Richardson and the novel they invented represent a thesis, to which Fielding, among others, opposed an antithesis; but the novels of the end of the eighteenth century, even Fielding's own *Amelia,* bore the marks of the thesis. By then Puritanism was in alliance with other social forces which it had fought before—that is the crucial point.

The Puritan army (at least in its lower ranks) had been radical, but the economic sinews of Cromwell's Commonwealth, the London merchants, were conservative. Though Presbyterian, they were luke-warm about even the Scots' Presbyterian Church, and grew tired also of supporting Cromwell's adventurous militarism. They made an alliance with the conservative forces in England, on which the subsequent settlement was based, and to this settlement the Brahmins (scholars, writers, clergymen) gradually subscribed.

These merchants even brought the Stuart Charles II back to the throne. A pamphlet of 1680* claimed that Presbyterians were not radicals, did not oppose either king or state, but were rather the natural heirs of the Elizabethan Puritans, men who wanted a *moral* revolution. That was what the Restoration Puritans engineered after 1688, by means of their Societies for the Reformation of Manners (led by Queen Mary and Archbishop Tillotson), and their Dissenting Academies, of which there were forty-seven by 1702. These were essentially merchant caste reforms, in education and morality, and as vital to the modern world system as the new habits of work imposed on the factory hands.

*H. G. Plum, *Restoration Puritanism,* 1943.

Literature cooperated, in the persons of Addison and Steele, and all that their famous journals, *The Tatler* and *The Spectator,* stood for. These immensely successful innovations in taste brought literature and culture into alliance with the merchant caste. Defoe felt that *The Tatler* continued the work he had begun with his *Review.* Together, they saved literature from the control of schoolmen, rakes, and aristocrats. On the stage the New Comedy, for which Steele's *The Conscious Lovers* set the model, did the same. And Defoe and Richardson created the novel. Pope and Swift, on the other hand, felt a loyalty to older and fiercer modes of literary intelligence; and the reason is that they would not identify themselves with the merchant caste, or with the new gentleness, the glorious and bloodless moral revolution, which was in its service.

This moral revolution redirected spiritual intensity toward home life, marriage, and sex; away from older objects of devotion, like the liturgical life of the church, and the cults of the aristomilitary caste. When the spirit of religion came out of the monastery, to adapt a famous phrase, it settled in the home as well as in the marketplace, making its altar the bedroom and the bed. Indeed, as far as the serious novelists were concerned, it was the home and *not* the market that was important; the treaty of mutual support between the merchant caste and the serious writers referred exclusively to the private life of the former, and did not cover the public life of commerce in England, much less in the empire. (By the same token, that treaty referred exclusively to the moral concerns of the serious writers, and did not cover their theological or specifically religious interests.)[12]

The colonial enterprise did not attract the participation of Brahmin seriousness, so it did not undergo the imaginative transformation that serious writers gave to family life in the courtship and domestic novel.[13] Serious writers facing the colonial theme felt an inhibition or a prohibition, from which they turned away, to the courtship theme. This is what the novelists above all took up (one sees that theme treated crudely in *The Family Instructor*) and the greatest example is Richardson; that is why there is that extraordinary concentration on sex in *Pamela* and *Clarissa* which has misled so many commentators. Of course it was a Puritan kind of sex that Richardson could celebrate. It was passive and feminine sex which was idealized in such novels, while the chivalric romance had idealized the active and masculine kind. Passive sex and spirituality were most seriously and inextricably wedded, or identified, by that author and those readers.

Thus even the theological and spiritual heritage of Puritanism did not entirely lose connection with the serious novel. We can find a structure of feelings closely related to Richardson's in the hymns of Isaac Watts, perhaps the major representative of Puritan piety in eighteenth-century England.[14]

> We are a garden walled around
> Chosen and made peculiar ground
> A little spot enclosed by grace
> Out of the world's wide wilderness.

And

> Watched by the world's indignant eye
> Who load us with reproach and shame
> As servants of the Lord most high
> As zealous for His glorious name,
> We ought in all His paths to move,
> With holy fear and humble love.

Clarissa persecuted by Lovelace, even Pamela persecuted by Mr. B., was, I think, the heroine of feelings like these. Persecution is a main mode of action and fantasy in Richardson.[15] You don't find anything comparable in the adventure novel.

Out of the negative and shadow figures of the Puritan drama, moreover, out of Milton's Satan and Richardson's Lovelace, comes the Byronic hero, and the Nietzschean superman. Such figures, when transvalued, are spiritual adventurers. They appear even in domestic novels, where all the action is transferred indoors, and almost all inside personal relations, and are moral imperialists. Lovelace says, "I have three passions that sway me by turns; all imperial ones. Love, revenge, ambition, or a desire of conquest." He often sees himself as "an imperial personage." While Clarissa takes modesty as her motto, and desires to slip through life unnoticed.[16] She is anti-imperialist. (These are puns, of course, but it is history that is making them.)

This disapproval of the military, aristocratic, and adventurous hero was a very powerful impulse within English seriousness, which persisted a long time, even though it always evoked some contradictions (voluntary contradictions in Fielding, Swift, Scott, as well as the involuntary ones in Milton and Richardson). For instance, Harriet

Byron in *Clarissa* attacked the aristocratic concept of honor from the mercantile-bourgeois point of view of duty. "Murderous, vile word, Honour! . . . the very opposite to duty, goodness, piety, religion." But we find Thomas Arnold in the nineteenth century saying something very similar.* "I confess that if I were called upon to name what spirit of evil predominantly deserved the name of anti-Christ, I should name the spirit of chivalry—the more detestable for the very guise of the 'Archangel ruined,' which has made it so seductive to the most generous spirits—but to me so hateful, because it is in direct opposition to the impartial justice of the Gospel, and its comprehensive feeling of equal brotherhood, and because it so fostered a sense of honour rather than a sense of duty."[17] Presumably Arnold meant to condemn Scott's novels and adventure novels, in general, for spreading the spirit of chivalry. In fact, the most serious voice in Scott comes down for duty against honor; and Defoe's adventure tales are not in the least chivalric. But serious moralists like Arnold (and Dr. Johnson) were sometimes impressed by the domestic novel as a spokesman for seriousness; never by the adventure tale.

Thus of the two genres which Defoe helped to found, only one was embraced by morality and by literature. Of course, one must take into account Defoe's weaknesses as a writer: his failure to achieve interiority, personality, with language and with literary form; his lack of artistic and intellectual scruple, which meant a lack of intensity of meaning. But in the case of the courtship novel there was a Richardson to take up where Defoe left off, and to create that intensity; in the case of the adventure novel there was not, even though *Robinson Crusoe* was much more of a success than *Religious Courtship,* by every measure of success. The adventure novel never became serious enough literarily for moralists like Arnold and Johnson to read.

We tend to think of that unseriousness as the *cause* why moralists (and the most gifted writers) neglected it. But it was *effect* just as much—writers were never told how to combine the adventure subject with political seriousness. Clearly English literature had organized itself into a system, of which the central seriousness was hostile to the material of adventure and therewith of empire and frontier. The writer who took up that material knew that he was providing entertainment.

*Quoted in John Lord, *Duty, Honor, Empire,* p. 83.

# III

# *Defoe*

## Defoe and his England

IN a work of this size and purpose, there is no room for any but
the most schematic biography of the authors. But Defoe acted out
his temperament and represented his caste in a dozen different political and economic roles.[1] He was a representative man of his times.
So it helps to remember his social activity while reading his adventures. Therefore I am going to pick out those "themes" of his life
story which relate most importantly to *Robinson Crusoe* and *Captain
Singleton;* and to my general subject, the modern world's imagination. I would say that Defoe embodied that imagination.

First, then, he was born into a Dissenting family, and knew, at least
by family tradition, some religious persecution. It always remained
one of his major interests to speak for and to Dissenters; and he could,
on occasion—for instance, in his *Memoirs of the Church of Scotland*
—talk the old Puritan language about "persecuted saints" and the
"worldly men," the "men of blood," who oppressed them. But more
characteristically, his stress fell on reconciliation, in religion as in
politics. He had a modern kind of tolerance, and wanted to reconcile
the Dissenters to the rest of England, and vice versa—put a modern
stress on moderation. Thus in "An Appeal to Honour and Justice"
(1715) he says, "I was from my first entering into knowledge of public
matters, and have ever been to this day, a sincere lover of the consti-

tution of my country; zealous for liberty, and the Protestant interest; but a constant follower of moderate principles, a vigorous opposer of hot measures in all parties. . . ." (p. 232). Both parties, he says, have succumbed to hot opinions. But he has been loyal to the country and the king.

This stress on England-as-a-whole, as an escape from factionalism, is also very characteristic of Defoe. The bitter memories he cherished were of civil war rather than of class or sect persecution. The happy future he foresaw was of prosperity and respectability, with the Dissenters fully members of the middle class.[2] This is modern system Puritanism, as distinct from earlier kinds.

Equally significant, and a second trait to stress in Defoe, is his loyalty to the king. Royalty rose above faction and above all ideologies except that which it embodied, the ideology of the nation-state itself. And for Defoe there was one king above all kings, William III, the Dutch prince invited to ascend the throne in 1688. Defoe was twenty-eight at the time of the Glorious Bloodless Revolution. He joined William's forces as they approached London, and cut something of a figure in the City of London's processions of welcome. He defended William in his poem "The True-Born Englishman," gave William a lot of advice, in pamphlets, saw him face-to-face, and claims to have been a valued consultant. And indeed his loyalty to William's memory after the king's death was unequivocal and warm in a way almost unique among Defoe's political passions. He always celebrated the anniversary of William's landing in England.

What William meant to Defoe was probably what he meant to most people; which was expressed in the official toast to the king's memory: "To the glorious, pious, and immortal memory of the Great Deliverer . . . who rescued us from Popery, Prelacy, Brass Money, and Wooden Shoes." Financial probity and material progress there go hand in hand with religious liberty, all supreme values of the merchant caste.

And it is not irrelevant to remember also that William III was a Dutch prince. In him the two leading core states came together; you might say that Amsterdam yielded precedence to London finally in 1688.[3] Certainly the contrast between the Protestant Dutchman and the Catholic Stuarts, who were half-attached to France and even to Spain, was a contrast full of meaning to those who believed in what we are calling the modern world system.

Then, born a Dissenter, Defoe began adult life as a tradesman. His family had been Flemish artisans, who had fled the persecution of Philip II; a group whose migration helped establish the English wool trade—a crucial element in English wealth of Defoe's time. He was also an economic journalist, indeed a major propagandist for exponential growth and all the changes that brings. But Defoe himself was not a successful merchant. From his early thirties on, he was never clear of debt, and he went bankrupt in 1692, for £17,000. He was one of nineteen marine insurers ruined in the French wars. (Insurance was one of the key new professions, a keystone in the great structure of finance capitalism.) He paid off all but £5,000 of his debt in ten years, but lost a lot again in 1703. At that time he was in jail for a political offense, and while there his Tilbury brick and tile works failed. Between 1688 and 1694 he was defendant in eight lawsuits, all accusing him of sharp practice. Thus he had profound, as well as varied, experience of modern capitalism.

(It is, I think, no accident that three of the writers I am treating at length, Defoe, Scott, and Twain, all went bankrupt; and failed on the scale of firms, not merely of private individuals. They did so because they *were* firms, commercial enterprises, as Jane Austen, George Eliot, D. H. Lawrence were not. They participated in the capitalist activity, and the other three did not.)

Defoe was also a journalist, most notably in *The Review,* which he edited, and largely wrote, from 1704 to 1713. As such he was engaged in political propaganda, and semipolitical intrigue, and was one of the Grub Streeters whom Pope put into the *Dunciad.* As Pat Rogers shows in *Grub Street,* Defoe was very representative of the group which Pope repudiated, the group from whom he dissociated himself and literature, as being sordid and semicriminal. (Between 1720 and 1726 Defoe was *Applebee's Journal*'s reporter, interviewing criminals in Newgate prison.) Literature at its most dignified maintained a distance between itself and the modern system; but Defoe did not belong to literature.

As a journalist, he can be associated with Twain and Kipling; and the work of all three is more made up of newspaper fact and newspaper interest than the work of, again, Austen, Eliot, and Lawrence. Indeed, it is no accident that the first three, and this time we can add Scott also, were very interested in hoaxes. In Defoe's case, the most famous is the pamphlet, *The Shortest Way with Dissenters,* which earned him a spell in pillory and jail. In Scott's case, I am thinking of his long denial of being the author of the *Waverley* novels; in Twain's and Kipling's, stories like "The Man Who Corrupted Hadleyburg" and "The Village That Voted the Earth Was Flat" show their fascination with fraud and hoax.

Then Defoe was a government agent, a secret agent, sent to Edinburgh to facilitate the Union of England with Scotland, which was forced through—against a lot of Scottish opposition—in 1707. The Scottish parliament was abolished, and the Scots were given forty-seven seats in the English House of Commons and sixteen in the English House of Lords. Defoe discharged his duties by writing pamphlets and poems, but also by masquerading as a merchant—dropping hints, picking up information—his glee at being in disguise is obvious in his letters to Harley, the minister who employed him. "I am perfectly unsuspected," one letter begins, and closes, "I am all to everyone that I may gain some." This glee he took in disguise seems peculiarly characteristic of the heroes of the modern world system, especially the literary heroes (it is prominent in *Kim*, for instance) and is related to the taste for hoaxes. Defoe delighted in the idea of secret policy, and made a minor cult of Cardinal Richelieu.

But it is just as important that this work was done for the union with Scotland, the foundation of the British empire. Defoe believed in that Union not merely as extending English power but as improving Scottish life—introducing the benefits of progress, of the modern world system, where they were not known before. (Of course, those two values, Empire and Progress, were natural twins to his mind.) The Scots, and particularly the Highlanders, were for Defoe men on the very periphery of the system, psychologically and sociologically—and to bring them inside the Union was to benefit them. This was true for many others beside Defoe, and remained so throughout the two centuries we are studying. It will be interesting for us to watch the different figures that Scotland cuts in relation to England's modernist idea, in subsequent adventure novelists, like Scott and Kipling.

One last point; Defoe was a rationalist. Not in the most philosophic sense: he was very interested in supernatural and providential phenomena, and quite ready to accept explanations in such terms. But in the more literary sense of a distaste for myths and fables, he was a rationalist. His "The Storm" is, like *Journal of the Plague Year*, a nonfiction novel which professes to give us all the facts about a natural phenomenon. In the Preface, he says that ancient history is mostly lost to us by the empty flourishes and romance of ancient historians, and the lives of great men, who could have been of use to us, are "drowned in fable." For instance, the true story of Daedalus, a man who cleverly made his way out of an Egyptian maze by using a clue of thread, "is grown into the fable of making himself a pair of wings, and flying through the air." A drought in Samaria gets turned into a tale of Phaeton. And so we have the silly romances of Arthur, St. George, Guy of Warwick, Bevis of Southampton, all "legends of fabulous history which have swallowed up the actions of our ancient predecessors." These are the native equivalents of *Amadis*, the fiction of the feudal system in England.

And in *The New Family Instructor*, Defoe derives the words "romance" and "romantic" etymologically from "Roman Catholic"; saying that they were first applied to the saints' legends and supposed miracles of that religion. That derivation indicates pretty clearly the revulsion felt by the merchant caste for romance, and their own affiliation to adventure instead.

A Dissenter and a rationalist, therefore, a journalist and a secret agent, a merchant and a patriot, Defoe embodied many of the dominant forces of the modern system in England, and was admirably equipped to devise the literary form of its energizing myth.[4]

## Defoe's Fiction

Defoe wrote many kinds of fiction, was a first practitioner of many subgenres, as *Moll Flanders*, *Memoirs of a Cavalier*, *Journal of the Plague Year*, *Roxana*, and *Colonel Jack* will remind us. Indeed, one aspect of his importance to my argument here is that he was so generally gifted and inventive as a writer of fiction. That he in effect invented the novel for England and therefore for the world, is part of that sense of him I want to invoke, in order to give importance to *Robinson Crusoe*, or to that significance of *Robinson Crusoe* which I am going to describe. But I trust the reader to supply that himself, for there has been a good deal of interest in those books in literary circles recently; and what I would say is not so very different. The only ones I shall talk about are his tales of adventure.

It is generally accepted that all Defoe's adventure fiction derives from (one might say, crystallizes out of) the flood of travel writing of his own youth and Elizabethan times. William Hallam Bonner tells us, in *Captain William Dampier,* that the Term Catalogues of 1668–1709 show voyages to have been the most popular genre of literature published then, and that this was a new popularity. Voyages were popular in Elizabethan times also, but there had been a falling off after 1626 for two generations. But Defoe's personal library included forty-nine voyages, and he styled himself a master of geography—he wrote the text for the very large and expensive *Atlas Maritimus et Commercialis.* And when an interest in pirates developed, after Exquemelin's book* appeared in 1684, Defoe produced the first English book on the subject.

Among particular titles that constituted precedents for Defoe's work, one could cite Dampier's *New Voyage Round the World.* Dampier was a roughly parallel figure to Crusoe and Singleton, almost certainly something of a model for them, and in fact sailed on the expedition which brought home Alexander Selkirk, the major model for Crusoe. Dampier also brought home a Friday figure, a "painted prince," from the Spice Islands, who was put on exhibition in England, but died soon after of smallpox. Dampier's book came out in 1697, and had three editions in nine months. He personally had a great success—dined with Pepys and Evelyn, and appeared before the Council for Trade to describe the Isthmus of Darien.

The major such title, however, is Hakluyt's *Voyages—The Principal Navigations, Voyages, Traffiques, and Discoveries of the English Nation,* in three volumes, 1598–1600.[5] The volumes include letters, ruttiers, navigation training manuals, battle reports, logs, diaries, official reports, and projected and imaginary voyages as well as real ones. When merchant adventurers formed companies, they consulted Hakluyt. He and his uncle founded geography in England, and prepared England for empire, by—in the *Voyages*—praising England, hailing its great captains, rallying support to the navy, recommending colonization, describing new lands, revealing Spain's weaknesses. Irwin R. Blacker, editor of the 1965 edition of the *Voyages,* says they are "the very papers of Empire," and "the epic of the

*A. O. Exquemelin, *The Bucaniers of America,* London, 1684–1685.

English people as they told it themselves." Defoe's novels retold that epic, but in fiction and a new kind of fiction—formally appropriate to the modernist material involved.

One of the fiercest episodes in the *Voyages,* fierce in its imperialist exultation, is Raleigh's account of Grenville's last fight on the *Revenge* and of the defeat of the Armada. Raleigh was one of Defoe's heroes; in 1719, the year of *Robinson Crusoe,* he also brought out a *Voyages of Raleigh.* But there was a difference between the styles of imperialism of the two men, the difference between the modernist and the Elizabethan. Raleigh's *History of the World* spread the dream of English empire far and wide, infecting amongst others Cromwell. But his idea of Guiana was all made of gold. Hidden in the interior was supposed to be a race of Incas of fabulous wealth; with a capital city, Manoa, full of gold, and a king, El Dorado, who was smeared with turpentine and then daubed with gold dust for his coronation. Manoa was sought by European adventurers, including Raleigh himself, for 240 years.

That sort of material—or more exactly, the reflection in the general English mind of that sort of material—is what Defoe started with when he began to write adventure tales. But he made something different out of it. I want to summarize briefly two other works of his of that kind before I come to *Robinson Crusoe* and *Captain Singleton.* The first is *A New Voyage Round the World,* in 1725, in which the anonymous captain-narrator describes a career in trading, exploring, privateering, from which he returned rich. The adventures he meets are largely typical of the genre. At the Cape of Good Hope the captain cleverly put down a mutiny. At Madagascar he enlisted hundreds of pirates, who were fed up with their leaderlessness and self-dividedness. In Borneo he traded with trinkets, and in New Guinea got gold from innocent savages; these were vegetarians, who had had no contact with the world, and so had no rapine or violence in their manners or their agriculture; whose faces were "singularly honest and sincere."[6]

The most interesting episodes occur at the end of the book, in South America. As he traded along the west coast, the captain kept inquiring about the Andes and how to cross them. He captured a Spaniard who owned a villa near Baldivia, and won his trust and affection—won him away from his national loyalties. The Spaniard became a sort of Montezuma to the captain's Cortes. He told the captain how few Spaniards there were in Peru, and how they did not deserve to own that country. There were only 7,000 Spanish families there, and they neither worked nor explored. "Seignior," says he, "we have so much pride that we have no avarice, and we do not covet enough to make us work for it" (p. 361). (Pride was the quality characterizing the Spanish, according to modern system characterology.) The English would make a valuable property out of Peru; there were several mountains as rich as Potosi that had never been worked.

The Spaniard invited the captain to his villa, and treated all the Englishmen like kings—also leaving his sons on board the English ship as hostages—and gave them much gold and silver plate. (Gift-giving is an important motif in Defoe.) He led them up into the mountains, where the volcanoes light up the valleys by night, and they saw a river of fire, etc. (p. 396). (This is one of the great landscapes of adventure fiction; it recurs notably in Rider Haggard and Conan Doyle.) Half the streams and pools had gold in them, ready to be picked up. But the captain led his men, and Defoe leads us, on past that, down the mountain's other side, onto a great plain. This is what Defoe wants us to reach out toward. The Spaniards, we are told, don't care about this land (which is what we now call Argentina).[7] The land is like Salisbury Plain, and they see vast herds of black cattle, wild, and think of what the land would be like "if it had but half the art and industry of a European nation to assist the natural fertility of the soil." The gold, as always in Defoe, is a semisinister value; it breeds a fever among the men, who break discipline more than once. But the land, empty land, asking to be worked, is the beatific vision of modernist adventure, recurring in Rider Haggard and Conan Doyle at the end of the nineteenth century. This marks the difference between Defoe's imperialism and Raleigh's.

Indeed, that England should occupy that particular piece of land was a message Defoe returned to several times during his life. In *History of the Principal Discoveries,* for instance, he recommends a colony 120 miles south of the Rio de la Plata. Defoe was an enthusiast for colonies generally. He wanted England to occupy Canada, Max Novak tells us, and to claim California, on the basis of Drake's explorations. In 1711 he was considering emigration himself. *Moll Flanders* and *Colonel Jack* are, amongst other things, propaganda for emigration to Virginia and Maryland. Indeed, all Defoe's adventure and picaresque fiction can be regarded as propaganda for emigration. An Act of 1717, just before he began his career as a fictionist, made it possible to deport much larger numbers of criminals than before, and Defoe consistently depicts the experience as regenerative. The land and the gold are, then, two adventure motifs in the *New Voyage.*

The other adventure tale is even more interesting: *The Four Year Voyage of Captain George Roberts* (1726). The book is anonymous but usually attributed to Defoe; as in several other cases, it is quite possible that he acted only as its editor or even its scribe, but that makes little difference to its interest for us. Defoe is not important for the idiosyncrasies of his style, or even the integrity of his individuality, but for the way he represents by participation, the way he merges into the whole activity he describes.

The tone of this book is very severe, factual, sober, and the narrative implicitly develops the captain (the narrator) as WASP hero, that is, as modern world system hero. He is contrasted, implicitly, with other men (for instance with his first commander, Captain Scott), all of whom turn out to lack crucial WASP qualities, to be either incompetent or untrustworthy.

There is a long episode with some pirates who capture his ship. The quartermaster general of the pirate company, though normally of remarkable intelligence and generosity, takes a dislike to Roberts; jealous (one gathers) of his greater piety, firmness, virtue. Roberts refuses to join the company, and the other pirates are willing to let him go free, but the quartermaster becomes vindictive, persuading Roberts' mate to desert him, denuding his ship of all provisions, and all sails but old ones, and leaving him with only "a boy" and "a small boy." It is a remarkable study in the jealousy and malignity that can feed on virtue itself in the close quarters of ship life; a precursor of Melville's and Conrad's studies of that kind; for this motif will often recur in later adventures.

After the pirates disappear, there is much Crusoe-like detail about Roberts making do with inadequate materials. Then he falls sick, and cannot look after himself properly. The boy goes ashore at St. Nicholas, in the Cape Verde Islands, and does not return. Then seven young blacks come aboard, and the other interesting episode of the book begins. They profess to help Roberts, but in fact get drunk, do everything wrong, and leave; except that three have hidden aboard. These three are very affectionate and helpful—in intention—but entirely undisciplined. They refuse to man the pumps at Roberts' command, and, giving up all hope, lie on deck like dead men. Then one of them claims to know the coast and its ports—to be able to guide the ship to anchorage, but in fact cannot do so.

This man jumps overboard, and swims ashore, abandoning the captain, who cannot swim, and soon after the other two do likewise. However, they and their friends on the island come back to the ship, and get the captain ashore, on a narrow beach at the foot of unclimbable rocks. There he is stuck for a whole month, still sick and helpless, and they look after him. Domingo puts Roberts' head on his lap so that he may sleep. Manuel gets killed by a falling rock while tending him. Roberts reflects on their virtues; humility, hospitality, reverence for age; "how vastly they exceed us . . . who pretend to so much learning and knowledge." The book ends with a long factual description of the Cape Verde Islands, calculated to be of use to merchants and sailors, including maps. But it is the mythic aspect that concerns us—though it is important to note how closely that relates to the factual aspect. Mythically it gives us the fullest and most complex picture of "natives" and—more implicitly—of the WASP captain confronting them, two of the most important motifs of the modernist adventure.

## Robinson Crusoe

And so now we come to Defoe's best-known work. I must, in order to economize time and space, pass very lightly over those features of my interpretation which I expect to be assented to easily, however important they are to my argument. I expect a consensus (not of course a total one) on the following points: the imaginative importance of tools and techniques in the story—the exploration and dramatization of work—as in the famous passage about the complex operations necessary to bake a loaf of bread;[8] the imaginative predominance of reason and prudence—so vivid that the passages of emotional melodrama (for instance, Crusoe's reactions on first arriving) fade from the view, or never grip the mind, of most readers;[9] the literary achievement of formal realism, to use Ian Watt's term —in Defoe's case, a how-to-do-it realism, as when Crusoe does not notice the rope dangling from the wreck until the second time he swims by it; the striking lack of interest in erotic feelings—Crusoe's marriage barely mentioned, and only the portrait of Friday having a strong (though innocent) erotic coloring; the role of religion, as a powerful engine for the virtues which make Crusoe the hero, but as a perfunctory mechanism from other points of view. All of those features of the book are important, in making it correspond to the modernist imagination, but I count on their being obvious.

Nor shall I spend much time arguing, what I can expect no consensual agreement to, that the spiritual autobiography aspect of the book is unimportant. There is no question that Defoe made use of that form, that framework, for his story. But it seems to me that he used it up in doing so—that it would never occur to another writer to use that framework again, for that purpose, because everything that is vivid and exciting in the book is independent of that framework. He got where he wanted to by means of that crutch, but in arriving he let it go. This brusque declaration cannot hope to convince those scholars who have invested their energies in the opposite idea. But I hope to carry with me the rest.

Among the ideas I do want to put some stress on is that of value. What Crusoe does on his island is primarily to create value. He brings together the ship and the island, two things which before were of no use to anyone, and he creates—and we participate in the creation—something that is very valuable. That is the central pathos of the story, I would suggest, and it makes *Robinson Crusoe* a central myth of the modern system. The ship is a wreck; it is no longer any use; the island is a desert; it has never been of any use. But Crusoe, swimming out to the wreck, and paddling back with loads of planks, ropes, nails, carpenters' tools, sews the two together and creates something new out of the two of them; creates a property.

It is always in jocular terms that Defoe names the island as property: "my castle," "my bower," "my country estate," "my subjects," and at the end the elaborate masquerade of playing royal governor to fool the mutineers. ("My property," taken to an extreme, becomes "my kingdom"—this is the mercantile feeling about kingship.) But there can be no doubt that Crusoe *feels* it as property, that the feeling is an excited one, which runs deep, and that the reader, unless alienated from the book, shares that feeling.

We are made to share it by means of a number of other, simpler feelings—or perhaps they are parts of this larger one. There is the feeling of glee, first of all. I quote from pages 57 through 58 of the Penguin edition. "Neither was this all; but my goods being all English manufactures, such as cloath, stuffs, bays, and things particularly valuable and desirable in the country, I found means to sell them to a very great advantage; so that I might say I had more than four times the value of my first cargo, and was now infinitely beyond my poor neighbour. . . ." I'd suggest that that note, that innocent gloating over possessions and achievements, runs through the book, and makes the experience of reading it very different from what we call serious fiction. The lust for possession is something "literature" is very nervous of.

Related to glee is luck. I quote from page 74. "But that which comforted me more still, was that at last of all, after I had made five or six such voyages as these, and thought I had nothing more to expect from the ship that was worth my medling with; I say, after all this, I found a great hogshead of bread, and three large runlets of rum or spirits, and a box of sugar, and a barrel of fine flower. . . ." That which one does *not* deserve, has *not* planned for, can be taken by the virtuous and prudent man as even sweeter profit, as confirmation that grace is with him. It is first cousin to another feeling I want to call greed, though it is not a matter of appetite but of possession, and is excited by the counting over of what one has, the arranging of them neatly, or the dividing of them up into convenient packages —as when "I finished this work in about a fortnight, and I think my powder, which in all was about 240 lb. weight, was divided in not less than a hundred parcels. . . ." (p. 79).

Closely connected to glee, luck, and greed are the more anxious emotions of possession, like the need for security; and no literary reader of *Robinson Crusoe* needs reminding how much effort and emotion the hero puts into his defenses, his stockades and his muskets and his cellars, his caves and his camouflage and his movable ladders. But those readers, being of literary interests, and so deeply suspicious of and hostile to the modern world system, will find that those features jump to the eye. I am concerned to argue that Defoe in fact gives us a very complete and all-round exploration of the emotions of possession—the *relationship* of possession, which is also a relationship of creativity. The creation of value, the joy of possession, the anxiety of security, they are all there, and their interdependence. The

modern system feels itself quite specially the creator of value, and
Defoe's book answers to that feeling.

So much for the book's themes. I have not said anything radically
different from what Ian Watt said, I believe; how could I, since to
anyone not blinded by literary "science" it has always been obvious
what *Robinson Crusoe* is about.[10] (Of course, as one's general vocabulary shifts, one wants to phrase the idea a little differently.) But I
have promised a structuralist criticism here, and so it is the motifs
I must say most about, though I want, in nonstructuralist fashion, to
give them an imaginative context from imperial history.

The first group I want to draw attention to includes trifles, objects
of use, and gold. In Guinea, Crusoe finds how easy it is to purchase
"for trifles, such as beads, toys, knives, scissars, hatchets, bits of glass,
and the like, not only gold dust, Guinea grains, elephants' teeth, etc.,
but Negroes, for the service of the Brasils, in great numbers" (p. 59).
This became an idea of great potency in the core states, so it recurs
often in their adventure tales; that the bright, brittle, valueless trifles
or toys they made in large quantities could be exchanged for gold. It
is an image that relates to that of their own solidity, for the trifles
are eminently fragile and impermanent (not stout or sturdy). Gold
is the opposite, a refulgent source of power, like the sun. In *The
Review*, III (4), page 13, Defoe says in so many words that gold and
silver have an intrinsic value and appropriateness to be money, as
opposed to "insignificant and unvaluable trifles, as beads, shells,
feathers, and stones."[11] Gold is heavy and shining, the opposite of
the brittle trifles, so soon rusted. But the weight suggests guilt, the
gleam is of blood, the whole thing means passion and fever. In the
polarity of gold and trifles nothing is wholly good or reliable. What
stands independent of that fatal polarity is the tool, the object of use
—the holy emblem of the modern system.

Crusoe values "that most useful thing called a grindstone. . . ."
This is perfectly sincere, and he takes deep satisfaction from tools and
devices, so that a phrase like "a snug contrivance" contains a great
deal of feeling. But of course the gold, though from a higher point
of view to be despised, is in fact always worth acquiring, as Crusoe
shows in the famous passage where he moralizes over the uselessness
of gold in his shipwrecked situation, but nevertheless appropriates it.

This group of motifs will recur in many other adventure tales, but
it is perhaps worth putting it into a historical context here. The idea

of trifles is a widespread myth of imperial power, which covers un-truth as well as truth. For instance, the Chinese got gold dust, spices, etc., in return for trifles (coins, combs, lacquer-boxes) in Indo-China. On the other hand, they paid lavishly in real values for the trifles they relished like swallows' nests. And just so, as Braudel points out, England paid lavishly for turtles to make turtle soup, and Holland paid lavishly for tulip bulbs, and both paid highly for porcelain. In such cases, the imperialist power handed out gold, and got trifles in return.

Trade between the modern system and other empires never did conform to the "official" model. In the East it was England that paid gold; the Indians and Chinese did not want our goods as much as we wanted theirs; and that trade, and the East India Company itself, was disapproved by Defoe, for instance, because it took bullion out of England. One thing we did sell to Turkey and India was gunpowder; in 1606, 500 barrels went from England to Turkey, in 1629, 1000 barrels to India. And in North America fur trappers, Indian and white, were often paid in guns and powder, which was the key transaction between the state government and the Cossacks in Russia also. But this was all subsumed, or obscured, under the image of the shrewd man, who himself cared only for objects of use, selling trifles and getting gold.

Of course there was a feverish imagination of, and appetite for, gold. John Smith in his *Generall Historie* (1624) says that among the English colonists in America, "there was no talk, no hope, no worke, but dig gold, wash gold, refined gold, load gold." And back in England the gold they found (and silver and jewels) were much dis-played. It is calculated that 20 percent of what came back was used in decoration; gold and silver lace and embroidery, cloth of gold, silver plate and toilet sets, rings, watches, chains, etc. The voyages made a big difference to such styles.[12] Raleigh and Charles I wore earrings, Queen Elizabeth was famous for the quantity of jewels she always wore. Not to mention the new perfumes, and tobacco, and slaves. The slave trade was called England's silver mine—her consola-tion prize for not getting Potosi. Thus most *objets de luxe* can be considered forms of, or allusions to, gold.

The next group of motifs includes guns, natives, slavery, and canni-balism. Guns and powder are of the first importance to Crusoe always, and Defoe dramatizes their arrival on the island very effec-

*Defoe*

tively. "I believe it was the first gun that had been fired there since
the creation of the world; I had no sooner fired, but from all the parts
of the wood there arose an innumerable number of fowls of many
sorts, making a confused screaming, and crying every one according
to his usual note. . . ." (p. 72). That is surely a very eloquent evocation
of the theme of guns; all the more eloquent for its aesthetic and
intellectual innocence, its lack of development, of larger design.
Defoe's art is in a sense no-art, almost totally transparent. The gun
itself pokes through the page at us.[13]

And guns are related to natives as directly—and fatefully—as gold
is related to trifles. Guns were the supreme tool, the supreme example
of the modern technology, on which the modern system was built.
It was at the sight and sound of guns that natives fell on their faces
and worshiped—as Friday does in the novel. Any unnatural conjunction of the two motifs, as when a native himself fired a gun—as
Friday does—gave the reader an almost sacrilegious thrill. These two,
and slavery and cannibalism, define the most aggressive aspect of the
modern system.

The idea of slavery is charged with very strong feeling, because it
is imposed on Crusoe by his Moorish captors, and is the very worst
of fates; freedom being a specifically modern system idea. And yet
Crusoe sells his faithful Xury as a slave, when he has the chance; and
he determines to enslave a savage—"to get a savage into my possession"—before Friday arrives. To be a slave is a fate worse than death;
to have a slave—from a race outside the system, of course—is almost
better than ordinary life. Like gold and guns, it raises the pitch of life
thrillingly. In the relationship with Friday, as has often been observed, Crusoe achieves a warmth and ease of feeling he has not
displayed before, and will not display toward his wife, at least in the
narrative.

And the slavery is justified above all by the natives' cannibalism.
". . . all my apprehensions were bury'd in the thoughts of such a pitch
of inhuman, hellish brutality, and the horror of the degeneracy of
human nature; which, though I had heard of often, yet I never had
so near a view of before. . . ." (p. 172). And when seen as threatening
white men, cannibalism resolves all Crusoe's doubts and hesitations
about killing the natives.

Cannibalism is heavily stressed in adventure tales. It is the archetype of everything monstrous and appalling in primitive cultures.

The books' feeling against it seems to be connected with the horror and fascination of abandoning oneself into the hands of men of another color and culture. In India, one of the luxuries of native servants was they would shave a man while he was still asleep—as well as dress and undress him, etc. That image, turned sinister, is for instance taken up by Melville in "Benito Cereno." No doubt there are fantasies of homosexual rape at work beneath the surface also. But it is cannibalism (in *Omoo,* for instance) which is named as the ultimate horror.

I hope it is not irrelevant to introduce here the thought of Lévi-Strauss, who remarks on how vividly cannibalism reversed and antithesized the process whereby the European nations filled their colonies—a process he calls anthropoemic; they vomited forth by exile or imprisonment those people who caused them trouble. Cawley tells us that that idea of social spitting or spewing forth was habitually used in Elizabethan times in describing the settlement process. Colonies would rid England of her idle and her incendiaries. Thus Rome too had used its colonies, to get rid of its beggars, its idle, and its mutinous. The same was true of Spain; and Cortes himself was a natural rebel, as was Clive; the great conquerors themselves did not fit happily into their native societies, and were in some sense forced to go abroad. Australia was the most famous example of a prison colony, with convicts sent there from the late eighteenth century on. But all England's American colonies save those of New England were penal settlements. So, though I claim no historical connection between anthropoemia and cannibalism (or the horror at cannibalism), I think that an imaginative connection must hold them together in our mind.

The most important motif is the most obvious one, that Crusoe is a man absolutely alone, and on a desert island. This appeals to our imaginations in many ways, some of them, especially the magical-subconscious, not directly relevant to imperialism or the modern world system. But in Defoe's novel these other appeals are subordinated to the island's function as a perfect setting for adventures in reason and work and the creation of value. That becomes clear if you compare Defoe's story with the true story he began with, the story of Alexander Selkirk, a much gloomier and more violent man than Crusoe, psychologically. Defoe minimized that material; though it seems it would have found a ready response from his audience. Max

Novak says that seventeenth- and eighteenth-century discussions of man's beginnings often worked with the image of an individual alone, and often assumed that a man in Crusoe's position would go in constant fear, and would probably go mad. Pufendorf, whom Defoe read, describes such a one creeping into a cave, covering himself up with leaves, and trembling at the approach of fellow creatures. When Crusoe does such things, they are subsumed into a larger image whose main emotional scheme is quite different—the triumphant emotion of modernist adventure. "Island" as Defoe uses it means the perfect setting for that adventure.

And finally we must remind ourselves that *Robinson Crusoe* is basically a romance, though one radically transformed to become appropriate to the modern world system. If we take Frye's definition of romance, in *Anatomy of Criticism,* we see that many traditional elements he mentions, like the necessary mutilation, and the redemption of a "loathly" lady, are not to be found in this book; nor, except by very far-reaching displacement, can we speak of buried treasure or even a quest. And where it is possible to recognize the presence of traditional romance in Defoe's mind, it is dysfunctional.

Sometimes an incident will occur which belongs to an older kind of romance—for instance, when one of the men Friday rescues turns out to be his long-lost father, an incident which belongs in Greek or chivalric, but not in modernist, romance. That sort of coincidence does not pay enough tribute to realism, which Defoe introduced into romance as a constant pressure, in adapting it to the modern world system. However, the three main stages of a romance, according to Frye's scheme: a journey, a crucial struggle (in this case Crusoe's struggle with the inertial forces of nature), and an exaltation of the hero; these are recognizably the three main stages of *Robinson Crusoe.* So are the reader's intense feelings of identification with the hero; Frye says romance offers the reader the ideal heroes and villains of the current ruling class. And most romance-like of all is the very strongly shaped curve of feeling, which is quite crucially carried, I think, by a young man hero. Crusoe's father begs him not to "act the young man," but he does, and the reader is of course delighted that he does, without needing to feel that the father is wrong. It is, I think, misleading to talk of Crusoe's *sin* of disobedience; that is what he says, but it is not what the reader can feel. Crusoe is being a young man.

Formally speaking, this is a romance device, but here again I find a historical perspective useful. Empire, frontier, exploration, have been peculiarly associated with that "young man"; the key content of that phrase being not so much youth as bachelorhood. The 186 young men who rode north into Mashonaland with Cecil Rhodes to found the city of Salisbury in 1890; the young men advertised for in St. Louis in 1822, to go up into the Rockies for two or three years (Mike Fink was one); the Cossacks who moved out from the settlements into the free land of the Russian frontier—these are the men (not all of them so young in the literal sense) for whom Crusoe stands.

One of the most vivid expressions of this young man idea is to be found in *Roughing It,* where Twain describes the California he first knew as "an assemblage of 200,000 *young* men—not simpering, dainty, kid-gloved weaklings, but stalwart, muscular, dauntless young braves, brimful of push and energy, and royally endowed with every attribute that goes to make up a peerless and magnificent manhood—the very pick and choice of the world's glorious ones. No women, no children, no grey and stooping veterans—none but erect, bright-eyed, quick-moving, strong-handed young giants . . ." (p. 132). It is worth remembering that Twain was known as "Youth" to his wife, and made a good deal out of embodying young manhood even in his old age. "It was that population which gave to California a name for getting up astounding enterprises and rushing them through with a magnificent dash and daring. . . . It was a wild, free, disorderly, grotesque society: *Men*—only swarming hosts of stalwart *men*—nothing juvenile, nothing feminine visible anywhere" (p. 133). America was a young man's country—was that country for all Europe—and in America young men went west.

Subsequent history brought out these meanings to the phrase "young man," but the concept was a potent one for Defoe to use because these meanings were always potential within it. *Robinson Crusoe* is a central mythic expression of the modern system, of its call to young men to go out to expand that empire; and the more you know about the latter, the richer the meanings you find in the former.

*Defoe*

## Captain Singleton

This is the story of an orphan who goes to sea, takes part in a mutiny, leads his fellow mutineers across Africa, makes a fortune and loses it. In the second half (the book is divided in two with mathematical exactitude), Captain Singleton becomes a pirate and makes another fortune, undergoes conversion, and returns to England in disguise, to enjoy a peaceful prosperity and do good works. In the second half of the book, also, the captain finds a comrade, but Defoe's stress does not fall on that comradeship so much as on the isolation of the man in command.

The story of adventure, as Defoe tells it, is always built around an isolated individual, who leads subordinates against alien opponents. He emphasizes the figure of the solitary captain. But seen in a larger generic conspectus, that story seems to be a linked alternate to a story of brothers, or comrades, or brothers-in-arms, who are loyal to or in love with each other. Thus in Greek epic the *Odyssey,* an isolate's story, structurally like *Captain Singleton,* is linked to the *Iliad,* a story of brothers-in-arms. (Hindu epic, as I pointed out in a note to Chapter II, is about literal brothers, bonded also by being all in love with the same woman.)

To link the two structurally seems paradoxical, since they are so different, but history presents them so linked; it is clear that the imaginative character and cultural purpose of both versions is the same. Moreover, we have a comparable case in the story of marriages, the story of the sisters; for famous examples of that story are *Pamela* and *Clarissa,* both about very isolated figures; and yet clearly linked to the sisters' stories told by (among others) Jane Austen. And the link is not that of fragments to a whole. *Clarissa* is no more a fragment of, shall we say, *Persuasion,* than *Captain Singleton* is a fragment of *Westward Ho!* or *The Three Musketeers.* The connection is quite different; they are alternative fictional forms, alternative versions of a mythic form.

They are linked alternates, the story of the isolate and the story of the band, and they bear the same mythic message. Therefore we can call Defoe's adventures, on certain occasions, examples of the story of the brothers—which is generically distinct from and quite unlinked to the story of the sisters. The former of course has a longer history, going back to epic, while the latter seems to arise only where there is a highly developed leisure culture, and not always there. Presumably its development in eighteenth-century England had something to do with the status of women then; just as the character of capitalism then had presumably something to do with the early development of the isolate alternative in both the sisters' and the brothers' stories. We begin with dramatically solitary figures, Robinson Crusoe and Pamela; it is not until we reach the works of Scott and Austen, both minds in which the Puritan thesis had been matched and mellowed by something opposite, that we get the stories of the groups. This is the historical development of fiction, as a genre of the modern imagination.

Many of the same motifs appear in *Captain Singleton* as in *Robinson Crusoe,* because it also is a modernist adventure. Thus I shall say very little about its treatment of Eros, gold, guns, natives, etc. But there is an important difference in this being not the story of an individual alone on an island, but of a group on the move across the world; in the first half of the book, on land across Africa, in the second half on a ship across the oceans.[14] In some sense it is *not* the story of a group, since the story takes no interest in group psychology, and scarcely any in individual psychology. It is the story of a captain, and, in the second half, of his comrade also. Nevertheless, it *is* a group story, in a *formal* sense, as the contrast with *Robinson Crusoe* brings out; many of its features are tied to the idea, however unrealized that may be artistically, that this is about a group of men on the move. And quite as many later romances have followed *Singleton* (using the group pattern) as have followed *Crusoe.* The immensely popular *Westward Ho!* is a Victorian example.

Another important innovation is Captain Singleton's career as pirate. Defoe wrote several narratives of pirates; in fact he is the inventor, so far as England goes, of that pirate genre that went on to become one of the most popular the modern world has told itself (equalled only by the much more recent cowboy story). But the reader must note, in *Singleton,* the curious equivocation that most of the time the narrator sounds like a merchant. In Defoe's time the lines separating merchant, privateer, and pirate were often blurred, and in certain times and places could be crossed without invoking the ordinary moral sanctions. Defoe makes use of that in *A New Voyage Around the World.* But in *Captain Singleton* the blur is of a different kind. Except when he *says,* at the beginning of each half of the book, what a wicked fellow, he, Singleton, is, the narrator writes in the same reasoning, prudent, constructive voice as Crusoe used—and of course Moll Flanders, and all Defoe—because that modern system voice was the one Defoe thought in. The cause of this is no doubt Defoe's habitual haste and carelessness; he didn't imagine things intensely, or perfect them esemplastically. But the effect is to create an effective artistic equivalent for the blur in the adventure-reader's mind, the blending of the desire to preserve the law in general with the desire to break it oneself. (The artistry is effective only for adventure-readers —not for those trained in the school of "serious" fiction.)

A third motif is explosion. This is closely related to that of guns and gunpowder, but is sufficiently distinct. When Singleton's group of sailors is baffled in a fight with some Indians, who retreat into a cave, they blow the latter up. The captain has said it was time to give up the struggle, even though "it would vex any Body to be so baulked by a few naked ignorant Fellows." But William, the captain's Quaker comrade, is determined to have some "Satisfaction" of them, though he acknowledges that there is nothing but "Curiosity" to be gratified in the attempt. He and the gunner fetch two barrels of powder out of the ship and put them in the mouth of the cave and set light to them. The force of the powder bursts out of some bushes on the other side of the hill, and they run to look.

"First, we saw that *there* was the other Mouth of the Cave, which the Powder had so torn and open'd, that the loose Earth was so fallen in again, that nothing of Shape could be discerned; but there we saw what was become of the Garrison of *Indians*—too, who had given us all this Trouble; for some of them had no Arms, some no Legs, some no Head, some lay half buried in the Rubbish of the Mine, that is to say, in the loose Earth that fell in; and, in short, there was a miserable Havock made of them all, for we had good Reason to believe, not one of them that were in the Inside could Escape, but rather were shot out of the Mouth of the Cave like a Bullet out of a Gun" (pp. 213–214).

This will immediately remind readers familiar with *Connecticut Yankee* of various scenes in that novel. But in fact, explosions, producing human debris, usually native, are a motif in much adventure fiction. Jules Verne, Conrad, Kingston, for instance, make much use of them. Defoe's distinction in the use of this subject matter—as in his use of others—is his candor. Like Crusoe's shot, this petard of William's reverberates in the reader's mind, uncontained by literature, and so unconstrained.

But the major motifs that *Captain Singleton* introduced are three figures, each of which embodies a contradiction, in the way that myths often do, according to the structural anthropologists. First of all, William, the bloody Quaker. He was a surgeon on a sloop the pirates captured, and lets them know that he wants to join them, but that they must make it seem that they are forcing him. He takes no part in actual fighting, but gives them military advice, even in the midst of battle—he tells them what to aim at and where to charge. But he is not so much murderous as mercenary. He reminds them often that their real interest is not in killing but in making money.

At the same time, William remains the representative of morality and religion in the story, and at the end effects the captain's conversion. The major means by which Defoe reconciles these two opposing sides of the character is by describing William as "merry"—alluding to his dry wit, "the cunning rogue," and so on. I need hardly say that this device does not work, for a reader trained in serious fiction. The indignation aroused by William's behavior cannot be pacified by anything to be called "humor." But Defoe was genuinely fascinated by Quakers; the theme of Quakerism turns up often in *The Review*, and in *Roxana*. It is a theme he characteristically *played* with— rather than treated seriously. Defoe or his characters *disguise* themselves as Quakers, in costume or dialect; but they also clearly regard Quakerism as the purest of moral positions. This is the source of half its fascination for them; the other source is the impulse to desecrate that purity. The paradoxical combination of Quaker and pirate expresses many feelings about this disparity, but one surely is the wish to find the former no better than the latter. And so it is not surprising that other writers have invented bloody Quakers too, notably Cooper in the Leatherstocking tales, R. M. Bird, in *Nick of the Woods,* and Melville in *Moby Dick.*

The second such figure is the Black Prince—a phrase used by Defoe himself. When the group have defeated a band of natives in Africa, "There was among the prisoners one tall, well-shap'd hand-som Fellow, to whom the rest seem'd to pay great Respect, and who, as we understood afterwards, was the Son of one of their Kings" (p. 57). They cure the Prince of his wound, and he takes a vow of loyalty to them (swearing by the sun, whom his tribe worship) and it is through him that the captain manages the rest of the natives. This man represents older modes of being, those we associate with epic; his language, mostly of gestures, is much grander and more mythic than the Englishmen's. He tames a leopard, which follows him around. He commands an extravagant devotion from his followers, and in turn offers an extravagant devotion to the captain. He is handsome, splendid, a noble human being, which one would not say of the captain; but clearly he is of so much simpler an order as to be of a lower order.

This figure also appears in later adventure tales; notably as Chingachgook in *Leatherstocking Tales,* and as Dain Waris in *Lord Jim,* and other such figures in other Conrad novels. Quite often he moves in an atmosphere of tragedy; but simplified tragedy, because his principal function is to serve as an opposite pole to the white man. The other is dry, calculating, managerial, functional; and it is our shame for imposing a dry, calculating order upon other men which is discharged by building up this lay figure of nobility.[15] Besides successors there were predecessors for the Black Prince; most notably, Othello, Oroonoko, and Montezuma. All three are in different ways interesting figures, and much more fully worked out than Defoe's Black Prince; those precedents are in a sense the content to Defoe's concept, and show how much there was in his readers' minds, ready to respond to his barest phrases. (Incidentally, it is worth keeping the Black Prince motif separate from that of "my man Friday," who is essentially a slave-companion, a devoted servant, a figure of comedy rather than of tragedy. The two are similar in certain ways, but if we regard them as functions, they are worth keeping distinct.)

Finally there is the figure of the English hermit—not Defoe's phrase, but the title of one of the popular imitations of *Robinson Crusoe, The English Hermit* published in 1727, which focused on this figure. This is "a White Man indeed, but stark naked," (p. 120) whom the group find living alone—that is to say, living among Negroes. "He appeared to be a Gentleman, not an ordinary bred Fellow, Seaman, or Labouring Man; this shewed itself in his Behaviour, in the first Moment of our conversing with him, and in speight of all the Disadvantages of his miserable condition." He embraced the captain "very passionately, the Tears running down his Face," and "never was without Tears in his Eyes for several Days" (p. 121).

"As he was naked, and had no Clothes, so he was naked of Arms for his Defence, having neither Gun, Sword, Staff, or any Instrument of War about him, so not to guard himself against the Attacks of a wild Beast, of which this Country was very full" (p. 124). It is this nakedness which distinguishes him from Crusoe, and suggests a word like "hermit." I have not found any full-blown successors to this figure in the authors that interest me, but of course the strain of feeling he satisfies enters into Tarzan and Tabu Dick, and into Ike McCaslin laying aside watch and compass to enter the wilderness, and into Mailer's heroes doing the same in *Why Are We in Vietnam?*

Thus *Captain Singleton* foreshadows the adventures of the next two centuries almost as vividly as *Robinson Crusoe*. It contains fictional possibilities at least as striking as *Religious Courtship*. And yet it and its genre, even its author to some degree, were rejected by literature proper. Defoe's motifs were to be found in later adventure tales, as some of my examples indicated, but their potentialities are scarcely realized, and their development is scarcely worthy of the name. Adventure motifs are likely to seem more promising when enumerated by a critic than when met in fiction, while the reverse is true of courtship motifs. This is the result of rejection by literature-as-a-system.

## Defoe, Literature, and Culture

The peripheralization of the adventure tale within the system of literature, and of Defoe's work in general, can be seen reflected in Defoe's relations with Swift. These relations can be described as a kind of polar opposition. Biographically there was an antagonism between the two men; ideologically they were on opposite sides; and in terms of literary achievement and consequent reputation, they are in the important sense irreconcilable. Swift established himself, in his own lifetime, and for futurity, at the center of literature. He and Pope and their friends were the arbiters of literary taste of their age. And by that token, Defoe was on the periphery.[16]

In *Swift and Defoe* John F. Ross says that the two men were antagonists for twenty-one years, from 1705 to 1726, and that it was Defoe who made the attacks. Swift was in the position of security and superiority, and by ignoring Defoe, his aggression could be merely negative. In 1705 Defoe's satiric fantasy, *The Consolidator*, attacked Swift's *Tale of a Tub*. In 1710 the two men became rivals, because both were working for Robert Harley. But Harley received Swift at his front door, and saw him occasionally at the Scriblerus Club, which met in Arbuthnot's rooms at the Palace, and at two other clubs. Defoe went to Harley's back door, and did not belong to any fashionable clubs. Literary and social values were in alliance. Though Defoe was put in the pillory and jail for "The Shortest Way With Dissenters," nothing happened to Swift for "A Modest Proposal." Defoe appeared in *The Dunciad* because everyone thought him a Dunce; he belonged completely to Grub Street, as Pat Rogers has pointed out—by his activities, by his associates, by his politics, by the kind of thing he wrote. Swift and Pope had won the battle for the leadership of literature; had made, for instance, classical models and classical learning necessary to authors, and by those standards Defoe failed. He himself said that his verse and his prose were addressed to the unlearned.[17]

In 1710 they were on different sides politically. On November 16, 1710, Swift's magazine, *The Examiner*, called "Mr. Review" a "stupid, illiterate scribbler, with a mock authoritative manner." Defoe answered from Scotland in two issues, saying that Swift was very learned, but "a cynic in behaviour, a fury in temper, unpolite in conversation, abusive and scurrilous in language, and ungovernable in passion. Is this to be learned? Then may I still be illiterate."

In the very first issue of his *Examiner*, Swift announced his position as spokesman for the landed gentry against tradesmen and stock-jobbers. (Defoe often said that land, when compared with trade as a source of wealth, was like a pool as compared with a stream.) Swift hated "money-men" and opposed the institution of the National Debt. ". . . the wealth of the nation, that used to be reckoned by the value of the land, is now computed by the rise and fall of stocks, . . . such a complication of knavery and cozenage, such a mystery of iniquity, and such an unintelligible jargon of terms to involve it. . . ." Like most serious writers, Swift hated exponential growth.[18] Then in No. 22, he complained that the Whigs wanted England to become, "a common receptacle for all nations, religions, and languages, a system only proper for small populous states, but altogether unworthy and below the dignity of an imperial crown; which with us is best upheld by a monarch in possession of his just prerogatives, a senate of nobles and of commons, and a clergy established in its due rights with a suitable maintenance by law. But these men come with the spirit of shopkeepers to frame rules for the administration of kingdoms." This is so directly the opposite of Defoe's opinions, at several points, that it could have been aimed at him. Swift's grandfather had been a royalist under Charles I; he hated the colonization of Ireland, and he was of course an officer of the Church of England. In him, literature allied itself to the military caste rather than the mercantile.

But literary considerations were also important in their antagonism. Mr. Ross maintains that Defoe was not an ironist at all but a realist—which shows how Swift's judgment still prevails in literary matters. But he is right to call Defoe's ordinary style a "copious, breathless gossip," and one can see how that styleless seriousness would irritate Swift. He called Defoe "so grave, sententious, dogmatical a rogue, that there's no enduring him." Swift knew he would be read by Berkeley, Bolingbroke, Pope, Addison, Arbuthnot, and by their equivalents of the future. Such a consciousness, which shaped Swift's style, is indeed a crucial element in serious writing at all times, and Defoe—who aimed at being a serious writer early on—was gradually convinced that he must give up such ambitions. His style lacks that shapeliness. And it was probably Swift's hostility, and a similar hostility in others, that helped convince him.

*Gulliver's Travels* contains some expression of the antagonism. *Robinson Crusoe* was one of the "traveller's tales" which Swift took off from; and he satirized the material they contained. For instance, when Gulliver offers gunpowder to the King of Brobdingnab, the latter rejects the idea with horror. And in the very last chapter we find this account of modernist adventure (*Works* XII 378–379):

"A crew of pirates are driven by a storm, they know not whither; at length a boy discovers land from the topmast; they go on shore to rob and plunder; they see a harmless people, are entertained with kindness; they give the country a new name; they take formal possession of it for their king; they set up a rotten plank or a stone for a memorial; they murder two or three dozen of the natives, bring away a couple more by force for a sample, return home, and get their pardon. Here commences a new dominion, acquired with a title by divine right. Ships are sent with the first opposition; the natives driven out or destroyed; their princes tortured to discover their gold; a free license given to all acts of humanity and lust; the earth reeking with the blood of its inhabitants; and this execrable crew of butchers employed in so pious an expedition is a modern colony sent to convert and civilize an idolatrous and barbarous people."

A passage like that makes it clear how Swift set himself against the spirit of the times. And making himself the center of literature-as-a-system, he made his own posture in such matters paradigmatic for other writers. Not that they must hold his opinions, but that they must display his independence of judgment, his self-dissociation from "the spirit of the times," while Defoe's strength derived from participation in that spirit. (Of course, the phrase is ambiguous; some *literary* things that could be called in the spirit of the eighteenth century were Swift's more than Defoe's; in this discussion it refers to things like colonies—the *new* forms of wealth and power and expansion.)[19] By and large, the writers did follow Swift.

For instance, amongst eighteenth-century men of letters who take a hostile attitude to the empire material one could mention Cowper, whose "Alexander Selkirk" and "The Castaway" use the Crusoe story but only in a highly moralized and unadventurous manner, and who is very severe against slavery and the East India Company. And Dr. Johnson, who in 1784 observed of Cook's *Voyages,* that no one would read them because "One set of savages is like another." Boswell tells us that Johnson was very incredulous about "particular facts."

But that does not mean that the triumph rested wholly with Swift. Literature is a system within a larger system of culture, and in the terms of that larger system *Robinson Crusoe* was an enormously successful book. Compare the pages it takes up in any large library catalog with the number of entries for any popular serious novel, like *Sons and Lovers.* By 1895 there had been 196 English editions, 110 translations, 115 revisions, 277 imitations. Defoe did not need to establish adventure as a genre. His book was a genre in itself. I must say more about that in a minute, but for the moment let me note the keenest irony against Swift. Despite his satirical intentions, *Gulliver's Travels* was read as yet another traveler's tale. It became a children's classic, but a classic of adventure. It was Defoe who triumphed, and Swift was carried along in his wake. One hears for instance that Daniel Boone was reading *Gulliver* one day when he was interrupted by an Indian attack, and to commemorate the occasion he named a nearby creek by a name out of the book. Now Boone was not a literary man; one can be pretty sure that he was reading *Gulliver* for its Defoe content, not for the ironic slant Swift gave to that content. And thus Swift's book came to play a part in the history of the frontier and empire and adventure—despite the effort of mind and will the author had directed against them.

To return to the career of *Crusoe*, one may say that it was an international genre also. There were forty-nine French translations, beginning with one in 1720, and twenty-one German. Of the German imitations, J. H. Campe's *Robinson Der Jüngere* (Hamburg, 1799) (in which Robinson started off with no utensils at all) itself had 117 editions by 1895, and was translated into twenty languages. Another very famous adaptation was *The Swiss Family Robinson* by Johann Wyss. This substituted a family for the isolated individual. It was published in 1814, written probably twenty years before; translated into English in the year of publication, it became nearly as popular and as often adapted as Defoe's story. These are obvious examples of a story being modified in the course of compulsive retelling. (Such modifications are less radical than the transformations we shall come to in Scott.)

And among testimonies to *Robinson Crusoe*'s influence, we might select Rousseau's use of it in his ideal education, in *Emile* (1762). *Crusoe* is to be the whole of Emile's library for a long time—"the text of which all our discussions of natural science will be a gloss. I would like him to be infatuated by it. I want him to identify himself with Robinson." Thus at the end of the eighteenth century *Robinson Crusoe* came to life again in France, and Germany, and all Europe; it remained alive all through the nineteenth century. All the political economists, including Marx, made use of the story. Missionaries took it with them, along with the Bible, to pagan empires and primitive tribes. It was a part of their gospel. The colporteur, George Borrow, writing in 1851, tells how he himself was first induced to learn to read (having long resisted his teachers) by hearing the story, and how he absorbed himself in it. ". . . it was a book which has exerted over the minds of Englishmen an influence certainly greater than any other of modern times, which has been in most people's hands . . . a book, moreover, to which, from the hardy deeds which it narrates, and the spirit of strange and romantic enterprise which it tends to awaken,

England owes many of her astonishing discoveries both by sea and land, and no inconsiderable part of her naval glory. Hail to thee, spirit of De Foe! What does not my own poor self owe to thee?" (*Lavengno*, p. 24). But still Defoe was not a figure in literature proper.

Of course, literature's rejection of Defoe in the eighteenth century was to some extent a passing phenomenon, not a permanent literary institution. There were, as I have said, contradictions within the system of literature which ultimately produced a revolution, which we call the Romantic Movement. This was from one point of view a revolution in the status of authors and genres, and it brought about a change of rank for Defoe and for Swift. For instance, Coleridge explicitly contrasted the two men, in 1818, to Defoe's advantage. "Defoe makes one respond to the experience, not to his comment on it, as Swift does." He said the character of Crusoe is a representative of humanity in general, and his story always interests, never agitates. Coleridge compared Defoe to Hogarth and Shakespeare, as being peculiarly English, and this is the note struck by other Romantic critics—Lamb, Hazlitt, Scott, and Carlyle. Defoe was a great Englishman, a great Protestant, patriot, and democrat. It was the nineteenth-century biographies (Wilson's in 1830, Lee's in 1869) that established his reputation, rather than critical appreciations. He became accepted as a sort of proto-Cobbett.

All this, obviously, was more effective as a cultural rehabilitation than as a literary one. Thus Scott praised Defoe's plain language and his realism in the handling of coincidence and supernatural events; he did not praise anything that could be called Defoe's imagination. As long as the reaction against the Augustans was strong, Defoe had an assured place as a reproach to them. But he was no precursor or pre-Romantic. If the Romantic system of literature was anti-ironical in tendency, it was Carlyle who was the great exemplar of that tendency, and he was closer to Swift than to Defoe. Carlyle spoke for the heart and for the people, against eighteenth-century wits, dandies, and ironists. But his weapon against them was a greater irony. Defoe could be no ally to Carlyle. While Wordsworth's and Coleridge's weapons against the eighteenth century were taste and theory, they spoke for plain and simple meanings, strong and deep feelings, but under the aegis of literature at its most sophisticated. Neither of them was any Defoe.

Thus by these writers Defoe was used rather than imitated—used against the Augustans or as a source of new material, as the voyagers were used, by Coleridge in "The Ancient Mariner," for example. The Romantics did not mean to be like Defoe themselves, as men of letters, any more than they meant to be like the Dampier or Hakluyt they also used. Once the defensive movement against the Augustans was over, I think it is true to say, Defoe again found himself on the periphery of literature, and a serious writer would not think of apprenticing himself to Defoe or of writing an adventure tale.

Defoe's meaning and message were carried to later generations not by the novelists or poets but by moralists like Benjamin Franklin and Samuel Smiles. (And by the Encyclopaedists in France.) Franklin's link with Defoe is explicit in more than one dimension. He says in his autobiography that he learned a lot from Defoe, both stylistically and intellectually; mentioning Defoe's "Essay Upon Projects" in particular. Biographically, we know that Samuel Keimer, who printed Defoe's writings in London in 1715, went to America six years later, employed Franklin in his printing house, and brought out more Defoe there in 1723. And the *Autobiography* contains adventures like Crusoe's in spirit, though confined in scope.

Smiles' anecdotes are very often of full-blown adventure, and his famous *Self-Help* (1859) has a final chapter entitled "Character: The True Gentleman," which is very close to Defoe's *Complete English Gentleman.* Defoe's definition of the gentleman is essentially in terms of maturity, seriousness, and responsibility; and so he claims the title for tradesmen and dissenters, and denies it to most squires, whom he depicts as red-faced, hard-drinking boobies. Smiles describes the distinction as being between "gentlemen" and "genteel men" or "gents."[20]

But I shall return to Smiles, in Chapter VII. Franklin is worth dwelling on for a moment here, because he was of great importance in the eighteenth and indeed the nineteenth century, as a propagator of modern system values in other lands. He was in his lifetime made a member of thirteen academies, from London to St. Petersburg, and there were many books for children with Franklin for hero; for instance, in England, Thomas Percival's *A Father's Instructions,* London, 1775.* In France, Franklin was of course a cult by the time of his death; in a book on Franklin and Germany he is described as

---

*Michael Kraus, *Atlantic Civilization,* Ithaca, 1949.

the living presence of the new age there; and in *Benjamin Franklin and Italy,* Antonio Pace puts special emphasis on his nineteenth-century reputation as a moralist. "Franklin's posthumous success as a moralist is, unlike his predictable reputation as a scientist and a statesman, quite extraordinary and a fact of considerable importance for the cultural historian. . . ."

That career as a moralist indicates the spread of modern system values—of the Defoe gospel. *Poor Richard* became very popular in Italy around 1830, and remained much read until after the achievement of national unity. "The fortune of Franklin's moral writings and his personal popularity prove in fact to be a sensitive indicator for gauging the formation of Italian bourgeois self-consciousness. . . ." Max Weber and Werner Sombart have both shown Franklin to be a touchstone of the European middle-class temper. "Moreover, the connection between Franklin's vogue as a moralist and the nationalistic movement is of great interest. . . . Franklin's rise from obscurity and poverty to prestige, power, and independence seemed prophetic of the course Italy had to take in order to achieve regeneration and her national destiny" (Pace, *Benjamin Franklin and Italy,* p. 234).

It was in the nineteenth century, we may say, that Franklin's and Defoe's message really reached the semi-periphery. Smiles' *Self-Help* was also very popular in nineteenth-century Italy. While Sarmiento, the great liberal hero of nineteenth-century Argentinian nationalism, as a young man devoted himself to Franklin, reciting the famous Turgot epigram, "Eripuit caelo fulmen, sceptrumque tyrannis," as his motto. Meanwhile, in the core countries a powerful reaction was developing, of which one expression was D. H. Lawrence's attack on Franklin in *Studies in Classic American Literature.* By the 1920s the keenest minds in England felt they'd had their fill of Franklin's virtues, not to mention Smiles' and Defoe's. (H. G. Wells, in many ways a twentieth-century equivalent of Defoe, could not maintain his literary reputation after 1918.) Those writers had never been allowed into the circle of literature, and now they were to be driven out of high culture altogether. That is why it is necessary, fifty years later, to remind ourselves of how living those ideas were for two centuries and more, whether conveyed in essays or in adventure tales.

# IV

## *Scott*

ALMOST a century stretches between *Robinson Crusoe* and *Waverley.* During that time the myth of adventure, with its message of empire, was spread by a variety of means. By the revisions and adaptations of *Robinson Crusoe* itself—very frequent in the second half of the century; by the biographies of adventurer heroes and the descriptions of exotic lands; by the teaching of history and geography. But it was not spread, to any significant degree, by fiction, and scarcely at all by the fiction of serious and ambitious authors.

All through that century, however, the power and pride of England were swelling, and the power and pride of the modern system generally. The rulers of England and the empire wanted fictional images to stimulate and educate their sense of self. When Scott finally devised such images, their grateful response was immediate and tumultuous. But the same cultural inhibitions that had so long restrained men of letters from creating such icons, now disguised and distorted the images they produced. Scott's stories did not express contemporary exploration and conquest as simply as Defoe's did. They seemed to bear no likeness to Defoe's.

And later writers followed Scott. That is why, if we accept the idea that Defoe was the founder of modernist adventure, and so the progenitor of a line of writers that runs down to Kipling and Conrad, we are likely to be puzzled by the occurrence in the work of these later writers of traditionally romantic features of just the kind that

Defoe exorcised from his stories. In many of them, perhaps particularly in Conrad, one finds that the atmosphere is far from factual, prosaic, or utilitarian; the landscape, charged with grandeur, is oppressively present; the hero, and even more the heroine—her very existence denied by Defoe—are figures out of opera; and so on.

All of this is so because of Scott's work—because of what Scott made of the Defoe heritage. Without really abandoning the modernist scheme of imaginative fiction, Scott introduced into it new materials—deriving from romantic history—which were superficially, and perhaps profoundly, too, antagonistic to the form. The measure of the resultant complexity is that he was often read as an antithesis to Defoe; for instance, he was so read, it seems, in the South of the United States, and certainly by Twain when he made his celebrated charge that Scott was to blame for the American Civil War. I don't think that antithesis was complete, as I shall explain, but certainly Scott represented the aristomilitary caste, and introduced into the adventure tale literary materials bearing the ideology of that caste.

Scott's reader was invited to imagine himself a knight in armor, engaging in tournaments for points of honor, and commanding the devotion of savage retainers; or else an Elizabethan courtier, or a Highland chieftain; or something else equally remote from the banks and counting houses and trading companies most readers saw as contemporary reality—as the source of the wealth around them. To some extent, then, Scott sold day dreams, dealt in illusion. But he also served a reality which their common sense ignored, being a mercantile common sense. For England was in his day depending more and more on its soldiers and sailors and rulers of colonies and makers of treaties, and so on. The imperial wealth and power was not the work of solitary Crusoes and freebooting Singletons. It was a ruling class, an aristomilitary caste, that wielded the power and took the responsibility; and that caste had been denied a voice and an image in the serious literature of the culture. Scott supplied a stream of rather fanciful images, rather obliquely related to reality, to the sons and daughters of that caste, and to those of the rest of the nation who admired them. Romantic, fanciful, merely historical as those images now seem, they clearly gave a satisfactory form, and a fuller life, to the aspirations of a large audience.

As I have said, Romanticism was a revolt of the genres within the system of literature. To a considerable extent, as its name indicates, it was a revolt of romance in a general sense; that is to say, of everything not realistic—legend, superstition, the saga, the epic, the exotic, and all the motifs of the marvelous to be found in Greek or Spanish romances. But in a more particular sense, this material was linked to the military caste, in Scott's world as in earlier times.

The great Romantic poets incorporated that new material into their verse, in various ways acceptable to the system of literature; they evolved the categories of sense and sensibility appropriate to it; and —except in certain cases—cut its connections to the military caste.

It was not so easily accommodated into fiction, and at first was restricted to subgenres, the Gothic and the historical novel. Of these, the first only gradually and partially became respectable, but the second leaped into enormous popularity with a very large audience. For Scott's contemporaries, he was a great writer because he incorporated a great deal of romance material into fiction, and did not fall into moral or intellectual nonsense—that is, he contained that material by means of suitable categories of sense and sensibility. After his death, critics declared those categories literarily inauthentic. The system of literature rejected or at least degraded him. From my own point of view, concerned with the caste character of literary materials, it was a great achievement that he incorporated romance into modernist adventure.

Scott, I may as well say here, knew Defoe's work well. He edited what was then thought to be a complete edition—the first. In *Rob Roy* he used Defoe's *The Highland Rogue,* though without realizing its authorship. He also used the *Tour* in that book. And in *Old Mortality* he used an episode from *Memoirs of the Church of Scotland.* Almost certainly there are other such particular borrowings, but the interesting point is the general connection, the tradition of thought. For instance, Defoe had plenty to say about Scotland and its relation to the modern system, which is not really unlike Scott's theory.

When Defoe writes about Scotland he stresses its antiquity, and the contrast between that and English modernity. In "Caledonia" he writes,

> The antiquity which other nations boast
> Would here turn modern, and in age be lost . . .
> Here mighty ancestors preserve their style,
> From long prescription, ancient as the isle.

And in *The True-Born Englishman* he says that the Scots aristocracy is older than the English. His interest in this idea (like Scott's interest, later) focuses on the ethos it betokens—is a cultural-anthropological interest. Thus in the Review III (12) he says that in Scotland people wear a national habit, and so put on the same suit until it wears out. In England, people wear a suit only until it ceases to be fashionable. And that interest inspires his fascination with the Highlanders. In a letter to Harley he says,

Indeed, they are formidable fellows, and I only wish her Majesty had 25,000 of them in Spain, a nation equally proud and barbarous like themselves. They are all gentlemen . . . [as opposed, we might add, to citizens] . . . will take affront from no man, and insolent to the last degree. But certainly the absurdity is ridiculous, to see a man in his mountain habit, with a broadsword, target, pistol or perhaps two at his girdle, a dagger and staff, walking down the street as upright and haughty as if he were a lord—and withal driving a cow. Bless us—are these the gentlemen! said I—" (*Letters*, pp. 146–147).

His tone there is as urbane and citified as Steele, but his interest went deep; as you can see when you consider how much that portrait resembles Robinson Crusoe crossing his island. Defoe was fascinated, as were all the great adventure writers in this series, by the contrast between the modern world citizen and those who embody another mode of being; and the fascination included admiration and emulation, as well as less positive emotions. In *Review* V (10), page 3, he wrote that Highlanders are "The best body of raw men in the world; they are all provided with arms, and understand them; they are entirely under subordination to their superiors, and may be perhaps the most formidable little body of men in their rude circumstances in these parts of the world." His criterion there is military—these are England's Cossacks—but there is also some sense that they are more *men* than others.

## The Novels

We shall find the equivalent in the *Waverley* novels, but let us note first that the whole series is dedicated, in the edition of 1829, to the King's Most Gracious Majesty; and different as were the two kings and the two authors, Scott's feeling for George IV *is* parallel to

Defoe's for William III. In both cases, the king represented the order and dignity which the writer needed to find at the apex of the social system.

Scott says that he hoped to do for Scotland what Maria Edgeworth had done for Ireland. She had accomplished "more than all the laws towards completing the Union" (of England with Ireland), and Scott had worked on that other union, of England with Scotland. This is the political character of his work. So we, from our point of view, may say that he tried to complete what Defoe began. Francis Jeffrey, the *Edinburgh Review* critic, said he did complete the Union.[1]

Let us note also the date of the individual novel, *Waverley.* It is significant that it came out in 1814, for the Waverly series as a whole arises naturally out of England's long struggle against Napoleon. To English eyes, as Alexander Welsh puts it,* Napoleon was an embodiment of will, ambition, passion, while England herself seemed an embodiment of reason, prudence, realism—humbler but stronger qualities, merchant-caste qualities, opposing the aristomilitary. Scott himself was an unequivocal patriot, whose opposition to Napoleon and admiration for Wellington was quite as strong as Defoe's feeling against Louis XIV and for Marlborough.[2] And his fiction was (as Defoe's was not) a literary equivalent of the national resistance.

In the General Preface, Scott tells us of the formation of his mind. As a boy he told his friends tales of knights-errant, and at fifteen, when he was ill a long time, he filled his head with "the romances of chivalry." But also with histories, memoirs, and voyages. That is the double heritage of adventure fiction, both military and mercantile myths. Scott began his literary career by writing ballads, and his first project in prose narrative was a *Castle of Otranto* fantastic romance. But then he saw the advantage of Scottish history as a subject; "the ancient traditions and high spirit of a people, who, living in a civilized age and country, retained . . . manners belonging to an early period of society" (p. 8). This historical change was his subject, and the need to accept both terms and their interrelation was his point, as Jeffrey and Coleridge, for instance, saw immediately. Jeffrey said that the novels' interest was that "in our own country and almost in our own age," we discover "manners and customs we had been accustomed to consider as belonging to remote antiquity or extravagant ro-

*In his *The Hero of the Waverley Novels,* New Haven, 1963.

mance."\* And Coleridge defined the main theme as the transition
from an age of heroism to one of prudence.

To connect this with Defoe, let us say that both authors treat the
theme of a conflict between the modern world system's life-style and
its alternatives. In *Tristes Tropiques*, Lévi-Strauss speaks of "that
crucial moment in modern thought when, thanks to the great voyages
of discovery, a human community [Europe] which had believed itself
to be complete and in its final form suddenly learned, as if through
the effect of a counterrevelation, that it was not alone, that it was part
of a greater whole, and that, in order to achieve self-knowledge, it
must first of all contemplate its unrecognizable image in this mirror.
. . ." (p. 367). That moment of thought is not something which took
place, once and for all, in the sixteenth century; Lévi-Strauss describes it to explain his own experience in the 1930s in approaching
the Tupi-Kawahib. And it is what Defoe was writing about in the
eighteenth century, and Scott in the nineteenth, though both presented the idea in fragmentary and oblique form. Defoe does not
contemplate the unrecognizable image of man—he conjures up an
unrecognizable environment; Scott places the unrecognizable image
in the past. But both writers evoke the passionate interest—mingled
glee and anxiety—which the modern citizen takes in his unique
situation.

But what one might call the axis of sensibility has rotated through
perhaps 90°, from geography to history; whereas Defoe's motto might
have been " 'Tis a Thousand Miles Hence," Scott's was " 'Tis Sixty
Years Since." And therewith the place of nature (the alien conditions
with which Crusoe had to struggle) has been taken by culture: the
mode of life of the Highlanders. And so naturally the interest in
technology has been replaced by an interest in ethnography. The
form has also developed toward an interest in larger historical units;
larger units of time, and larger institutions; the armies are larger and
the battles last longer. Instead of Singleton's band of pirates, we have
the 1745 rebellion, a doomed rising, larger in every way.

Of course, there are other differences, which don't fit into so
simple a scheme. For instance, the central position, narratively speaking, is no longer occupied by a man of action, but by an observer-
participant. The effect of this is discussed by Alexander Welsh, in his

\*Quoted on p. viii of James C. Corson's Preface to the Everyman's edition of
*Waverley*, 1969.

*Hero of the Waverley Novels.* The dominant virtue of the novels is prudence, he says (in this the continuity from Defoe is obvious) but Scott's heroes are all passive (while Crusoe is a model of active prudence). Scott's heroes are not even calculatingly prudent, and they allow social authority to win their rights for them—even their sexual rights. They deserve the girl they love by being good, and they inherit the property they end up with. They do not make money by trade or in any other way, or make love; though a hero may often seem to, or seem about to, kill an enemy or seduce a woman, this always turns out to be mere seeming. The novels' scenes of violence and disorder are soon over, and have the character of being a disturbance of reality, while the Byronic villains, dark figures of passion that at first glance look more lively than the heroes, are in fact more merely literary. It is significant that they belong often to some geographically as well as morally remote origin—Fergus to the mountains, Saladin to the desert, Staunton to the West Indies. Reality is characterized by a middleground in every category, including character. Scott's values, despite his love of aristocratic stylishness, were more passive and compromising than Defoe's—perhaps because his position was a compromise between the chivalric and the mercantile.

In the Introductory to *Waverley,* Scott compares the spirit of the past with that of the present contrastively, but rather ambiguously.

"The wrath of our ancestors, for instance, was coloured gules; it broke forth in acts of open and sanguinary violence against the objects of his fury. Our malignant feelings, which must seek gratification through more indirect channels . . . may be rather said to be tinctured sable. But . . . the proud peer, who now can only ruin his neighbour according to law, by protracted suits, is the genuine descendant of the baron, who wrapped the castle of his competitor in flames, and knocked him on the head as he attempted to escape from the conflagration" (p. 65). A passage like that suggests the complicated scheme of feelings and values which Scott offers. The contrast between gules and sable is to the advantage of the past; but the Cockney cynicism of "knocked him on the head" alerts us to a realistic assessment of that "open and sanguinary violence." Scott's judgment of things feudal is often not much different from Twain's. Indeed, he often made exactly the same point as Twain, that in medieval times rooms were too cold, and behavior too hot. Although Twain saw Scott as the romantic, and therefore as antithetical in spirit to Cervantes the ironist, in fact Cervantes was favorite reading of Scott's. Scott was a skillful homogenizer of moral feelings, as Welsh puts it. He minimized antitheses.

Scott's purpose was more conciliatory, in literary terms too, than Defoe's. He genuinely liked both the modern world adventures and the old world romances, and tried to satisfy both the military and the mercantile castes. This is the source of his weakness, as we shall see, his lack of authenticity; or perhaps that derived from his attempts to conciliate his public's various tastes, rather than express his own. There is a fatal gentility to the *Waverley* enterprise; one aspect to it is a game with chivalric trappings for readers who make their money in trade—a literary equivalent for the social pursuit of titles and coats of arms. Like the snobbery of genre in the eighteenth century (the greater prestige of epic poetry), and the shame of trade among families like the Bingleys of *Pride and Prejudice,* the *Waverley* enterprise also derives from a distaste for the public face of the modern world system, and amounts to a kind of concealment. But this compromising and conciliatory purpose is also a sign of Scott's strength. He is much more knowledgeable and much more ambitious than Defoe in literary matters. He clearly had some sense of literature as a system, and set out to manipulate it, and succeeded, temporarily.

## Waverley

We can perhaps divide the story of *Waverley* into two main parts. In the first, the observer-participant is moved from his place of origin in Hanoverian England (a commercialized and rationalized England, where he can find romance only in a debased and literary form) up north to Scotland. There an older form of social organization survives, most intensely and purely in the Highlands, supporting a life which gives a central importance to the passion, gallantry, and death, which elsewhere seem banished to a moral periphery. On the borders of the Highlands, Waverley enters a village described to us in terms of its poverty, its discomfort, its comic picturesqueness (described, that is, from a modernist perspective); and this impressionism rests on a detailed analysis of the crops, the agricultural methods, the drainage, the ownership, etc., from the same point of view. Then Waverley enters Baron Bradwardine's manor house, which is seen as both grotesque and picturesque, and is dominated by carvings of bears, the family emblem, here rendered in so many sizes and materials as to carry some totemic and tribal suggestion. And the first person Waverley meets is a Shakespearian fool. All this, I am suggesting, is the equivalent, in historical, cultural, ethnological terms, of Crusoe's discovery that he is alone on a desert island, and must defend himself against its wild animals, its storms, its unknown fruits, etc. The representative of our modern life meets a challenge that we the readers are usually exempt from.

But this is only a halfway stage on Waverley's journey into the Highlands. Rose Bradwardine describes to Waverley an incident—seen by her at the age of ten—in which real Highlanders were involved.

Three of the Highlanders were killed, and they brought them wrapped in their plaids, and laid them on the stone floor of the hall; and next morning, their wives and daughters came, clapping their hands, and crying the coronach, and shrieking, and carried away the dead bodies, with the pipes playing before them. I could not sleep for six weeks without starting, and thinking I heard those terrible cries, and saw the bodies lying on the steps, all stiff and swathed up in their bloody tartans (p. 148).

Waverley's reaction to this anecdote is the essence of Scott's meaning.

"Waverley could not help starting at a story which bore so much resemblance to one of his own daydreams. Here was a girl scarce seventeen, the gentlest of her sex, both in temper and appearance, who had witnessed with her own eyes such a scene as he had used to conjure up in his imagination, as only occurring in ancient times, and spoke of it coolly, as one very likely to recur. He felt at once the impulse of curiosity, and that slight sense of danger which only serves to heighten its interest." He feels himself in "the land of military and romantic adventures," and determines to have a share of them himself. (Scott had a clear if intermittent sense of the interplay of chivalric and mercantile caste sensibilities in his stories.)

When Highlanders appear on the page, the first one is described as a figure of epic poetry, in terms of his costume and arms; the dirk and pistol, the broadsword, target, and fowling piece. And from his mouth we hear epic speech.

"Fergus MacIvor Vich Ian Vohr," said the ambassador, in good English,

greets you well, baron of Bradwardine and Tully-Veolan, and is sorry there has been a thick cloud interposed between you and him, which has kept you from seeing and considering the friendship and alliances that have been between your houses and forbears of old; and he prays you that the cloud may pass away and that things may be as they have been heretofore between the clan Ivor and the house of Bradwardine, when there was an egg between them for a flint, and a knife for a sword (p. 151).

This is the equivalent in language (and in a work of literature of course language has a very special potency) of romantic styles of behavior and relationship, and of patriarchal modes of authority, land tenure, land cultivation, etc. This is life in the grand style—attractive, impressive, challenging, threatening. Waverley is led by Evan Dhu on a visit to Fergus MacIvor, and on his way he hears of the latter's retinue.

There is his *hanchman*, or right hand man; then his *bard*, or poet; then his *bladier*, or orator, to make harangues to the great folks whom he visits; then his *gilly-more*, or armour-bearer, to carry his sword, his target, and his gun; then his *gilly-casfluich*, who carries him on his back through the sikes and brooks, then his *gilly-comstrian*, to lead his horse by the bridle in steep and difficult paths; then his *gilly-trushharnish*, to carry his knapsack; and the piper and the piper's man, and it may be a dozen young lads beside, that have no business, but are just boys of the belt, to follow the laird, and do his honour's bidding (p. 153).

As they talk, they see the mountains rising around them, and the eagles flying, and in general the landscape suits itself to a grander moral and social scenery, grander in various ways. Waverley feels conscious of an imputation (p. 155) "which Evan seemed to entertain of the effeminacy of the Lowlanders, and particularly of the English." For it is manhood that is under test, here in the Highlands as it was on Crusoe's island. And at Glennaquoich Waverley meets Fergus and Flora MacIvor, the principal embodiments of this virility and splendor.

In the second part of the story, the spectacle of Highland life, that has been unrolled before Waverley like a painted panorama, is replaced by the 1745 Rebellion, in which the MacIvors involve him. Essentially his role in this second part is as passive, or at most as tentative, as his role was in Part I, but geographically he moves a great deal, and socially he moves up and down the ranks of Scottish society, reaching the circle of the Young Pretender himself. But at the battle of Prestonpans he meets Colonel Talbot, a forceful spokesman for English reason at its best, and under Talbot's guidance realizes the weaknesses and dangers, practical and moral, of the romance world he has entered. This education coincides with, and rationalizes, the defeat of the Rebellion, and the retreat of Waverley to private life in England again.

But Waverley has gained much from the experience. At the end of the story he has become a man, and has won a highly desirable though entirely domestic bride. (There is less conventional rounding-off in Defoe's story, but—by the same token—the sense of reward and relief at the end is stronger; Crusoe's triumphs as mock-governor of the island, like Charles Edward's triumphs as Pretender, have to end; but Crusoe's financial investments, so lavishly detailed, and his difficult journey home, are less conventional than Waverley's rewards.) And clearly the curve of Waverley's experience is to be echoed in the sympathizing reader, who has tempered his own loyalty to modern reality by indulging a yearning for the opposite, in a measured and controlled experiment that leaves him all the more firmly what he was before.

If we examine *Waverley* structurally, we find that the rotation of the romance axis already described has made confusion of most of the old motifs. We must be struck by the profusion of new ones, like the historical figures and local details (costume, houses, food, etc.), the epic speech, the romantic landscape, and the heroines. These last are a feeble invention, who bring with them an operatic sensibility badly at odds with modernist adventure.[3] Flora MacIvor's "effects" (in both senses, theatrical properties *and* splendid tableaux; her harp and her diamonds, but also her political passion and her tragic fate) turn every place and event she enters into papier-mâché. Rose, the inheriting blonde, is less recalcitrant but no more rewarding. But from Scott's time on, romance was burdened down with a stock of such lay figures, Cooper's narrative pace being particularly hobbled.

Fergus's function is like that of the Black Prince, but it would be stretching that term too far to apply it to him. "Black" is not inappropriate, but it will not apply in Defoe's sense—the sense of belonging to another race and culture; Fergus is black in the moral sense. He is a prince, but because the hero has become passive in *Waverley* his opposite number has to become active, and this makes another development to the figure as Scott used him. He is much more of a threat, to the hero and to the story, than Defoe's Black Prince was.

Perhaps Scott's most successful invention in the way of romance motifs is the large scene; like the ball at Holyrood, the army on the march, or the battle. This is something Defoe did not attempt in his modernist adventures, though in *Memoirs of a Cavalier* he came closer. Scott had of course read *Memoirs of a Cavalier,* and one might say that his whole achievement was to blend together material from several of Defoe's kinds of books. But that is not true in any sense derogatory to Scott's originality, for in large scenes of this kind his extraordinary feeling for (and knowledge of) how institutions work, both the formally and the informally organized, finds truly vivid literary expression.[4]

## Scott's Career and Reputation

We know much more about Scott than about Defoe, but it isn't feasible in his case either to develop biographical detail here, except in the matter of his literary career, which is peculiarly representative of the adventure novelist's.

Scott began his literary career with narrative poems, and immediately showed that he knew how to make literature pay—how to make it popular. In 1809 he published *The Lay of the Last Minstrel,* the first best-selling poem. A significant predecessor was Defoe's *The True-Born Englishman,* but Defoe's sales and even more his earnings could not compete, because of the underdeveloped state of publishing then. Scott's poem had sold 44,000 copies before the Collected Edition of his works appeared in 1829. Then came *The Lady of the Lake,* which sold 25,000 copies in eight months, and made the western Highlands a tourist attraction forthwith. Houses and inns there were filled that season, and posthouse duty in Scotland rose from the date of its publication. In 1813 came *Rokeby* and *Triermain.* The first sold 10,000 copies, which would have been a great success for anyone else, but he regarded it as a failure. In fact, Byron had begun to write similar poems, and since he could charge their Romantic heroes with autobiographical excitement, he outshone Scott. Scott said to his publisher, "Since one line has failed, we must stick to something else." So in 1814 he produced *Waverley*.

On his deathbed, he is supposed to have said (according to Samuel Smiles, *Character*, p. 187), "It *is* a comfort to me to think that I have tried to unsettle no man's faith, to corrupt no man's principles, and that I have written nothing which on my deathbed I should wish blotted out." The phrasing of that is implausibly mealy-mouthed, but one can imagine that he said something to that effect. Scott did mean to reinforce the constructive energies of his people; that is just what makes him, and the other adventure-tellers, so unlike serious writers. That remark is after all not so far from another entry in his Journal for June 16, 1826, "I am sensible that if there be anything good about my poetry, or prose either, it is a hurried frankness of composition which pleases soldiers, sailors, and young people of bold and active disposition." As opposed, obviously, to people of literary taste. (In our day, Donald Davie has said it is science students, not literature students, who read Scott.) In fact, in 1831 a cruise in a warship, on the Mediterranean, was arranged for Scott, because he was such a favorite author of the navy's; a favor extended later to Kipling, but not to George Eliot or Henry James.

The system of literature gradually moved Scott to its periphery in the course of the nineteenth century. At the beginning, the novelty, the profusion, the pleasure given, the very popularity of *The Waverley Novels*, overbore all criticism. That popularity was quite unprecedented. Ten to thirty journals reviewed each one as it came out, and copies were eagerly awaited from the packet from Leith. Weeklies had advance copies rushed down by coach. *Waverley* sold six printings in one year, *Old Mortality* (1816) sold 4,000 copies in six months, *Rob Roy* (1816) 10,000 in two weeks, *The Fortunes of Nigel* (1822) 7,000 by 10:30 of the first day it was for sale. They earned him £10 to 15,000 a year. So England found in Scott the stories it wanted to hear, and not only England.

French translations came out within the year of publication in English, and the rest of Europe was not far behind. *Ivanhoe*, for instance, was translated into French, Spanish, and German by 1832, Portuguese by 1838, Italian by 1840, Greek by 1847, Polish by 1865. Cheap editions in England began in the 1860s, while in 1871 Scott's biography sold 180,000 copies.

Soon after 1870 he began to be relegated to children, and versions of his work adapted to their taste appeared. This is a sure mark of relegation to the periphery of literature, though that very shift may be a move to something like the center of culture; for the books that shape ourselves as a nation or as a class are surely the books we read as children.[5] What we read as adults, at least what we read seriously, cannot have that effect, just because serious critical attention disinfects the reading process. (I am thinking of that infection which Tolstoy said was the great power of art.) Ideally, of course, critical reading is a process which ensures that we get infected or excited only by those ideas and images which deserve to excite us. Practically, however, critical reading is often more aggressive than that. The reader's mind acts upon the text, and in doing so crushes its seeds of meaning.

The best reviewers understood what Scott was doing from the beginning. Jeffrey reviewed *Waverley* enthusiastically in the *Edinburgh Review* in 1814, and spoke of how it showed "feudal chivalry in the mountains, and vulgar fanaticism in the plains; and startled the more polished parts of the land with the wild but brilliant picture of the devoted valour, incorruptible fidelity, patriarchal brotherhood, and savage habits of the Celtic Clans. . . . [elsewhere] so long superseded by more peaceable habits, and milder manners. . . . When the glens of the central Highlands . . . were opened up to the gaze of the English, it seemed as if they were carried back to the days of the Heptarchy."*

Generally speaking, Scott was seen as being morally affirmative and effective, at least by conservatives. He inspired the nation; particularly its military men, as we have seen, but not exclusively them. Newman in 1839 said Scott's novels prepared men for conversion to Catholicism, and gave them nobler ideas, and, set beside Pope and 18th century literature, "look almost as oracles of truth confronting the ministers of error and sin." On the other hand, Hazlitt was always largely hostile, in the name of political radicalism; and Carlyle delivered the crucial Victorian verdict, which in the long run relegated Scott to the periphery. Reviewing Lockhart's biography of Scott in 1838, for the *London and Westminster Review,* he said the latter had no faith in anything but power. Nor did he disbelieve. He "quietly

---

*Scott: The Critical Heritage,* John O. Hayden, (Ed.), p. 80.

acquiesced, and made himself at home in a world of conventionalities."* He was at ease, not in Zion, but in Babel. A man of letters, Carlyle implies, is not supposed to be at ease with the world around him. He is supposed to be a hero of resistance.

Twain's criticism of Scott, in *Life on the Mississippi* (1883), is in a sense irrelevant to our argument, but deserves a short comment, just because we are concerned with both Twain and Scott. Twain says Scott set the world in love with dreams and phantoms; "with decayed and swinish forms of religion; . . . with the sillinesses and emptinesses, sham grandeurs, sham gauds, and sham chivalries of a brainless and worthless long-vanished society" (p. 375). This is partly a political attack. In the same chapter, Twain praises Napoleon and the French Revolution for their permanent services to liberty, humanity, and progress; and Scott was Napoleon's major literary antagonist in England. But it is partly literary criticism, and that part is purely modernist. Twain is attacking Scott (and the same is true of his attack on Cooper) for not being enough like Defoe.

His attack is not quite relevant to our argument because Twain is not thinking of the Scott represented by *Waverley,* but of the author of *Ivanhoe* and other such novels; and even more of what the plantation aristocrats of the South made of *Ivanhoe,* with their mock-tournaments, etc. But (of course) I must acknowledge that the Scott of whom I speak also wrote *Ivanhoe,* and several other books, in which his nostalgia for the past is not effectively balanced or shaped by his moral realism and by that interest in cultural anthropology which was its intellectual expression. The Waverley novels were not all like *Waverley;* but the best ones are, and the form I described is potentially present within the whole enterprise.

If Carlyle delivered the verdict against Scott, and relegated him to the periphery of the Victorian literary system, it was Coleridge who played a part closer to Swift's part against Defoe. Coleridge was the genius who seemed to his literary contemporaries to sit at the very centre of the system, and to incarnate its best qualities of judgment and discrimination. The antagonism between him and Scott, and his refusal to "accept" the other man, is of crucial importance. Coleridge understood the Waverley novels. He said Scott's stories could never be obsolete, because their subject is† "the contrast between the two

---

*Scott,* Hayden, p. 347.
†Quoted in David D. Devlin, *Author of Waverley,* Lewisburg, Pa., 1971, p. 53.

great moving principles of social humanity; religious adherence to the past and the ancient, the desire and the admiration of permanence, on one hand; and the passion for increase of knowledge . . . on the other."

But he thought the novels not serious enough in their treatment of that subject. In a letter of 1821, he described Scott as popular reading that aimed "to amuse without requiring any effort of thought and without exciting any deep emotion. The age seems *sore* from excess of stimulation." And when he heard of Scott's financial failure, in 1826, he wrote, "When I think of the wretched trash that the lust for gain induced him to publish for the last three or four years . . . even my feelings assist in hardening me. . . . I should indeed be sorry if any ultimate success had attended the attempt to unite the Poet and the Worldling."

Scott took a tone of philistine heartiness about Coleridge. He referred in his *Journal* in 1828 to meeting him—that extraordinary man—"Zounds, I was never so bethumped with words," and told Mrs. Davy in 1831 that most of Coleridge's prose was nonsense. But in effect he accepted his own banishment from the central position Coleridge and Wordsworth held in literature. In an entry for 1827, he says Wordsworth is unwise and unjust to himself in choosing subjects which the popular mind cannot sympathize in. "He fails to receive the universal suffrage he deserves because too subtle in subject, too blunt in expression." He compared himself rather with Tom Moore. "We are both good-humoured fellows who rather seek to enjoy what is going forward than to maintain our dignity as Lions. . . ." (*Journal*, p. 6).[6]

## Scotland and India

Most of Scott's fiction made only indirect mention of the colonies as such. At the end of *The Heart of Midlothian*, Effie's son kills his (illegitimate) father and goes to America to escape justice. There he conspires against his master, and finally renounces white culture altogether, joining an Indian tribe. His parents' sin works itself out in his loss of white identity. This is one of the rare occasions when the colonies appear in Scott's fiction. The function assigned to them is eloquently "anthropoemic," but rudimentary. (Other Victorian novelists also made this use of them.)

Another tantalizing reference comes in Appendix III to the General Preface to *The Waverley Novels,* in which Scott describes a subject for an adventure novel, with which his brother Thomas toyed, and which derived from an incident in their youth. The Scott brothers and their friends engaged in boyhood battles against the poor children of their neighborhood, and "one very active and spirited lad . . . a youthful Goth," who led their armies, got wounded rather severely. Scott and his brothers tried to bribe him to silence, but he refused either to "sell his blood" or to inform on them. "Such was the hero whom Mr. Thomas Scott proposed to carry off to Canada, and involve in adventures with the natives and colonists of that country" (*Waverley,* p. 50). Scott shows himself much struck with the boy's "nobleness of sentiment," and calls him an Achilles and an Ajax, so the anthropoemic elements of the story are enriched by antithesis. He says nothing about the boy's lowly origins, but of course that is another element of interest. It is indeed a very promising subject for an adventure story of a kind closer to Defoe's than anything Scott did in fact write. For of course the striking fact this calls our attention to is that Scott's adventure tales do not involve either empire or frontier. So that even that limited respectability which he won for adventure did not extend to the crucially important contemporary subject matter.

But in the Prefatory to *The Surgeon's Daughter,* he says he has been advised to write a story about India. "India, where gold is won by steel; where a brave man cannot pitch his desire of fame and wealth so high but that he may realize it, if he have fortune to his friend." He has been advised to take a story from Robert Orme's 1763 three-volume *History of the Military Transactions of the British Nation in Indostan 1745–1761.* This is the story of Clive, and Scott sees its adventure potential. He agrees that the subject is wonderful. All the English soldiers "are distinguished among the natives like the Spaniards among the Mexicans. What do I say? They are like Homer's demi-gods among the warring mortals. Men like Clive and Cailliaud [a 19th century French traveler in Africa] influenced great events like Jove himself. . . . Then the various religious costumes, habits, and manners of the people of Hindostan—the patient Hindoo, the warlike Rajahpoot, the haughty Moslemah, the savage and vindictive Malay. Glorious and unbounded subject! The only objection is, that I have never been there, and know nothing at all about them" (p. xiv).

But that is not a sufficient explanation, since he had never been in the rebellion of 1745, for instance. And it seems clear that Scott did "know something about them," in fact, did think of going to India. He spoke of it in 1810, when there was some chance that his friend, Lord Melville, might go out as governor general. Scott's wife's brother had made a fortune there. Indeed, his family, like other Scots, had many connections with the colonies. His brother Thomas went out to Canada, his brother James to the West Indies. Scott was very aware of the world destiny of the British—that, ultimately, was his subject. But the connection between Scotland and India was particularly close.

The East India Company was of course a large part of the British empire, and a very striking fact from our point of view; that an empire —a subcontinent much larger than England itself, in every sense of large—should be ruled by a commercial company, is a striking example of how the modern world system worked—how it blended empire with nonempire. The Company was, among other things, a huge source of wealth to England. It paid £400,000 a year to the Treasury, as well as making very large loans on occasion. It is usually now considered that this was the wealth which financed the Industrial Revolution in England.[7] One example of the profits involved is the case of the E. I. C. ship *Berrington,* which in 1784 carried to India a cargo of lead, copper, steel, wool cloths, naval stores, worth £27,000, and brought back cotton goods, yarn, indigo, silk, and saltpeter, worth £120,000. And the effect in terms of imperialist psychology was also huge.

Like other parts of the empire, India was a living promise of lordship or royalty to Englishmen. In *Adventures of a Younger Son* (1831), his purported autobiography, Trelawney says, "If the English conspired against our liberty . . . India, with her thousand kings, was open to us . . . In India Europeans lorded it over the conquered natives with a high hand. Every outrage may be committed almost with impunity, and their ready flexibility of temperament has acquired a servile subordination. . . ." (p. 46). One example of what he is talking about is given us by James Morris in *Pax Britannica.* Sir David Ochtherlony, East India Company Resident at Delhi in the eighteenth century, used to travel with thirteen wives, each on her own elephant.

This was just one of the facts that made nineteenth-century liberals and radicals deeply suspicious of and hostile to the empire. It attracted the wrong kind of Englishmen from their point of view, and brought out the wrong tendencies in them. And this feeling was closely related to caste loyalty. Cobden and Goldwin Smith described the colonies as being linked to the army, the navy, the established church, and the aristocracy. "Merely accessories to our aristocratic government," Cobbett called them in 1836; and in 1838 Bronterre O'Brien said, "Our aristocracy and merchants possess colonies all over the world, but the people of England—the real, veritable people of England—do not possess a sod of ground in their own country, much less colonies in any other."* It was the military caste who governed the colonies; the public schools were training boys' characters, and the new boys' literature was training their imaginations, in the ways of the military caste. Nineteenth-century imperialists like Froude saw the colonies as a way for England to return to farming and landowning, and to get away from trade and commerce.

Morally, too, the effects of this imperial wealth were manifold, and most of them the cause for disapproval by the serious mind of England, perhaps especially the serious literary mind. Cowper's *Expostulation,* line 82, says

> Hast thou, though suckled at fair freedom's breast,
> Exported slavery to the conquered East . . .
> With Asiatic vices stored thy mind
> But left their virtues and thine own behind?

Burke's attack on the East India Company as birds of prey and birds of passage is well-known. And in 1770 Chatham said to Parliament, "For some years past there has been an influx of wealth into this country, which has been attended with many fatal consequences, because it has not been the natural produce of labour and industry. The riches of Asia have been poured in on us, and brought with them not only Asiatic luxury but, I fear, Asiatic principles of government. Without connections, without any natural interest in the soil, the

*R. Hyam and G. Martin, *Reappraisals in British Imperial History,* London, 1975, p. 9.

importers of foreign gold have forced their way into Parliament by such a torrent of corruption as no private hereditary fortune could resist."*

The special importance of India for Scotsmen can be given in Scott's own words, when he described the India Board as "this corn chest for Scotland, where we poor gentry must send our youngest sons, as we send our black cattle to the south." Young Scotsmen, above all young gentry, could retrieve their family's fortunes there. The connection was made largely via his friend Henry Dundas, Lord Melville, who was Pitt's political manager of Scotland, and who dispensed a large patronage in the East India Company after 1784. Englishmen commonly said that no one but a Scot could get a job in any Indian province where the chief was a Scot, and Boswell in 1762 spoke of knowing a Scot who saw London only as a place to join the Company. Men spoke of the Indian-and-Scottish interest in politics, and James MacIntosh said you could see "a little stream of Indian gold" in Scotland "spreading cultivation and fertility and plenty along its narrow valley."

For thirty years another channel of Company patronage to Scotsmen was Charles Grant. Though also a friend of Dundas, Grant was very unlike Scott in his views, for he was a fervent Evangelical, a powerful member of the Clapham sect, and an agent of the Victorianization of the Company, the substitution of missionary moralism, which Scott would have hated, for the old Enlightenment tolerance. Nevertheless, it is worth saying something about Grant here, because both his family and history and his own career bear importantly on the operation of the modern world system, in Scotland and in India.

He was born in 1746, and his father, called Alexander Grant the Swordsman, was a very colorful figure in the 1745 rebellion. Charles was named after the prince, and was baptized just before his defeat at Culloden, having to clasp the hilts of two swords held crossed over him. He grew up to be the very opposite of Jacobite romanticism—to be an embodiment of Evangelical seriousness. After Culloden, Alexander, like many other Jacobites and Highlanders, went out to the West Indies. He died soon after getting there, but another Alexander Grant became Charles's protector and patron. This Alex-

*R. A. Huttenback, The *British Imperial Achievement*, p. 7.

ander had also fought at Culloden, but then emigrated to India, and fought under Clive at Plassey and won prize money there amounting to £11,000. Charles went to London to work for him in 1763, and then to India. (It is interesting to note, as an example of Scots-Indian nepotism, that Charles had two brothers and two cousins in India with him, besides his wife's sister.) He became Secretary of a Board of Trade in 1774 and made a lot of money, and was converted by the Danish missionaries out there.

This was the time of such conversions, the time of missions abroad and the Evangelical movement at home. There was a general reaction against the eighteenth-century rationalism and skepticism. From our point of view this shows the modern system recharging itself with primitive energies which had begun to drain away from at least the conscious mind and will of the system—primitive both in the sense of crude and in the sense of original. The conviction of righteousness, individual and collective righteousness, strong in Defoe and Raleigh, much eroded in Hume and Gibbon (and their readers in, for instance, the East India Company), was renewed in Macaulay and Grant.[8]

The latter's case is especially interesting for us, because of his close biographical connection with the forty-five, and all the colorful Jacobitism which his father represented and which Scott celebrated. Charles Grant, after his conversion, turned away from that colorfulness (predominantly aristomilitary colors) toward the black and white of Puritanism. This was the movement of the whole serious mind of England then, and it meant that the adventure novel as Scott wrote it was swimming against the tide, morally speaking, and would not become a major literary genre.

Between 1780 and 1790 Dundas imposed government control on the Company. Grant came back to Scotland in 1790, and became M.P. for Inverness in 1799, keeping the seat for fifteen years. In 1794 he became a director of the Company, which he is said to have dominated after 1804 because he did so much of the work. He attacked Sir William Jones and the other Orientalists, who had studied and celebrated Indian culture. Grant saw that culture as being in a state of decadence and India as needing redemption by means of an infusion of English culture; for instance, he wanted to have missionaries sent out there and to have support be given them by the Company. He spread a nondialectical, single-valued view of history and progress. But the point for the moment is that in this typically Victorian form the patronage connection between Scotland and India continued.

So when we read Scott celebrating the ancestral virtues of Scotsmen—virtues no longer rife in modern England—we should think of India as being implicitly referred to. Those virtues habitually found an important political function and a large economic reward, in the administration of India. And also that ancient character-structure, and the social structure behind it, explained India and Indians to his readers. Scott was in a sense writing about the nineteenth-century empire under the guise of writing about feudal Scotland. That is another reason why his readers were so engrossed by him, until the system of literature persuaded them he was not serious.


## Emigration and Empire


But this sketch of a historical context for Scott must be expanded still further. That connection between Scotland and India is only part of a larger pattern connecting the British Isles with the colonies, and that in turn is part of the modern world system migration. In "The Migration of Human Populations," (*Scientific American*, September 1974) the demographer Kingsley Davis tells us that in the sixteenth and seventeenth centuries the world was dominated by a single migratory network, built around the advanced states, and it was thanks to this network that they were able to achieve their Industrial Revolution. The first territories to be exploited were tropical and uninhabited (that is, no "civilized" people lived there); lands like the Caribbean islands, where the Europeans grew spices, sugar, rice, coffee, etc., by means of slave labor. Between 1451 and 1870, 11 million slaves were exported from Africa and 9.6 million reached their destinations. When the slave trade was stopped, indentured labor, from India, China, and Java took its place. Some 16.8 million left India, 4.4 million for good.

The second sort of lands to be exploited were temperate and uninhabited; and these attracted the European migrants. They were moving in considerable numbers from 1720 on, but it was after steamships began to operate in 1827 that those numbers expanded; by 1830, it is estimated, 52 million had changed their land of residence. In 1897 145,000 emigrants left Britain alone, 50,000 for the colonies. Associated with migration is a remarkable increase in population. C. F. Carrington says that in the course of the ten generations following the days of Raleigh and Drake, the population of Britain increased (counting those living in the colonies and the U.S.) from 7 to 140 million, a rate unexampled among other races. Davis says that between 1840 and 1930 Europe's population rose from 194 million to 463 million, a rate of growth twice the world's average, and Europeans abroad increased at a rate even faster. Between 1750 and 1930 the European-occupied areas of the rest of the world increased their population by a factor of 14, while the world rate was 2.5. In 1750 these areas held 3 percent of the world's people, while in 1930, 16 percent. Caucasians increased by a factor of 5.4, Asians by a factor of 2.3.[9]

One importance of this to us is to remind us of the literature that necessarily accompanied this vast shift of population. Two categories that jump to mind are first the literature of promotion, from the poems of Marston and Chapman to the twentieth-century pamphlets of the Canada office in London; and second the flow of correspondence by means of which emigrants kept in touch with family and friends at home. This literature kept the idea, in some sense the experience, of the empire in the minds of the home population, however the serious writers of the time might slight it. From this point of view we can discern two different meanings of the word literature, and can say both that there was no significant literature of empire in nineteenth-century England, and that there was a very rich and significant one. Scott's leatherbound volumes, with their indirect mythic message, joined forces with millions of pamphlets and letters and miniatures and mementos of those abroad. The swarming of WASP's over the rest of the globe was being recorded and celebrated.

Another literature of that kind, to do with missions, developed in Scott's time. Although the Roman Catholic church had sent missionaries to foreign parts from the beginning of the age of exploration, Protestant missions, much more important from our point of view, did not begin effectively until the 1790s. In 1792 William Carey founded a London Missionary Society (Baptist); in 1795 a group of mostly Presbyterians founded their London Missionary Society; in 1799 Evangelicals founded the Church Missionary Society, who began to publish the *Christian Observer* in 1802, and so on. The

Moravians (the first Protestant missionaries generally) had gone to Bengal in 1777, the first English missionaries followed them the next year, but it was not until 1813 that the numbers became considerable. But more considerable, on the whole, was the homeland role played by missionaries in pious Victorian society. Probably the greatest hero of the whole nineteenth century for that half of England was the missionary Livingstone. And we must imagine all the church- and chapel-goers hearing sermons and reading church-magazine reports about missionaries in foreign parts, regularly. On the whole, that segment of Victorian culture remained distinct from the literary segment, but there were figures who crossed the line, like George Borrow. He also showed the connection between missions, empire, and adventure, when he said it was a "crown of glory to carry the blessings of civilization and religion to barbarous, yet at the same time beautiful and romantic lands."

This aspect of modern system ideology also can be associated with Scotland.

Livingstone of course was a Scot, as was his missionary father-in-law, Moffat, and many other missionaries. The African Lakes Company that ruled Nyasaland did so on the behalf of both the Free Church and some Glasgow merchants. And the missionary enterprise blended with others in which the Scots were prominent. Scots explorers, like James Bruce and Mungo Park, were famous for their journeys. And Scots soldiers, like Charles Napier and Colin Campbell, were famous in India. The Hudson's Bay Company was largely Scottish, in fact largely Orcadian, and whole villages considered themselves "Company folk." And the Canadian Pacific Railway was carried through by Scottish financiers and engineers.

It is clear that Scotland had, as England's subordinate partner, a special destiny in the modern world system.[10] John Galt the novelist founded a Canada Company in 1824 to organize emigration there (70-acre land grants were being made in Canada in the 1820s) and there was a British-American Land Co., appealing to Highlanders, in 1834. During the nineteenth century a high proportion of Scots emigrants were skilled workers; engineers, shipbuilders, iron smelters. A typical Scots emigrant city was Pittsburgh, and its great success story was Andrew Carnegie.

It is no wonder that when R. L. Stevenson went out to America by emigrant ship in 1879, he described emigration as "this great epic of self-help. The epic is composed of individual heroisms. . . . For in emigration the young men enter direct and by the ship-load on their heritage of work; empty continents swarm, as at the bo'sun's whistle, with industrious hands, and whole new empires are domesticated to the service of man" (*From Scotland to Silverado,* p. 10). His tone is ironic, for he sees on his ship that most emigrants are in fact already defeated men. But on board the emigrant train to California he is caught up by the old excitement, at the building of the railroad. Think, he tells us, "how at each stage of the construction, roaring, impromptu cities, full of gold and lust and death, sprang up and then died away again, and are now but wayside stations in the desert; how in those uncouth places pig-tailed Chinese pirates worked side by side with border ruffians. . . . If it be romance, if it be contrast, if it be heroism that we require, what was Troy Town to this?" (p. 129).

Stevenson saw the subject. But then Scott had done that much. And neither one could in fact marry that subject to the serious writer's modes of sense and sensibility. The trick could be turned in children's literature; vivid narratives of that kind were produced; they were written by Stevenson, as by Ballantyne before him—both Scots writers. If anyone could have written the serious novel of adventure, it probably would have been a Scotsman, because of the mode of Scots participation in the Empire—the disengagement (compared with England) despite the deep involvement. But it seems that the polarity holding literature always in some opposition to that genre and subject-matter was too strong.

## Historians and Historical Novelists

Despite his "official" demotion from literature, Scott exerted an enormous influence on writers, partly just because of his sales. (The same was true of Defoe before him, and it is one reason why students of literature need to study both of them.) But Scott (and Defoe) also exerted influence in the larger realm of high culture—were, odd as it sounds, intellectuals. They were Whig ideologues. This influence constitutes another imaginative context for the adventure tale, explaining its potency by naming its allies. In Defoe's case, the influence was felt in the field of economics. In Scott's case, this influence centered in the realm of history, where the deeds of kings, generals, and armies always bulk larger than they do in literature. He was himself a historian. His *Life of Napoleon,* which appeared in nine volumes in 1827, earned him £18,000, and is said to have shown Carlyle and Macaulay how profitable a work of history could be made. But his greater influence on history-writing was exerted through his novels. Via Scott, the adventure ethos entered history, in the work of the nineteenth-century Whig historians of England and America, carrying in solution also nationalism and historical romanticism. Even Macaulay, in some ways a Utilitarian, wrote patriotic ballads (about the Armada) which would have shocked Hume. It was the infusion of adventure that made the difference between eighteenth- and nineteenth-century historiography, and it was Scott who made the infusion.

In many ways Scott himself was an eighteenth-century Whig historian, as he was an eighteenth-century sensibility in general. His Toryism, and his Romanticism, though they seemed to his contemporaries so unlike the attitudes of his predecessors, are rather superficial changes from the point of view of anyone considering the progress of the modern world system. He only introduced a dialectic, which complicated but also enriched the Whig historians' system of ideas.

In *The History of Historical Writing,* J. W. Thompson calls the period, 1715–1789, the Age of Reason. (We might call it the Age of the Encyclopaedists, and imply Defoe also.) In those years, historians' ideas were derived from Descartes, and their metaphors were derived from mechanics. They promoted peace and prosperity, fought superstition and splendid tyranny. Their ethos was neither adventurous nor zealous; especially in France, historians tended to oppose both the army and the church, and to mock both kings and empires. Voltaire is an example. Scott reacted against much of that. His sense of history was unlike Voltaire's. On the other hand, another of the representative French historians of that time was the more conservative Montesquieu, whose political model was constitutional monarchy in the English style, and whose enemy was military despotism in the style of Louis XIV. And that was Scott's position as much as Defoe's. Scott's Toryism (his aristomilitary sympathy) was not of a kind to divide him from Montesquieu, or from the English Whigs.

History, in the Age of Reason, seemed to be on England's side. Thompson says that eighteenth-century writers throughout Europe used history as an arsenal with which to bombard the ancien régime with irony, in the name of freedom. In England, with all its faults, historians felt that they had freedom; or at least that the worst cases of unfreedom were abroad. The greatest ironist of them all, Gibbon, served the same cause. He first intended to write the history of liberty in Switzerland, then one of the holy places of Protestantism and freedom. And freedom represented all the values of progress; the Scots historian, Robertson, said his *History of Charles V* would mark the steps by which Europe advanced from barbarism to refinement. These historians spoke as clearly for modernism—as Defoe himself.

The difference between their attitudes and Scott's is that his loyalties were more divided, even in *Waverley*, where he made the issue to the conflict clearer than usual. The comparative narrowness and simplicity of the eighteenth-century historians' view is clear in this remark of Robertson about Loyola. "The wild adventures and visionary schemes in which his enthusiasm engaged him equal anything recorded in the legends of the Roman saints; but are unworthy of notice in history." Robertson also deplored the reading of conqueror's exploits while "the useful arts and the branches of commerce sink into oblivion." One glimpses there an aridity and narrowness of mercantile rationalism which Scott and the Romantics reacted against.

But he was not really skeptical of the values of progress and modernism. He merely held those values dialectically. Avrom Fleishman, in *The English Historical Novel*, has shown that Scott was consciously a sociologist, in the Scots school of speculative history, which had its roots in 18th century Whiggery, but refined upon it. His Whig friend Adam Ferguson, in his essay on the *History of Modern Society*, warned against the effects of wealth and liberty (in polished and commercial nations) because they dissolve the bonds of patriotism, loyalty, blood brotherhood, etc. That is exactly Scott's message. And Dugald Stewart, another such friend, made a sharp distinction between natural and historical aristocracy, which, as Fleishman says, is a very important distinction for Scott, as a way to refurbish aristocracy for the modern world. Scott ". . . throughout his poetry and fiction may be said to have worked towards a refinement of the aristocrat ideal [towards creating] . . . a paidea for modern life" (p. 52). He carefully analyzed the idea of a gentleman. (In this work, of course, Scott was next in line from Defoe and next before Smiles.)

Thus Scott's adventures, though less directly than Defoe's, translated the Whig interpretation of history into fiction.

In his famous essay, *The Whig Interpretation of History* (1951), Herbert Butterfield defines this interpretation as "The tendency in many historians to write on the side of Protestants and Whigs, to praise revolutions provided they have been successful, to emphasize certain principles of progress in the past, and to produce a story which is the ratification if not the glorification of the present. . . ." (Preface, p. v). Clearly this is a specification, in terms of historiography, of the general line of thought and sensibility we are studying. On page 4, Butterfield says that "the great patriarchs of history-writing" divided people between those who furthered history and those who impeded it, and introduced value judgments at every turn, so that history might be their judge and their defender. Butterfield's irony is of course another sign that by 1951 people were feeling that this long historical movement was over, and that other intellectual attitudes must be devised. But in the period we are concerned with, that could not or did not happen. The modern enterprise dragged the modern mind after it.

In the nineteenth century, Thompson says, we should consider Thiers and Guizot Whig historians, while in England the supreme example is Macaulay; no other history has ever approached Macaulay's *History of England* in popularity. Three thousand copies were sold within ten days of publication, 13,000 in four months; and in America, Harper sold 40,000 in a cheap edition, more than anything else but the Bible.

The specifically Victorian note is perhaps struck by Macaulay's confident declaration on page 516, "No *state* has achieved anything by a breach of public faith, and the British government in India has gained everything by having always kept its promises." Scott would have found that a bit much to swallow. But in "The State of England in 1685," Macaulay puts the stress where Scott put it—and even more exactly where Defoe put it—on the excitements of progress. North of the Trent, England in 1685 was in a state of barbarism. Middlesex was to Northumberland as Massachusetts is to America west of the Mississippi, where settlers impose the law of the gun and the knife. A quarter of England has been turned from a wilderness into a garden in little more than a century. There has been an immense increase in wealth of every kind, and of refinement, arts, skills, learning and specifically comfort. Macaulay was, as Herzen says somewhere, the Scott of his generation, and the poet of the middle class.

The nationalist and racist historians of later in the century, Froude, Freeman, Green, etc., who more clearly owed a lot to Scott, were nevertheless Whig in Butterfield's sense. They wrote histories that were also adventures. Froude produced *A History of England from the Fall of Wolsey to the Defeat of the Spanish Armada*—a foundation epic—between 1856 and 1870; and *English Seamen in the 16th Century*—a book of heroes—in 1895. Freeman made heroes of Harold and Godwin, using the idea of the Norman yoke which Scott had employed in *Ivanhoe*. And J. R. Green described his *Short History* as a chronicle of the English people, showing their development from primitive democracy.[11]

But all this, though relevant to the larger subject of the modern world's imaginative transactions with its empire, is rather remote from Scott. Let me conclude this chapter by describing his influence on subsequent novelists, especially on historical novelists. Their number was enormous; at times in the nineteenth century, half a year's new fiction was historical. Of course not all had serious meanings, and among the serious books, not all held by Scott's ideas. But it is clear that for some years Scott was at the center of fiction as a production system, and his kind of novel promised rich rewards even to serious writers. A high point seems to be the early 1860s, as far as quality goes, when we have Flaubert's *Salâmmbo* in 1862, and George Eliot's *Romola* in 1863, and Charles Reade's *The Cloister and the Hearth* in 1861. Even in the '80s we have *John Inglesant* (1881), and *Marius the Epicurean* (1885) and the works of George Moore; but by then the influence of Scott was quite adulterated by mixture with other ideas. The big producers of historical fiction in England were of course lesser writers, such as G. P. R. James, who wrote about sixty novels, beginning with *The Life of Edward, the Black Prince* in 1822. Harrison Ainsworth (1805–1882) was closer to Dumas in style. Lytton and Kingsley, for that matter Dickens and Thackeray, wrote historical novels. R. D. Blackmore introduced a somewhat new style in 1869, with *Lorna Doone;* and Stevenson another, with *Treasure Island, Kidnapped,* and *The Master of Ballantrae.*

More important, in terms of the quality of minds shaped by Scott's influence, and as testimony to his place in the system of literature, was his imitation abroad. In the other modern system countries, writers had every incentive to become proto-Scotts, in the field of their own national history. Among the early works in France, we can list de Vigny's *Cinq-Mars* (1826), Balzac's *Les Chouans* (1829), Dumas's *Henri III et sa Cour* (1827), Mérimée's *Chronique du Règne de Charles IX*, and Hugo's *Nôtre Dame de Paris*, as early specimens from drama and fiction, not to mention the historical painters who clearly owed a lot to him. The great nineteenth-century passion of nationalism was largely shaped by such works of art. It is obvious that Scott had found a formula, which would for the time being produce a notable work every time a talented writer worked on it. (The same was true, in a less spectacular degree, of Defoe's *Tour*, and other of Defoe's nonfiction work; but in his fiction he did not fully develop his formulas.) Then in Italy we must mention Manzoni; in Germany Ebers, Hausrath, and Freytag; in Poland Mickiewicz and Sienkewicz; in Russia Tolstoy and Merezhkowski. And why did this formula work so well? Why was there this avid interest in the past for writers to tap? Because of the nationalist passion, especially in countries still struggling for independence. Because the change from the past, once rightly named, was the energizing myth of the modern system. The Scott novel could be adapted to any European public, because indirectly it celebrated the triumph of the whole white race.

Meanwhile in America, as we shall see, Cooper twisted the formula in some ways back towards Defoe, so that the material of contemporary and frontier adventure could be included. That was the privilege of the American, which other writers could only envy. And Cooper's extraordinary success in other countries, despite the manifest ineptitudes of his performance, seems to be a proof that such material had a very privileged status in the imagination of readers everywhere.

## Scott and Defoe

But before turning to Cooper, I should like to sum up the development of the adventure genre so far, the transformation of motifs and themes. What is missing from Scott is the sharply modernist interest of Defoe. His stories breathe no sense of "how to do it." When they have any sense of "how things are done," it takes the form of "how *they* did it *then*"; for instance, Fergus's banquet, or Donald Bean Lean's cave life. And there is less interest in guns, weapons, explosions; these are not *our* explosions. And consequently the adventures themselves tend to be escapades, like Baron Bradwardine hidden in his hole. Such an episode does not give the reader the Defoe-sense of a practical emergency he should prepare for imaginatively since— just by virtue of his being a civilized person—it lies in wait for him.

What is obtrusively present in Scott is the formal elaboration of "literature"; the prefaces and notes, the folklore and history, the pseudonarrators and the class conventions, the archaisms and the humor. Scott is dignifying the adventure tale by making it a high genre, with large claims on our seriousness. It is very characteristic of Scott that this attempt is clearly conscious, but also self-conscious and artful—self-deprecating. This is an artificial and synthetic genre he has invented, including a love interest, a Gothic interest, a comedy of manners, high tragedy, and above all, the materials of romance; all any reader could ask for in a single book. It might even be called a pseudogenre, since the formal elaboration does not function "organically." At its best the machinery reminds one of the form Northrop Frye calls the anatomy, which is the very opposite of adventure; anatomy devices let the air out of a fictional balloon. Scott's devices don't intensify the essential feelings of his stories so much as assure the reader that he is getting a lot for his money—like the formal devices of Victorian furniture.

Above all, Scott brought into the form of the modernist adventure motifs and feelings which represented the aristomilitary caste. Their kind of heroes, their kind of virtues, their kind of exploits, their *romance*, were fitted into the framework of prudential and realistic reflection and narrative. Merchants and men at arms were brought together—and men of letters too, to begin with.

But if in those three ways Scott is very different from Defoe, and almost his antithesis as an adventure-writer, he does continue Defoe's expression of the excitement of empire and frontier in deflected form. He (and his followers in other European countries) may be said to dodge the issue, asking not "what are we doing to other forms of life," but "how did it all start?" But they were responding to the excited awareness of Europe's world triumph, the spreading dominance of the modern system. Their response was deeply deflected, but then so was Defoe's; and it was more of a response than the serious novelists made.

And one aspect of Defoe's work Scott did carry to completion and crown: he made the adventure tale into a foundation epic of England. Here one would compare him with Shakespeare rather than with Defoe. He retold the stories of British history so that they made sense for modern readers, and sense of the energizing kind. The Hanoverians were for him what the Tudors were for Shakespeare; the Rebellions of 1715 and 1745 were his Wars of the Roses; Elizabeth was his Henry IV, Mary Stuart his Richard II, Richard the Lion Heart his Henry V, and so on.

Of course there is ambivalence in Scott's piety; particularly evident in the way his story culminates in the subordination of Scotland as a necessary feature of the triumph of England. One always has to ask about Scott, whose side is he on? And the answer is always, both. Moreover, his way of being on both sides suggests moral laziness and mental cynicism rather than anything nobler. But still there is no denying that he guided the adventure tale to a higher position and a wider scope than it had before, or since. He blended into its mercantile character that aristomilitary character which the upper class of England demanded for its myths; and he took it beyond romance to epic.

# V

# *Cooper*

IN ORDER to make the transition from Scott to Cooper, we have to overcome the intellectual prejudice that there are always immense differences between England and America, in matters of both history and literature—immense distances between Empire and Frontier. In reality, the United States were just as imperialist as the English Colonies in America. The case of Daniel Boone and the invasion of Kentucky shows how local and popular, how American, the imperialist dynamic was, even before 1776. In pouring through the Cumberland Gap, and driving the Indians out of their lands, the settlers were going against the treaties and the wishes of the government in London. The frontier—not the court—was where one saw the empire in action. And American high culture, though reluctantly, followed and reflected that action. As the U.S. gradually became the leading edge of the modern system, so did its literature develop the leading form of adventure.

## Frontier and Empire

The historian whose work is most useful to us in this matter is Walter Prescott Webb. In his *The Great Frontier* he analyses the relations of modern Europe with the rest of the world as a political system relating a Metropolis to a Frontier.

The term frontier, Webb points out, has meant something different in America from what it has in Europe. In the latter it has been a line between two powers, to cross which means danger; in the former, it has been an area that invites entrance and promises opportunity and riches. But this difference in usage is deceptive. Europe, without acknowledging it, has had the same experience as America, because it has had new worlds as its frontier ever since the fifteenth century. (Clearly, when Webb says Europe, he thinks of what, following Wallerstein, I have been calling its core states; and in general Wallerstein's theory refines upon Webb's usefully.) America is the most notable case, but the Boers in South Africa, and the English in Australia, etc., also lived on a frontier. The difference is that Europe's high culture kept that experience at arm's length, did not name it or know it, did not acknowledge the frontier. By the same token, moreover, America was an unnamed empire, and its experience was unacknowledgedly imperial.

When Webb calls Europe a metropolis, he means that it was a cultural center, holding within it everything pertaining to Western civilization. But he is more concerned with the frontier experience, which was opposite in character to the metropolitan, and with the legend that centered about it. The frontier, he says, wore away European and metropolitan institutions—entail, titles, primogeniture, for instance—as on an abrasive grindstone: it set men free—made them rich—made them bold. "The frontier experience from 1500 to, say, 1900 was without doubt among the most memorable adventures mankind has had in modern times. On the rim of the Metropolis, always at its yonder edge, the beacon fires of its Great Frontier was luring men outward, stirring them to mighty deeds, achievements and sacrifices. This was indeed a heroic period, heroic for the individuals and the nations involved. People love their heroic periods, make legends about them, and vaguely hope that they will come again. . . ." (p. 280). Webb seems to me to make this nostalgia too simply chronological. "Heroic periods" can be quite contemporary, as the Frontier was. The contrast is with something different, not past, and the nostalgia it evokes is for something culturally out of style, not for something literally nonexistent. But economically, in any case, it was clearly an overwhelming force, acting on the Western world as a whole.

Webb argues that the frontier was, for Europe, above all other things, a windfall of natural resources: precious metals, furs, ambergris, slaves, pasturage; things that brought immediate profit or things into which little work had to be put. And the windfall created a boom, and the boom modified economic and political structures. He says that most of the institutions Western man has developed since 1500 are boom-born; which means that "the modern age was an abnormal age . . . with exceptional institutions. . . ."

This way of naming the excitements of Empire makes us realize that they are to be found on the frontier as much as in the metropolis. The modern empire has not meant so much a scepter and an orb as a rifle and an axe, and Natty Bumppo embodied those excitements better than George III. This should remind us of the extraordinary response, all across Europe, to *Robinson Crusoe*. That was a response to the new kind of empire. And observers at the right distance saw the identity of that empire with frontier. Alexander Herzen habitually coupled the images of Crusoe and Natty, to name a single concept, the free spirit, the man creating his own life, modifying the conditions of nature, and rejecting the conditions of civilization. And the social-political consequences of releasing this free spirit in the citizens of the core states were empire.

After 1500, Western man's condition improved, Webb says, not in a moderate way, but extraordinarily. But around 1830 the land-population ratio, for Europe and its frontier together (that is, for the modern system) reached the same level it had been at in 1500 for Europe alone; that is, about twenty-seven persons per square mile. The rate of expansion began to slow down, although it took a long time for the full effects of the arrest to show themselves.

Historians have criticized Webb's theory quite severely, on the grounds that he does not know in sufficient detail what the complicated economic relations of Metropolis and Frontier actually were. And I myself would say that in literature, Europe's sense of its frontier was significantly different from America's, and so the American word can be used for the colonies only metaphorically in literary studies. Nevertheless, that metaphorical use of the word seems to me brilliantly illuminating, for one striking difference between literature (and high culture generally) in England, and literature in America, is that the latter made much more of the frontier experience and the boom. There were many justifying reasons for that difference. But it may be possible to say, as a generalization, that England's indifference to, or undisturbedness by, what was happening on its frontier, amounted to a falsity, and falsified the values her high culture was enunciating.

The great virtue of Webb's theory is to suggest an analogy between American experience and British, and so a propriety in holding up British literature against the model of American—and against American real life. If we look at Robinson Crusoe as being a first cousin to Daniel Boone, we shall be struck by new features of the way Defoe presents him. And we shall better understand Natty Bumppo, too, for American studies also will benefit from breaking down the false isolation in which they have so long worked. *Robinson Crusoe* is, as John Seelye has pointed out, the true archetype of much American as well as English fiction.

## Cooper's Books

In Cooper we find an exaggerated version of Scott's posture (his blending of the aristocratic style with the mercantile) set in a cultural situation which makes that posture seem eccentric to begin with. The American situation was much more hostile than the English to anything aristocratic. For that reason, Cooper in his forest tales chose an aggressively unaristocratic and unmilitary hero; but tried to make him answer to the aspirations, satisfy the sensibility, *represent,* his own aristomilitary caste. It was an absurd project, and the debris of literary disaster is everywhere in those tales; and yet the ruins are impressive.

Cooper's father was a self-made man, or rather a self-made aristocrat, as we shall see. And Cooper himself was a military man, in the American navy; imaginatively though not literally a captain. Those were the two determining experiences of his imaginative life; partly because they were not approved as determining experiences by official American culture. Thus he had a special vocation to speak, as novelist, for the aristomilitary caste. He had to defy the overreaching claims of the mercantile mind, but at the same time to conciliate American culture—to make his own caste the favorite son of the American imagination.

Within Cooper's writings, the Leatherstocking Tales are what most concern us, and within them, Leatherstocking himself. They, and above all he, mark the next great stage in the growth of the WASP adventure tale and adventure hero. Taking them in the order of their publication, we have *The Pioneers* (1823), *The Last of the Mohicans* (1826), *The Prairie* (1827), and *The Pathfinder* (1840) and *The Deerslayer* (1841). Taking them in the order of Natty Bumppo's biography, the first is last and the last is first; and we also find a change in the mode of his depiction, from realism to romance. As indeed their respective titles indicate, the first published book is more "about" the beginnings of American society, while the last, though describing a much earlier historical period, feels less distant in time —because it relates to those beginnings only symbolically. A change from realism to romance sounds like a change from Defoe to Scott. But in fact Cooper showed very little sense of, or awareness of, Defoean realism, even in *The Pioneers*. That unDefoean quality is, I think one may say, Cooper's greatest weakness as a writer of modernist romance—his feeble interest in fact and process, and his flimsy caterings to our interest in them. He was very heavily influenced by Scott; from beginning to end, one needs nothing more than Scott's varying styles to explain all the variations amongst Cooper's fictional forms. The difference between *The Pioneers* and *The Deerslayer* is rather that between *Waverley* and *Ivanhoe* than that between *Waverley* and *Crusoe*.

In his Preface to the Leatherstocking Tales, Cooper says that his hero is a man "with little of civilization but its highest principles as exhibited in the uneducated; and all of savagery not incompatible with those great rules of conduct." The complicated phrasing obscures the meaning, and is perhaps related to the paradox in the idea itself—to the elements of self-contradiction in Cooper's enterprise. Natty is a savage, except that he has the highest principles of civilization, in simple form. As such he represents both the best of what Cooper sees around him, and the direction in which America *should* move—a direction which is only one option among many facing the country and indeed one already losing out to the others.

In both ways Cooper is pointing out the American ideal to readers who are presumed to feel themselves very remote from it—from Natty; not necessarily because they are not Americans; just being a reader of novels is enough to ensure that you are of a class to whom Natty must be a very strange figure. When he is first described,

Cooper stresses Natty's *coarse* physique, his skinny body, lank sandy hair, enormous mouth, single tooth; and his flannel underwear, his silent and ironical laugh, and his wiping his nose with his hand. All those traits are in marked contrast with those of Gilbert Stuart's portraits, for example; those pink, plump, smooth faces, every detail of physique and costume "finished" as if by a salon. That is what Cooper's readers thought they saw in each other, I would suggest. And in fact, Stuart painted just such a portrait of William Cooper, the novelist's father, who is depicted as Judge Temple in the first novel, and who is the civilized, reading American, as contrasted with Natty.

In *The Pioneers,* Natty represents natural law, and so finds himself in conflict with Judge Temple, who represents civil law; both are indignant against various kinds of waste endemic in the frontier community; but the Judge fights that with regulations which Natty feels are an infringement on personal liberty. The situation is richly symbolic, and the theme of waste, the spoliation of natural resources, is a very valuable extension of the subject matter of modernist romance. So is the conflict between law and individual liberty—both are typical of American experience, of the Frontier as opposed to the Empire; the English, in India or Africa, did not experience those problems half so acutely. But of the two, the first, waste, is felt by Cooper more deeply and originally.

Another such theme is the Indian tribes (represented by Chingachgook), in treating which Cooper employs motifs already familiar to us. In his passion and pride, and in his loyalty to Natty, Chingachgook is a Black Prince of the kind we met in Defoe and Scott. In this book, however, the Prince is degenerated into Indian John for most of the time, ruined by addiction to drink and by being uprooted. His death too is related to the conflict between his people and the whites, and is caused by the symbolic means of an explosion of gunpowder. At the end of the novel, Natty declares his intention to leave the settlement for the wilderness. The Judge's daughter, Elizabeth, goes up the mountain to take Natty a canister of powder as a farewell gift (his rifle, bullet mold, and powder keg are his constant accoutrements). Not finding Natty, she gives them to Chingachgook, who promises to hand them over but says, "This is the great enemy of my nation. Without this, when could the white man drive the Delawares? [sic] Daughter, the Great Spirit gave your fathers to know how to make guns and powder, that they might sweep the Indians from the land" (p. 418). A fire breaks out on the mountain, surrounds Chingachgook, and the powder explodes, wounding him fatally.

Such gunpowder explosions are to be found in Defoe, but the very parallels demonstrate how remote Cooper is from the spirit of Defoe; the mechanism of his explosion is so theatrical—a whole mountain set ablaze to get one spark into a canister of powder—and so implausible—if Chingachgook was being showered with sparks, surely he would put the can down? And how could it happen that the fire, having been about to consume him, retreated as soon as he was killed? Cooper's indifference to these questions (even if there are answers to them, it is fatal to arouse such questions) shows his failure to grasp something essential in modernist romance.

And indeed the central plot of *The Pioneers* is not modernist-adventurous but chivalrous-romantic. Its theme is the legitimation of the Temples' post-Revolution possession of the land, which used to belong to a family named Effingham when the colony was under British rule. The Temples are legitimized by inheritance and marriage; Elizabeth Temple marries Oliver Effingham, and the long-lost Major Effingham turns up out of hiding at the end to bless the union. The mechanism of the plot also is all romance—disguises, concealments, and mysteries; and there even seems to be a network of allusions to *As You Like It* (the "usurping" Temple is called Duke —short for Marmaduke; the inheriting Effingham is called Oliver, the old major is called a king, and there is a banishment and a forest and so on). Indeed the legitimation of an American aristocracy—by aristocratic and romantic means of legitimation—is one of Cooper's concerns in other books. He was always writing chivalric romances almost as much as modernist adventures, and he was not skillful at combining the two sets of conventions.

*The Last of the Mohicans* takes place at the time of the wars against the French and the Indians. Its basic story-motif is one we can identify with Cooper in general, the group-flight—something distinct from the group-quest in *Captain Singleton*. At first, Major Duncan Heyward is guiding Cora and Alice Munro to meet their father, with the help of Magua, the Mohawk scout; but Magua turns out to be a treacherous Mingo in reality, and the journey becomes a flight. This book also introduces another motif that was to be very important in frontier romance, that of the-fate-worse-than-death.

The idea that the forest (or other such environment in another novel) is bristling with savages lusting for a white woman, who will subject her to the unspeakable if the white man's vigilance lapses for a moment, is a very powerful motor for this sort of romance—and for white race-consciousness outside literature. Obviously it is parallel to the fear of cannibalism which Defoe made much of; this adds the manifold energizing force of explicit sex. Cooper derives it from the captivity narratives, so popular in America, beginning with Mrs. Rowlandson's; the white woman, abducted and then imprisoned by a screaming horde, becomes the ark of the covenant for white men. But it is worth considering that serious fiction in England had also made use of a similar motif of abduction, in Richardson and his successors.[1] Cooper does not owe anything to Richardson directly, but insofar as he inherited the romance pattern from Scott, he benefited from Richardson's work. Cooper brought together these two strands of Puritan sexual melodrama, one with the prestige of polite fiction, the other with the power of frontier racism. In this story sex and death are closely linked; above all, miscegenatory lust is fearfully punished. Chingachgook is accompanied by his son, Uncas, a good Indian. Magua lusts after Cora; but Uncas modestly loves her. When Uncas and Cora are both captured and tortured by Magua, Natty offers himself as a sacrificial captive in exchange for her. A savage kills Cora; Uncas kills him; Magua kills him; Natty kills him.

In *The Prairie* the-fate-worse-than-death is again prominent. Ines is the dainty and delicate prisoner of Ishmael Bush and his sons—a coarse-grained crew—but she is in no danger of rape from them. It is the lust of the Indians she arouses, and with barely controllable intensity. Even Hard-Heart the Pawnee, a good Indian, cannot take his eyes off her. "Nothing so fair, so ideal, so every way worthy to reward the courage and self-devotion of a warrior, had ever before been encountered on the prairies" (p. 268). Mahtoree, a bad Indian, tells his favorite wife to look at Ines, and then at her own reflection; the effect is instantaneous; the wife takes off her ornaments, and hands them, and her baby, to Ines. Ines is a heroine of civilization, of progress; with her "intellectual and nearly infantile beauty," she embodies a degree of sexual differentiation, and produces a pitch of sexual-moral excitement, undreamed of by more primitive races. Other white women are defined in terms of their coarseness compared to her, and the ultimate opposite are the withered and remorseless crones of the Indians, who mock and torture white captives. (The active and working women to be found in primitive societies are always a focus of horror for the novelists in this tradition.)

Another motif in this novel is the physical size of white Americans of the frontier states; size being closely related to atavism and degeneracy. The Bushes are Tennessean, and are described as colossal, vast, gigantic, and so on. Ishmael is dull and listless, his face's lower features coarse, extended and vacant, the nobler parts low, receding, and mean. His costume is motley and gaudy, with a sash, three watches, silver buttons, silver-plated knife and rifle. His sons are indolent and inert, sullenly resistant to authority, ideas, education, and politeness. Among the Bushes even family feeling has dried up —their moral substance all transmuted into physical.[2]

This idea of the size of frontiersmen powerfully struck the American imagination; men like James Hall and Timothy Flint commented on the size of first Virginians, then Tennesseeans, then Kentuckians, as the frontier moved west and south.[3] And the idea of degeneration on the frontier was also to be found, for instance in Crèvecoeur's *Letters of an American Farmer*. But the two ideas are not usually combined, and Cooper's combination of them has a very disconcerting effect. Literarily it is a striking effect, but largely because it is out of place, as it were out of date—it would be in place in Frank Norris. It derives, presumably, from Cooper's profound dividedness. His Americanism was no stronger than his conservatism, and the spectacle of these huge new men struck him mainly with dismay. He contrasts them with Natty, the good American, but the contrast is ineffective. The difference between the two is fictionally uninteresting, and its didactic message is more dismal than Cooper intended. Natty dies in the course of this novel, and leaves no heir; he was the last, indeed, the only, one of his kind. It is the Bushes who are destined to breed, and settle the country, in their wasteful and destructive way. And one day, says Natty, "They will turn on their tracks like a fox that doubles, and then the rank smell of their footsteps will show them the madness of their waste" (p. 79). With such a vision, how can Cooper be an Americanist?

In the last two novels the religious and moral note of warning grows stronger, and conflicts even more with the adventure dynamic. Natty, who is now thirty-two years old, says on page 20 of *The Pathfinder*, "They that live in the settlements and the towns have confined and unjust opinions concerning the might of His hand; but we, who pass our time in His very presence, as it might be, see things differently. . . ." He thinks sadly of the men killed in the recent wars. "Generals and privates, they lay scattered throughout the land, so many proofs of what men are when led on by love of great names and the wish to be more than their fellows. . . . 'If you think I pass my days in warfare against my kind, you know neither me nor my history. . . . No, no; bloodshed and warfare are not my real gifts, but peace and mercy. . . .' " (p. 86). But he is a scout. "My real calling is to hunt for the army, on its marches and in times of peace" (p. 86). What scope does *this* give him to exercise his "real gifts"? We are bound to think of Defoe's William.

And when in Chapter 27 Natty tells of being morally tempted three times, the last and worst was when he found six Mingoes asleep and could have killed them. He overcame the temptation; but this means that he waited till they awoke, then peppered them with shot till only one limped home—Chingachgook having scalped the rest.

Yet Natty is clearly presented as a religious and moral hero in this book. When at the end Mabel Dunham appeals for peace "in the name of our holy religion," Natty endorses her plea with his forest wisdom. He's not been personally Christianized by the Moravians, but he respects them, and says, "I'm in church now; I eat in church, drink in church, sleep in church. The earth is the temple of the Lord, and I wait on him hourly, daily, without ceasing, I humbly hope" (p. 402). We are told that "His feelings appeared to possess the freshness and nature of the forest in which he passed so much of his time; and no casuist could have made clearer decisions in matters relating to right and wrong" (p. 121). And this was of course a powerful idea in American culture. Jefferson had said, in his *Notes on Virginia*, "State a case to a ploughman and a professor. The former will decide it as well, and often better than the latter, because he has not been led astray by artificial rules." That myth persisted for a long time to come. Even F. J. Turner, so much later, said, "Political wisdom is not sealed up in books and parchments. It welled up in the forests, like waters from the hillside." But Natty's claims to moral wisdom are concentrated in his manner. His actual behavior is that of a killer.

And in *The Deerslayer,* there is again talk of how Natty's sweetheart is in the forest; like his religious life, his love life is not differentiated or defined in the way that other men's are. He lives in a prelapsarian innocence, in which all things merge. The price of this is his inability to choose any one creed or any one woman. In this story he is chosen by Judith Hutter, but declines. All of which amounts to a pretty total disability, in a hero of adventure. He is the victim of his author's ambivalence. Critics have often spoken of Natty's renunciations, but it is of course Cooper who has on Natty's behalf renounced all sorts of definite action for him, except self-sacrifice—in this novel, as in *The Pathfinder,* he voluntarily surrenders himself to wicked Indians. Insofar as he does act aggressively, he has to apologize immediately after, because such actions are not in accordance with his beliefs.

This book tells the story of how Natty came of age, by going on his first warpath; how he kills a man. This is greeted with joy by all his friends and acquaintances, but he himself cannot take any satisfaction in it. The novelist has to engage in a lot of aesthetic casuistry to provide him with an occasion on which he *can* kill someone; and then Natty engages in a lot of moral casuistry to justify the act. Later in *The Deerslayer* he is first given his famous rifle, and displays his prowess by shooting an eagle; but must descant immediately on why he shouldn't have done that. And it is this paradox which has such fatal aesthetic consequences; the action is intolerably slow because each action has to be elaborately prepared for and retroactively justified; and Natty, though described as silent, talks incessantly, because he has to rationalize everything he does. He's a moral hero who performs immoral acts, so his moral life has to be all in his speeches. And at the end of the book, with the rescue of the whites, comes the official slaughter, for which Natty was clearly the outrunner.

And though there is usually no profit in dwelling on an author's failings, in this case it is necessary to insist—since literary critics have often argued or implied the opposite—that these are very bad adventure tales. Moreover, Cooper's failure is interesting, because he was perfectly capable of writing a decent adventure, as his sea-novels show. In the forest stories he fails to adapt the Scott formula to the conditions of the frontier—the operatic conventions with which he handles his heroines, for instance, fundamentally conflict with any realistic sense of where they are and what they are doing. One must put some of this down to personal literary ineptitude, but it still remains puzzling, because he did so much better with other fictional problems. One is bound to suspect that the root of his difficulty lies in Natty; in the paradox of the American hero, a man who derives his moral principles from the Moravians, but achieves his manhood as a killer.

This, however, may be the place to say that Cooper's difficulties are typical of the problems of American writers in the nineteenth century; Melville's problems with, notably, *Moby Dick*, Whitman's with verse form, Twain's with the novel. All of these are genre problems, and derive from the fact that the genres (the code of the system of literature) which America inherited from England were not adapted to the imaginative material forced on her writers by her frontier experience (which irresistibly established itself as her essential experience). That maladaptation was in part cultural; the new material was associated with cultural attitudes which were hostile to gentility, and so to "literature-as-a-system." That system continued to dominate critics and publishers, and the book-buyers who put down the money for novels and poems. But it was badly at odds with the imaginative experience that pressed upon the writers, and which was in certain ways formless. That is, it existed only in minor forms —pungent dialectical anecdotes—forms outside the system, and hostile to it, in just the way the Indian tribes, and to some degree the frontiersmen, were outside the political and economic system. However, we are concerned only with Cooper's version of this problem.

Cooper inherited these conflicts, along with a strong filial pride and affection, from his father, William Cooper, the founder of Cooperstown, New York. He was one of the most energetic and successful promoters of new settlements in eighteenth-century America. He published in 1782 a do-it-yourself *Guide in the Wilderness,* and moved his own family to central New York State in 1790. William was something of a Crusoe figure, but one who had, by the time his son knew him, risen to be a gentleman, to belong to the aristocratic caste.

James Fenimore Cooper had a great admiration for his father and everything he represented. He must surely have thought of him when, in *Wyandotte,* he says, "There is a pleasure in diving into a virgin forest and commencing the labours of civilization, that has no exact parallel in any other human occupation . . . [it] approaches nearer to the feeling of creating, and is far more pregnant with anticipation and hopes, though its first effects are seldom agreeable, and are sometimes nearly hideous" (p. 42). William Cooper was, like

Judge Temple in *The Pioneers,* born a Quaker, but became an Epis-
copalian and a Federalist—an American aristocrat. He was the lord
of his manor, a modified patroon, and died violently in 1809, at the
age of fifty-five, killed by a blow from behind by an opponent at a
public meeting.

William Cooper came to own tens of thousands of acres, but
continued to assert himself against his opponents by means of direct
physical contact, as well as by the socially privileged means of law and
wealth. He would wrestle with, after arguing with, those who disa-
greed with him; on occasion challenging all comers, and promising
to give 100 acres to anyone who could throw him. In *The Pioneers,*
Judge Temple is placed in opposition to Natty the true hero; the
Judge has renounced his Quakerism (as so many did during the War
of Independence) and become a judge, a man of wealth, and so on.
Natty is a kind of shadow self for Temple/Cooper, more really and
primitively American, one who embodies all that other men have
renounced. He moves off at the book's end to a purer life:—"I'm
weary of living in clearings, and where the hammer is sounding in my
ears from sunrise to sundown" (p. 473). But as Natty's fictional career
works itself out—in response to Cooper's experience of America over
nearly twenty years—it becomes clear that Natty too is living against
his principles as much as Judge Temple—that to be "really American" was no escape.

By his marriage to Susan DeLancey, James Fenimore Cooper
moved even further inside the American aristocracy. The DeLanceys
had owned vast estates before the Revolution, and owned them by
the patroon system of land tenure. Even after the Revolution they
still owned a good deal of Westchester County in New York State,
described by Robert Spiller as the most aristocratic bit of American
soil in those days. So that Cooper became by marriage a sort of
thirteenth-century English baron, to use Spiller's formula.

It is therefore not surprising that he was full of the pride of caste.
And it is worth noting how conscious and clear he was about what
caste meant. In *The Chainbearer,* the hero says, "I had got the
notions of my caste, obtained in the silent, insinuating manner in
which all our characters are formed. . . ." (p. 188). His was, of course,
the aristomilitary caste. And he defines a gentleman at some length.
The most general idea is that a gentleman is a man who will not stoop
to meannesses, and Cooper is ready to develop that idea in distinction

from other, more "Christian" ideas of morality. The gentleman
". . . is truthful out of self-respect, and not in obedience to the will
of God; free with his money, because liberality is an essential feature
of his habits, and not in imitation of the self-sacrifice of Christ;
superior to scandal and the vices of the busybody, inasmuch they are
low and impair his pride of character . . ." (p. 172). One of Cooper's
major themes is the fate of this caste in America, a country which
dedicated itself so definitely to the modern system and the mercantile
caste.

But I must revert to structuralist criticism. Essentially, Cooper
adapted Scott's formula to a frontier condition, and to a sense of
distance that was as much geographical as historical. That phrase
suggests a return to Defoe, but there is little in Cooper's way of
handling geography that is Defoean. However, his way has its own
intermittent grandeur. Its sweep is enormous, in physical and historical geography. The Introduction to *The Prairie* begins "The geologi-
cal formation of that portion of the American Union . . ." and invokes
the largest scientific categories. Moreover, Chapter I relates the story
to come to the Louisiana Purchase, and all American history. However, there is one really striking change away from Scott toward
Defoe, in the character of the hero, away from being an observer-
participant, to being a man of action. Natty *is* much closer to Crusoe
than Waverley was. The action in question, moreover, is of Defoe's
kind, insofar as Natty does everything with his own hands and a few
essential modern-system tools, mostly the rifle and the axe, and a few
techniques in woodcraft. (On the other hand, Cooper being a philosophical novelist, Natty embodies a touch of sadness, a sense of
failure, unthinkable in Crusoe.)

There is nothing in Natty to make one think that Cooper had been
reading Defoe, but it is undeniable that Natty is much the same
figure as Crusoe. There are artist's drawings of the one that could be
used to illustrate the book about the other; the rifle, the fur cap, the
leggings, the knife. If we take Defoe's geographical axis as a horizon-
tal line, and Scott's historical axis as a vertical, it would be possible
to represent Cooper's axis as a line bisecting the 90° angle between
the two.

Natty is another do-it-yourself hero, who earns his power over our
imaginations by commanding our participation and making us believe he in fact does solve problems we would be unable to. Cooper

being such a fictional blunderer, we often refuse Natty our participation, but when we yield, it is of this kind, and not of the kind we give to Waverley. And it is time to admit, also, that Natty commands us in some other remoter way, not when we are actually reading about him, but when we think about him at a distance from the text. After all, if Natty gave Cooper fictional difficulties he didn't meet elsewhere, he also gave Cooper his greatest fictional success. It is Natty he is famous for, and when one reads the tributes of remarkable men of letters, but when also one consults one's own experience, one can see why. Fictional characters, fictional subjects in general, can have a vitality and power which is independent of the normal criteria of realization in fictional terms. That happens—in this case at least— when a writer has linked together a number of powerful ideas which stay linked and stay powerful in our minds, despite the ineptitude of dialogue, action, characterization, etc.

Of course the power I am attributing to Natty, if unearned by fictional realization, *is* earned by Cooper's general impressiveness as a writer and thinker—and to some extent by his mere reputation. Those powerful ideas were linked together in our minds by the name of Natty partly because we were forced to read Cooper and not someone else.

Otherwise, I suspect, we would be more moved by Nathan Slaughter in R. M. Bird's *Nick of the Woods,* 1837, a much better adventure tale. Nathan is a bloody Quaker of a much fiercer kind than Natty—or than Defoe's William; and most of the themes of the frontier novel are better rendered. There is for instance a family of large Kentuckians called Bruce—of colossal stature, like Cooper's Bushes; and the proportions of their frame are "as just as they were gigantic"; with the same "lounging indifference of carriage, and something like awkwardness or uncouthness . . . but real native majesty." Bird's apter realization of the idea is evident in Mr. Bruce's commendation of his son as coming from the best stock in Kentucky for loving women or fighting Injuns; the boy took his first Shawnee scalp before he was fourteen. Cooper is too genteel to give us that sort of tone, and therefore too genteel for this sort of story. The same contrast holds true of the two representations of Western humorous boasting; by Cooper in Paul Hover (in *The Prairie*) and by Bird in Ralph Stackpole. The latter leaps, howls, boasts, cavorts, with much more power. And Bird himself enters into the spirit of farce much more completely. When Stackpole is thrown at wrestling, "his heels were suddenly seen flying in the air, his head aiming at the earth, upon which it as suddenly descended with the violence of a bombshell; and there it would doubtless have burrowed, like the aforesaid instrument of destruction, had the soil been soft enough for that purpose, or exploded into a thousand fragments. . . ." (p. 77). Bird here participates in that Western humor (which continued down to Disney) which Cooper was far too stiff to capture.

But, as I said, Cooper was to achieve his greatest fictional successes in nautical fiction. His forest adventures he never imagined with any intensity, and they are realistically implausible; while the way people talk and behave, especially the women, is generically inappropriate, because he has not imagined the genre either. He has mixed up drawing-room diction and gestures, and theater entries and exits, with the evocation of endless rolling plains and virgin woods. (In *The Prairie* Hard-Heart leaps into our view out of undergrowth that is palpably a stage trap, and exits—across the dreary and interminable plains—as if slamming a door.) But in the sea-novels, though there are lapses with the women characters, Cooper clearly knows and loves the medium of the adventure, and consequently his imagination does not stumble and flounder over plot and episode. One might take as an example of his success there, his vivid rendering of the personality of ships, their characteristic lines and movements, their human and usually feminine personalities.

One explanation of that superiority is biographical. Cooper became a midshipman as a teenager and mastered that world of experience for himself, while his experience of the forest and the frontier came to him via his father. It seems that he met only decrepit and degenerate Indians himself, and the frontier history of Cooperstown was something he knew only by anecdote. Ships he discovered for himself, and he found a ship's severely hierarchical and yet practically egalitarian social structure very congenial.

I find such an explanation quite convincing, but it leaves us facing the paradox that the sea-novels are not rated so highly—and are not in fact so interesting—as the badly flawed forest-novels. The reason for that, I believe, lies deep in the cultural history of America.

To put it briefly, after 1850 the American imagination turned decisively toward the West and the continent. But though that may explain Natty Bumppo's later reputation, it cannot explain his creation; the Leatherstocking stories had been written before that, at a time when in his essays Cooper was still declaring that America was not an agricultural but a maritime nation. Perhaps those declarations had always expressed a wish rather than an observation. As a sea-power, America could have a less threatening future greatness than as a land-power, precisely because great land-powers were empires; the British empire was sea-based, and Cooper and Americans like him implicitly exempted Britain from the infamy generally attached to "Empire." It was Austria and Russia, and France under Napoleon, that were empires in the opprobrious sense. England was essentially a trading nation, and the home of liberty, which is what America should become.

That belief, I think, explains the reluctance of Cooper's imagination to accept Natty as the agent for America's westward advance. That was the wrong direction, geographically, politically, imaginatively. ". . . the tide of emigration, which has been so long flowing westward, must have its reflux . . ." (*Notions,* p. 48). But that reluctance, that conflict of feelings and sense of doom, though it made the craftsman in Cooper so clumsy, made the artist in him rise above himself, because it generated intensity. Natty's first and last appearances in *The Prairie,* his two sunset hilltop scenes—once one knows he is in effect barring the way to the west, warning the whites back—have an intensity which nothing in the sea fiction can match.[4]

## Cooper's Reputation

In the case of Cooper, some study of his reception and reputation is especially rewarding, because his readers' response was both vivid and also expressed in terms close to those of this study. For instance, W. H. Gardiner's review of the very early novel, *The Spy,* in the *North American Review* in 1822, included advice to Cooper on how to write "an American novel." The advice was very sympathetic to Cooper, in both senses; and in fact Cooper followed it. Gardiner told him to stress the sectional variety of American society (to replace the class variety of Europe, which Scott had at his disposal); and to choose subjects from the settlement period, the Indian wars and the revolutionary wars; and to celebrate the American landscape—which he should describe "with that deep moral feeling that unites the soul to beauty and breathes its own freshness and fragrance." And in fact, Cooper went on to write five novels about the revolutionary wars, and six about the Indian wars, and stressed sectional variety and landscape in exactly that way.

Gardiner was a friend of Prescott, one of the Brahmin intellectuals; and despite Cooper's prejudice against New England, he and they were on the same side culturally, being all representatives of the "responsible" class in America, the reading class. (I mean those who felt themselves responsible for America's values and cultural images.) Cooper's project was recognized, in its very earliest manifestation, as a group project in that sense, and was promoted and cooperated in by his readers.

Cooper was very successful with that class. *The Spy* went through three editions in six months, *The Pioneers* sold 3,500 copies the day after publication, and *The Pilot*'s edition of 3,000 was quickly exhausted. He was unpopular with reviewers after 1830, but this was for political reasons. (They attacked him ostensibly for introducing political ideas into his romances, but their antagonism owed more to their belonging to the opposite party to him.) Cooper took Horace Greeley and four other newspapermen to court for libel. And between 1840 and 1851, when he published sixteen novels, only four were reviewed. But this was less significant than it might seem. His sales were as high in those years as they had been in the 1820s. One guesses that this was because the people who bought his books, the responsible class, were independent of the opinions of newspapers, who directed themselves to a different audience.

We should not identify this responsible class with "advanced" literary opinions or taste. They were not responsive to, for instance, writers like Edgar Allan Poe. Poe never sold anything like as well as Cooper, and he has an interesting essay of 1843 in which he reflects on that fact. Poe says that the interest readers take in Cooper "has no reference to plot, but to theme, a Robinson-Crusoe-like detail, and the figure of the half-civilized Indian. The theme—life in the wilderness—is one of intrinsic and universal interest; appealing to the heart of man in all phases; success or popularity is, with such a subject, expected as a matter of course. So also is life at sea. . . ." (*Fenimore Cooper: the Critical Heritage,* p. 208). Here one sees the conscience of literature considering the adventure tale, and condemning it for its spiritual commonplaceness, its subservience to the dominant interests of the culture. One might say that Poe is to Cooper as Coleridge is to Scott, and Swift to Defoe, though I am not aware of a comparable intensity of antagonism. He continues, "There are two classes of fiction, the popular, read with pleasure but without admiration—in which the Author is lost or forgotten . . ." This is Cooper's; and such fiction merely feeds a well-established appetite. ". . . and then a class . . . in which, at every paragraph, arises a distinct and highly pleasurable interest, springing from our perception and appreciation of the skill employed, or the genius evinced in the composition. After perusal of one class, we think solely of the book—after reading the other, chiefly of the author. The former class leads to popularity—the latter to fame" (p. 208). He names Hawthorne, Simms, and Charles Brockden Brown in the latter class—and thinks almost certainly of himself, too. What is most striking in those remarks for us is their candor—their attribution of egotism, and thirst for fame, to his own party, the men of literature. This is the point of view we must adopt in order to study this story of the conflicts between literature and the adventure tale.

Other essays also bring out the strong alliance between Cooper and the men of action—the party of action in American culture. A review of 1827 speaks of "this naked and masculine power" and says of the author, "A sailor, and an American, he has had noble opportunities of forming an acquaintance with her [Nature], and nobly has he used them! He is not her poet, but her secretary and copyist . . . compared to him, our poets are freshwater sailors, who know nothing of the matter; he alone gives us the plain but mighty truth" (p. 121). And in 1842 William Gilmore Simms wrote that we are interested in Cooper's hero (he is talking about *The Pilot*) "by the fact that he promises nothing, yet goes to work, without a word, in a manner that promises everything. . . . He shows the capacity for work, and this constitutes the sort of manhood upon which all men rely in moments of doubt and danger . . . with ship and man we grow fascinated beyond all measure of ordinary attraction. . . ." Hawkeye he finds the same as the Pilot; a figure of self-reliance; clearly Simms sees both Cooper's heroes as heirs to or versions of Robinson Crusoe, as distinct from other fictional heroes—and distinct by being more manly. We do not love such heroes but admire them in their progress through sea and forest. "But *manhood*, true manhood, is a sight,

147

always, of wondrous beauty and magnificence" (pp. 222–223).

It is in Cooper that we see most clearly in literature the close alliance ever potential in American culture, between manhood, adventure, and national destiny. And America was the model state of the modern world system, acting out its collective dream. Cooper, as the voice of America, was extremely popular in Europe, and translated into almost every language. Between 1820 and 1853 there were 105 German translations of individual works of his, and five collected editions; while in France, Gosselin brought out thirty volumes of the *Works of Fenimore Cooper* between 1836 and 1852. He was often set by French writers in political antithesis to Scott. Scott was seen as the celebrant of the feudal past, Cooper of the modern world system. A review of 1827 made him the emblem of everything which Europe and the Bourbons had denied. And a review signed F. A. S. in *Le Globe,* in the same year (June 19 and July 2) said, "We do not see much resemblance between the entirely new culture portrayed by the republican author, and the feudal customs which the Scotch baronet has exhumed from old chronicles" (p. 127).

Scott, the writer says, has no moral idea except the Voltairean ideal of tolerance, based on indifference and skepticism; while Cooper is full of moral energy, because he sees a moral society around him— the most reasonably constructed society in the world. It is true that America's population is divided into two colors, and that the whites hold the reds in bondage. "And yet, everywhere in America one senses a spirit of enterprise, of braving all obstacles, of pursuing one's fortune over the seas and through the wilderness." Cooper's books are a magnificent epic of the wilderness (while a French treatment of similar themes, like Chateaubriand's *Atala,* is only a work of the imagination). "On the borders of the wilderness and civilization, hosts of pioneers are rolling back the limits of the wilderness, men strongly shaped by these two influences, men who combine the vices and virtues of these two opposing orders. And in the depths of the wilderness, there is a race of men almost unknown, generous and ferocious, crafty and brave, independent and savage, despoiled of a dominion formerly their own, beaten down but never enslaved, a race for whom the light of civilization has never been anything but a devouring fire. . . ." (p. 127).

One sees there how completely the response to Cooper is part of a response to America. The critic is quite blind to what seems so vivid to us—the military caste-character of Cooper's images. But it is still a response—a marvelously intelligent one—to the books. It describes Hawkeye as embodying the first dream of Rousseau, the natural man, and Hawkeye's problems as dramatizing the conflicts between that and Rousseau's second dream, the social contract. The point couldn't be better made.

French criticism continued to be particularly illuminating during another quarter century. (Russian criticism of Cooper is also very interesting, but that will be discussed in the next chapter.) Balzac knew Cooper's work very well, and admired it; and George Sand, in 1856, named Cooper and Scott as the two great poets of the middle class. "They have no grudge against God, or society; no eccentricities, no sacred joys like Shakespeare and Byron" (p. 262). This is a point of view close to Poe's, but more generous. "The foundation of their power is this wisdom, this doggedness, this apparent simple good-heartedness which characterizes industrial society and practical education" (pp. 262–263). She recognizes them as spokesmen for the modern world system; at a moment when, in France, nearly all serious writers were already turned against it. She sees Cooper as an American hero, to whom America owes as much as to Franklin and Washington; but also as a tragic hero—because of the tragic history of American power; "This fateful situation of a power acquired at the cost of suffering, murder, and fraud, pricked his heart with a deep philosophical remorse" (p. 263). But after this decade of the 1850s, Cooper dropped down from the serious level to the popular in France.

In America, too, this happened after 1852, when Cooper died. The note struck in that year by the contributors to the Cooper memorial was most strikingly a stress on his manliness. His novels contained an elixir of the qualities needed by men of action—and other adventure writers were linked to him in that. In an essay in *North American Review,* Jan. 1852, Parkman said that Cooper and Scott were "both practical men, able and willing to grapple with the hard realities of the world. Either might have learned with ease to lead a regiment, or command a line of battle ship. His readers are not persons of sedentary and studious habits but of a more active turn, military officers and the like, whose tastes have not been trained into fastidiousness. . . ." (p. 252). Cooper deals with realities, whereas Bulwer Lytton and Hawthorne never cheat us into a belief in the reality of their conceptions. This manly realism was what the New Englanders took from him. R. H. Dana said how he and all his friends were stirred by *The Spy* when it came out, and how immediately they connected the book with the man who wrote it. Parkman said the books were his boyhood friends, and influenced his own choice of career and work. Prescott said Cooper's books were "instinct with the spirit of nationality."

Dana and Parkman are especially interesting as representatives of that "responsible class" who actually sought out adventures, and then wrote them out, in the spirit that Cooper had implicitly recommended. (This responsible class adventurism seems to have been more American than English; one might point to Borrow and Brooke as comparable English cases, but their books don't convey the same sense that these men felt their caste challenged.) In Dana's and Parkman's books, we see both the individuals and their class asserting a leadership in modern system affairs, on the strength of a capacity for adventure. Theirs was a class which American history was forcing to assume the posture of the aristomilitary caste, despite a powerful heritage of quite opposite character.

The Brahmins of New England, who had always felt themselves the enemies of English aristocrats, were now feeling themselves much more the enemy of the frontiersmen of the West of their own country; and so in need of a strenuous manliness. R. H. Dana, who was born in 1815 and entered Harvard in 1831, left the university in 1834 because his eyes were weak, and sailed all around America, to California and back, as a common sailor. In *Two Years Before the Mast* (published in 1840) he makes much reference to Cooper in the Preface, and stresses the value of such a voyage in acquiring manhood. We should also be reminded of Cooper when he describes the autocratic character of the captain's power on board ship and the discipline he exerts, but says that that is necessary and valuable.[5]

But the aristocratic qualities are combined with the mercantile adventure qualities we associate with Defoe. Adventure by 1840 combined both; or at least the New Englanders were determined that it should. Dana's voyage took him to Crusoe's island of Juan Fernandez, which he describes as "the most romantic spot on earth that my eyes had ever seen. I did then and have ever since, felt an attachment to that island, altogether peculiar. . . . [It is made sacred by] the associations which everyone has connected with in their childhood from reading *Robinson Crusoe*" (p. 47). Like Cooper he makes much of Spanish lethargy (and Indian loutishness) in California settlement society; the moral geography of the modern world system is strong. And he has his handsome sailor, Bill Jackson, "the best specimen of the thoroughbred English sailor that I ever saw" (pp. 24–25).

Parkman, who was also troubled by ill health, went out West a decade later than Dana, on the Oregon Trail; it was 1846, the year of decision in the Westward Movement and Manifest Destiny. He had been seized with a passion for the forest, like Dana's for the sea, at the age of fifteen. In *The Conspiracy of Pontiac* he says, "To him who once has tasted the reckless independence, the haughty self-reliance, the sense of irresponsible freedom which the forest life engenders, civilization henceforth seems flat and stale." His rhetoric was significantly different from Defoe's—much more romantic. "The wilderness, rough, harsh, and inexorable, has charms more potent in their seductive influence than all the lures of luxury and sloth. And often he on whom it has cast its magic finds no heart to dissolve the spell, and remains a wanderer and an Ishmaelite to the hour of his death" (*The Oregon Trail*, p. 27). He responded to the American adventure, and the world of young men, though to the idea of it rather than the actuality.

Parkman's mind was very like Cooper's, though fiercer. He was as unsympathetic to the emigrants on the Oregon Trail as Cooper was to the Bushes. He saw them as "some of the vilest outcasts in the country" not in love with liberty but "shaking off restraints of law and society" (p. 7). But he tried to ally himself with their energy, for in them "seemed to be revived, with redoubled force, that fierce spirit which impelled their ancestors, scarcely more lawless than themselves, from the German forests, to inundate Europe, and overwhelm the Roman empire" (p. 88). This idea, with all its racist implications, was to be a powerful one in the latter part of the century, especially among historians. But it was the Indians that most excited Parkman's romantic feelings, just because they were

151

doomed. He called them the conservatives of barbarism, who would not change and so must perish. "The stern, unchanging features of his mind excite our admiration from their very immutability." He went West chiefly to see an Indian war, and to study Indian character. He believed that only war saved the Indians from lethargy and abasement.

His feeling for the Indians is very like Cooper's—and probably Cooper's sympathy also owed something to a sense that they were doomed, as Parkman's certainly did. They are *his* young men, and quite unlike Twain's figures of triumphant aggression and innovation. Parkman often invokes Apollo in describing Indians, and stresses their static physical beauty. At one point he looks up to find that "superb naked figures stood silently gazing on us" (p. 155). And he is interested by the paint, the earrings, and the hair ornaments, worn by the warriors—their self-display—though he is interested just because "the proud and ambitious Dakota warrior can sometimes boast heroic virtues" (p. 155). Like Cooper, he is horrified by the withered crones, and the women who work while the men laze. He too makes a noble Indian friend, the Panther; and he invokes a moral landscape like Cooper's: "There is a spirit of energy in mountains, and they impart it to all who approach them" (p. 167).

Above all, he has a guide and bear-hunter, Henry Chatillon, who is his hero. (Melville, in a review of the book, called Chatillon the last hero, and compared him with Kit Carson. Natty Bumppo would have been more exact.) His "age was about 30; he was 6 feet high, and very powerfully and gracefully molded. The prairies had been his school; he could neither read nor write, but he had a natural refinement and delicacy of mind, such as is rare, even in women. . . ." (p. 14). In a cancelled passage, Parkman compared him with Napoleon and Nelson, but that was an excess of enthusiasm. In fact Chatillon "had not the restless energy of an Anglo-American. He was content to take things as he found them. . . ." (p. 14). This kind of passivity —not *like* Natty's, of course, but parallel in function—is partly what makes him attractive to Parkman. (The Indians had yet another kind of attractive passivity.) "He was a proof of what unaided nature will sometimes do." In these two books we see how Cooper's constituency of readers, and caste-comrades, cooperated with him in spreading the gospel of adventure; and we see another, more ruling class, character to that adventure.

## Historians

In America historians seem to have been particularly representative of the culturally responsible class for whom Cooper wrote. Butterfield remarks on how many of his Whig interpreters were American. The historians gave America a new sense of nationhood in the 19th century, and they got the feel of it, in part, from Cooper.[6] In the second half of the century they, like other people, read him primarily in boyhood, and Allan Nevins, writing as late as 1954, seemed still close to the experience. In that year he introduced a selection of chapters about Natty, called *Leather-Stocking,* and recalled his boyhood in Illinois, where he lived in the world of Cooper; and of Henty and Reid, two of the principal boys' adventure writers of England, and of "Oliver Optic" and John T. Trowbridge, their American equivalents. Nevins says, "Men do not easily forget an early devotion to Scott, Dumas, Maryatt and Lytton." (He might add that even when they do forget it, that devotion continues to mold their minds.) He calls the Leatherstocking tales "the nearest approach yet made to an American epic." They deal with "our rude heroic age, our Homeric period of national life."

Of course in 1954 Nevins's remark was out of period, and something of a curiosity. But the nineteenth-century historians all felt something like that, or at least the four whom David Levin deals with in *History as Romantic Art.* These four are William Prescott (1796–1859), George Bancroft (1800–1891), John Lathrop Motley (1814–1877), and Francis Parkman (1823–1893), all Brahmin authors; and some of the relevant titles are Prescott's *Conquest of Mexico* (1843), *Ferdinand and Isabella* (1838), and *Conquest of Peru* (1847); Bancroft's *History of the United States,* which came out between 1859 and 1876; Motley's *Rise of the Dutch Republic* (1856) and *Peter the Great* (1877); and Parkman's *Conspiracy of Pontiac* (1851), *The Discovery of the Great West* (1869), and *Montcalm and Wolfe* (1884). There were close connections between the four, and between the group of them and the other Brahmins. They all disliked Hume, Locke, Voltaire, and the irony, skepticism, and materialism of the eighteenth-century Whigs, which acted as a check on the expansive energies of modernist ideology; these nineteenth-century Whigs identified themselves with those energies. They were on the side of religion—which they interpreted in the nineteenth-century fashion as "faith" or earnestness. Thus Bancroft said that George Fox towered over Descartes morally and spiritually, though intellectually their "methods" coincided.

As the titles of their books indicate, the four men's histories tell the story—celebrate the epic—of the development of the modern world system. In their hands that development becomes an adventure tale. Prescott's Spain, Motley's Holland, Parkman's England and France, and Bancroft's America, were core states, and each in turn became the leading power in that system. Cooper too tells that story, insofar as it concerns America; and the philosophical remorse of his Natty is to be found in the historians.

The true hero of history, these historians said, was The People; but in practice they focused their feelings rather upon what they called Representative Men. For instance, Isabella of Spain, William the Silent, the older Pitt, and Washington.[7] Representative men were "natural," in the sense that Natty Bumppo was. Isabella and William the Silent wore simple austere dress, and had deep-lying passion, warmth, *nature*. They were, in their historical settings, what Natty was in his. In American heroes, naturalness tended to be associated with Nature herself. Bancroft said Washington went into the wilderness as a surveyor for three years, and "Nature revealed to him her obedience to serene and silent laws . . . from her he acquired a divine and animating virtue" (Levin, *History as Romantic Art,* p. 53). And he described Daniel Boone as being, "of a strong, robust frame, in the vigorous health of early manhood, ignorant of books but versed in the forest and forest life" (p. 52).

Of the four, Parkman was the most vivid temperamentally, and can remind us of T. E. Lawrence in his physical frailty, his hardness on himself and contempt for weakness in others too, his love of heroism and his enthusiasm for masculinity.[8] He was determined to keep up the spirit of adventure, to keep the reins of progress in his own people's hands. He once said, "An uncommon vigor, joined to the hardy virtues of a *masculine* race, marked the New England type. The sinews, it is true, were hardened at the expense of blood and flesh —and this literally as well as figuratively; but the staple of character was a sturdy conscientiousness, an undespairing courage, patriotism, public spirit, sagacity, and a strong good sense" (p. 35).

This is the late nineteenth-century Whig interpretation of history, for there was a marked transition from moralism to racism in the course of the century. That went naturally with the rising power of adventure. The story of the Teutonic race became an adventure tale. Bancroft and Motley were keen on primitive epic and saga; as were Kingsley and his friends in England. Stubbs and Freeman, in England, not only traced the history of political and legal institutions, but also refurbished Anglo-Saxon art and taste; made Beowulf and Caedmon great poets. (Whereas Gibbon and Hume regarded the Anglo-Saxons as barbarians, and despised historians who glorified their own peoples.) We touch here upon what one might call the saga modification of military caste sensibility, a development I must return to. For the moment it is enough to note that Victorian manliness, a very important element in the culture's morally serious thought and feeling, owed much to this strain of adventurism. And American manliness owed more, as we shall see.[9]

## The American Hero

The historians themselves are one element in the imaginative context for Cooper, as for Scott; but the most important single element is something the historians wrote about—the historical hero. The other culture-heroes of a period give the reader the crucial comparisons and contrasts for its fiction heroes. For the cases of Defoe and Scott I cited Marlborough and Wellington, and went into some detail about Cortes and Clive. In the case of Cooper, the comparable figure must be Andrew Jackson, the backwoods Napoleon, victor of the Battle of New Orleans and the Battle of the Bank.

Cooper ardently supported President Jackson's political policies against the Whigs (who were more suitable political allies for Cooper, in most ways) and ardently admired General Jackson's military victories over the British and the Indians. He liked Jackson's bluntness of word and deed, his attack on the money interests, and his strong government; he saw Jackson as embodying the moral virtue of the old rural republic, whose memory he himself cherished. Of course Cooper saw the difference, in breeding and gentlemanliness, between Jackson and the Founding Fathers, who commanded his deepest loyalty. And in *The Monikins* he satirized Jacksonianism and the political spoils system, operated by Jackson's followers. But such discrepancies only make more striking the general truth that Cooper himself was a Jacksonian.*

This is so striking because Jacksonian democracy represented what Emerson called the "savage" element in American culture, against which Cooper and his caste-comrades fought. In his essay on *Power,* Emerson wrote, "In history the great moment is when the savage is just ceasing to be a savage. . . . Everything good in nature and the world is in that moment of transition, when the swarthy juices still flow plentifully from Nature, but their astringency or acidity is got out by ethics and humanity." This was a central Romantic idea, closely related to the nostalgia for the frontier, and those Americans who chose to be sons of the Adamses and not sons of Adam were renouncing that heritage of power.[10]

The Hawkeye version of the WASP hero had been a literary attempt to resolve America's cultural dilemma in favor of the responsible class. But Hawkeye was only the most aristocratic profile of a multiform cultural image, only a mask of simple virtue dropped over one of a hydra's heads; it had only a doubtful claim to represent the cultural forces seething within that image. (In fact that dilemma is still a living one, because the responsible class has never made its case good. The irresponsible class has always seemed the more "savage.") In politics it was the presidency of Andrew Jackson that marked both the entry of "savagery" into the White House, and the defeat of the system of politicomoral ideas that corresponded to the responsible class.

Jackson was a culture hero, and his Presidency meant an alliance of the most official with the most unofficial elements in American culture, against "literature." Cooper, and the responsible class in general, had no chance against that alliance. All the eulogies of Jackson when he died said that he had embodied the spirit of his age; and his Battle of New Orleans was mythified from the moment it occurred, in 1815; it was declared to be a subject fit for Homer, Ossian, or Milton, because it showed the veterans of Europe beaten by an American militia. It showed God and Nature to be on America's side; or else it showed how American willpower and marksman-

*See John P. McWilliams, Jr., *Political Justice in a Republic.*

ship would always win the day.[11] This was the crucial event that turned America's aspirations west, away from Europe, J. H. Ward tells us, in *Andrew Jackson: Symbol for an Age.* The cultural nostalgia for the frontier mastered the country.

Out of the battle came the famous song, "The Hunters of Kentucky," which played an important part in subsequent Presidential elections. It was composed and sung first in 1822. The singer (a man called Ludlow) wore buckskins and moccasins, and carried a rifle over his shoulder; his appearance was greeted by an Indian war whoop from the audience, repeated at the song's climax; touches of Indian style that were directed against genteel propriety. The song itself was full of Southwestern boasting: "And if a daring foe annoys / Whate'er his strength and forces / We'll show him that Kentucky boys / Are alligator horses." This was always sung at Jackson Day dinners, thereafter. And that "Cossack" image was more successful, culturally, than Natty Bumppo.

Nature (the opposite of culture) was always invoked in the rhetoric of Jacksonianism. Bancroft introduced the subject of Jackson's presidency with the question, "What wisdom will he bring with him from the forest? What rules of duty will he evolve from the oracles of his own mind?" And he was also seen as God's chosen instrument and associated with thunder and lightning images.

The political concomitants were imperialism, as might have been predicted. The idea of manifest destiny was always historically attributed to Jackson, though it was in fact first used by John L. O'Sullivan in 1845, in reference to America's claim to Oregon. "By the right of our manifest destiny to overspread and possess the whole of the continent which Providence has given us for the development of the great experiment of liberty and self-government entrusted to us." In any case, Jackson gave political expression to that feeling. Already in 1843, indeed, he had spoken of the annexation of Texas as "extending the arm of freedom." Under his rule, America was quietistic in Europe, but aggressive in the West and toward the Indians.

Jackson was in fact the moving force behind Indian removal in the south. He was responsible for all but two of the eleven treaties of cession with the Georgia Creeks. He acquired for the United States three-fourths of Alabama and Florida, one-third of Tennessee, one-fifth of Georgia and Mississippi, and so on. Such was the political work of the real-life Natty. And this was continental imperialism, however it was named. Jackson forged the American identity, and the national state, in the struggle for westward expansion, says Michael Paul Rogin, in *Fathers and Children*. In 1820, 125,000 Indians lived east of the Mississippi; by 1840 75 percent of them had been involved in removal programs. And American politics as a whole bore the stamp of that imperialism. The years 1824–1852 are generally called the years of Jacksonian democracy, and during that period half the candidates for the Presidency were either Indian war generals or else secretaries of State involved in Indian removal.

But in Natty's case we have to contrast not only the historical hero, or his political policy, but also the frontier folk hero, a diffused cultural presence, of which four crystallizations are especially interesting—Daniel Boone, Davy Crockett, Mike Fink, and Kit Carson. These men form an indispensable context for Natty Bumppo, and bring out the purposefulness of Cooper's characterization.

To show that context we must first make clear the close connection, and then the sharp difference, between Natty and the American folk hero. The difference is that (by definition) a folk hero serves the purposes of an irresponsible class. The connection is that Cooper's idea was not a personal one; he borrowed and adapted it from— amongst other sources—the living legend of his time, Daniel Boone.[12]

In Chapter I of *The Prairie*, Cooper talks of the "swarms of that restless people which is ever found hovering on the skirts of American society," who invaded the lands of Louisiana, as soon as it was bought. The men of the new states led "long files of descendants, born and reared in the forests of Ohio and Kentucky, deeper into the land in quest of that which might be termed, without the aid of poetry, their natural and more congenial atmosphere . . ." (p. 10). One of whom was Daniel Boone. "This adventurous and venerable patriarch was now seen making his last remove . . . [leaving] . . . enjoyments which were rendered worthless in his eyes when trammelled by the forms of human institutions." We must be reminded of Boone when Ishmael Bush boasts, on p. 69, "that he had never dwelt where he might not safely fell every tree he could view from his own threshold, that the law had rarely been known to enter his clearing, and that his ears had never willingly admitted the sound of a church bell." In 1786 Jefferson had cited Boone as getting uneasy as soon as he knew there were ten people to the square mile where he lived. But if Bush is like Boone, so is Natty. (Indeed, the whole charm of *The Prairie* as a literary scheme—a charm not realized in effect—is that Bush and Natty stand for such similar ideas.) Natty had been associated with Boone since the publication of *The Last of the Mohicans,* at least; in that book Cooper borrowed significant features of Boone's Indian adventures—the rescue of the maidens, and the latter's leaving of a trail for their avengers to follow.

Boone's story was told many times in print, and in a way that testifies to innumerable tellings orally. Some of these versions of his character differ significantly from what Cooper (and other responsible-class writers) tried to make out of Boone. James Hall's *Letters from the West,* which appeared between 1822 and 1828, in Cincinnati, portrayed Boone as brave, adventurous, restless, delighting in danger and strife. (Letter 15, on "The National Character," says the Western version of that character is the most original, while Letter 16 is about Boone as a backwoodsman, the typical American.) Above all, Hall says, Boone was a hunter; devoid of selfishness and of softness; "an isolate being, professing tastes and habits of his own, and voluntarily supporting hardships, perils, and privations" (p. 407). (This can only remind us of D. H. Lawrence's famous description of the American hero—hard, isolate, stoic, and a killer.)

Hall describes seeing Kentucky men in Philadelphia in 1800, and admiring "their brawny limbs and sun-burned features . . . the rough hardy air . . . the blanket, bear-skin, and saddle bags—nay the very oil-skin on his hat, and the dirk that peeped from among his vestments. . . . He strode amongst us with the step of an Achilles, glancing with a goodnatured superciliousness." He showed, "a spirit quick to resent—he had the will to dare, and the spirit to execute; there was something in his look which bespoke a disdain of control, and an absence of constraint in all his movements" (Arthur K. Moore, *The Frontier Mind,* p. 68). This is, to use Cooper's terms, not Natty Bumppo but Hurry Harry, a nonhero; but it was Hall's version of the frontier hero who caught the general imagination.

Many figures in fiction were derived from Boone, as well as Natty, and it is interesting to note that most of them are notably old men —and each is paired with a young hunter, who is less uncouth than he, and often turns out to be genteel-in-disguise. We get something of this pattern in *The Pioneers,* where Natty is paired to some degree with Oliver Effingham, who is at first disguised as the young hunter Edwards. And in *The Prairie,* the other novel in which Natty is old, he is paired with Paul Hover, though also with Captain Middleton; in this novel, the two split between them the young man's role. The essential function of this character is to be an intermediary for the reader to the old man, and to inherit as the reader's proxy the old man's heroic qualities. Some other examples are to be found in *Westward Ho!,* a novel by Cooper's friend, Paulding; Charles W. Webber's *Old Hicks the Guide,* about the Texas Rangers; and Edward Ellis's best-selling *Seth Jones.* Of seventy-nine dime novels from 1860 to 1893 which Henry Nash Smith reports examining, forty contained old hunters.[13] They are old, presumably, because they represent the past—"America's Homeric age."

Boone was succeeded as national folk hero by Davy Crockett, who published three autobiographical volumes—two in 1834, and one in 1836, the year of his death. He was famous for killing; he says he killed forty-seven bears one month, which made 105 that year. Like Boone, and Natty, he had a much-beloved and personified rifle, Betsy. Like Boone, he was offered the chance to become a brave, by the Comanche tribe. But his story is more full of violence. He describes a truly savage fight with a cougar; and a comic scene of a man he overheard practicing eye-gouging and face-stamping, alone in the forest.

In 1835, politically disappointed—he had hoped to win the Western vote away from Jackson—Crockett set off for Texas, abandoning country, home, and family, for Texas still belonged to Mexico. He died defending the Alamo against the Mexican force sent to subdue rebellion. And the last part of his autobiography, describing his journey through the southwest toward the Alamo, is quite interesting from our point of view. It contains some vivid anecdotes that combine frontier ferocity with frontier humor in that blend which in American culture has so much force because of its implicit hostility to genteel values. Most strikingly, he describes picking up two companions, Thimblerig, a Red River boat gambler, and young Bee-Hunter, who is an erotic hero. (They also pick up later a pirate and an Indian, all on their way to the Alamo—the home of all lovers of freedom. The Bee-Hunter, he tells us, once sat down to breakfast in Texas with eleven men, all of whom were wanted for murder in their home states.) What is interesting for us is that the Bee-Hunter is so

like Paul Hover in *The Prairie.* Cooper seems to have rewritten
Crockett's material. It has been argued that in his last two Leatherstocking tales Cooper was reacting against the Crockett image, consciously or unconsciously; trying to rescue the Western hero from
those associations of rapacity and vulgarity. (That is why there is such
a heavy stress on Natty's nobility there.)

Then Mike Fink, famous as a boatman, who had in fact three
separate careers as a frontier hero. In the first he was a scout/ranger/
guide, like Natty, who defended Fort Pitt and spied in Indian territory. (He was always an expert rifleman, using a Kentucky rifle.)[14] In
the second he was a keelboatman on the Ohio and Mississippi rivers.
After the battle of Fallen Timbers, in 1793, a treaty of peace was
signed with the Indians near Fort Pitt, so scouts like Fink were left
with no employment. And they didn't want regular work; "they had
imbibed in their intercourse with the Indians a contempt as well as
disrelish for regular and steady labour."* Like the Cossacks, the
frontiersmen took on the cultural traits of the tribes they fought. So
they became boatmen, a trade which involved little contact with the
law, and was a part of the great migration movement. In 1787, five
hundred boats carried 20,000 people down the Ohio River, and the
keelboats were poled even against the current by muscular boatmen.
There was much singing, boasting, and taunting of rivals, as the boats
passed each other; while their relations with the shore-dwellers were
marked by drinking, wenching, and blackmail.

Fink's third career was as trapper and mountainman in the Rockies. This began in 1822, in St. Louis, when William H. Ashley and
Major Andrew Henry advertised for one hundred young men to
ascend the Missouri to its source, and to remain in the wilderness for
two or three years. Several of that hundred were to become legendary,
for their bear fights, human fights, or, as in the case of Fink, for being
murdered. (He was killed in a brawl in 1823.) The fur trade had just
then become important, and the trappers were the precursors of
empire.

Fink was always described as being of Herculean proportions,
perfectly symmetrical, of Indian coloring, and usually naked to the
waist. He is the most physical of these heroes, and the most erotic.
The language attributed to him is of the Southwestern-humor kind;

*Charles Cist, *History of Cincinnati,* 1845.

"I'm a Salt River roarer, and I love the wimming, and I'm chockful of fight." And his violence had a racist cast; two of his famous exploits with his rifle were first that he shot the heel off a Negro, and second that he shot the scalp lock off an Indian—both in jest. This is the sort of raucous folk image to keep in focus behind the figure of Natty, in order to appreciate Cooper's shaping hand.

Finally, Kit Carson. He was born in Kentucky in 1809, but his father believed that Daniel Boone was the greatest of Americans, and followed him to Missouri in 1813. In 1830 Kit answered an advertisement by Thomas Fitzpatrick, for men to go into the Rockies, and ultimately became the most famous of all mountain men.* Such men traveled in companies of fifty or a hundred, and often changed employers. Kit worked for the Hudson Bay Company for a time. They were also exemplars of the reckless, savage life, resistant to all laws or constraints, and inclined to Indian habits and ideas—rumored, for instance, to scalp their enemies. Timothy Flint, in *Shoshonee Valley* (1830) describes them as alternately indolent and laborious, aggressive and amorous.

When famous, Kit was offered a job with land speculators. But he met Fremont in St. Louis in 1842, and went with him to chart a route to the mouth of the Colorado River, for the U. S. Engineers; and then on a second expedition beyond the Salt Lake. He became Scout to the American army in California, and helped defeat large forces of Mexicans; he was offered a military commission during his visit to Washington.

Carson was therefore coopted by the established society, more clearly than any of the other folk heroes were. This coopting could be compared with Cooper's appropriation of the cultural image for establishment purposes. But it could also remind us of the way certain Cossacks (like Platov, or Skobelev's regiment) were employed by the Russian autocracy—exemplars of freedom employed as the agents of political discipline—disciplining those who had been freer than themselves from the modern system's laws.

For Carson later became an Indian agent. He fought the Apaches in New Mexico in 1854, and again in 1855–1856, the Apaches and the Utahs. In 1861 he was made a colonel in the Union army, and defeated a force of Texas rebels. By then he was the hero of many

---

*According to Noel B. Gerson, in *Kit Carson*, New York, 1964.

dime novels—the representative of America's unofficial imperialism; on one occasion he found such a novel amongst the debris of a wagon whose occupants he had been too late to save from Indian attackers. In such adventure scripts, of course, he was a brave loner; in real life, he was on the side of the big battalions. In 1863–1864 he had to fight the Navajo, and defeated them by the use of cannon; thereafter, it is said, his sleep was haunted by dreams of starving Navajo squaws and children. And he was of great assistance to General Sherman when the latter came out to arrange the treaty with the Indians in 1867.

On the political plane one may say that Carson, and the frontiersmen in general, were controlled and used by the Federal government. But on the cultural plane, it is clear that the folk hero image escaped the controls which Cooper and the responsible class tried to put on it. In literature itself Natty Bumppo has been successful, in some sense; readers have been induced to pay him quite exaggerated respect; but in the culture at large Mike Fink and Davy Crockett counted for more. Just as in literature, *Gulliver's Travels* was a masterpiece of irony, but in the culture at large it was just another adventure tale.[15]

# V I

## *Tolstoy*

I CHOSE Tolstoy as one of the authors to examine here for various reasons, one of the most important being that his books and his ideas, just because he is a Russian, throw a different light on the history of modern adventure. This is a light that comes in some sense from outside, because Russia and Russian literature lay on the periphery of the modern system, while England and America and literature-in-English lay at its center.

Russia in the nineteenth century was making a violent effort to acquire the technology of the modern system, without being infected by its ideology. That statement applies primarily to official Russia, not to the intelligentsia; but the latter too—at least Tolstoy's party, powerful within literature—opposed some Western styles of thought and feeling. Russian literature did not breathe the spirit of the modern system, or of the mercantile caste. There was no Russian Defoe. In Defoe's day, indeed, Russia had practically no printed literature. In the time of Dante and Chaucer, Russia had had no poetry, in the time of Shakespeare no drama, and before 1750 no novels. That made a difference, even in the nineteenth century.

Even more strikingly, Russian imperialism then was still under the control of the tsars, and not to be associated primarily with merchants. The merchants were a caste, devoted to traditional methods of trading, and the life-style that traditionally went with them. Not until the second half of the nineteenth century did they become

English-style merchants, entrepreneurs, and engage in capitalist expansion. Russia did have, in its advance eastward, some character of representing the modern system—spreading the benefits of civilization—but by and large it was a conscious and military imperialism; like that of sixteenth-century Spain, not that of seventeenth-century England. The nineteenth-century novel of adventure accordingly began as romance, heavily influenced by Scott (favorite reading of Tsar Nicholas I) and with a markedly aristomilitary character.

Indeed, in early nineteenth-century Russia, something like a caste system still prevailed, and the aristomilitary caste was dominant in literature. We see this in the early rise of the nobleman's genre of *Sportsman's Sketches*, in which Aksakov, Turgenev, and Tolstoy began their writing careers; and in the genre of childhood reminiscences, in which Aksakov, Tolstoy, and Herzen excelled, and which was also tied to the landowning caste. Later in the century, a different and somewhat opposed sensibility developed, in the work of priests' sons, like Chernyshevsky, and doctors' sons, like Dostoevsky, and the epigones of Belinsky (himself a doctor's son and priest's grandson). N. G. Pomyalovsky, whose *Seminary Sketches* appeared in 1862, was typical of a group of intellectuals of the raznochintsy—most of them priests' sons but outside the caste system themselves—whose naturalistic-satiric writing was very popular in the 1860s. *Seminary Sketches* is a childhood reminiscence, but very unlike Tolstoy's *Childhood, Boyhood, and Youth.* But these men are also unlike the English domestic novelists, and their related critics. There is for instance no implicit alliance to be detected, within such work or within the intelligentsia that read it, between the writers and the merchant caste in Russia. The intelligentsia dissociated itself from all other castes, except the peasants, and threw itself into a posture of aggressive dissatisfaction with society as a whole. Russia was a different case.

Tolstoy's position can best be understood as following from Pushkin's. In 1825 Pushkin wrote to a friend that "our writers are recruited from the highest social class. With them aristocratic pride is linked with their literary ambition. . . . Our poets do not solicit the protection of gentlemen; our poets are gentlemen themselves. [And, though the friend he was addressing, Ryleev, was a Decembrist, soon to be executed for his part in that revolt] The lack of esteem for one's ancestors is the first sign of wildness and immorality." Pushkin was proud of his six-hundred-year-old nobility. But more important, he and his friend, Prince Viazemsky, saw literature in Russia as threatened by the new nobility, appointed as noble by the tsars for services to the state—that is, to the autocracy. This threat was represented, in the '20s and '30s, by the literary journalist, Bulgarin, who, Pushkin said, treated literature as a commodity. Literature as represented by Pushkin and his friends—and by Herzen and Tolstoy later—was close to the politics of the Decembrists; who were rebels against the autocracy, but in the name of the aristocracy as much as of the lower classes (Gleason, *European and Muscovite,* p. 46).

This anachronism in the cultural style of literature (from a modern system point of view) was not accidental or atypical of Russia. Something similar was even truer in political matters. Even in its eastward expansion, Russian imperialism was not like the English kind. It was more the work of the autocracy, its armed forces, and above all its Cossacks. If that character was not reflected in the imaginative literature in any major way, it was because the conscience of literature-as-a-system was against it.

Thus in 1821 Pushkin wrote a verse tale, *The Prisoner of the Caucasus,* in which a Russian officer is loved by a girl among his Chechen captors, who helps him escape and then kills herself in despair. (Tolstoy was to write a prose tale with a similar plot and setting.) There is some fine description of the premodern life of the Chechen, and the poem was acclaimed as a triumph of Russian poetry; except that, in the epilogue, Pushkin celebrated the final victory of the Russian forces, under General Ermolov, the conquest of the Caucasus and defeat of the Chechens. (Pushkin much admired Ermolov, a military and imperialist hero, who had, he said, the head of a tiger on the shoulders of Hercules; he wanted to write his biography.) But his friend Viazemsky wrote that that epilogue stained Pushkin's verse with blood. "The blood freezes in one's veins, and one's hair stands on end, to read that Ermolov 'Destroyed and annihilated the tribes like a black plague.' " This, said Viazemsky, is an anachronism; poetry is not the ally of executioners; we should be educating the tribes, not executing them (Woolf, *Pushkin on Literature,* p. 63). This is what the conscience of literature would have said in England too, and later Russian writers were more obedient to it.

But the conscience of a literary system often unconsciously pays tribute to its connections with the political system too. By their silence Russian adventures slurred over the imperialist character of

Russia's advance east, and over the "continental" nature of Russian imperialism. In the section "Imperialism" of her *Origins of Totalitarianism,* Hannah Arendt says, "Nazism and Bolshevism owe more to Pan-Germanism and Pan-Slavism (respectively) than to any other ideology or political movement" (p. 222). And she goes on to talk about a continental kind of imperialism, in which there was no distance between colony and mother country (between frontier and metropolis, to use Webb's terms). She says that transoceanic empires sometimes suffer from a "boomerang effect," whereby the political methods and political ideas used on the frontier, usually much harsher than those approved for the home population, filter back and infect the home country. In the case of continental empires, there is no need for any such gradual effect. "Continental imperialism truly begins at home" (p. 223).[1]

There are indeed parallels between Russia's history and that of Prussia, and the Romanovs were traditionally friends and allies, even imitators, of the Hohenzollerns. (To some degree, the Russian autocracy may be seen as a sequence of German princes, dragooning a quite alien Slavic population.) But Germany as a whole did not become an empire until 1870, three hundred years after Russia. The preeminent example of continental imperialism must be Russia.

Moreover, Germany had nothing to compare with the thrust eastward, that enormous expansion of Russian power over unoccupied land—that is, occupied only by nomadic or mountain tribes who did not belong to the modern system. That expansive thrust was still continental, though it was not so consciously imperialist. Russia's conscious expansion was the territory it took from Sweden, Poland, and Turkey; the land it took from the tribes of Central Asia seemed as empty and unclaimed as Africa and the West Indies seemed to England. Historians sometimes say, comparing the expansion east with Russia's efforts to expand in other directions, that the former "happened of itself." This should remind us of the "absence of mind" in which England acquired its empire; and of America's "innocent" expropriation of the Indians.

As that reference suggests, there is much in Arendt's "continental" idea which applies particularly to the case of American culture. (While England, on the other hand, is preeminent amongst empires in which the boomerang effect was dodged and delayed.) G. A. Lensen, in *Russia's Eastward Expansion,* says in his Introduction,

"Russia's eastward expansion was part of the European tide that inundated Asia and America in the Age of Exploration," and it involved the same types—pathfinders, traders, missionaries, soldiers of fortune. They moved into Siberia in search of "the golden fleece," and during the 1630s Russia annexed territory at the rate of something like the size of France every three years.

Only America's thrust westward could compare with Russia's, and even that was smaller, in square miles occupied and in numbers of people moved. Moreover there was the difference, which made those two great powers politically antithetical, that in Russia the power of the state was concentrated in the autocracy to an extraordinary degree. Russia was the most backward state in Europe, from a modern political point of view; it had practically no liberties, even after it had begun to modernize its technology, and even after it began to produce its great literature.

Russia was the first in a sequence of modernized empires (imperial Germany and Japan were later examples) whose history is of the greatest importance in understanding the modern system. These were countries who continued to be ruled by military castes, even while they appropriated modern system skills. Their history in some sense caricatured or satirized the modern system; it mocked the hopes of countries like England that they had escaped from militarism and caste-domination, had exorcised the black magic of imperialism, had substituted the white magic of productivity, enlightened self-interest, and the pursuit of happiness.

Ever since the days of Boris Godunov, Russia had been either sending men to Europe to acquire the secrets of Western technology (sometimes these men refused to come home afterward) or recruiting European technicians to come to Russia (sometimes *these* men's passage was prevented by the kings of Sweden or Poland).[2] It was most typically military engineers the tsars wanted, and what they most definitely did not want was the liberal ideology that Europe had developed along with that technology. The economic development of Russia was not autonomous, in the Western style, but occurred under the direction of the tsars, out of phase with the "free growth of the free market," etc. It stopped and started at their behests. Thus Peter the Great had fostered the growth of a metallurgical industry, to the point where Russia's was one of the foremost in Europe. In 1800 her iron ore production was nearly equal to England's. But it was not a free-growing industry; by the end of Nicholas I's reign, in 1855, England's production had increased twelve-fold over the 1800 figure, while Russia's was much the same as before; and England was producing a thousand times as much coal as Russia.

Russia's intellectuals were bitterly conscious of belonging to an empire and not to a modern system country. Their efforts to create a great literature were bedeviled by the fear that "literature" as they understood the term—an idea derived from the literature of eighteenth- and nineteenth-century Europe—only could or only should flourish in a free country.

Thus Russian literature, in its relation to Russian culture as a whole, provides an interesting contrast to English. And amongst Russian authors, Tolstoy was a pre-eminent spokesman.

## Tolstoy and Cooper and Caste

But Tolstoy is also of special interest to our argument because, of all the writers of adventure tales, he is the only one who went on to write serious fiction of the very highest level—*War and Peace* and *Anna Karenina*.

Such novels are, by definition, not our concern here. But I should say a word about *War and Peace*, which contains elements of adventure—of the story of the brothers. It is after all about Napoleon, one of the three great conquistadors I cited as inspiring the modern idea of the historical hero. When Napoleon actually appears on the page, Tolstoy gives a very disparaging account of him, and the book's tone becomes hostile to adventure. But he figures in the book also as the focus of Andrey's and Pierre's early aspirations; as the symbol of glory and achievement, and youthful genius defeating established power unaided; in a manuscript note, Tolstoy said that each of the novel's heroes was ambitious à la Napoleon. Moreover, each hero's feelings for Napoleon is a young man's worship of another young man—that is a pattern in the book, most strikingly illustrated by Nicholas Rostov's feeling for Tsar Alexander. Seeing the tsar's handsome and happy face, Nicholas "experienced a feeling of tenderness and ecstasy such as he had never before known. Every trait and every movement of the Tsar's seemed to him enchanting" (p. 264). This is a military-caste story, suffused by the love of young manhood—a love felt by young men for young men.[3] This group of motifs and themes will remind us of Scott; and the big social and battle scenes we admired in *Waverley* are developed even further in *War and Peace*.

But this novel is also about girls and whom they should marry; notably Natasha, contrasted with Sonia and Vera; and Princess Mary, contrasted with Lisa and Mlle. Bourienne. And this group of motifs and the thematic material surrounding them will remind us of George Eliot, and the English story of the sisters. *War and Peace* is a great synthesis of a novel, as has often been said. I don't know that it has been remarked that the two elements most importantly synthesized are the story of the brothers and the story of the sisters. Of course there are other elements too, but from the point of view of the history of the novel, these are the most important. And they are held together not in equality but in a subordination (Tolstoy assigns "reality" to the story of marriages and "unreality" to the story of adventures) which is also part of the history of the novel.

Tolstoy went on from that achievement in serious fiction to renounce art and denounce Empire entirely. Following his conversion, about 1880, he took up a moral position outside the system of literature as a whole, and outside the modern world system as a whole. He disapproved of the direction of development of modern history, in Russia but also outside. And looking back, we can now see the origins of that final attitude always present in his mind.

During his youth, however, Tolstoy wrote not only serious novels but also some adventures. Indeed, he never wholly ceased to work on that kind of material, as we shall see, but after his conversion he was uneasy with it. His kind of adventure was in the Russian tradition. Besides Pushkin's verse tale, and similar tales by Lermontov, there was *Ammalet Bek* by Bestuzhev-Marlinsky. He was another Decembrist, who won a pardon. He fought in the Caucasus between 1829 and 1837 (when he died there in battle) and wrote this very popular historical novel, with a Byronic hero, about the fighting there in 1810. In the Scott tradition, there were verses interspersed, and some ethnological interest shown in the life of the Chechens. Novels about the Caucasus war were a well-established genre in Russia, the genre of transposed Scott, and that was the option Tolstoy chose when he began *The Cossacks*. But if we consider Tolstoy as a whole, we are likely to see a more intimate and revealing likeness between him and Cooper than between him and Scott.

In the course of Chapter 19 of *The Cossacks,* Tolstoy makes an explicit reference to Cooper which lights up his manifold debt to adventure in English. "The memory of Fenimore Cooper's *The Pathfinder* flashed through" the hero's mind, because he finds himself involved in an adventure like those he'd read about. (In another story, Tolstoy also invokes *The Pathfinder* to mean the beauty of the forest, and the happiness of living in it.)[4] Cooper was generally popular in Russia, and with serious writers. Belinsky compared him with Shakespeare. Lermontov thought him greater than Scott, and borrowed from *The Water-Witch* for his *Taman.* Gogol's Cossacks in *Taras Bulba,* like Tolstoy's, owe much to Cooper's frontiersmen and Indians. The heyday of his reputation there was 1825–1845, Tolstoy's youth, when Cooper's novels appeared in the magazine, *Notes of the Fatherland,* and the drift of the Russian critics' enthusiasm can be caught in this quotation from an essay by Belinsky in 1839. ". . . and as for the sea and ships, here again he [Cooper] is at home: he knows the name of every rope on board ship; like the most experienced of pilots, he knows its every movement; like a skillful captain, he . . ." (Dekker and McWilliams, *James Fenimore Cooper: The Critical Heritage,* p. 189). Belinsky is impressed by the same feature of Cooper as were the American readers, his practical knowledge and skills. Annenkov, Herzen, Chernyshevsky, were all enthusiastic. Cooper was referred to in the Epilogue to *Brothers Karamazov,* and by Chekhov, and by Gorky.

Cooper's stories (despite the elements of conflict we see in them) carried the message of hope in Russia; so they did in France, and in England, to judge by D. H. Lawrence's account of his boyish enjoyment of them. They carried the modern system's energizing myth. And it seems likely that Cooper exerted a more powerful influence in Russia than anywhere else, because America was such a mirage of freedom to people living under the tsarist authority, and also because of the similarities between the two countries' geopolitical situations.

In Tolstoy's case, however, there were also personal reasons for a special affinity between him and Cooper. The latter was the youngest of five brothers; Tolstoy was the youngest of four, and the son of a father who impressed those who knew him, including his children, as remarkable. (The mother died when Lev was two.) Nikolai Ilyitch

## Tolstoy

Tolstoy was not a great achiever, as William Cooper was, but he was notably the center of his household, around whom everyone else revolved; he was not an adventure-novel hero, but he was a domestic-novel hero; he was adored by his mother, by his cousin Toinette—who did the most to bring up the children—by the servants, and by the children themselves. There were two Cooper girls, one Tolstoy girl, but in both families it seems clear that the masculine principle was dominant. Tolstoy described what he felt at the age of five, when he was moved downstairs from the nursery to join his brothers and to receive lessons—to enter the world of men, of horses, dogs, and hunting. For Cooper, too, the initiation into manhood, and aristocratic manhood, was of crucial importance.

For there were, also, certain sociocultural similarities between the two families. In *Fenimore Cooper: Critic of His Times,* Robert Spiller describes the Cooper house as a curious mixture of pioneering crudity and baronial grandeur, a description that would fit the early Yasnaya Polyana. (The house and estate at Aksokovo, which S. T. Aksakov describes at the beginning of his *Family Chronicle,* is in some ways even closer to Cooperstown.) The houses of the Russian nobility contained trophies of European culture, like grand pianos and marble statues, while they lacked the comforts of quite modest English houses. Spiller says on p. 28, "The tin-plate stove must have held curious conversations with the plaster busts in those pedimented doorways during those long northern nights." English travelers made very similar comments on Russian houses in the early nineteenth century.

That was the time when Sidney Smith asked the famous question, "Who reads an American novel?" in the *Edinburgh Review.* And in 1804, when Karamzin's *Letters of a Traveller* was published in English, Henry Brougham said, in the same magazine, "a book of translations from Moscow is like a horse in Venice or a tree in Scotland—its amusing badness is all that deserves attention." In some sense, everyone thought that, about both America and Russia. The *Edinburgh Review* critics were famous for sharpening to the point of insult prejudices other people softened to the mumble of shame.

The obverse side of that prejudice was the enthusiasm felt for both America and Russia as places where a new life could be begun, a new and purified European civilization. Herder, early in his career, dreamed of becoming the Luther and Solon of a new nation of the

Ukraine; Bernardin de Saint-Pierre thought a new Pennsylvania might grow up around the Aral sea. And it was in Russia and America that the radical Protestant sects persecuted in Central Europe found a place to live and grow. Moravianism, for instance, was not without its effects on both Cooper and Tolstoy, and is even reflected indirectly in their fiction. Natty Bumppo and Karataev are both figures of radical Christianity, figures of renunciation, passivity, simplicity—essentially negations of the worldly culture around them and ahead of them.

The incongruities of furnishing, etc., reflected contradictory pressures on the people who lived there, which could cause the anxious questions, "How do really modern people do this or that?" or "Is this country really civilized?" or "Do I want it to be?" Both our authors asked those questions. They were too intelligent for that self-questioning to inspire mere cultural snobbery in them. But they felt that anxiety and were angry to feel it.

They responded in part negatively to the pressure to be liberal and democratic and advanced; they asserted an aristocratic caste identity which always seemed reactionary. Here is one example of that in Cooper, from *Satanstoe,* a novel largely preoccupied with the differences between the author-representing hero and a New Englander, Jasper Newcome, who is in some ways the better educated and more earnest of the two, more the modern system hero, but who is not a gentleman. Newcome, we are told, was "ultra-levelling in his notions of social intercourse, while I had the opinions of my own colony, in which the distinction of classes are far more strongly marked than is usual in New England." The tone is of course defiant, for Cooper had to defy the pressure of all modern system ideology, to say such things. But he needed to claim a place in the modern world for his own caste. And the likeness between him and Tolstoy centers in their caste identity.

An equivalent to such caste opinions are the caste sports, like skating and riding and shooting, in which Cooper's heroes excel, and their enemies do not. And of course the same is true of Tolstoy. Hunting above all is of great importance to the aristomilitary caste. Then Cooper became a sailor, while Tolstoy became a soldier, and served in an imperialist war in the Caucasus.

In that war, Russia was putting down the resistance of mountain tribesmen, who had never before been subdued by any civilization, and who were inspired and led by their imams; it was a muridic rising, religious and populist in character, while the imperialist power they faced justified itself by its civilizing mission.

It is also worth remembering that Tolstoy was an artillery officer in those wars. Artillery, cannon, were the supreme weapon of the modern system against the rest of the world. (When he arrived in St. Petersburg, and began his career as a man of letters, he was still, officially, military inspector to a munitions factory there.) And though Tolstoy's part in the war was to some degree that of an observer, it was not entirely so. He took part in battles. Indeed, on February 17, 1853, he distinguished himself in a major attack, in which his battery silenced the enemy's guns; and that was the engagement which broke the back of Shamil's resistance. Thus he belonged to the military caste by experience—the experience of modern war —as well as by birth.

In Tolstoy's case, the most striking expression of this caste feeling in writing is this extract from a discarded chapter of *War and Peace.* "I am not a bourgeois, as Pushkin boldly said, and I boldly say that I am an aristocrat by birth, by habits and by position. I am an aristocrat because I am not only not ashamed, but positively glad to remember my ancestors—I was brought up from childhood in love and respect for the highest orders of society and in love for the refined as expressed not only in Homer, Bach, and Raphael, but also in all the small things in life. . . . I am an aristocrat because I cannot believe in the high intellect, the refined taste, or the absolute honesty of a man who picks his nose and whose soul converses with God."[5] That last sentence is Tolstoy's fling at the Jasper Newcomes of his society. And it is no accident that both novelists' heroines are often what Cooper describes as "a spirited horsewoman." On horseback, everyone is a figure of chivalry, and we shall see in discussing Kipling how powerful that image is. In the case of Natasha Rostov, the concept has a good deal more content than it does in Cooper's usage, but as a caste index it has still the same meaning.

Tolstoy's animus against Speransky in *War and Peace* (which is probably mirrored in the more full-length portrait of Karenin in *Anna Karenina*) is another example of caste feeling. Mikhail Speransky (1772–1839) was the great bureaucrat of nineteenth-century Russia,

---

*Quoted in R. F. Christian, *Tolstoy's War and Peace*, pp. 102–103.

the bureaucrat as genius, and responsible for much of the modernization and Westernization of the country. According to Marc Raeff, he was "the model and teacher for an entire generation of government officials, at least in the techniques of bureaucratic work" (*Michael Speransky*, p. 350). He was a village priest's son—the typical origin for the Russian bureaucrat—and educated at a seminary.

This means more than it may seem to do at first glance, because the Russian priesthood was in effect a caste.[6] At least this was true of the "white" priests (and deacons and psalmodists, and so on) who officiated in the village churches, and who married before they took orders. Their sons almost always went to a seminary for their education, and their daughters sometimes were given a benefice as a dowry, to help them find a husband in a seminary. (The "black" churchmen were the monks and the higher ecclesiastics.) Thus, though there were of course exceptions, a priest's father was usually another priest, and so was his son. Turgenev said Belinsky was of the purest Russian blood, because he came of a priestly family—who could only intermarry with other such families. Turgenev also complained to the de Goncourts that he had been seated next to a priest at a banquet given by the Russian ambassador in Paris; in Russia, he explained, the nobles had nothing to do with the priests. And indeed, if the white priesthood was a Brahmin caste, it altogether lacked the Indian associations of purity, learning, and refinement; the parish priests of Russia were associated rather with ignorance, drunkenness, and tyranny. They had to keep records for the central authorities, and make them political reports. Even Speransky had to draw up a code of laws for Nicholas, and act as chief prosecutor of the Decembrists.

But Tolstoy's feeling was against the psychological type as much as against the cultural function: it was the feeling of the free nobleman against the office-bound clerk, of the military caste against the bureaucratic, and one can see something similar in Nabokov's treatment of Chernyshevsky in *The Gift*. Speransky became an expert popularizer and report-writer, with the traits, intellectually, of the French Encyclopaedists and the English Utilitarians, and had remarkable powers of work and self-dedication. He married an Englishwoman, and clearly his function in Russia was very parallel to that of the Evangelicals in contemporary England; the men like Grant, who recharged England with neo-Puritan certitude. Speransky asserted himself by means of mind and morality, not by manliness and human warmth; he manifested himself as a Brahmin, not a Kshat-triya. Socially he was always on guard, and relaxed only with inferiors with whom he felt sure of every superiority. With equals his personality was marked by a cold aloofness, which masked a hypersensitive need for admiration and consolation. This figure played an important part in Tolstoy's emotional life (as it did in Russian culture as a whole) and he discharged upon it strong caste prejudices; although in *Anna Karenina* that prejudice is counteracted by opposite feelings, and later in life he attempted to divest himself of that caste persona.

Speransky was apparently destined to be an important character in *War and Peace* from its first conception in Tolstoy's mind, and he survived the many changes that engulfed other originals. K. B. Feuer establishes this, in her study of the *War and Peace* manuscripts cited in the bibliography. She also establishes that there was a connection between Speransky and Napoleon in Tolstoy's mind—a connection Shklovsky had more intuitively pointed to, on the strength of the detail Tolstoy uses to characterize both, their plump, small, white hands. In one draft Tolstoy said that Speransky was a civic Napoleon to Prince Andrey, and in another he applied to both the same prejudicial term for seminarians, *kuteynitski.* It is clearly a nobleman's caste-dislike for them that Tolstoy is expressing; when Andrey gives vent to his disillusionment with both, in another place, Pierre says to him *"quel esprit de caste."* Such feelings were strong in Russian literary circles, even in the second half of the century. Tolstoy's friend, Strakhov, was told by a fellow conservative, Leontev, that he couldn't understand the aristocracy because "You are still just a seminarian," in a quarrel in the '70s. And both Dostoevsky and Chekhov declared they felt a handicap in matters of form and aesthetics, because they were not nobles—Chekhov said this as late as 1889.

Such caste-feeling in a novelist is important also because it bears on the sort of adventure and adventurer he imagines. Tolstoy, true to his caste, does not give us a do-it-yourself hero; he is much closer to Scott than to Defoe. His heroes are—or rather they become, for his stress is on their becoming—fiery figures of manhood, eminent in courage, and honor, and ardor—essentially, though not simply, chivalric types. His caste-loyalty persisted, against his will, all his life. In his diary entry for December 31, 1904, he wrote about his desire for a Russian victory over the Japanese, "This is patriotism. I was brought up on it and am not free from it, just as I am not free from personal egoism, from a family and even an aristocratic egoism, and from patriotism."* The literary proof of that caste-character persisting is *Hadji Murad,* the masterpiece of imperialist adventure he was working on—ashamedly—at that very time.

Earlier in his life, however, he asserted his caste-identity unashamedly and voluntarily—rooted himself in it. When he entered the University of Kazan, he began smoking, set up a horse and trap, and became a dandy. He was much impressed by his brother Sergei, who was perfectly comme il faut. Tolstoy scorned the gymnasium graduates and scholarship boys at the university, consorted only with fellow aristocrats, refused to bow first when he met someone, froze the overfamiliar. And this aspect of his personality recurred, though intermittently, over some fifteen years. In 1851 he went to Moscow with the express intent to (1) gamble, (2) marry, (3) get a post; and he wrote out for himself some Rules for Society: that he must associate only with men of higher status, dance only with important women, never express his feelings, always punish a sarcastic or insulting remark.

And this was not merely a matter of personality style; when Tolstoy became a famous writer after the Crimean War, he quarreled with his fellow contributors to *Sovremennik,* because he felt they lacked aristocratic honor, even in their intellectual life. They represented the modern system mind in literature. He doubted the quality of their convictions, found them morally flabby, and insisted on the criterion of man-to-man combat as a test of intellectual sincerity. Turgenev complained bitterly of Tolstoy's "nobleman's pride." And it is clear that Tolstoy was asserting just that by his behavior toward this group. He always wore his military uniform with them, flaunted his grooming and physical condition, and in return for their domestic hospitality entertained them at a hotel, with gypsies. He was using a caste-rooted integrity and authenticity against them, just as in our century working-class writers have used their class against their colleagues.[7]

And his close relations with his brothers are important because their mutual affection despite incompatibility of belief was the nuclear model for the caste loyalty he was asserting. In 1854—by which time Nikolai would be thirty-two—the four of them reunited at

---

*Quoted in Ernest J. Simmons, *Tolstoy,* p. 208.

Yasnaya Polyana, and talked far into the night, and then made up a bed on the floor and slept together. This speaks of an intensity of man-to-man warmth which can remind us only of Kipling. And this warmth is one of the sources of all stories of the brothers.

Tolstoy put his faith in caste-loyalty through much of his life; and, after marriage, supplemented that with a faith in family life; and both were for him alternatives to modern system values and personality styles. Both were forms of silent resistance to modern civilization— though also to the empire of Nicholas I. Thus in his hands (as indeed in Cooper's) the adventure story served antimodernist forces of the mind, too.

## Tolstoy and Peter and Modernization

But one tendency in the adventure novel, one ideological implication or alliance, was in the long run repugnant to Tolstoy. This was its being finally on the side of the modern system; it might counter that tendency by an opposite sympathy with Nature and the primitive, but it could not seriously oppose it. (Tolstoy was also disturbed by the violence of adventure, but that is a separate issue.) He was nearly always uneasy about the modernization of Russia, and a natural ally of the Slavophiles rather than the Westernizers—the two great parties of the Russian intellectual debate. As time passed, his temperamental ambivalence came down more and more against the latter. It might be said that he undertook to wrestle against Peter the Great, the great modernizer of Russia, who had brought her into line with western Europe. Nicholas I, the tsar of Tolstoy's youth, saw himself as another Peter, and the spokesmen for "official nationality" made a cult of Peter. Egor Kankrin, Nicholas's minister of finance, even proposed that Russia should be renamed Petrovia and Russians Petrovians. Tolstoy, like Herzen, picked a determined quarrel with Nicholas, especially in certain late stories and essays.

All the Slavophiles, and most Russian writers, had to quarrel with the agents of their country's modernization, at one point or another. "Peter I" said Herzen, "drove civilization into us with such a wedge that Russia could not stand it, and split into two layers" (*My Past and Thoughts*, p. 1576). And Dostoevsky, announcing a new journal in

1863, said, "The reforms of Peter the Great have been too expensive for us: they have separated us from the people." It is true that Belinsky in his final phase, when he bitterly concentrated all his will and contracted all his sensibility into the demand for modernization and enlightenment, declared that Peter was his model and his religion. And in 1854 Granofsky angrily reproached Herzen with having betrayed their cause, when the latter began to write against Peter. But such incidents only show how alive an issue Peter remained to all Russian intellectuals—when he was repudiated, he was sure to be defended. As Herzen said, apropos of Granofsky's reproach, in Russia Peter's image grew more colossal every year.

Much of Russian cultural history could be written around the Bronze Horseman, the statue to Peter set up by Catherine, and a symbol of autocracy in Pushkin's poem of that name. It is the symbolic center of the modern system city Peter conjured into being— the Dutch-style naval base subsequently embellished by Elizabeth and Catherine. When Herzen first visited St. Petersburg, in 1839, he tells us he went immediately to gaze upon that statue, and to wish that the cannon that crushed the Decembrists had instead pulverized that image. Peter, his statue, and his city, were the symbols of modernism and state power to Herzen, Pushkin, Dostoevsky, and most other writers. Pushkin said Peter had made all Russia rear up like a horse when he got on her back.

Tolstoy had, moreover, a personal connection with Peter the Great, for the founder of the Tolstoy family fortunes, Lev's great-great-great-grandfather, was a personal favorite of that tsar. He went to Italy on Peter's bidding in 1697, to study naval science, as part of the modernization program. He became the first Russian ambassador to Constantinople, 1701–1710. And in 1717 he tricked Peter's recalcitrant son, Alexei, into returning to Russia from Germany, where he is thought to have been murdered to suit Peter's plans. After the death of Alexei, Peter Tolstoy was "one of the most intimate and trusted persons about the Emperor," according to Paul Birukov, the later Tolstoy's biographer.

The tragic confrontation of Peter and his son has continued to fascinate and trouble the Russian imagination. Ge, a friend of the novelist Tolstoy, painted a famous picture of the two facing each other; and D. S. Merezhkovsky wrote a famous novel, *Peter and Alexis,* in 1905, in which Peter reproached his son with listening too

much to priests and with taking no interest in military matters—
"through which we have come from darkness to light."

The part of the Petropavlovsk Fortress in which the Tsarevitch was
put to death was known afterward as the Alexis Ravelin, and it
remained an evocative name in Russian culture, because it was the
prison's death row. It was a place impossible for outsiders to visit, and
Tolstoy himself, even though the prison governor was an old friend
of his, was refused permission when he wanted to do some research
there. It was also where the famous revolutionaries of his lifetime, like
Nechaev and Kropotkin, were held. Thus there were many reasons
for Alexis, and Peter Tolstoy, and Peter the Great, to recur to the
novelist's mind.

Peter the Great was known as the Tsar Preobrazovatel, the Transforming Tsar, and what he transformed was Russia, and into a part
of the modern world system. Earlier rulers had wanted to reform
Russia, Marc Raeff tells us, "But not at the price of a loss of its
traditional spiritual and cultural identity. For Peter, on the other
hand, this identity did not have any absolute value or particular
meaning, quite the contrary perhaps" (Raeff, *Peter the Great*, p. x).
And on the next page, "Power was the most easily perceptible and
most dramatic manifestation of the new spirit of Europe. It was this
very modern and Western trait that Peter possessed to a high degree." He forced on Russia a new chronology, new script, new costume; he set up a newspaper, shaved off people's beards, reorganized
the Church, and created that metallurgy industry which was in the
eighteenth century the most advanced in Europe.

And he was a modernist in the detail of his personality, as well as
in the design of his reforms. V. O. Kliuchevsky says, "Whenever he
could, he used his hands, which were never free from calluses. When
he was young and still inexperienced he could never be shown over
a factory or a workshop without trying his hand at whatever work was
in progress. He found it impossible to remain a mere spectator,
particularly if he saw something new going on. His hands instinctively
sought for tools; he wanted to work at everything himself." He was
an epitome of the modern world system. "Even during his first
foreign tour, the German princesses who talked with him came to the
conclusion that he was a master-craftsman in fourteen different
trades" (Kliuchevsky, *Peter the Great*, p. 13). He was a royal Robinson Crusoe, but he had a populous empire to work on, not an empty

island. As B. H. Sumner says, in his *Peter the Great*, "He had, in fact, a craftsman's bent, an inventor's, an explorer's" (p. 23).

Peter evoked awe-struck loyalty from his subjects. One of his contemporaries called him, "Our Lord, Peter the Great, who has drawn us from nothingness into being," and Derzhavin said, "Was it not God, Who in his person came down to earth?" But in *Notes on Ancient and Modern Russia* (1811), Karamzin, who at first also idolized him, said that Peter had made Russians citizens of the world, but stopped them being citizens of their native land. And the revival of nationalism, after the defeat of Napoleon, strengthened this feeling. The Slavophiles glorified pre-Petrine Russia. The peasants had always resisted Peter's reforms, and had rumored that he was the Anti-Christ, because he was leading their country into the modern world system.

It cannot have been a matter of indifference to an imagination like Tolstoy's that his family's fortunes were founded by a favorite of this tsar—in a sense by Peter. He tried for a long time to write a novel about Peter and his work, but had to give it up. According to D. S. Mirsky, he failed because he became so disgusted with the person of the great emperor—"the embodiment of all he hated."

Tolstoy himself was not without modernizing and westernizing sympathies, especially early in his life. When he was young he read Rousseau with passionate enthusiasm, and imitated Benjamin Franklin by keeping a Franklin journal to record his faults and his progress in correcting them, and so on. In middle life he spent much of his energy on educational and agricultural experiments. And in his comments on the English and French soldiers he met when they were prisoners of the Russians in the Crimean war, he used modernist criteria himself. He admired their independence and skill and fully developed individuality, and contrasted the Russian soldiers with them unfavorably.

He wrote to his brother Sergei during the Crimean War (Birukoff, *Leo Tolstoy*, Vol. I, p. 176), "You should see the French and English prisoners (especially the latter); each one is better than the last, I mean morally and physically; they are a *splendid people*. The Cossacks say that even they feel pity in sabring them, and by their side, you should see any one of our riflemen; small, lousy, and shriveled up, in a way."

One of the official papers Tolstoy wrote as an officer in that war was about the fact that the Western armies had rifles, and the Russians only muskets. It was entitled "Massacre by Small-Arms." In fact, half the English and French soldiers had guns with a range of 1,200 paces, while 95 percent of the Russians' range was only 300. And they were not trained in marksmanship (Harcave, *Years of the Golden Cockerel,* p. 155). Thus Tolstoy was involved in those practical and even military affairs which involved acknowledging the superiority of the West. When he turned against Peter, he turned against part of himself.

Intellectual Russia as a whole may be said to have turned against modernization—which again meant turning against part of itself—in the course of the nineteenth century. The populist movement was in part inspired by Tolstoy, in part by Herzen and other writers. It can be seen, as James Billington has argued in *The Icon and the Axe,* as a continuation of the various forms of resistance and protest recurrent in Russia since the times of Peter himself. "The central fact of the populist era," Billington says, "which haunted the imagination of its creative artists, was that all of Russian life was being materially transformed by modernizing forces from the West" (p. 402). But this was not a new concern. The student martyrs of the populist movement in the 1870s and '80s were the heirs of the 20,000 Old Believers who had burned themselves to death two centuries before rather than accept the modernization of the Russian Church. They were the heirs of the Cossacks who had risen in defense of their liberty, and of the peasants who had declared Peter the Anti-Christ himself. And Tolstoy was one of their literary heroes.

Moreover, seeing Tolstoy as opposing Peter is also of interest to us because Defoe wrote a history of that tsar, and made him into one of his heroes of modernization. They were of course on the same side on most issues. Defoe's hero, William III, was the western king Peter most admired, and on his trip to England he visited William and was presented with an English yacht. And when Peter sent Vitus Bering exploring in 1725, the Great Northern Expedition took with it nine wagons of instruments and books, amongst which were the very recently published *Robinson Crusoe* (and *Gulliver's Travels*).

In his *Impartial History of the Life and Actions of Peter Alexandrovitz,* Defoe points out that the tsar had altered "the economy, the customs, manners and commerce of his own people. By this means, he has brought a nation, who were before the most blind and ignorant, and the greatest contemners of knowledge, and of all manner of learning, to be searchers after wisdom, studying sciences and eagerly bringing home books, instruments, and artists, from the most learned parts of the world, for their instruction. By this means, he has brought his soldiers, who were before the most scoundrel undisciplined crowds, rabbles rather than soldiers, and just good for nothing, to be regular disciplined troops, clothed, armed, and paid like other nations, and behaving on all occasions in a manner sufficient to make them formidable to those who used to despise them. By this means, he has reduced his people in general, to a legal kind of obedience to their governors; not the same kind of blind homage they used to pay to their princes, who they rather worshiped than obeyed; but, a more polite regulation, so that now the czar endeavors to convince their reason, of the real advantages which his new laws are to them, at the same time that he exacts their obedience. . . ." (p. 3). He brought them into the modern world system, taught them freedom, productivity, enterprise, enlightened self-interest.

It was not Defoe but Voltaire who wrote for Catherine the Great the official biography of Peter. Lomonosov collected the materials, and Voltaire wrote them up—and fell, like so many other philosophes, philosophically enamored of Catherine. But this was a very appropriate conjunction of personalities, which can only reinforce our sense of the greater affinity between Defoe and Peter. Voltaire and the philosophes were in many ways the more elegant heirs and belles-lettres epigones of Defoe, just as Catherine was the more elegant and belles-lettres edition of Peter; just as her Italianate St. Petersburg was the rococo efflorescence of his Dutch-style naval base.

Defoe returned to the subject of Peter quite often in other books, notably in *The Complete English Gentleman*, where we are told, "He sought wisdom, thro' the whole world; he applyed for knowledge, in every branch of science. . . ." (p. 36) and, "It was his usual saying, that every cobbler that came but from Germany or Holland knew more than he did" (p. 27). When Peter came to the throne, there was no printing press in Moscow, and the boyars didn't want the one he forced on them. "Their best surgeons knew nothing of anatomy; their best astronomers knew nothing of eclipses; they had not a skeleton in the whole empire, except what be natural in their graves; their geographers had not a globe, their seamen not a compass (by the way they had no ships) even their physicians had no books . . . even their handicrafts had no tools; there was not a Russian clock-maker or watch-maker to be found in the whole empire. . . ." (p. 67).

And though Russian intellectuals in the nineteenth century necessarily had angrier and more complicated feelings about Peter than Defoe did, still the affirmative half of their dialectic followed the lines of this argument. There were moments in Tolstoy's life when he would have assented to this account of Peter, and even when he dissented, it remained a very important idea to him.

## Tolstoy's Adventures

Through much of his writing career, then, Tolstoy believed in the modern system and therefore in adventure; and even after he ceased to believe in the former, he was strongly drawn toward the latter. I will just mention, among his adventure tales, "A Prisoner in the Caucasus," "The Raid," "The Bear Hunt," and "Stories of My Dogs." Moreover, he planned a great novel about Russian history and national destiny, which would have contained elements of Cooper and even of Defoe. We find in his diary for March 3, 1877,[*] "In *Anna Karenina* I cherish the idea of the *family,* in *War and Peace,* in view of the war of 1812, the idea of the *people;* the central idea of my new book will be the *power of expansion* of the Russian people."

He saw this expansion in the constant migration of Russians to the new lands in the southeast, in southern Siberia, in the Belaya Reka region, in Turkestan, etc. "A great deal is heard about all this migration nowadays. We spent last summer in the Samara region, and the two of us drove to a Cossack settlement some fifteen miles from our Samara farm . . ." and met on the way a long procession of such migrants (p. 63). Just recently he'd heard of a hundred Tambov peasants going to Siberia on their own initiative; they finally found some abandoned land on the Manchurian border. "And so, although the land originally belonged to China, it became Russian soil, conquered not with blood and war, but by the agricultural strength of

[*]Copied into his wife's diary; see Sonia Tolstoy, *Diary of Tolstoy's Wife 1860–91.*

the Russian moujik. Occasionally the Manchurians attack them, but the Russians have built a fort and are able to protect themselves." This is in a sense a scene out of American experience which he is recording, and he is finding an inspiration for his new novel in a modern system story. On October 25, of the same year, he says this book's "main theme is the people and their strength, which reveals itself exclusively in agriculture." In Part II there will be a Russian Robinson Crusoe, who will settle on new land in the Samara Steppe. This could have been the great *serious* adventure tale. But that novel never got written; no doubt Tolstoy came to feel that "the strength of the Russian people" was a divisive theme, and that such strength was not and could not be manifested only in agriculture.

Nevertheless, even at the end of his life, Tolstoy wrote one of his finest adventure tales, *Hadji Murad;* again about the war in the Caucasus, but its sympathies directed against the Russians, or at least with the Chechens. Alexandra Tolstoy, in her *Life of My Father,* describes how Tolstoy worked on "How to Read the Gospels" and allowed himself also to write *Hadji Murad* as an indulgence. Thus in his diary for August 5, 1902, he says, "I have been writing on Hadji Murad, partly with pleasure, partly against the grain, and with shame."

Its origin is in a diary entry of 1896, about a thistle plant he saw. "There were three shoots on it: one was broken and a white, muddy flower hung from it; another was broken and splashed with mud, the stem was shattered and dirt-stained; the third shoot stuck on sideways; it was also dark with dust, but it was still alive and the centre of it was turning red. It reminded me of Hadji Murad. I'd like to write about it. It clings to life right up to the last, and it is the one thing in all the field, and somehow it has clung to it" (A. Tolstoy, *Tolstoy: A Life of My Father,* p. 371).

It is a passionate empathy with all living things that triggers this memory and this inspiration. That was a faculty which Tolstoy possessed in unusual degree. And it is connected with the values his art embodies, the worship of life. The thistle is a triumphant emblem of life surviving in spite of all difficulties—life, as distinct from beauty or goodness or anything else; and the same is true of the character Hadji Murad. And the fact that his art—and much modern art—is inseparable from life-worship, is the reason why the late Tolstoy (whose values were spiritual) was ashamed of writing the story.

In the introduction to the actual story he describes gathering flowers, and seeing the red kind called Tatar, always avoided by pickers because of its cruel thorns, and its toughness. This specimen took him five minutes to pluck, and then was too coarse for his nosegay. A little later he saw another such plant thrown away on a ploughed field, and he thought how destructive man is to other species.

" 'What a destructive creature is man, how many different creatures, how much growth he destroys to support his own life!' I thought, involuntarily striving to discover something living amid the black and lifeless fields." His attitude is very close to Lévi-Strauss's, if we make an equivalence between Tolstoy's "man" and the other's "European man" or "civilized man." When he sees the second Tatar thistle: "one of its arms lopped off, an eye put out, still it stood up, refusing to surrender to Man, the destroyer of its many brothers all around it. 'What energy!' I thought."

But all of this translates also into quite specific reference to the story he is going to tell. "Tatar" was a general name for all the savage tribes against whom the Russians made war in their expansion east. They were tough and cruel and too full of vitality to be sentimentalized, but as the empire expanded with its ploughed fields, these tribes were one by one subdued or slaughtered. One of them was the Caucasians (also called Circassians, or Chechens), against whom a Russian army was fighting in 1850, when Tolstoy joined it, and when Hadji Murad was a leading figure on the opposite side.

It is notable that Tolstoy wrote so often about this situation, rather than about, say, the Crimean War—apart from the reports he wrote at the time from Sebastopol. The Caucasian situation was explicitly imperialist—very like, in fact, the North-West frontier in India which Kipling wrote about—and that was the subject Tolstoy turned back to, time and time again. The main leader of the Caucasian resistance then was Shamil, a religious as well as military figure. In Tolstoy's story, Hadji Murad, having quarreled with Shamil, has to flee to the Russians for protection; we see him only when he arrives among the Russians; he dictates his life story, which is very bloody, at their request; he makes friends with Butler, a handsome officer in the Cossack regiment; finally he makes a suicidal attempt to return to his people, in order to save his family there, but is killed and decapitated.

Hadji Murad, the man and the story, is fierceness incarnate. The idea of a doomed rebellion, and the hero's position, vis-à-vis Shamil, roughly like Fergus's position vis-à-vis the Young Pretender, may remind us of Scott and his adaptation of the Black Prince motif. But the difference is that Tolstoy's story has no Waverley and consequently no Rose or Flora; nor, indeed, any plot, in the sense of the mild interests and satisfactions connected with Waverley himself. Tolstoy confronts us very directly with Hadji Murad, which has a much more shocking and sobering effect. But underneath and behind that sobriety is the ineluctable exhilaration of adventure. We identify with fierceness incarnate. This is a late-style adventure, closer to Kipling than to Scott. Fifty years after the event, and fifty years later in the history of the modern system, Tolstoy had to see imperialist war in more radical terms. To enjoy its excitements, one had to swallow blood, cruelty, and destruction.

## The Cossacks

But Tolstoy wrote *The Cossacks,* also about that war, at the beginning of his writing career, between 1852 and 1862. This *is* another Waverley story, with an author-representing central character called Olenin, who leaves Moscow because he feels his mind and his heart going to seed in the center of a civilization, and joins the Russian army in the Caucasus as an observer-participant. While there he meets some powerful excitements and severe challenges to his manhood; from an old Cossack hunter, Eroshka, a figure of vitality, freedom, boldness; from a beautiful Cossack girl, Maryanka, with whom Olenin falls in love but does not dare marry; and from Luka, a Cossack brave whom Maryanka does marry, and who represents in many other ways all that Olenin wants to be. At the end he goes back to Moscow, defeated but enriched by the experience, like Waverley. And the background is another doomed rising (of the Chechens); though there is less bloodshed here than in *Waverley.*

The novel is significantly autobiographical. There was an Eroshka (in real life Epishka) and a Maryanka (in real life Solomonida) and a Chechen brave called Sado, who made Tolstoy his *kunak* (comrade or blood-brother). Most significant, Tolstoy felt the challenges and promises of Cossack life just as Olenin felt them. He felt the cultural nostalgia we saw in Cooper; writing to his aunt about becoming Sado's *kunak*, he told her how ancient the custom was, something "by now" honored mostly in the memory.

At the same time, *The Cossacks* is very completely and straightforwardly a translation into the terms of Russian culture of the Scott-Cooper version of modernist adventure, and somewhat closer to Cooper's rendering. Tolstoy puts, for instance, a stress on guns and hunting, and takes an interest in geography and contemporary history, which is more like Cooper's. And Eroshka, though very unlike Natty Bumppo in his psychosexual type, and the intensity of his physical presence—which is rendered in terms of a smell of blood, sweat, and gunpowder—is nevertheless a version of the old hunter. One of the diagrams of tendency in the book is a triangle of emotional vectors, in which Olenin and Luka both aspire toward Eroshka, as rival heirs to his virtue.

The triangle is the same as one in *The Prairie,* though the tendency and the conflict are blurred in Cooper. (Captain Middleton and Paul Hover aspire to be Natty's heir.) But we also think of *Waverley.* Luka is a Black Prince of the Fergus MacIvor kind, in that he is the man of action whom the observer-participant yearns to be. We switch back to a Scott-comparison here, because Luka is not separated from Olenin by race, as Chingachgook is from Natty. Moreover, Maryanka is a heroine of the Flora type (with some touches of Marina/Malintzi); she embodies the wild and barbaric virtue of her race, which Olenin could only possess by possessing her. (This was a motif Conrad was to make much use of—Nina in *Almayer's Folly,* Jewel in *Lord Jim.* )[8] There is another triangle of vectors, with Luka and Olenin both aspiring to her.

Had the novel been completed (what we have is only Part I of three projected parts) it would have reminded us even more of *Waverley.* In Part II Maryanka was decisively to choose Luka over Olenin, but the two men were to go together up into the mountains to take part in the war there. In Part III Olenin was to return alone to marry Maryanka, but the marriage was to turn out badly, and he was to be murdered, either by her or by some rival for her favors. This is a rearrangement of Scott's scheme in *Waverley;* making Flora Fergus's beloved instead of his sister; and then—a more significant change but still true to the theme—ending the story tragically and not comically. Waverley–Olenin's attempt to assimilate the wildness of the Cossacks–Highlanders is here shown to be impossible and doomed to bring about disaster.

The important new idea which Tolstoy brings to the adventure is that of Nature—his idea being a much more metaphysical and psychological one than Scott's or Cooper's. Tolstoy's is even a religious idea and so more a kind of cult. (Tolstoy's beloved brother Nikolai, the day before his death, said, "Only one thing remains—the vague hope that there is in Nature, of which in the earth one will become a part, something which will abide and will be found.")

This is what gives so much more depth to the characterization of Olenin than there was to Waverley. Olenin's motivation for leaving Moscow, what he sees as he looks at the Cossack village, his desire for Maryanka, his excitement in the fighting, all this as much as his feeling for the actual forest is a cult of nature. It is an idea very well suited to the modernist adventure story, in which the thematic crux is the exchange of values between a more primitive and a more civilized culture.

But there was something else in Tolstoy which made him avoid some of the adventure possibilities of this story; at the end of Chapter 32, Olenin is awakened by the sergeant major and told that the company is leaving on a raid into the Chechen country. This raid lasts four days, and is the most considerable military operation described —except that it isn't described. The narration jumps ahead to Olenin's return from it. The paragraph that begins with the raid ends with, "Then Olenin sat all evening long on the porch staring at Maryanka, and the whole night, without a thought in his head, he aimlessly paced the yard" (p. 145). This makes *The Cossacks* into a love-adventure, which is to say, no adventure. The writing of the story took a long time, including some complete breaks, and Tolstoy was heading towards the domestic novel by the time he finished. He had committed himself to marriage, in life and letters.

Tolstoy was always serious, always spiritually ambitious—more than Defoe and Scott, for example. He aimed at greatness always, and however skeptical he might be of the received ideas of his time, he could not resist the pressure that pushed him away from the adventure and toward the domestic novel. He did resist the pressure to write about lower- and middle-class characters, as we saw, but he yielded to the fundamental teaching of literature-as-a-system; and in *War and Peace* wrote a masterpiece of the subordination of the adventure to the other form; and in *Anna Karenina* a masterpiece of the domestic novel at its purest.

Perhaps, however, he missed one opportunity, to make a masterpiece out of *The Cossacks*. The most striking feature of Tolstoy's treatment of that story is the one indicated by the title: his presentation of Cossack life. This is striking because so appropriate, skillful, and beautiful; but it was not original, in literary terms, for it is very like Scott's treatment of the Highlanders. It was a treatment already conventional in Russian literature; the Caucasus had been for Pushkin and Lermontov already the land of nature and of heroism. Russians in general held that, as Tolstoy said of the Chechens, "These people live as nature does; they die, are born, intermingle, give birth to children, fight, drink, eat, are happy and die again, and their lives are not conditioned, except as nature herself inexorably rules the sun, the grass, the animals, the trees, and them. They have no other laws" (A. Tolstoy, *The Cossacks*, p. 123). Nor does Tolstoy stress—and this was his opportunity—those features of the Cossacks that would have distinguished them from Scott's Highlanders; their double function as both examples of freedom and agents of discipline.

Those distinguishing features he does stress, or does allow to emerge, are those which align his picture with Cooper's. For the Russian situation was strikingly like the American in certain ways. The idea of the natural or primitive that was represented for Scott by the Highlanders, for Cooper and Tolstoy was split into two figures that were at war with each other: the Cossacks versus the Chechens, the frontiersmen against the Indians. The Cossacks were fighting for the Russian state against the Chechens, though they were not part of the Russian army, and were in fact resentful and scornful of Russian individuals—seeing them as overcivilized. When Olenin joins the Russian army as observer-participant, he faces three social groups, of which the Cossacks are the middle term; they are something of a stepping stone for his imagination toward the fiercer and unimaginable primitivism of the Chechens. Perhaps they are not so much a stepping stone as an arrow pointing the way, for some Cossacks have already adopted Chechen ways, particularly the young men, and Luka and Eroshka have Chechen friends; respectable families like Maryanka's aspire to be Russian, but the young people with whom Olenin is concerned aspire to be Chechen. This is of course very like frontiersmen's feelings for the Indians (Natty's heart is with the Indians) and their *being* half-Indian, half-white. The situation is very emblematic of imperialism; Kipling's heroes too intensely admire the tribes they war against—Stalky on the North-West frontier is said to have *become* a Sikh—and are very uneasy with the Englishmen they meet in London. But not even Tolstoy took full imaginative advantage of the situation.

Of course, neither Scott nor Cooper offered him a good model. Scott's Highlanders were more like the Chechens than the Cossacks, and Cooper's frontiersmen were depicted stiffly and distortedly. While in Russian fiction, Gogol's Cossacks were almost purely picturesque. Tolstoy portrays his Cossacks close up with wonderful vividness, but fails to find the larger historical perspective they deserve, and the sterner historical seriousness that would go with that.

Thus the greatest interest Tolstoy has for us here does not derive from his artistic success with the genre of adventure. Judged from that point of view, *The Cossacks* is charming and even distinguished, but not a major achievement. Its greatest interest is of the kind it shares with *Robinson Crusoe*—the importance of the facts (including the myths) it engages our imaginations with. Tolstoy's achievement is to persuade us that there is something out there—not in *The Cossacks* but in the Cossacks—which has fixed his attention and so deserves to fix ours. The power of his treatment lies in its historical truth. This is an important imaginative context for not only his own work but all adventure fiction. And it is important in more than one way. Tolstoy's resemblance to Cooper also brings out the *international* character of modern system imperialism. This is not an American or a Russian, but a world-historical phenomenon. The Cossacks reveal to us the tendency so mutedly expressed in the frontiersmen of America and the transoceanic empires.

The American frontier too was advanced westward by the means of bands of *men;* men on their own, that is; as were the frontiers of the empires of European powers.[9] In the case of France, we find the Foreign Legion, who won Vietnam for France between 1865 and 1885; in the case of England, the Canadian Mounted Police, who rode west from Winnipeg in 1873; and the young pioneers Rhodes sent north in 1890 to occupy Mashonaland. But there were fewer of them than of the Cossacks, and they counted for less, in the running of the homeland and the character of the government. It seemed a metaphor when Marx or Herzen called the African troops of Napoleon III "Cossacks." But it was more than a metaphor, and it meant more than Marx intended. It meant not only that Napoleon III's France was getting to be like Russia, but that Russia was only like France—her Cossacks had always had their counterparts in Western Europe. Russia was in many ways—in its relation to China, the Caucasus, Tibet, the Tatars—culturally WASP. It was the agent of expansion of the modern system, in its relation to the rest of the world, although it was the patient in its relation to Western Europe.

## The Cossacks

Their origin seems to go back to Muscovy's rise to power in Russia, when the national enemy were the Mongol states ruled by the successors to Genghis Khan. Mongol or Tatar parties raided Russian settlements by night, bringing baskets to carry off babies, and taking slaves to sell to the Turks. So some groups of "free" Tatars sold their services to the Russians as border guards to defend them against these raids. Then Russians who disliked settlement life moved out into the "wild" or "free" country to do the same. At first they lived out there in the summer months only, returning to the settlements in the winter. But then the authorities exerted tighter controls, and these frontiersmen had to choose —and those who chose to live like Cossacks all the time were of course the fiercer ones. The first leader of Russian Cossacks was probably Ivan Russo, who is mentioned in 1468. By 1570 there were seventy-three watchposts along the frontier manned by such men, who were granted land and hunting rights in return for their services. These were called "town Cossacks" because of their comparatively organized condition.*

They were in flight from the taxation and legalism of the settlements. From 1500 on Russian peasants had been fleeing the imposition of authority by the central government. As Muscovy established

*See Philip Longworth, *The Cossacks.*

its empire over the rest of Russia, it gave the nobles imperial rights over their peasants.

According to Wallerstein, serfdom was introduced into periphery states like Russia just as it was being ended in core states like England. The bonded peasant class was created in Western Europe between 1100 and 1300, but in Russia between 1500 and 1700. They remained bound. The last serfs were emancipated in France in 1791, but in Russia nearly all the peasants remained serfs until 1861. Feudal dues and duties increased decade by decade, and it was as late as 1581 that the decree was passed forbidding peasants to leave the village they were born in—tying them to a particular landowner. The Cossacks were those who escaped that process, from a variety of motives. They were strongly influenced by the Tatars they fought against. They used the horsetail standard of the Mongols (Genghis Khan's standard) and mated with Tatar women, whom they often abducted. For many of them, marriage was not a part of life. One of the famous settlements, the Zaporozhian Sech, was officially bachelor, and women were not supposed to enter it. They used Tatar words, like *ataman,* for their leader, *esaul* for his lieutenant, and *yassak* for tribute. They called farming a kind of slavery, and promulgated decrees against it. The plough was for them a mark of bondage. The word Cossack itself, *kasak,* is a Turkic word used since the tenth century by the Mongols to mean adventurer.

They were not, then, an ethnic group, in any strict sense; in a loose sense they were an ideological group, with an ideology of freedom. Their economic activities were to sell to the settlements the fish, fur, and hides they had caught, plus honey and wax, in return for grain and cloth, nails, and lead, powder and guns. This must remind us of the American frontiersmen; and it is typical of many similarities that when attacked on the march, the Cossacks formed their carts into a triangle (called a tabor) and fired upon the Tatars, who circled the formation on horseback, galloping and shooting arrows. (Longworth says the Cossacks were closer to our image of cowboys than were the real cowboys.) But of course their main activity was hunting and fighting; the boys were trained to gallop, to stalk, to swim horses across streams, etc.

Of all the companies of Cossacks, that of the Terek—the one Tolstoy wrote about—was generally considered the most romantic. Alexandre Dumas had written about them, in his *Adventures in the*

*Caucasus.* They had adopted the Chechen cloaks, Chechen war cries, Chechen riding style, just as American frontiersmen adopted the Indians'. And the situation of their lives was as adventurous and romantic as any adventure-romancer would wish; bare-chested, shaven-headed Circassian braves, who one day came to the Cossack village to trade, the next day lurked in the reeds by the river to kill. The Cossacks were Old Believers—and thus religiously too they were in resistance to modern Russia—and they were defending a narrow strip of land along the Terek river, fifty miles long but only about 700 yards wide. They were fighting against mountain tribes first aroused to a holy war against Russia by Kazi Mullah in 1829, who did not capitulate until 1859.[10] Indeed, Russia had annexed Georgia in 1801, and the mountain tribes had been fighting sporadically ever since then. The conquest of the mountains had been begun by General Ermolov in 1816, but it was not easy. General Velgaminov wrote, "The mounted natives are very superior in many ways both to our regular cavalry and to the Cossacks; they can ride between dawn and sunset a hundred miles. They are born on horseback, their weapons, carefully selected, are private property, and kept in excellent condition" (W. Laqueur, *Guerilla,* p. 73).

But how did the Cossacks feel, that they should be attacking the Chechens on behalf of Russia, while their sympathies ran as much in the opposite direction? This was in fact a very typical situation for them. They had always been the advance guard of the Russian empire, Russia's frontiersmen (and also shock troops and arm of terror), but they were also rebels against the settled life of citizenship; they imposed the discipline of civilization on primitive tribes, while at the same time in flight from that discipline themselves. They played the same role as Natty and Daniel Boone, only armed to the teeth and organized into hordes of thousands.

Politically, they stood for freedom, as far as their own social organization goes. Each host, or *voisk,* governed itself by means of a general assembly, called a *krug,* and theoretically the land was communally owned. In the seventeenth century there were about ten thousand Don Cossacks, egalitarian and libertarian, unruly and marauding. And they saw themselves, and were seen by others, as free; singing and dancing were a part of their image; and even free-thinking writers were praised as "Cossacks." They were mythical heroes for the rest of Russia, embodying the myth of freedom and expansion, just as the frontiersmen were for America. Pushkin's Decembrist friend, Ryleev, wrote a famous ballad, "Voynarovsky," about a Byronic Cossack hero, the heir to Mazeppa (the Cossack rebel against Peter the Great). Herzen referred to himself as a Cossack, and to his circle of friends as a Cossack brotherhood, because of their love of freedom. At the same time, he referred to the troops who put down the revolution of 1848 in France as "African Cossacks."

This is surely the most vivid example of the anthropoemia Lévi-Strauss discusses, and shows how that could serve the purposes of an imperialist power. For seen in terms of their relations with the outside world, the Cossacks were the agents of political discipline. In the 1650s the tsarist government created a military community of five regiments of Cossacks around Kharkov; other such settlements came later, and the Cossacks were pressed to conform to that pattern. (The government's control of ammunition gave them leverage over the Cossacks.) In 1654 the Zaporozhian Cossacks, who had been employed by the king of Poland as border guards, against, amongst others, the Russians, transferred their services to the tsar. This was a very important step in the development of Russian power in Europe, and brought, as its first fruits, the acquisition of the Ukraine. But even more important was the expansion of Russia toward the East, which was also the work of Cossacks.

The Cossack leader Ermak had led 540 men across the Urals in 1581, and the four hundred of them who reached Sibir there defeated a force of two thousand Tatars. This is a story like that of Cortes and Raleigh, in date and historical significance, and in frequency of retelling. (It is, incidentally, a subject Tolstoy devoted a story to.) They were sent out by a rich trading company, the Stroganovs, and they won partly because they had guns. Ermak's success advanced the Russian frontier, at one point, four thousand miles east. By 1600 a million skins were being sent back to Moscow every year. Whole areas were hunted out in twenty or thirty years. Ten percent of the state's revenue was derived from that trade, and foreigners were rigidly debarred from it. (The Cossacks acted as tribute collectors from the trappers, when they weren't the trappers themselves.) Their advance is comparable in many ways to the American advance west, but by 1630, the Russians had settlements on the Pacific coast, while the Americans had only reached the Appalachians. And the Cossacks here were the advance guard of the modern system—culturally WASP.

In the eighteenth century, however, they developed a loyalty to the tsars in particular. The government used them for military purposes, expansive or repressive. In 1792 Catherine the Great created the Kuban host, to protect and develop the North-West of the Caucasus, recently taken from Turkey. In 1867 a Seven Rivers *Voisk* was created to do the same for Central Asia. During the nineteenth century there were twelve main groups; by 1900, 7 million Cossacks were estimated to live on 230,000 square miles, and to provide the Russian army with soldiers, mostly cavalry. In peacetime they formed 45 percent of Russia's cavalry, in wartime 70 percent. Every Cossack male had to serve in the army twenty years. Napoleon called the Cossacks a disgrace to the human race, but dreamed for a time of creating a similar force in France.

Repressively they were used, for instance, against Poland, after the annexation of that country. In 1798 60,000 Poles took up arms, mostly pikes and scythes, with a few muskets; and the same happened in 1831 and 1863, when the Russian superiority was ten to one. Polish veterans of those aborted revolutions went to fight in revolutions elsewhere: Mieroslavski in Baden and Sicily; Dembinski and Bern against Austria in 1848; Mickiewicz in the Roman Republic. This was the kind of history that shaped, for instance, Conrad's feeling about Russia and about politics in general. The Cossacks played a very sinister role in that history, and—inside Russia—against Jews and students and striking workers.

On the other hand, there were Cossack revolts within Russia in the name of freedom. For instance, in the seventeenth century, the revolt led by Xmelnitski; in the eighteenth those led by Stenka Razin and Pugachev. These men were heroes of liberty to nineteenth-century revolutionaries in Russia like Bakunin and Nechaev. For that matter, Byron had made a hero out of Mazeppa, the Hetman of the Ukraine who rebelled against Peter the Great. And gradually their loyalty to the tsar wore out at the end of the nineteenth century, when they were used more and more against striking workers and protesting students. They played a major part in defeating the Revolution of 1905, but soon after they began to refuse to fire or to charge against certain kinds of rebels, and in 1917 they effectively deserted the tsar.

The Cossacks' is the great story which explains so much—not only about Russia—and which challenges and denies as well as explains; and yet it did not get taken into literature.* And behind the Cossacks themselves, a great body of Russian people, mostly peasants, moved east. Migration has, as we know, an important connection with adventure writing. And there was, in Russia, an ever-mounting drive eastward. Between 1894 and 1914, five million migrated east across the Urals, more than in the whole three hundred years preceding.

In his *Survey of Russian History* B. H. Sumner says, "Throughout Russian history one dominating theme has been the frontier; the theme of the struggle for the mastering of the natural resources of an untamed country, expanded into a continent by the ever-shifting movement of the Russian people and their conquest of and intermingling with other peoples" (p. 9). Sumner draws several parallels between Russian history and American and English imperialism. The Caucasian mountains were the equivalent of India's North-West Frontier; and Gogol's *Taras Bulba* is like Parkman's *Oregon Trail.* The agriculturalists continually advanced against forest-and-plains nomads, and the edge of the wave was the meeting with savagery—"a return to primitive conditions on a continually advancing frontier."

As in Anglo-Saxon imperial history, part of the motive power was mechanical, part political, part military. In 1886 the Trans-Caspian Railway reached to Merv, in 1888 to Samarkand, in 1898 to Herat. But there was also a Russian equivalent to the American doctrine of manifest destiny, preached by Prince Ukhtemsky. And Russia had acquired Vladivostok in 1860, and most of Central Asia between 1864 and 1878; for instance, in 1866, General Romanovsky defeated 40,000 Bokharans and took Khodjent, and in 1871 a part of Chinese Turkestan was seized. Then during the Boxer Rebellion in China in 1900, Russia acquired Manchuria, and during the Boer War, while England was otherwise occupied, Russia pushed ahead in Persia, Turkey, and Afghanistan. Here we touch on imperialism in the conventional sense.

Intellectually, Russian imperialism used the same racist and cultural apologetics as did the English and French. The explorer Przhevalsky wrote in 1887, "These poor Asiatics look to the advance of Russian power with a firm conviction that its advent is synonymous

---

*Sholokhov's novels come closest to a full-scale treatment.

with the commencement of a happier era, a life of greater security for themselves." And the philosopher Solovev wrote in 1890 that inferior races must either submit or disappear. Let us take the explorer as a final example of the historical hero, to stand beside Olenin, and Tolstoy's other heroes, to define them by contrast.

## Przhevalsky

Because Tolstoy was so divided in his sympathies, the enemy as much as the celebrant of adventure, we cannot naturally associate him with the historical heroes of his time. If we look for an equivalent to Andrew Jackson and Cooper's fascination by him, the best we can do is Peter the Great, who aroused Tolstoy's hostility rather than his fascination. And though Tolstoy was as much the historian as Scott, in *War and Peace,* we cannot associate him with the writing of nationalist or racist history in nineteenth-century Russia. (There was plenty of both; the myth of the coming of the Varangians to rule the Slavs, and thus to found the Russian state, is the same Teutonic race-myth as we found in nineteenth-century America.)

We do of course associate Tolstoy, the adventure-writer, with the war in the Caucasus. But he was too young to have known Ermolov, the conquistador who captured Pushkin's imagination; while Paskevich, the general who succeeded Ermolov, was not a heroic figure. Moreover, the conquest of the Caucasus was completed in 1859, and during Tolstoy's maturity Russian imperialism was directed toward Central Asia; under the direction of the minister of war, Miliutin, who came to power in 1861 and remained there until 1881. He avoided trouble with Turkey (which was under the protection of the European powers) but was aggressive in Turkestan. He advanced the careers of General Kaufman, the dashing conqueror of that territory, and later its viceroy; and of General Skobelev, whose victory at Gek Tepe excited many people, including Dostoevsky. The last words of his *Diary of a Writer* were, "Yes, hail the victory of Gek Tepe! Hail Skobelev and his soldiers, and the eternal memory of the heroic knights who were 'withdrawn from the rolls.' We shall inscribe them on our rolls." (E. C. Thaden, *Conservative Nationalism in 19th Cen-*

*tury Russia,* p. 85.) There we see Dostoevsky, though not congeni-
tally of a military temperament, succumbing to military excitement
under the influence of nationalist ideas.

But we must seek a more appropriate figure to set beside Tolstoy
amongst those who represent more specifically modernist forms of
expansion, who represent (though equivocally) the forces of enlightenment, the explorers. The figure of Nikolai Przhevalsky (1838–
1888) is an interesting one for us, partly because of a specific resemblance between him and Stanley, but more generally because he
represents in Russian terms forces we are familiar with in English
history. Donald Rayfield, in his *Dream of Lhasa,* describes
Przhevalsky as explorer, adventurer, zoologist, and conquistador.
Though he despised China and the East, he also loathed European
society—"The breath of mankind is more terrible and more destructive than all the misfortunes of nature." Though, like so many nineteenth-century boys, he dreamed as a child of being another Livingstone, his adult temperament was in fact much closer to Stanley's.

His father was of a Polish Cossack family, so he inherited something of that tradition. But in 1863 he helped to crush the Polish
rising against tsarist rule. He belonged to the military and ruling
caste, which took its leading part in the modernization of the country;
his stepbrother directed the extension of the Trans-Caspian Railway
to Samarkand—a significant step in the Russification of the East.

As a boy, Przhevalsky (like Stanley or Clive) hated school, loved
hunting, and read only books on travel. He joined the Russian army
in 1855, but still hoped to explore "the black heart of Africa," like
Livingstone. In 1862 he published his first book, *Memoirs of a Sportsman,* in the aristocratic genre which Aksakov, Turgenev, and Tolstoy
had made famous. And gradually he established his status as an
explorer.

His personality conformed to one of the more distorted adventur-
er-models, least like domestic novel heroes in general, and Tolstoy's
in particular. He was an enormous eater, especially of sweets. He took
no interest in women, didn't drink, and went to bed at nine. He
preferred boys as companions, and imposed a playfully sadistic relationship upon them. In 1866, when he began his explorations in
eastern Siberia, he took with him a young companion, who had to
promise implicit obedience in advance. When the boy got homesick,
he was sent home in disgrace. In 1867 Przhevalsky took another

sixteen-year-old with him into the Siberian jungle, armed with twenty-five pounds of gunpowder, fifteen pounds of shot, and so on. He was passionately fond of guns, and dazzled the natives with displays of marksmanship. But he was also passionately fond of Nature and of natural science, and he returned from this trip with 130 new species of flowering plants from Lake Hanka.

Later he went still farther afield, and got to Peking in 1870. He liked the company of the Buryat Mongol Cossacks whom he employed—they were horsemen of freedom. "Like a free bird in a cage, I cannot get on with this 'civilization,' where everyone is first and foremost a slave to social life" (Rayfield, *The Dream of Lhasa*, p. 187). But for non-European civilizations he had even less sympathy. "In my opinion, only the rifles and cannons of the Europeans can do any good here," he wrote from China. "Missionary preaching, in which Europe puts its hopes, is the voice of one crying in the wilderness" (Rayfield, p. 52). On this trip he (like another Connecticut Yankee) won a reputation among the natives as invulnerable, and also as a miracle doctor, because of the cures he worked with quinine.

His great desire was to get to Lhasa, for official Russia during the last quarter of the nineteenth century hoped to create a satellite kingdom in Tibet. In 1872 he set off on an expedition there, with a Martini machine gun, two Schneiders, thirteen revolvers, and a quarter of a ton of ammunition; and a rich store of trifles, such as mirrors, magnets, kaleidoscopes, and picture postcards of actresses. He reported to the general staff that, "A thousand of our soldiers would be enough to subdue all Asia from Lake Baykal to the Himalayas. . . . Here the exploits of Cortes can still be repeated" (p. 69). He wrote a three-volume book about this expedition before setting out on the next; and that was the pattern of his life; a journey, lectures and a book, another journey. He had to give lectures and go to dinners when he was in St. Petersburg, collecting funds for his next trip, but hating to do so, and always fell sick there.

In 1876 he again set out for Tibet (which he never reached) with two new teenage companions, whom he had jovially promised would get thrashed side by side whenever that was necessary. He won their devotion; in 1928 one of them recalled how "the deep gaze of his strict, handsome blue eyes seemed to penetrate right into your soul" (p. 154). He always praised his own Spartan education, because it had hardened him, and that was what he promised his boys—that he would harden them. On this last trip he took a new £100 Lancaster Express rifle, which he called Lyan, and which he fired and polished every day of his life till his death.

Such was Russia's explorer-conquistador. He was admired by men of letters too. Chekhov wrote an obituary, and said, "One Przhevalsky or one Stanley is worth twelve polytechnics and a thousand good books. Their loyalty . . . etc. . . . makes them in the eyes of the people heroes who personify a higher moral force" (p. 203). What Tolstoy thought, we don't know, but we can be sure he would have understood and admired, during the expansive moments in his own development, and would have bitterly condemned in the other moments. Przhevalsky embodied one force in the dialectic of tendency in Russia and in Tolstoy. That conflict was in some ways fiercer in them than in England and Tolstoy's equivalents there, just because of Russia's position on the periphery of the modern system. Rebecca West, in her life of St. Augustine, draws some interesting parallels between that saint's peripheral and provincial relation to the Roman Empire, and Tolstoy's to what we call the modern system. Tolstoy, like St. Augustine, was on the periphery, and he loved and envied what he saw at the center; but he also identified himself with the opposite to all that.

After *War and Peace* and *Anna Karenina*, no one was able to drive Tolstoy out of the center of literature-as-a-system in Russia, by attacks such as those on Defoe, Scott, and Cooper. (Though there were, and are, savage claims that he *ought not* to have been a great novelist, holding such opinions as he did.) But there was a comparable contemporary criticism of the early work, *The Cossacks*, before he became so established. This was written by Eugenie Tur, a highly respected novelist and critic of the time. She described Tolstoy's novel as "a poem in which the praise is sung, not by a commonplace talent, but a very real one, of daring prowess, thirst for blood and booty, man-hunts, the heartlessness of a beast-like savage. Side by side with this beast-savage is the abased, disparaged, broken, debauched representative of civilized society. . . . The author is at great pains to prove that savages are magnificent and happy, and cultivated people are low, petty, and unhappy" (A. Tolstoy, *Tolstoy*, p. 165). This is somewhat different from the attacks on Defoe and Swift, because the critic does not deny Tolstoy's talent; but just for that reason her ideological thrust—the thrust of literature's criticism of the adventure tale—is brought out. Tolstoy is said to betray the cause of civilization; we might interpret that to mean that he betrays the Brahmin caste of writers. (In Kipling's case, the critics felt the same, but made more of purely literary deficiencies, too.)

The conscience of later Russian literature, in the form of the writers of the 1860s, like Pisarev and Dobroliyubov, made to Tolstoy similar reproaches. He accepted the challenge. He told everyone he did not want to be "a writer"; and, as we have seen, he declared his inability and unwillingness to write like a bourgeois. He wrote like and for his own caste, the military and aristocratic. (A similar defiance can be seen in modern American novelists who have been struck by the claims of adventure—Hemingway, Mailer, Faulkner.) Then he wrote two of the greatest serious novels the world has; and then he repudiated literature altogether.

And behind all his shifts of stance, which have often been condemned as uneasy egotism, competitiveness, desire to be different, lay internecine struggles of sympathy and tendency in his nature, set off by the dialectic of the modern system.

# VII

## *Popular Literature*

## *and Children's Literature*

T OLSTOY gives us the sense—proper to high culture and especially to art—that he is questioning and testing whatever he describes; both the modern system, and the adventures of its expansion. Now we must look to narratives and discussions which seem not to test but to advertise their values, which work at a lower artistic and cultural level.

Turning to popular literature will bring out the importance of the how-to-do-it strain of adventure, the Defoe/merchant-caste strain, which gets overshadowed by the chivalric romance when we restrict our attention to works of literary value (serious art being reactionary, and often allied to the aristocracy) but which was very powerful at the popular level. That strain of feeling was also more powerful in nonfiction than in even "democratic" fiction, because art at its purest recoils from predominant truisms, and perhaps especially from mercantile ones. It is in popular biographies and advice books that Defoe's adventurer lived on and inspired others, not in brilliant novels.

Books of this kind had been appearing ever since Defoe's time, though they are meagerly represented in the histories of literature. I have mentioned one or two eighteenth-century writers like Dilworth; there were the stories of the sea and sailors; and of course there was the unending sequence of reissues and adaptations of *Robinson Crusoe.* But in the nineteenth century, this literature changed its character somewhat, as did more serious literature, in response to changing cultural forces, and also found new forms of expression. In the first half of this chapter, then, I shall not be tracing the development of fictional motifs, or evoking the historical background that gave those motifs resonance, but categorizing the culture heroes of the time—those that were in effect variants on the adventurer theme, and reinforcements of that idea. In the second half I shall describe motifs in the children's and popular literature of the time, or that part of it that was adventurous.

My discussion in the other chapters is restricted to writers of first-class intelligence and sensibility. Even Cooper, though far from being a great novelist, was a man of great intelligence. Since we are dealing with a cultural image as it got expressed in literature, and dealing with it in a literary way, it was necessary to choose material one can respect from that point of view. But it is necessary also to remember the other expressions of that image, less respectable and substantial from that point of view, but as effective or more so as a cultural influence. (For evidence of that effectiveness I rely on sales figures; no one seems to know what happens to books once bought —what they do inside the reading audience's heads.)

First of all, the work of Samuel Smiles, who was born in 1812, and became famous in 1859 with a book called *Self-Help,* which sold 25,000 copies in its year of publication, and 250,000 by 1900. It was translated into nearly every European language, and several Indian ones, plus Japanese, Arabic, and Turkish. In Italy there was an edition which substituted examples of self-help from Italian history for those British anecdotes which Smiles had chosen—anecdotes which made up nine-tenths of his book. This book was subtitled "Illustrations of Conduct and Perseverance," and it promised in effect to explain the secret of the superior energy and success of the Anglo-Saxons, their superior adaptation to the modern system. The *Revue des Deux Mondes* review took it as that, and only feared that Frenchmen's chauvinist prejudice might deny them access to this new source of moral energy. In his *Autobiography,* Smiles said that he wrote it to illustrate PERSEVERANCE, the great word of George Stephenson, the railway engineer.

Smiles was a Scotsman, a Utilitarian, and something of a radical in early life. Not an adventurer, then, but something of a Puritan. (He was a friend of Ebenezer Elliott, the Corn Law Rhymer of Sheffield.) And what this book teaches is how to acquire, by making a cult of these examples of great men and great actions, the standard virtues of Victorian England. What those are is perhaps sufficiently indicated by the titles of his later books: *Character,* 1871, *Thrift,* 1875, and *Duty,* 1880. They contain much warning against drink, and praise of savings banks; but basically these are collections of anecdotes about great men, noble boys, and Mothers (no need for an honorific for *them*). Some of the men most often cited are Washington, Wallerstein, Wellington, and Scott—a list somewhat equivalent to Defoe's list of Protestant heroes. Cobbett is described as the typical Englishman in character, and contrasted with Herder and Fichte; he was coarse and vulgar, compared with such Continental intellectuals, but had a strong undercurrent of poetry in his nature, and the tenderest regard for the character of women; though anything but refined, he was a true Englishman—pure, temperate, self-denying, industrious, vigorous, and energetic.

In the intellectual line, the greatest man who ever lived was Newton. (This is what Defoe and the Encyclopaedists said, but it's worth recalling that Swift dismissed Newton as a mechanic; Smiles is clearly on Defoe's side—the Encyclopaedists' side—in the Swift-Defoe battle.) More controversial choices of exemplars of virtue, but characteristic of Smiles, are Savonarola and Grace Darling, the lifeboat heroine. Both of these are puritan, and in their different ways, modernist figures. On the other side, Goethe, though a great poet, is not a man to copy, because he was amoral and an aesthete. Smiles has his suspicions of art, and warns us against certain kinds of literature— the leprous book, the scrofulous book, and even the giggling book. (Petronius? Pope? Nabokov?)

Considerably more interesting are his *Lives of the Engineers,* which began with *The Life of George Stephenson,* the great railway pioneer, who lived from 1781 to 1848. Smiles complained that history had been monopolized by kings and warriors and war, and claimed attention for engineers, the heroes of peace. Some phrases from the English reviews will indicate the kind of interest this biography has. "Few romances possess so strong an interest as this life, so brave, so simple, so strenuous in its faith . . . the true history of a working man." Stephenson was a true Victorian hero, and his rise from poverty to fame and fortune was felt to be adventure in the best sense—something in competition with, though not in hostility to, literal adventure in the Crusoe sense. "We see the vast achievements and the epic story of this age of ours more than half comprised in the feats of its strongest and most successful worker . . . we may designate him a hero . . . To young men faltering, it gives lessons which should supply fresh vigour. The continuous effort, the persistent valour, the daring ingenuity, and ever-active intellect of this collier boy . . ." Crusoe's virtues are seen at work in a somewhat different setting.

Smiles's importance is that he was so typical of nineteenth-century opinion. It is easy to recognize in his idea of manliness a vulgarized version of Emerson's, and indeed of other Victorian moralists. Stephenson was a *man;* he hated foppery and frippery above all things; he didn't drink, but ran and wrestled, and above all, worked. Emerson in fact, as Smiles tells us, said it was worth crossing the Atlantic just to meet Stephenson, he had such native force of character and intellect.

Smiles connects the cult of manliness, again in no unique way, with the cult of machinery. The ideas of work and workman subsume both. "There is indeed a peculiar fascination about an engine, to the intelligent workman who watches and feeds it. It is almost sublime in its untiring industry and quiet power; capable of performing the most gigantic work, yet so docile that a child's hand may guide it" (p. 28). Such a workman often speaks of his machine "with glowing admiration." All the improvements to machinery have come from workmen, not from scientists or philosophers. "This daily contemplation of the steam engine, and the sight of its steady action, is an education of itself to the ingenious and thoughtful workman." Defoe, I want to suggest, would have assented, would almost certainly have come to some such judgment, had he lived in the nineteenth century. It is a suggestive crystallization of the technocratic idea, which was powerful all through the century, though it rarely reached high levels of expression, literarily.

It figured largely in Mark Twain's life, however (his experience with the Paige type-setting machine constitutes a sardonic comment on the last sentence quoted), and he developed it literarily in *Connecticut Yankee* and other stories. It was also quite brilliantly expressed in fiction by Kipling and Wells; and commented on by Henry Adams, in "The Virgin and the Dynamo." The cult of the engineer may be said to have replaced in the nineteenth century Defoe's eighteenth-century cult of the merchant, as the former came to seem more the hero of peace, constructiveness, and the modern system.

Smiles's later *Lives of the Engineers* are particularly interesting for us because, alongside the biographies, they include histories of particular cities from a point of view very close to Defoe's, and continue the imaginative work he did in *The Tour.* We are shown England from a modern system point of view. Thus, in the Introduction we are told that England *is* not fertile—it has been *made* fertile by its industry, its canals, and other works of its engineers and improvers (p. 74). This work is moreover quite new. Not long ago, our wool was made into cloth in Flanders, our mines dug by Germans, our windmills built by the Dutch, and so on. Our apparent luck is based on our self-help—and will last only as long as our virtue does. This is exactly the approach Defoe took in his *Tour,* and his *Essay on Projects,* and Smiles emphasizes exactly what Defoe emphasized. He tells us for instance that the roads recently built in the Highlands of Scotland have had a moral influence. Telford, the engineer in charge, called the road-building a Working Academy, which turned out eight hundred improved workmen every year, and he meant improved as citizens too. (The image, and the tone, are very close to Twain's "factory of men" in *Connecticut Yankee.*) The change this road-building has made to Scotland can be measured in the fact that back in the 1745 Rebellion, when the district of Balmoral was remote from civilization, a whole regiment of Jacobite rebels was raised there, in a district "where *now* our Queen is so beloved."

Volume I is mostly about James Brindley, who built his first canal in 1761, but it also gives an account of Manchester in 1740. Volume II is mostly about Rennie and Smeaton—the latter built his first lighthouse in 1759—but it also gives a history of docks and bridges, and of the pirates who flourished before these modernizations. Volume III is mostly about Telford and Scotland; and it is notable how many of these men were Scots. Volume IV is about Watt and Boulton—Watt's first steam engine was built in 1766, and Arkwright's spinning jenny was built three years later; but also about

Birmingham. Thus these four volumes are a history of England during its Industrial Revolution, complete with exempla and heroes, exactly what Defoe wanted, and very like what Defoe produced in that line.

In *Self-Help* Smiles also took many examples of heroism from the suppression of the Indian Mutiny, which had only just occurred; and in *Duty* he praised Sir Charles Napier, John and Henry Lawrence, and Outram, as military heroes of the Indian Service. This gives us the cue to put that kind of Victorian hero beside Smiles's engineers; such kinds of men surround and support figures like Stanley—perhaps the most famous Victorian adventurer—in a cultural pantheon. The Indian soldiers are not Cortes or Clive types, military conquerors on the grand scale. They are suitable heroes for merchants, and their allies in the modern world system. But they assimilate as much of the conquistador material as could be assimilated into a Crusoe form.

As our example of the Indian hero let us take the Lawrence brothers, and their work in the Punjab in the mid-nineteenth century. They administered this province, after England took it away from the Sikhs in 1848, and made it the showpiece of British India. It was 74,000 square miles, of which the population was only one-fifth Sikh, though they were dominant. The British built the Grand Canal of the Punjab, nearly 250 miles long; and in four years built 3,000 miles of road, and surveyed 5,000 more, that was to be the Grand Trunk Road which Kipling celebrated.

The Lawrences were a Scots-Irish military family, very poor and in most senses underprivileged. John was the sixth son and eighth child, and said that at school "I was flogged every day of my life, except one, and then I was flogged twice" (Bosworth-Smith, *Life of Lord Lawrence*, p. 15). But it must have been a ruling-caste training place, for there were other boys at the school who were to become Indian heroes—besides the Lawrence brothers themselves. There was, for instance, Lord Gough, later to be the victor of Chillianwallah and conqueror of Gujerat. It was a school like Kipling's United Services College, in effect. These poor but ruling-caste Ulstermen (like but unlike the Ulstermen prominent on the American frontier) provided much of England's imperialist strength.

Bosworth-Smith's characterization of John Lawrence in his official biography is particularly interesting. Of Herculean physique, we are told, he had the cut of the Jats he ruled, with their handsome prominent features and tall bony frames; and the Jats are said to be descended from the ancient Goths. There was no ounce of superfluous fat upon John Lawrence, and he could hold a cannonball at arm's length. His friends, we are told, called him Oliver, after Cromwell, "the greatest and most downright and God-fearing of Englishmen" (p. 100). It was of course Carlyle's *Heroes and Hero-Worship* essay on Cromwell that they and Bosworth-Smith were thinking of. And the latter's whole account draws heavily on Carlyle's value-images.[1]

Lawrence was brave and strong and rough as a giant, but tender as a woman and simple as a child. He was heroically simple; he had the rough humor, the boisterous pranks, the wild spirit of adventure we associate with the Norwegian troll. When the rugged lineaments and deep furrows of his grand countenance are described, Bosworth-Smith quotes Milton's lines describing Satan. But the Satanic associations could be misleading. Lawrence was above all things a moral hero. Smiles says, in *Self-Help*, that Delhi was taken and India saved during the Mutiny by the personal character of Sir John Lawrence. His eye glared terribly when he saw anything mean or cowardly or wrong. They called him King John on the frontier. He was made Viceroy in 1864, and came home a peer in 1869, one of the great Victorian heroes.

Comparing the Lawrence brothers, Bosworth-Smith (a schoolmaster at Harrow) categorized John as Scots in character, Henry as Irish. The latter was, it seems, the more imaginative, the gentler, the more literary. He married a rather literary woman, his second cousin Honoria, a governess who had been a great friend of his sister Letitia, who herself was an Evangelical in the circle of Wilberforce and Thornton. (This illustrates the range of ruling-class types, and the alliance between them.) John, we are told, was passionately fond of Scott, but otherwise seems to have been aesthetically philistine. Henry and Honoria were more imaginative. The brothers quarreled over the administration of the Punjab, though with great dignity and mutual respect. Henry went into semiretirement, but he emerged again to be Resident at Lucknow, where he died, a martyr, during the Mutiny.

Henry gathered around him a number of young men, who were destined to have remarkable careers in India. There were, for instance, William Hodson, famous for the corps he formed, Hodson's Foot; John Nicholson, famous for the relief of Delhi during the Mutiny; and James Abbott, who was, we are told, accepted as prophet, priest, and king, by the fierce Yusupzais of the Hozara country. This phrasing I take from Maud Diver's biography of Honoria Lawrence, and it reminds us of Kipling, but more importantly it reminds us of the enormous imaginative charge of these Indian careers, where it seemed that everyone English was a Man Who Could Be King. Another of Henry Lawrence's young men was Herbert Edwardes, who was sent to Jummu to be, as he said, a Lieutenant of Foot advising the King of the Mountains. Edwardes, who wrote remarkably well, again and again in his letters names that kind of excitement. "I found five countries oppressed by one tyrant—and I removed him. I found three chiefs in exile—and I restored them. Those countries and those chiefs rallied round me in the hour of need. When I held up my hand for soldiers, they came. When I left the province, during an imperial war, peace reigned behind me" (Maud Diver, *Honoria Lawrence,* p. 319). John Nicholson was literally worshiped by a sect, the Nikkulseynites, whom he cursed and flogged for doing so. Edwardes's obituary comment on Henry was as Carlylean as Bosworth-Smith's on John: "How much of the *man* there was in him. How unsubdued he was. How his great purposes, his fierce will, generous impulses, and strong passions raged within him, making him the fine, genuine character we knew. . . ."

One final quotation from Edwardes will make clear the moral and imaginative tone of the Victorian cult of Empire itself. In a letter of 1846, after a satirical description of some Sikhs, he continues, "These barbarous phases of society, into which an educated man descends as into a pit of lions, have, after all, a wild, almost terrible interest. There is something noble in putting the hand of civilization on the mane of a nation like the Punjab (if I may borrow Spenser's allegory) and *looking down* brute passions. What a victory! to bind a bullying people with a garland—to impose security of life, good order, and law as fine, upon a whole nation."* The military impulse and military pride were sanctified and subdued to other caste values.[2]

There we have a kind of Victorian hero, obviously carrying a very potent image, who might have seemed quite unrelatable to the engineer and the merchant. In fact, India was a theater of empire where the military caste provided the leading actors, and even quite displaced the merchants from public view. But administrative civilians

---

*\*Memorial of Herbert B. Edwardes,* ed. by Lady Edwardes (his wife), p. 76.

were heroes in India; their tasks more constructive, but their powers still exhilarating. I take as an example H. M. Kisch, whose letters were published as *A Young Victorian in India* in 1957. Mr. Kisch, who was born in 1850, arrived in India in 1873, and immediately found himself in charge of "198 square miles of famine" (p. 24). He wrote home that he gave employment to 5000 people every day, and fed another 3000 a day free. He had an establishment of 300 and ruled a population of 100,000. In 1874 he recalled with pride that when he arrived he couldn't dig a tank, build a grain store, or anything else. And a little later he wrote, "Since I last wrote, I have dammed several of the rivers in my circle. . . ." (p. 45). In 1876, his subdivision was 782 square miles, and contained a population of 154,000—mostly of an aboriginal tribe, "far superior to Bengalis." (That prejudice against the Hindus, and particularly the Bengalis, was a large feature of English rule in India; an imperial power prefers to deal with a primitive or aboriginal tribe.) They treated even his music box as a god.

It was in India that the institution of Guides originated; although guides and scouts were obviously famous long before, in the American colonies; perhaps I should say, it was in India that something was instituted on the British side which was called Guides. In 1839 Henry Lawrence proposed such a corps, trained to work in forest and jungle (to discover enemy positions) where regular troops could not operate. In 1845–1846 Harry Lumsden created the Queen's Corps of Guides (he himself being only twenty-five) and Hodson was his second in command.

The institution much struck the general imagination; Kipling for instance always found such irregular troops much more exciting than the regulars. (This excitement was a fraction of that attaching to the Cossacks in Russia, for the Cossacks were irregulars.) And after the Boer War Colonel Baden-Powell, with Kipling's advice, set out to create such an institution for boys, to save England from the softness and degeneracy threatening it. Baden-Powell designed the Boy Scouts to foster specifically English-boy qualities. He wrote, "Your Englishman . . . is endowed by nature with a spirit of practical discipline. . . . Whether it has been instilled into him by his public school training, by his football and his fagging, or whether it is inbred from previous generations of stern though kindly parents, one cannot say" (Ellis, *The Social History of the Machine Gun*, p. 105). That practical discipline was what the Empire required of its administrators, and the public schools supplied. He set out to develop that English quality by means of simulated and controlled adventures. The Boy Scouts and the public schools are examples of those institutions of large cultural effectiveness which did not operate through books, and which were hardly at all expressed or reflected in serious literature.

One final hero-type in the Victorian constellation is the missionary. In *Self-Help* Smiles tells, for instance, the story of John Williams, a London Society missionary, who died a martyr on Erromanga, a South Seas island. And a book-length version of that sort of narrative is James Paton's *The Story of John G. Paton: or 30 Years Among South Seas Cannibals.* The hero was born in 1824, and after a very severe and pious Scots Presbyterian childhood, set off as a missionary for the New Hebrides in 1858. There he engaged in a thirty-year-long and more or less fruitless struggle with naked savages, who practiced horrid heathen rites, including cannibalism. And the whites he encountered were nearly all rough, swearing traders, who mocked and jostled him. It is an intensely grim life that is described, but it is offered as a call to imitation; John G. Paton is a Christian hero of Christian adventure.

But in Smiles's book there is also much about Livingstone, which gives quite a different image of missionary work; stressing how Livingstone dug canals, built houses, cultivated fields, as he labored among the Bechuanas; he taught them to work as well as to worship. It was by using this stress on the missionaries' work that a man like Smiles could best assimilate it to the work of the explorers and administrators—the work of civilization. And this was a stress by no means foreign to the missionaries themselves; they sometimes took copies of *Robinson Crusoe* with them as well as Bibles. The practice, and later theory, was that the missionary should be a trustee for Western civilization. He taught his tribe habits of work, of justice, of reason, and collected information about their language, culture, natural habitat.

Seen as such, he was first cousin to the heroes of adventure stories; and in fact R. M. Ballantyne blended both images. In his very popular boys' stories, including *Coral Island* itself, he included a strong strain of missionary feeling, quite like that of *The Story of John G. Paton.*

Beside the missionary stood the colporteur, of whom the most famous and the most literary was George Borrow. His *The Bible in*

*Spain,* 1842, told the adventures of an Englishman, attempting to circulate the Scriptures in Spain; but it was also full of picaresque adventures, romantic settings, and chauvinist opinions. "Yes, notwithstanding the misrule of the brutal and sensual Austrian, the doting Bourbon, and above all, the spiritual tyranny of the court of Rome, Spain can still maintain her own. . . ." And it might be Defoe himself who tells us that for two hundred years Spain was the she-butcher of malignant Rome.

Borrow learned to read on *Robinson Crusoe,* and maintained a kind of cult of it. For months, he tells us, "the wondrous volume was my only and principal source of amusement. For hours together I would sit poring over a page till I had become acquainted with the import of every line. . . ." (*Lavengro,* p. 10). Borrow was described as an Elizabethan born out of his time, and in fact illustrates that revival of primitive WASP energies in Victorian England. He traveled far and riskily with his Bibles; he went to Russia in 1823 for the London Missionary Society, and to Spain in 1835, where he told everyone that the Pope was Satan's prime minister, and that they weren't Christians, for they were ignorant of Christ and his teaching. It can give one a valuable insight into the imperialist aspect of the Victorian temperament to remember that Borrow was a pupil at grammar school together with James Brooke, who became Rajah Brooke of Sarawak.

Moreover, people in the nineteenth century continued to read the travel literature of earlier times, which made the explorer one of the great heroes of nineteenth-century culture. One reader we happen to know about is Thoreau, thanks to the researches of J. A. Christie, reported in his *Thoreau as World Traveller.* Thoreau read the collections of Hakluyt, Purchas, and Drake; but also the works of the Spaniards, like Columbus, Balboa, and Ponce de Leon; and also Frobisher, de Soto, Cartier, Hudson. But three-quarters of his travel-reading was written after 1800, and half of that was contemporary —written between 1832 and 1865. This meant books about travels in Japan, the Arctic and Antarctic, the West and South America, and, more latterly, Africa and Asia. He read, Mr. Christie calculates, about twelve such books a year.

One favorite was Alexander Henry, whose *Travels in Canada 1760–76,* Thoreau said, was "like the argument to a great poem on the primitive state of the country and its inhabitants." This—the relation to legend and myth—was Thoreau's main interest in such reading. In his *Journal* for March 16, 1852, he writes, "The volumes of the 15th, 16th, and 17th centuries, which lie so near us on the shelf, are rarely opened, are effectually forgotten and not implied by our literature and newspapers. When I looked into Purchas's *Pilgrims,* it affected me like looking into an impassable swamp, ten feet deep with sphagnum, where the monarchs of the forest, covered with mosses, and stretched out along the ground, were making haste to become peat. These old books suggested a certain fertility, an Ohio soil, as if they were making a humus for new literature to spring in." His language implies fertility even when it asserts decay. And indeed a new literature did spring up—that of Kingsley and Kipling. Whether Thoreau would have approved of that literature we cannot say; but it is clear that he was concerned for the tradition of thought we are following. (We should note a certain likeness between life at Walden and life on Crusoe's island; and a certain fondness in Thoreau for guns and hunting.) He read even the boys' books of the period; notably those of Captain Mayne Reid, whom we shall come to. He read each Reid tale, *Desert Home, Boy Hunters,* and *Forest Exiles,* as they came out in the '50s. (The last is a Swiss Family Robinson set in Peru.) He read and reread Reid's *Young Voyagers; The Boy Hunters in the North.*

Thus the engineer, the explorer, the missionary, and the Indian soldier, all in different ways continued and developed the Crusoe image of heroism. Nineteenth-century readers, at many levels of literacy, made a cult of those heroes. And at the end of the century, boys were urged to do the same, by a variety of institutional means.

If we turn now to fiction, we can begin with Captain Marryat, who wrote very popular books, first for men and then for boys, in the first half of the nineteenth century. He and Cooper together invented the genre of sea fiction at a significant level of intelligence and taste. Marryat was often said to be the best recruiting officer the British Navy had. His *Mr. Midshipman Easy* (1836) is an adventure tale of the kind we have studied, but set on shipboard. The hero's father had been mad about equality and other French Revolutionary ideas, so Jack has some hard lessons in discipline to learn when he joins a ship of the Royal Navy, but he is fundamentally good-natured—being a typical adventure hero. Thus in the course of many adventures he acquires a Black Prince, Mesty, who has tales to tell of savage despotism; a devoted friend and comrade, Gascoigne; and an exotic bride, Donna Agnes, whom he rescues from the clutches of wicked priests. Marryat used several of the motifs that Cooper used (in *The Prairie*, for instance) and which Defoe or Scott had used before him. He modified rather than transformed the energizing myth of the system.

But *Mr. Midshipman Easy* had something of Regency jauntiness, and in 1841 Marryat showed his alertness to the new Victorian mood by writing a more serious, an *Evangelical* adventure tale for children, *Masterman Ready*. This is the story of the Seagrave family who are shipwrecked on to a desert island while on their way to Australia. They learn to survive there in Robinson Crusoe fashion, their adventures rising to a climax with a battle against savages and a last-minute rescue. The differences from Defoe's book largely arise from the fact that the central figure is not an individual but a family. This change was introduced by Wyss in *Swiss Family Robinson* and Marryat consciously set out to improve on Wyss. The change brought with it not only a domestic life-style in the wilderness, but a narrative change, in the more moralistic differentiation of roles played by the different children (and the adults, but they are less important). Here William is definitively a good boy, while Tommy is naughty, and precipitates the catastrophe. By letting the water out of the drinking cask the family relies on while it is besieged by savages, he creates a critical emergency; Masterman Ready saves them by crawling out of the stockade to get water for Mrs. Seagrave and the babies, but is killed.

Ready is Marryat's crucial invention, and one that opened the way for many Victorian adaptations of the adventure tale. He is a common seaman, who has been fifty years at sea, and attaches himself to the genteel Seagrave family, and especially to William, even before the wreck; after the wreck he is their instructor in the practical arts of survival. He is a Natty Bumppo figure, except that he has a wild past to repent—which he narrates serially and edifyingly to William —and that he holds by a more Evangelical morality. His function is indicated by the name "Masterman"; he introduces the principle of social hierarchy even into the wilderness and adventure setting.

The book's Victorian prudence is indicated by its teaching about Empire and about discipline. Ready tells William, ". . . there is more work got out of men in a well-conducted man-of-war than there can in the merchant service in double the time . . . I should never have known what could be done by order and arrangement, if I had not been pressed on board a man-of-war. . . . I found that everything was done in silence" (p. 120). And William is even taught that all empires grow old and decay, that the British Empire will, too, and one day it may be the turn of black races to be great. This, then, is a highly moralized version of modernist adventure. The balance between Brahmin and merchant has shifted in favor of the former, and aristomilitary values are largely repudiated.

That story reflected the early Victorian mood, full of the vigor of English Puritanism, but at odds with the imperial situation. It was replaced in the second half of the century by something almost opposite. English readers soon passed from semi-Defoe adventure to ultra-Scott romance; to, for instance, Charles Kingsley, another extremely popular Victorian writer, and with higher intellectual claims.[3] His Elizabethan adventure tale, *Westward Ho!* was published in 1855, but reprinted very often. It was, for instance, officially distributed to English troops in the Crimean War, and after a new edition in 1857, it was reprinted three times in the '60s, twelve times in the '70s, eight times in the '80s, and altogether thirty-eight times by 1897. It was dedicated to two men, Rajah Brooke of Sarawak, and Bishop Selwyn of New Zealand, both of whom possessed "a virtue even purer and more heroic than the Elizabethan." That suggests Kingsley's key contribution to Victorianism and to the adventure tale —the idea of recapturing Elizabethan vigor (in somewhat purified form)—of assimilating the two ages to each other.

The hero is a "glorious lad," Amyas Leigh, who is much closer to the fiery hero of chivalric romance than to the prudent Crusoe-type, but who represents a new stress, derived from the sagas, on primitive and simple-minded strength. Kingsley describes him as a savage but simple-hearted giant, but also "a symbol of brave young England longing to wing its way out of its island prison, to discover and to traffic, to colonize and to civilize, until no wind can sweep the earth which does not bear the echoes of an English voice" (p. 10). The shout that greeted Amyas's victory was, we are told, "the birth-paean of North America, Australia, New Zealand, the Pacific Isles, of free commerce and free colonization over the whole earth." He is contrasted with his clever consumptive brother, Frank, and his hysterical Catholic cousin Eustace, who has been corrupted by Jesuit teachers, and whose face often writhes with envy, malice, and revenge. Amyas has been brought up by his widowed and martyred mother, and by stately Sir Richard Grenville. There is a lot of North Devon scenery and legend, and many historical characters, with elaborately Elizabethan language, verse, pageants, etc. (Kingsley's method is derived from Scott at his most "historical.") Defoe-virtues are represented only in the merchant, Mr. Salterne, a minor character and not much favored by the author. Romantic chivalry is the keynote of the author's values, and Spenser, Raleigh, and Sidney are his historical heroes.

Unlike Scott, Kingsley is very Protestant and even anti-Catholic. This, like the saga influence, derives from Carlyle, and reflects a recharging of the modern world system with moral righteousness of a more imperialist and military kind. Rose Salterne is the beauty of North Devon, and Amyas and five other glorious lads who love her form a chivalric Brotherhood of the Rose, and take an oath to all go away for three years and not court her, for fear that mutual competition may injure their mutual brotherhood. (This curious way to express their love is to be explained by the author's covert malevolence against Rose, and women, and sex.) While they are away, Rose is seduced by a Spaniard, Don Guzman, and elopes with him to Spain, and subsequently to South America, where Don Guzman is associated with the rape of Peru. Amyas sets off in pursuit of her, but she has been abandoned by Don Guzman and fallen a prey to the Inquisition, in whose hands she dies. Amyas then pursues Don Guzman, finally kills him in the battle that defeated the Armada, and—having been blinded in that battle, and so reduced to a status for which marriage is not inappropriate—marries Ayancora. She is a new and much-to-be repeated motif—adapted from Cortes's Marina; Ayancora is an Indian princess Amyas picked up in his travels, but is really an English girl abandoned in the jungle as a baby and worshiped by the savages because she is white. Marrying her, Amyas incorporates—without any real miscegenation—primitive powers. *Westward Ho!* tells the story of the ousting of Spain by England from the leadership of the modern system, one of the key episodes in the history of that system. But morally and aesthetically it is a lurid fantasy of power and revenge and hatred, on quite a different, and lower, level, from the other adventure tales.

It is worth taking a brief look at some nonfiction by Kingsley, because he was a central figure in the Victorian propaganda for empire and adventure. In *The Heroes or Greek Fairy Tales for My Children* (1868) he says that "heroes" used to mean (when nations were young) men who dared more than other men. Then it came to mean men who helped their countries. And now it means men who suffer pain and grief. (This idea is linked, paradoxically, to the atavistic worship of animal vigor in Amyas Leigh; Kingsley's moral imagination accords the primacy to pain and grief—to passivity—and as a result his historical and political imagination has no effective moral component.)

And his *The Roman and the Teuton* (1864) warns England against the fate of Rome and other empires. In the early years of Christendom, the Teutons were "Forest Children," a young and strong race, like English sailors and navies now, while the Romans were subtle and sophisticated. (William Morris took up this story in his late romance, *The House of the Wolfings.*) The Roman palace was "a sink of corruption," where eunuchs, concubines, spies abounded. Kingsley warns his listeners, who were the undergraduates at Cambridge, where he was Professor of History, to beware of a similar corruption at home. "Forget for a few minutes that you are Englishmen, the freest and bravest nation upon earth, strong in all that gives real strength, and with a volunteer army which is now formidable by numbers and courage. . . ." (p. 32). It can happen in England, too. Unbridled indulgence of the passions produces frivolity and effeminacy, as we see in the French noblesse of the ancien régime, in the Spaniards in America, and in the Italians in their once-great cities. National life is grounded in morality, that is, on the life of the family. "The muscle of the Teuton" was always combined with moral purity, and this gave him, "as it may give you, gentlemen, a calm and steady brain, and a free and loyal heart; the energy which springs from health; the self-respect which comes from self-restraint". . . and so on (p. 38). Here we see the late Victorian version of the WASP hero, containing recognizable elements of Defoe and Scott, but also something else. That hero now embodies racist and atavistic energies.

Kingsley draws several contrasts between the Roman Empire and the British Empire in India, where the moral roles of imperial power and native population are reversed. "The Goth was very English; and the overcivilized, learned, false, profligate Roman was the very counterpart of the modern Brahmin" (p. 114). Only the English among the Goths' descendants preserved the Gothic heritage of freedom, and so they are anti-imperialist even in India. Kingsley's main hero in this book is Dietrich of Bern, who "went adventures." Dietrich, he says, has been criticized on the grounds that his civilized qualities only went skin-deep; that if you scratched him you'd find a barbarian. But this is really a high compliment, he argues. For Kingsley's message is always to cultivate the barbaric qualities in the individual and the nation; and that is one of the messages of most nineteenth-century adventure tales after him.[4]

That call sounds loud and clear in Kipling and Haggard, who form the climax to this chapter, but there are several other writers who modified or extended the range of the adventure-myth, before I come to them. For instance, there is Alexandre Dumas, one of the adventure tellers with the most international and long-lasting audiences. He will remind us of the pan-European character of modernist imperialism. Dumas was born in 1803, the son of one of Napoleon's generals, and though he lost his father at the age of three, he grew up on the tales of his father's exploits, and on the tales of adventure and bloodshed which the Napoleonic era left behind. His work is a literary equivalent to his father's career. Hippolyte Parigot said, "If Danton and Napoleon were exemplars of Gallic energy, Dumas, in *The Three Musketeers,* is the national novelist who puts it into words."*

Having read Scott, and seen Shakespeare performed in Paris, Dumas wrote *Henri III et sa Cour* (staged in 1830), and set out to do for French history what the English writers were doing for English, and the American writers for America. (In 1838 he adapted Cooper's *The Pilot* as a serial for *Le Siècle,* and it attracted five thousand new subscribers in three weeks.) In 1844 he produced *The Three Musketeers,* also as a serial; drawing his historical material, incidentally, from Courtilz, the French Defoe.[5] The confrontation at the heart of that book, between Cardinal Richelieu, compact of old-man wisdom—cold, inhuman, unhealthy—and the four healthy young men, who are a composite representation of France's young-man vitality, is an important new motif of adventure. It reconstitutes the framework of the story of the brothers. That motif was to be repeated again and again, notably by Kipling, in the *Puck of Pook's Hill* stories.

*Quoted in André Maurois, *The Titans,* p. 179.

## Popular Literature and Children's Literature

Then Dumas's *Count of Monte Cristo* (1846) made triumphant use of that romantic revenge motif which was employed by later adventure writers, like Jules Verne in *Twenty Thousand Leagues Under the Sea*. And Dumas himself was another example of the writer as entrepreneur, on the largest possible scale. From the beginning he planned to put all French history into fiction; he made a fortune, built himself a great house (called Monte Cristo) like Scott and Twain; and went bankrupt, like Scott and Twain. He translated into literary terms (though terms which literature-as-a-system rejected) the energies of nineteenth-century France. And he distilled a version for child-readers—the new class of readers.

*The Critical History of Children's Literature**\* says "During the years from 1840 onward, boys were exploring remote regions, sailing the high seas, escaping from cannibals or redskins in the company of heroes . . ." (p. 237). This was something radically new. The genre of children's literature had been invented, we may roughly say, by the Puritans; in verse quite explicitly by Bunyan and Watts; Bunyan's *Book for Boys and Girls*, 1686, and Watts's *Divine and Moral Songs for Children*, 1715, which was influenced by Bunyan's example; in prose, more accidentally, by Bunyan and Defoe, with *Pilgrim's Progress* and *Robinson Crusoe*, not written for children, but soon given to them to read. The only Tory who contributed was Swift, in *Gulliver's Travels*, and that was read as if Defoe had written it. Later in the eighteenth century there were big successes like *Giles Gingerbread* and *Goody Two-Shoes*, but the message and the myth remained the same. Prudence and piety were the values recommended. The new nineteenth-century development (apart from *Alice in Wonderland*, which stands by itself) was in stories which operated on almost opposite values.

The middle of the nineteenth century saw a very striking and very significant change in the culture's idea of children. Their literature was in effect captured by the aristomilitary caste. Adventure took the place of fable; and the adventure took on the characteristics of romance. Children's literature became boys' literature; it focused its attention on the Empire and the Frontier; and the virtues it taught were dash, pluck, and lion-heartedness, not obedience, duty, and piety. For instance, "Oliver Optic" in America (where children's

---

\*See under Meigs in Bibliography.

literature had been *very* pious), wrote a Starry Flag series 1867–1869, and an Army and Navy series 1865–1894. Another dominant interest was science and invention, and that was only slightly indirect in its support of the same values. Edward Stratemeyer wrote a long series about Tom Swift, boy adventurer, full of grit and ginger, who goes up in balloons, drives an electric car, fires an electric rifle, and so on. Stratemeyer started a syndicate of writers to use his name in 1903, because he was so successful. In 1926, 98 percent of the children questioned in a survey listed a Stratemeyer title as a favorite and in the '20s and '30s the Tom Swift series sold fifteen million.

Kingsley, and for that matter Scott, were read also by children, but some authors were read only by them, and these authors too were aristomilitary by affiliation. Among English writers of boys' adventure books, one of the most notable was George Alfred Henty. He wrote nearly eighty such books, with titles like *With Clive in India, With Roberts to Pretoria,* and so on, stories of the achievements of the British army in colonial settings. Henty borrowed a good deal from standard histories and geographies, so his books were also educational. They rely on Anglo-Saxon racism, assigning stereotype identities to Latins, Easterners, and "natives." *By Sheer Pluck* describes Africans as being "just like children. . . . They are always laughing or quarrelling. They are good-natured, and passionate, indolent, but will work hard for a time, clever up to a point, densely stupid beyond."[6] (It is the idea implicit in Defoe's *Four Year Voyage of Captain Roberts.*)

Most of Henty's books begin with a letter addressed to "My dear lads," and teaching some homely truth. He had himself been a puny and sickly boy, who spent most of his childhood in bed, and was bullied at school. Then he took up boxing and yachting, became a man and a war correspondent; and as a writer, became a preacher of manliness. His biography by G. Manville Fenn (published in 1910) says, "There was nothing namby-pamby in Henty's writings. . . . 'No,' he said, 'I never touch on love interest.'" His study was full of pipe-smoke and native weapons, and he had a "Johnsonian" manner with the effete and impudent. When met in the Strand, he had always just returned from wide open spaces, and was sternly silent about subjects of mere chatter. Fenn says his books are "essentially manly, and he used to say that he wanted his boys to be bold, straightforward, and ready to play a young man's part, not to be milksops. He had a horror of a lad who displayed any weak emotion and shrank from shedding blood, or winced at any encounter" (p. 334). He contributed stories to boys' magazines like *Captain, Chums, Great Thoughts, Young England,* and *Union Jack.*

In *The Great War and Modern Memory* Paul Fussell says that the soldiers in that war had learned the language of patriotic duty from Henty and Rider Haggard among the novelists, and from Robert Bridges and Henry Newbolt among the poets. Newbolt was famous for "Lampaida Vitae," with the famous refrain, "Play up, play up, and play the game." He will remind us of the important part played in this manliness propaganda by the public schools. In that poem, and many others, the subject moves from a public school to a colonial battle, and the first is shown to be essentially a preparation for the second. Newbolt was the poet of Clifton College, and wrote a famous poem, "Clifton Chapel," which begins with the stanza,

> This is the Chapel: here, my son,
> Your father thought the thoughts of youth,
> And heard the words that one by one
> The touch of life has turned to truth.
> Here in a day that is not far,
> You, too, may speak with noble ghosts
> Of manhood and the vows of war
> You made before the Lord of Hosts.

(We should not take this school militarism for granted. It was something new, and Thomas Arnold would have been shocked by it.)

At the end Newbolt added a note, "Thirty-seven Old Cliftonian officers served in the campaign of 1887 on the Indian frontier, of whom twenty-two were mentioned in dispatches and six recommended for the D.S.O. Of the 300 Cliftonians who served in the war in South Africa, 30 were killed in action and 14 died of wounds or fever." Then he added a supplementary stanza.

> Clifton remember thy sons who fell
> Fighting far oversea,
> For they in a dark hour remembered well
> Their warfare learned of thee.

Fussell tells us that General Haig, Commander in Chief during the Great War, was a lifelong friend of Newbolt's, and that the latter sneered at Wilfred Owen and poets of that kind as "broken men."

Literature of this kind was spread largely by means of the boys' magazines to which Henty contributed so much. The most famous of these was G. A. Hutchinson's *Boys' Own Paper*, which brought Henty, Ballantyne, Michael Fenn, and W. H. G. Kingston to a large audience, and, as *The Literature and Art of the Empire* says, made patriots of its readers. It began in 1879, belonged to the Religious Tract Society, but was above all patriotic, though it printed foreigners like Jules Verne as well as all the famous English ones. A typical title from Volume I is Kingston's *From Powder-Monkey to Admiral;* the navy had a whole chapel to itself in the cathedral of British patriotism. There were also publishing projects like a series of biographies, edited by Sir Harry Wilson, called "The Builders of Greater Britain" and another edited by Sir William Hunter, called "The Rulers of India." (This is the background against which to see Kipling.) There was, this volume says, a literary empire, consisting of Kipling's India, Haggard's South Africa, Gilbert Parker's Canada, and inspired by the songs of Tennyson, Henley, Newbolt, and Masefield.

Comparable with Henty in popularity, and even more popular internationally, was Captain Mayne Reid, 1818–1883, for a time the most popular English author in Russia, for instance; also translated into French, German, Italian, Spanish. He was born in Ireland of Presbyterian parents, and left for America in 1839. Reid was a militant and indeed military liberal. He fought in the Mexican War, and was the first man in the U.S. force to enter Mexico City. In 1848 he published *The Rifle Rangers,* his first romance, read and admired by Dumas and Lamartine. In 1849, stirred by the news of the revolutions in Europe, he organized a legion to go to Kossuth's support in the revolt of Hungary against Austria. Then his romance *The Scalp Hunters* sold a million copies in England, and was translated into as many languages as *Pilgrim's Progress.* Another book of his published that year, *The Desert House or The English Family Robinson,* began a series.

But he also continued his political activities, and it is important to note their anti-imperialist character. He had become Kossuth's friend, and in 1852 they planned to go together to Milan to fight against the Austrians for Italian freedom. In Reid the connection between book adventure and real-life adventure was especially close. But though he was a Liberal, and Kipling a Tory, both men established rifle clubs, so that young Englishmen should get some military training; and there is no real discontinuity between them culturally, despite the political difference. Like Henty's, Reid's books care as much about geography and history as about moral ideas or narrative —*The Castaways,* 1870, for instance, quotes Wallace and Livingstone for a page at a time, and has a trivial plot that seems not seriously meant. Indeed, because of the predominance of the killer albatross and the hammerhead shark over the human characters, the book produces an effect quite like those of Crane and Conrad.

A very important development in the boys' books of the second half of the century was the synthetic, framework story, like *The Three Musketeers.* One very popular example was W. H. G. Kingston's *The Three Midshipmen.* Kingston (1814–1880) wrote 150 books for children. This one begins at a school, and puts together an English, a Scots, and an Irish boy, who were to appear again and again in a whole series of books. The English boy, Jack Rogers, takes the lead; he is a squire's son, solid and pugnacious; Alick Murray is serious, clever, and cautious; while Paddy Adair is full of fun, lovable, but thoughtless. This trio is the United Kingdom in literary form, and they act out the same function—of dominating the rest of the empire.

At school the boys have to deal with a soft, fat sneak called Bully Pigeon, who embodies the least attractive aspects of Englishness and turns up later in their lives as a cowardly civilian in the Mediterranean, and then as a would-be sophisticate on their ship to China. Bully Pigeon boasts himself an atheist, but whines when he gets into trouble, and soon dies. Aboard ship, Honest Dick Needham, of the lower classes, comes to the help of the young gentlemen time and time again. In the Mediterranean, the three chase Greek pirates and smash Mehmet Ali on the Sultan of Turkey's behalf. Their adventures frequently lead to explosions, in which human limbs mingle with fragments of stone and iron. Then they go to Sierra Leone, where they chase slavers, and first meet the Portuguese villain, Dom Diogo, whom they pursue through several episodes. (England had gained great moral prestige by suppressing the slave trade in its own dominions, and Portugal great infamy by not doing so.) They meet a Black Prince and acquire a faithful Friday-style Negro, Wasser. Later they go to Singapore and Hong Kong, where they chase opium clippers. Thus they cover the whole empire, and make it, by their adventures, vivid and glorious to their readers.

Rather similar in synthetic form is R. M. Ballantyne's *Coral Island.* In this adventure three boys are wrecked on an island; Jack Martin is eighteen and a natural leader; Ralph, who tells the story, is fifteen and serious and "old-fashioned," and Peterkin Gay is thirteen or fourteen, little and quick and mischievous.[7] Like Crusoe, they land with an axe, an oar, an iron hoop, a telescope, some whipcord and a broken penknife, and have to make do. But Ballantyne puts much more stress than Defoe does on the Paradisal beauty of both land and sea, and the heroes are seen more romantically and chivalrically than Crusoe. (Ballantyne was much influenced by Scott.) Jack is lion-like; tall, strapping, broad-shouldered, handsome, good-humored; Peterkin expects him to become king of a native population. When cannibals arrive (looking more like demons than human beings) Jack goes berserk while fighting them. (The idea of an Englishman going berserk, when pushed too far, was a much-repeated device, derived from the sagas.) Later they get to Fiji, where the natives, being pagans, feed their eels with babies, and fill their temple with human bones. The story contains some Evangelical teaching, but puts more stress on the related secular virtues, for instance, cold bathing and training in observation. (This is the book which William Golding transvalued to write *Lord of the Flies*, one of the clearest cases of post-1945 reversal of sentiment.)

Another major force in fiction and ideas at the popular level in the nineteenth century was Jules Verne, and his followers. Though Verne imitated Dumas to begin with, he had more in common with Defoe than with Scott, while Dumas's affinity was the reverse. Verne's work is thought of usually as science fiction, but it is just as much adventure fiction, and his heroes are adventurers. And his case is an interesting one for us because there have been some studies of his work, in French, which are not too far removed from ours in point of view.

Jules Verne was born in 1828, and though he trained in law, always wanted to write. He met Dumas in 1849, sat in his box for the first stage performance of *Three Musketeers*, and became a sort of secretary to him. But he also made friends with Jacques Arago, a blind explorer, whose brother was an astronomer. Verne had always loved science, and also the sea and ships. In 1862 he wrote *Cinq Semaines en Ballon*, the story of a British eccentric, Dr. Ferguson, who floats across Africa in a balloon. He took this novel to a publisher, Jules Hetzel, a liberal who had been Lamartine's Chef de Cabinet in his Ministry in 1848, and thereafter for a time exiled by Napoleon III.

(This liberal connection expresses an important tendency in the books.)

Hetzel gradually saw the immense potential in Verne's work. In 1866 the latter produced *Les Aventures du Capitaine Hatteras,* about an English explorer, who races against his American rival, Altamont, to discover the North Pole; and for this book Hetzel wrote an advertising explanation of Verne's work in general: "Son but est, en effet, de résumer toutes les connaissances géographiques, géologiques, physiques, astronomiques, amassées par la science moderne, et de faire, sous la forme attrayante et pittoresque qui lui est propre, l'histoire de l'univers" (M-H. Huet, in *L'Histoire des Voyages Extraordinaires,* p. 20).

He used as models for his heroes mostly explorers like Livingstone, Stanley, Burton, De Brazza, the heroes of the nineteenth century. It is notable how many of his leading figures were Anglo-Saxon; Huet counts ninety Americans, eighty English, thirty Russians, and so on. The French tend to appear as comic savants, like Paganel, or comic servants, like Passepartout. But Verne had in fact strong anti-English prejudices; though he admired their tunnels and bridges, and their energy, sense, and progress, he hated their cruelty and love of profit.[8] But still he judged them only by their own, modern system standards.

So it is not surprising that Verne wrote several Robinsonaden: *L'Oncle Robinson, L'Ecole des Robinsons, La Seconde Patrie* (an avowed continuation of *The Swiss Family Robinson*), and *Deux Ans de Vacances.* And his work is largely an energizing myth of the modern system. It is similar to Defoe's in emotional character. His works cannot be said to be novels, someone says, because they do not deal with love. He always declared he couldn't handle that subject; on the other hand he was proud of and conscientious about the science he included. Michel Corday says (quoted by Jean Jules-Verne) that he helped young readers to escape their "stupid jail. . . . He inspired in us a desire to know about the universe, a taste for science, a dedication to masculine forms of energy."

When Chesneaux says that Verne is a Utopian Socialist, he is thinking of the Saint-Simonian brand of socialism; and in particular of the technocrats. The Saint-Simonian, Enfantin, became administrator of the French railways under the Third Empire, and other Saint-Simonians were employed in big projects like the Suez Canal and the plan for a Channel tunnel. Verne's friend Nadar, who is depicted in some of the novels, was de Lesseps's secretary. He often describes possible engineering projects, like a giant lighthouse on Cape Horn, or a canal to irrigate the Sahara. Many of his friends were polytechnicians, and he assigned that status to some of his favorite characters. "Paganel" was an avowed Saint-Simonian, and *Indes Noires* is a technocratic fantasy.

This line of imagination, which runs through much science fiction, is one we can only assume that Defoe would have found very congenial, as did H. G. Wells, the modern Defoe. Chesneaux says that Verne was, like Wells, an author of politics fiction as much as of science fiction. And though Wells had a much more literary imagination than Verne, it is fair to bracket them together. What strikes one about *The War of the Worlds* is the vivid way England is imagined —and imagined as vulnerable; Wells evokes the anxiety of riches and a panic at the rout of civilization. He presents London as an enormous magnificent city, about to be destroyed, and England as an entirely tamed country, at the mercy of fierce invaders. This is of course the vision of much imperialist fiction—a soft, rich, splendid mother country, inviting rape by the hardy savage tribes outside. It is Kipling's vision; while on the other hand the narrative structure of Wells's book is that of Defoe's *Journal of the Plague Year*.

An interesting book which connects Verne with Defoe is Emile Cammaerts's *Discoveries in England*, of 1930. Cammaerts was a Frenchman long resident in England. He says he was struck as a child by the number of Englishmen who played leading roles in Verne's stories, and finally realized that his hero, Phileas Fogg (in *Around the World in 80 Days*), was just another version of Robinson Crusoe, whom he had been in love with a long time. Crusoe was for him as a child "the ideal type of adventurer—courageous, patient, as well as wise and just in his relations with the savages"; whereas Cammaerts knew that temperamentally he couldn't emulate d'Artagnan's bravado, or the military dash of French adventure heroes in general. (He was pointing to a contrast between mercantile and military heroes as well as between English and French.) Crusoe was a settler, and carried, "in a kind of frog, instead of a sword and dagger, a little saw and a hatchet, one on one side, one on the other." This is a highly significant contrast, for Cammaerts. The English adventure novel, he says, is geographical, where the French is historical; the English dream is in a sense outside history—at least the history of militarism and domination.

Cammaerts mentions Robert Louis Stevenson's voyages as an example of the compulsion felt by every English author to live out something of an adventure himself; and Stevenson was a symbolic figure as man as well as author to many readers of adventure at the turn of the century. His family were famous consulting engineers, who had built lighthouses all around Scotland, and harbors all around the world. They were examples of Defoe's and Smiles's engineer-heroes. He had difficulty in reconciling his parents to his vocation to be a writer, but in fact he turned their engineering work to fictional images as much as Dumas turned his father's military exploits into fiction.

Stevenson finished *Treasure Island* in 1882, and it was a tremendous success, both accepting and changing the conventions of adventure. In "How This Book Came To Be," he shows how much it was a composite of earlier books in that tradition. The parrot came from *Robinson Crusoe*, the stockade from *Masterman Ready*, the chest from Washington Irving, and so on. There is much reference to Scott, whom Stevenson was very conscious of rivaling, and in fact there is much more of him than of Defoe. Stevenson's is *historical* expertise rather than practical. He said that the story began with the drawing of a map and that it was told to his stepson, with his father's collaboration. It is palpably the fantasy of men-being-boys. There is no real interest in large historical forces. What is strikingly new about it in a generic way is that a boy plays the leading part and tells the story; and that the violence is much more open and important.

The end of this sort of adventure romance was announced by another Scots writer whom it is suitable to connect with Stevenson in many ways, J. M. Barrie. The servitor imperialism of the Scots writers from Scott on has played an important part in the reinforcement of modernist values in England, as we have seen.[9] (John Buchan, another Scot, was the last of the old-style adventure writers.) Barrie was no conscious or intentional rebel against tradition. As a boy, he read Defoe, Cooper, Stevenson, and at the end of his life, when he was guardian of the boys for and about whom he wrote *Peter Pan*, he was, they tell us, always eager for them to be involved in sports and athletics, and reluctant to see them concerned with the arts. He wanted Kims and Hucks about him, not Little Lord Fauntleroys.

But his own temperament, which was expressed in *Peter Pan*, was purely whimsical and playful, and deeply averse from serious adventure or violence of any kind. *Peter Pan*, 1904, is about a Boy Who Would Not Grow Up, and though it uses all the devices of the boys' adventure story, the Indians, the hollow tree, the underground house, the lost boys, the pirates, it treats them all as conscious fantasy, and so denies their connection with the real world, a connection which is the life line of any energizing myth. But of course a work so purely playful has a thousand faces, and this one was not what most people, or Barrie himself, saw. To them *Peter Pan* seemed like a continuation of *Treasure Island*, the same themes transposed into another key. But the end of Empire was at hand, as far as England was concerned, and that feeling is transmitted, all innocently, through Barrie's work.

*Treasure Island* had been a very great success of the old kind; W. E. Henley called it the best boys' book since *Robinson Crusoe*, and Andrew Lang said, "Except for *Tom Sawyer* and *The Odyssey*, I never liked a romance so much." (Implicitly that comment conjures up a whole scheme of literary tradition, which would relate literature closely to imperialism, and relegate the serious domestic novel to the periphery of the system.) It prompted, amongst other things, *King Solomon's Mines*, which Rider Haggard published in 1885. This too was very popular; it sold 31,000 copies in twelve months, was praised by literary men, and read aloud in public schools. And though Haggard didn't have Stevenson's finished artistry, nor anything like Kipling's talent and taste, still some parts of his work have some literary importance.

Haggard was born in 1856, and went out to Natal with Sir Henry Bulwer, when the latter became Lieutenant Governor in 1875. When England annexed the Transvaal in 1877, it was Haggard who ran up the Union Jack there. Then he went back to England in 1881, published *Cetewayo and His White Neighbors* (which urged the Government to be aggressive in South Africa) and *King Solomon's Mines* in 1885 and *She* in 1889. *She* is a curiosity from our point of view, because the myth is implicitly erotic and in some sense feminist—the major character being an immortal incarnation of femininity; it is the sort of idea D. H. Lawrence played with, and *The Plumed Serpent* is not totally dissimilar from *She;* and yet Haggard employs many of the traditional adventure motifs, which are so tied to opposite values. (The result is to embarrass the characterization of the young man hero, whom the story keeps turning into Chéri, despite the story-teller's determination to make him stay Tom Brown.) This is the only time when one of these adventure romances is told—in part—in the service of the Mother Goddess.

*King Solomon's Mines* is not very interesting, though one should note the treasure motif, taken over from Stevenson, and from now on standard; and the introduction of the old-hunter narrator, Allan Quatermaine. There is no striking similarity between him and Natty Bumppo. His literal model is probably African hunters like Frederick Courtney Selous, who advised Rhodes, and planted the Union Jack in Mashonaland in 1891—"the king of the white hunters." In literary effect, the important thing about Quatermaine is a certain almost-Cockney tone, a self-deprecating and antiromantic humor which proved an effective literary crystallization of the modern man's self-awareness in the presence of primitive grandeur and savagery. It combined intimations given by both Defoe and Scott, and was developed further by Kipling and Edgar Wallace.

Haggard was deeply impressed with both the grandeur and the savagery of tribal life, and felt them to be in some sense truer than the civilized ideas of Victorian England. "Nineteen parts of our nature are savage, the twentieth civilized, but the last is spread over the rest like the blacking over a boot, or the veneer over a table; it is on the savage that we fall back in emergencies" (*Allan Quatermaine*, p. 16). The deeper philosophic note of Haggard's romances is thus quite strongly stoic and melancholy. *King Solomon's Mines* introduced, as well as an old hunter, a Black Prince, Umslopogaas (modeled, Haggard tells us, on a Swazi aide-de-camp he knew in 1860). In *Allan Quatermaine,* in which the main characters of the earlier novel return, Umslopogaas says, "Man is born to kill. He who kills not when his blood is hot is a woman and no man." And in tendency the story endorses this.

For instance, even in *King Solomon's Mines,* Sir Henry Curtis, who is usually described as an Arthurian knight in Victorian dress, in battle turns back into a Viking and a Berserker. And on page 108 of *Allan Quatermaine* we are told, "The Englishmen are adventurers to the backbone; the colonies which will in time become a great nation, will testify to the value of this spirit of adventure, which seems at first sight mere luxury." Like Kingsley, Haggard saw the value of savagery, especially for a ruling race.

Like Kipling, Haggard was deeply impressed by Rhodes, his achievements and his ideas; Haggard's fiction is in effect propaganda in Rhodes's service. *Allan Quatermaine,* published in 1887, begins in England, and the narrator's picture of the country is charged with anxiety and indeed anger. "This prim English country, with its prim hedgerows and cultivated fields . . . now for several years I have lived here in England, and have in my own stupid manner done my best to learn the ways of the children of light . . . and found civilization is only savagery silver-gilt. . . . It is on the savage that we fall back in emergencies. . . . Civilization should wipe away our tears, and yet we weep and cannot be comforted. Warfare is abhorrent to her, and yet we strike out for hearth and home, for honour and fair fame, and can glory in the blow" (p. 16).

Haggard's most impressive book is *Nada the Lily,* which came out in 1892, and was inspired by the story of Chaka the Zulu king, who ruled from 1800 to 1828, and is said to have caused the deaths of over a million people. This subject also inspired Bertram Mitford's *The King's Assegai,* which was published in 1894, and has a similar epic grandeur and ferocity. The translations of Homer taught in the public schools, and even more the Norse and Germanic sagas that aroused so much interest in the nineteenth century, provided a literary model for which these African subjects were perfect.

Haggard compares Chaka to Napoleon and Tiberius, and then dedicates his book, in Zulu style, to "Sompsen, my father," the white man who had 3000 black warriors shouting for his blood, but calmly replied that for every drop of blood they shed of his, a hundred avengers should rise from the sea; so that they gave him the Bayete and said that the spirit of Chaka dwelt in him. This is a key idea— to show natives that white heroes have as savage a splendor as they.

In his Preface Haggard says that his intention is to convey "the remarkable spirit that animated these kings and their subjects." The Zulu military organization, "perhaps the most wonderful thing the world has seen," is already a thing of the past. He says he has learned to think and speak like a Zulu, in order to tell this story. The story is told to a white man by Chaka's witch doctor, Mopo, who has known Chaka from childhood. Mopo has some of Quatermaine's antiheroic realism. Umslopogaas is Chaka's son, but is brought up as Mopo's, and consequently as Nada's brother, since Chaka always has his children killed. Umslopogaas wins a comrade, Galazi the Wolf, who has won a great club by passing the night in a cave inside Ghost Mountain, where the Stone Witch sits forever, waiting for the world to die. In the cleft between her breasts are the bones of human sacrifice. Umslopogaas also wins a great weapon, an axe, but to get it has to marry, which spoils their comradeship. "Galazi was also great among the people, but dwelt with them little, for best he loved the wild woods and the mountain's breast, and often, as of old, he swept at night across the forest and the plains, and the howling of the ghost wolves went with him" (p. 153). (Galazi was the inspiration for Mowgli, Kipling said.) When disaster finally comes, and the comrades know they must die, Umslopogaas says, "May we one day find a land where there are no women, and war only, for in that land we shall grow great. But now, at the least, we will make a good end to this fellowship and the Grey People shall fight their fill, and the old stone witch who sits aloft, waiting for the world to die, shall smile to see that fight, if she never smiled before" (p. 285). This is *not* in the spirit of Defoe or Scott; but it takes something from Kingsley, Morris, and Carlyle.

The most impressive passages are those describing battle, or meditating on it. Their stychomythic dialogues and ritual and rhythmic formulas are not original, but they have some power.

Ah, the battle!—the battle! In those days we knew how to fight, my father! All night our fires shone out across the valley; all night the songs of soldiers echoed down the hills. Then the grey dawning came, the oxen lowed to the light, the regiments arose from their bed of spears; they sprang up and shook the dew from their hair and shields—yes! they arose! The glad to die! . . . The morning breeze came up and found them, their plumes bent in the breeze; like a plain of seeding grass they bent, the plumes of soldiers ripe for the assegai. Up over the shoulder of the hill came the sun of Slaughter; it glowed red upon the red shields; red grew the place of killing; the white plumes of chiefs were dipped in the blood of heaven. They knew it; they saw the omen of death, and, ah! they laughed in the joy of the waking of battle. What was death? Was it not well to die on the spear? What was death? Was it not well to die for the king? Death was the arms of Victory. Victory should be their bride that night, and ah! her breast is fair (pp. 48–49).

The feeling that passage expresses—and there is much of it in *Nada the Lily* and Haggard's other books—is rare in English literature. That literature on the whole, and certainly in the nineteenth century, had been in the keeping of what Haggard called "the children of light"; let us say George Eliot, Matthew Arnold, John Stuart

Mill, and the novelists Tolstoy approved in *What is Art?* What Haggard introduced was a lyrical or threnodic militarism, better fitting an army-focused culture like Prussia or Russia; and in *King Solomon's Mines* there is also a new emphasis upon regiments—their organization and training, but also their pride and glory.

There was to be something of this in Kipling, too; it was the two together who demonstrated in literary terms what Hannah Arendt called the Boomerang effect. The values by which the English on their frontier lived and imagined life, though the opposite of those which they proclaimed at home, crept home in novel form. The liberal values of the modern system, productivity and enlightened self-interest, etc., are undermined. The oppositeness itself took its toll, as we see in Quatermaine's alienation from England. The two effects together produced a kind of pessimism echoed in Mopo's remark, "Nothing matters, except being born. That is a mistake, my father!" (p. 39). The story of the Zulus made a particularly strong impression on the English imagination; they seemed terrible but noble, above all "worthy adversaries." They so appear, for instance, in one of Lady Butler's most famous battle pictures, "The Defence of Rourke's Drift"; and Cetewayo, who paid a visit to England, became a figure in the popular vocabulary—in music-hall jokes, for instance.

Haggard's friend, Andrew Lang, spoke in 1901 of a new "exotic" literature, "whose writers have at least seen new worlds for themselves; have gone out of the streets of the overpopulated lands into the open air; have sailed and ridden, walked and hunted; have escaped from the smoke and fog of towns. New strength has come from fresher air into their brains and blood . . ." (Brian Street's *The Savage in Literature*, p. 11). And it is significant that Lang was an anthropologist. There was a strong racist interest in anthropology then. The Anthropological Society itself declared in 1864 that black children develop only up to the age of twelve—an idea you can find in both Henty and Kipling. To such ideas Darwin's influence added others, of man's nearness to the apes, the struggle for survival, the persistence or sudden development of monstrous specimens, and so on. This made "primitive man" seem very horrifying but very exciting. It has been proposed to call a whole group of novels that arose in the 1870s with Henty's book on the Ashanti, "the ethnographic novel." And there is also the "anthropological romance" genre which

## Popular Literature and Children's Literature

Leo J. Henkin discusses in *Darwinism and the English Novel;* these are novels written between 1890 and 1940 about fossil races of men or near-men. And then there is the whole Tarzan oeuvre. These all expressed and reinforced the trepidation of the imperialist race at the height of its powers. The anxiety of possession we noted in Defoe was an individual thing; by the time of Wells and Haggard it was national.

# VIII

## *Twain*

TWAIN belongs in this sequence of writers just on the strength of his combination of great talent with enormous popularity. Because of his success alone I should have to ask what modification he introduced into adventure conventions. But he also made the idea of adventure and the frontier crucial parts of his subject-matter. He allied them to humor. His treatment of those themes was in some ways oblique and out of line with the other writers—because he was a humorist—but in one book he made a major statement out of them. And in that book he also made a wholesale attack upon the romance genre and the aristomilitary caste (in the form of a parody of Malory) and spoke himself in the voice of a self-styled modern Crusoe. Indeed, Twain habitually spoke in a version of that voice. It was natural to him, though he made full use of it only in *Connecticut Yankee*.

That voice is his great achievement—the brash triumphalism of the modern system made audible, at first self-confidently self-mocking, then savagely self-destructive. The first performance, which continues for three-quarters of the book, announces the American rebellion, the rebellion of the Defoes against the Scotts, the reself-assertion of the mercantile against the aristomilitary caste. (Scott came after Defoe, but Twain came after Scott, so he could avenge the taking over of adventure by the aristocrats.) The second, which is rather a breakdown of performance, announces the self-accusation of the whole modern system. The horror at imperialism, which men began to feel at the end of the nineteenth century, breaks down the decorum of literature, breaks through the mood of entertainment, with dramatic effect.


## The *Connecticut Yankee in King Arthur's Court*


The book by Twain I want to talk most about is, therefore, *A Connecticut Yankee in King Arthur's Court,* and I want to interpret it —that is, to put it into an imaginative context that is not entirely obvious, to light up an otherwise obscured context in which the book becomes alive, interacts with the experience we bring to it in a vivid and rewarding way. So I must comment on the text in a little more detail than I have used elsewhere. But my opening remark—that Arthurian romance is *not* the book's imaginative context—will take me away from the text.

It seems likely that Arthurian romance was important to Twain. When his wife died, for instance, he quoted a part of Ector's lament for Launcelot, in Malory, to express his grief; that, and other biographical testimony, suggests a richness and intimacy of feeling on Twain's part for the Arthurian story which could—playing against his opposite feelings of impatience and antagonism—have made a wonderful subject. But in fact it was not a wonderful subject, for Twain, and the critics who have read it in the context that subject brings with it have rightly neglected the book. The more experience of Arthurian literature you bring to your reading of it, the more disappointed you will be. Twain makes only the most obvious jokes—assumes the most philistine attitudes—never evokes the spirit of romance.

Why this should have been so is not my problem; but I would guess that the difficulty was Twain's habit of simplifying and dichotomizing. We see this also in his attacks on Scott and Cooper. He attacks them, I think, because they don't go far enough in the direction of modernist realism, but he makes it appear that they are going in a totally different direction, and attacks them wholesale. This is of course an effective rhetorical device, especially for a humorist, and it works well enough for a short-term, small-scale performance. But in a full-length novel, that wholesale and unqualified scorn for the thing satirized kills the reader's interest—denies the interest the writer in fact felt. Writing a full-length novel brought Twain many problems, and one of them was that his "official attitudes" bulked too large. Twain was essentially ambivalent, and could make very few judgments without starting to feel opposite sympathies. But in a full-length book he was on his dignity, and his attitude to the subject matter (in this case, Arthurian romance) became rigid, programmatic, dismissive. After the first few pages we know that he won't ever give Malory a fair chance, that there won't be any interaction between the two modes of sensibility. A humorist—someone who habitually sees things in terms of dichotomies—is likely to be more interesting, at least in a long performance, on a subject to which he doesn't have an "official attitude," a plan or a purpose—on a subject which engages him accidentally, though completely, and very powerfully. This, I think, is to be found in *Connecticut Yankee,* but that subject is not Arthurian romance, but modern imperialism or modernization.

Before Twain finally decided to make his novel out of the King Arthur burlesque, he had thoughts of using some old material about how civilization came to the Sandwich Islands; and if we look at what he had to say on that subject, we shall get a first glimpse of the imaginative context in which to set what he did write. Twain was sent to the Islands in 1866 by the *Sacramento Union,* because of a new American interest in them, created partly by the developing sugar trade. He stayed longer than he had intended to—four months—finding a lot to say about them; he sent twenty-five letters to his paper, amounting to eighty-five thousand words; and returned to the subject in later books.

It was during this trip that he began to find his vocation, to associate with the cultural elite of America, as distinct from the miners, prospectors, newspaper-bohemians, and so on, he had known before. He became friends with the U. S. Minister to China, the honorable Anson Burlingame, who gave Twain the advice—which he says in his *Autobiography* he followed for the next forty years— "Avoid inferiors. Seek your comradeships among your superiors in intellect and character; always climb." And the effect of the association was literary as well as social; in his letters from the Sandwich Islands, Twain first began to speak for the forces of refinement and respectability (though of course he continued to speak for their opponents also).

But what concerns us primarily is the interest Twain took in the Islands' cultural contrasts—between what he called "savagery" and "civilization." For instance, he described the president of the Assembly (who was also the king's father) thus, "This man, naked as the day he was born, and war-club and spear in hand, has charged at the head of a horde of savages . . . and revelled in slaughter and carnage; has worshipped wooden images on his devout knees . . . and now look at him; an educated Christian; neatly and handsomely dressed; a high-minded, elegant gentleman . . . a grave, dignified, statesmanlike personage. . . . How the experiences of this old man's eventful life shame the cheap inventions of romance." Surely it is another version of that idea that Twain evoked in the novel he did write. And perhaps it is an even more specific clue to the origin of *Connecticut Yankee*, that the Prime Minister of the Islands then was a renegade New Hampshire man. That quotation comes from *Roughing It*, page 206; for Twain returned to the subject of the islands in that book in 1871, and again in *Following the Equator* in 1897; it was a subject that stayed on his mind.

Thus I interpret *Connecticut Yankee* to be about modernization, and find it to be variously ironic, for and against that subject. Without any interpretation, of course we would find in it some comedy of irony at the Yankee's expense, an irony through which *some* complexity of feeling is engaged. He describes himself on page 14 as "a Yankee of the Yankees—and practical; yes, and nearly barren of sentiment, I suppose—or poetry, in other words." And on page 23, "I made up my mind to two things; if it was still the 19th century and I was among lunatics and couldn't get away, I would presently boss that asylum or know the reason why; and if on the other hand, it was really the 6th century, all right, I didn't want any softer thing; I would boss the whole country inside of three months. . . ." And so on. Let me just point out the Bob Hope-tone, the flat dry uneasy overself-confidence, and the comment on that in the word "boss," which is a central word. The Yankee's title in Arthurian England is Sir Boss. On the other hand, that irony is friendly and gentle, compared with the savage ironies directed against slavery and the droit de seigneur and feudal injustice, and so on. (The end of the book is not friendly or gentle to the technology which the Yankee has introduced, but the end of the book is quite separate from the rest, as we shall see.)

The theme of modernization is explicit, and even its connections with Crusoe and Columbus are explicit. On page 47, the Yankee says, "I saw that I was just another Robinson Crusoe cast away on an uninhabited island, with no society but some more or less tame animals, and if I wanted to make life bearable I must do as he did —invent, contrive, create, reorganize things—set brain and hand to work, and keep them busy. Well, that was in my line." And this comes at the end of a paragraph in which he has deplored the lack of gas or candles, or windows, of books, paper, pen, and ink, of coffee, tea, tobacco and sugar. And on page 232, like another Samuel Smiles, he praises "the creators of this world—after God—Gutenberg, Watt, Arkwright, Whitney, Morse, Stephenson, Bell." As for Columbus, he is invoked on page 38, when, "It came into my mind, in the nick of time, how Columbus, or Cortes, or one of those people, played an eclipse as a saving trump once, on some savages, and I saw my chance." And in fact eclipses were often "played" in contemporary romances of contemporary adventure, like *King Solomon's Mines.* [1] So there are explicit parallels and connections with Defoe-adventure and mercantile romance.

But what is only implicit in the novel is the similarity between the Yankee's modernization of sixth-century England and the core countries' modernization of lands outside their system, like the Sandwich Islands. A more notable example was the continent of Africa, to which general attention was just then being attracted by the Scramble for Africa. And the crucial case there was the Congo, which was being modernized, in matters of transport and administration, by a man with whom Twain had worked as a colleague—Henry Stanley. This was a crucial case also because in reaction against the Congo and Stanley there was arising that revulsion against modernization and colonization which disturbed the whole civilized world and paralleled exactly the revulsion which disturbed the end of *Connecticut Yankee.* (Twain began writing the novel in 1886; Stanley began his last journey, during which the worst scandals erupted, in 1887, and reached his objective in April 1888; the *North American Review* held a symposium on his expedition in December 1888; Twain finished the novel, of which the end is so disillusioned, in 1889.) Parallel cases included the modernization of Germany under Bismarck; a figure and a country which Twain, like other Americans, deeply admired; and the political position of the Boss is strikingly like that of Bismarck, the power behind the throne.[2] Also the modernization of Japan, once it was opened to American influence; a case which Thorstein Veblen compared with Germany's in *Imperial Germany.*

We are bound to think of both these countries (and Russia) when we read, on page 65, "My works showed what a despot could do with the resources of a kingdom at his command. Unsuspected by this dark land, I had the civilization of the 19th century booming right under its very nose." The opposition of the Church, which finally defeats the Boss, was the great opposition which Bismarck had to face in Germany; and Twain's characterization of the Church and the peasantry would have reminded contemporary readers of the church and the peasantry of Russia. Finally, let me point out that the use of modern military technology against much more primitive equivalents was to be found in contemporary American practice against Indians; Gatling guns, dynamite bombs, wires charged with electricity dangling from balloons, all were used in attacks on Indians at the end of the century.* This is the context, I want to suggest, in which to read *Connecticut Yankee;* put into this context, the book's enthusiasm, its anecdotes, and above all its growing uneasiness, which finally explodes, all become meaningful and moving.

We can discuss the way the book works in terms of a contrast between the Yankee and King Arthur. Twain does not put a heavy or at least consistent stress on Arthur; the contrast he draws is between the Yankee and Arthurian England as a whole; but we can, for the sake of neatness, use Arthur as a way to make the points. The Yankee represents democracy, which is good, while Arthur represents feudalism, which is bad. There is a great deal of teaching of that thesis in the book, to be taken quite straight. On page 84, "You see my kind of loyalty was loyalty to one's country, not to its institutions or its office-holders. . . . To be loyal to rags, to shout for rags, to worship rags, to die for rags—that is a loyalty of unreason, it is pure animal; it belongs to the monarchy, was invented by monarchy; let monarchy keep it." And with democracy we can associate free trade, a disestablished church, an established stock exchange, and organized competition—competitiveness is one of the Yankee's prime characteristics, as we see in his argument with Dowley. Turning to Arthur's England, we might put its Bastille-type prisons in contrast with the

*S. Moskowitz, *Explorers of the Infinite,* p. 106.

stock exchange, and its general dirt, squalor and nakedness with the Yankee's clean competitiveness, and its slavery and droit de seigneur with free trade and free worship.

Then the Yankee represents technology, while Arthur represents traditionalism. The Yankee loves technology, and it plays an essential part in two of his best performances, the blowing up of Merlin's tower and the restoration of the fountain. And with that we can associate for instance his knowledge of science; his prediction of the eclipse; and his confidence that "the world was not flat, and hadn't pillars under it to support it, nor a canopy over it to turn off a universe of water that occupied all space above. . . ." (p. 133). And his West Point military academy, and his machinery imagery, and above all his technocracy.

At the end of Chapter 17, he tells a grateful serf, "I'll book you both for my colony; you'll like it there; it's a Factory where I'm going to turn groping and grubbing automata into *men.*" This is a crucial idea, politically, to make the factory the means of humanization. And after he has restored the fountain, the people fell back before him, "as if I had been some kind of a superior being—and I was, I was aware of that" (p. 160). This is that divinization of the white man which we can trace from Columbus to Kipling. With Arthur's traditionalism we can associate superstition, and romanticism in general, like Sandy's; the Church and its doctrines and mysticism in particular; and the hermits and the monks and the knights and the barons.

Then the Yankee represents vaudeville, while Arthur represents legend. Both the Yankee's use of language, and shaping of anecdotes, but also the things he does, like the blowing up of the tower, are vaudeville, calculated to strike an audience with surprise, to deflate their pomposity, and to make them laugh. And we can associate that with his Cockney sensibility—the feeling of the quicker, cleverer, more knowing, townie, facing the slower-witted countryman or pompous aristocrat or tradition-bound native. And his elaborate and ingenious lying; and his journalism, in which he delights. ". . . when outside there rang clear as a clarion a note that enchanted my soul and tumbled 13 worthless centuries about my ears: 'Camelot *Weekly Hosannah and Literary Volcano*—latest eruption—only 2¢—all about the big miracle in the Valley of Holiness!' One greater than kings had arrived—the newsboy" (p. 186). While to the legends and legendariness associated with Arthur we can add the jousts, the ceremonies, the tournaments, the colorfulness, the figure of Merlin, and the quotations and pseudoquotations from Malory.

Finally, the Yankee represents brains, while Arthur represents brawn, or, to put it more kindly, physical splendor. When the Yankee challenges the chivalry of England, 25,000 knights, he says, "Therefore, you have no chance—none whatsoever. Reflect: we are well-equipped, well-fortified, we number 54. 54 what? Men? No, *minds* —the capablest in the world; a force against which mere animal might may no more hope to prevail than may the idle waves of the sea hope to prevail against the granite barriers of England" (p. 311). This is a challenging assertion—exactly the faith that modern prophets, like Susan Sontag and Norman Mailer, have blamed the modern dilemma on. And with those brains we might associate the Yankee's faith in argument, and in reason, and his delight in finding that as a slave he fetches a much higher price than Arthur. While with the latter's physical strength goes his natural royalty, and the splendor of Lancelot and the others, but also their childishness and stupidity.

It is easy to see how this novel fits into the genre we have been studying. It is a recrudescence and further radicalization of the Defoe model of mercantile adventure. David Beard, who illustrated the *Yankee,* wrote to Twain on November 12, 1889, that he wanted to see a copy in every American home, "because I consider the story a great missionary work to bring Americans back to the safe honest and manly position, intended for them to occupy, by their ancestors when they signed the Declaration of Independence." Beard's illustrations delighted Twain, and they stressed the book's antiaristocratic and antichivalric feelings, by introducing caricatures of English notables. Merlin was drawn from Tennyson, for instance. The mention of Independence, which is exactly right, will remind us of Franklin, and so indirectly of Defoe again.

Directly Twain does not mention Defoe much, and there seems to be no evidence of "influence," but there is plenty of evidence of similarity of mind. For instance, Twain played with statistics in the way that Defoe did—though Twain's play is more typically humorous. (I am thinking of pieces like "The Dangers of Lying in Bed.") And the love of figures is only a crystallization of the general love of fact, the preference for the empirical and the pragmatic over the imaginative and speculative and high culture generally. Both *Life on the Mississippi* and *Following the Equator* are books in the genre of Defoe's *Tour;* each gives a progress report on civilization.

Often when Twain says Cervantes, moreover, I think we have the right to think of Defoe, because what he means is that force which displaced chivalry from our imagination. Thus in *Life on the Mississippi* he says that *Don Quixote* swept away the world's liking for medieval chivalry—though *Ivanhoe* had such effect in the South that *Don Quixote* was a wasted effort there. "As far as our South is concerned, the good work done by Cervantes is pretty nearly a dead letter, so effectually has Scott's pernicious work undermined it" (p. 378). That good work was in fact done for the Anglo-Saxon mind by Defoe.

The Yankee is a latter-day Crusoe; he has the same practical ingenuity, the same love of material possessions and the same creation of value, and perhaps the most striking, the same glee. For three-quarters of the book the dominant tone is gleeful, though that dominance is more and more disturbed, and finally overthrown, by its opposite, guilt and horror. King Arthur, though not personally attached to, or subordinate to, the Yankee, like a Black Prince, is a development of the Black Prince motif; he represents his people, commands them magically or religiously, and through him the Yankee commands them. And Clarence is a development of the Friday figure. But we must be more struck by the differences—by the way these categories have become more formal than substantial as a way of linking this book with *Robinson Crusoe*. The reason is just that this is a fundamentally different *kind* of book; just because it is a humorous book, and as such contains no real adventures.

There are adventures, but they are unreal; because permeated by and subsumed in an alien spirit, the spirit of humor. That does not mean that adventure and humor are not allied here—it means that they *are*. One of Twain's interests for us is that he shows just how those two went together in nineteenth-century culture (low culture). Twain sums up and embodies the long tradition of American humor, which found its most pungent form in the Southwest humorists. (There were elements of something similar in English humorists, and elements of that humor in English writers from Defoe on, but in Twain's time the English sense of humor—let us cite Dickens and Thackeray as examples—was more gentlemanly. After Twain made his impact, however, English laughter became more democratic, in Kipling and Wells.) The central figure who unites adventure and humor is the shrewd and calculating trader who triumphs over various grander, grosser, or more traditional opponents. Thus Twain exemplifies an alliance between adventure and something else that resembles the alliance between adventure and history-writing in Scott. Such alliances are the crucial joints and gears in the workings of a culture.

There being no real adventures does not make the book so different as it might seem, for us, for we are concerned with the larger cultural *meanings* of those adventures in *Crusoe,* and the same meanings are treated in the *Yankee.* I said that the change from Defoe to Scott was like a 90° rotation of the axis of the first book, from geography to history. This change is like another 90° rotation, but in another plane, from adventure to humor. The point of each anecdote is different; or shall I say that the shape is different because in Twain it has much more point. The "reality" is different; the element of hypothesis is much stronger and livelier in Twain. And so on. But the writer's, and the reader's, adventure of spirit is the same in both authors—except that in Twain that adventure comes to a horrible end.

Some of the power of that ending, and of the book as a whole, is prophetic. When we read of, for instance, the setting up of the military academy, we can think that within the decade of the novel's publication, after the Spanish-American War, Harvard began its School of Business Administration (in the belief that an imperialist nation needed a trained foreign service) and the University of Chicago created a Department of Military Science and Tactics. When we read of the factories to turn groping and grubbing automata into men, we can think of the Congo, and the scandal that broke after Roger Casement's investigations. And when we read of the rings of barbed wire on which the knights hang dead, what can we think of but the Somme in 1916?

### Tom Sawyer, Huckleberry Finn, etc.

Although *The Yankee* is not an adventure novel, Twain was interested in that genre, and in fact most of his fiction carries the word adventure in their titles; but they belong to the genre of children's-adventure, and to the subgenre of children's-adventure-for-adults. That makes a considerable difference; the adventures of Tom Sawyer and Huck Finn are mock adventures, and their point is most often a humorous point, so that those books are halfway between *Crusoe* and *The Yankee*. That is why I shall not make a great deal of them here.

In *Life on the Mississippi*, Twain talks about Murel's Gang— desperadoes who hid out on an island in that river, a nineteenth-century equivalent to Rob Roy. But Twain could not tell their story, as Defoe and Scott told their equivalents'. Such stories made him too nervous to tell them full-scale. He wrote always about the world of adventure, but he could not take the adventurer's point of view—or he took it only to renounce it with a self-deprecating joke. His treatment of such material is represented by "The Private History of a Campaign that Failed," which is a vivid example of humor as an escape from painful truth. Twain is not as purely playful as Barrie about adventure, but he is of the same moment in the history of adventure. He is much more playful than Stevenson. His eye is on the adult reading over the child's shoulder, in collusion with that second reader. He is ambivalent, as always; and to some degree he undermines the adventure and the whole genre.

It is worth remembering that William Dean Howells had to convince Twain to promote *Tom Sawyer* as a book for boys. This was Howells's invention; not adventure but a new genre, whose real reference was to safe domesticity always. It was Howells who had heralded Thomas Bailey Aldrich's *Story of a Bad Boy* in 1870 as a landmark. He said that it was written with "so great desire to show what a boy's life is, and so little purpose of teaching what it should be" that it established a new pattern of fiction.* And Howells himself wrote books of that sort; boy's-life stories, rather than adventure stories. Their purpose was realism rather than excitement, though realism of a sentimental-nostalgic kind. They weren't part of an energizing myth.

Neither were Twain's, because he thought of the adventures as jokes for grown-ups. According to F. L. Mott, in *Golden Multitudes*, page 157, Twain wrote to Howells about *Tom Sawyer*, "It is not a boy's book at all. It will only be read by adults. It was only written

---

*Richard Darling, *The Rise of Children's Book Reviewing, 1865–1881.*

for adults." On the other hand, *Tom Sawyer* contains most of the motifs of adventure: the cave, the treasure, the captain, his comrade, and his band, a Friday figure, and a wicked Indian. There is even some development of those motifs, of a kind significant for later, more serious adventure. In *Huckleberry Finn,* Huck's relationship with Jim is clearly a development of the Crusoe-Friday relationship, and led on to Kim-and-the-Lama. The Crusoe-type practical ingenuity is now devoted to trick, fraud, and hoax purposes, as in Huck's disappearance from his father's house, or the release of Jim from imprisonment. And the King and the Dauphin carry some sardonic allusion to Scott-type romance.

What is importantly new—and antienergizing—is the sense of the sordid and horrible, which broods at the edge of the narrative, and is crystallized in the figure of Pap, his appearance at Huck's window, and his final appearance as a corpse. That whole sense of the sordidness of the frontier is something that doesn't appear in British adventures; and it is of course appropriate that it should be an American who brought it into relation with the rest, since the Americans always knew their Frontier more realistically than the English knew their Empire. Even the part of the book that is beautiful, Twain's lyrical evocation of the river, and all nature, and of drifting with the current, depends on that sense of the sordid and horrible. The innocent stressless beauty is evoked in revulsion from the incidents of frontier life. One is bound to remember that at eight Samuel Clemens found a stabbed body on the floor of his father's office one night, and at nine he witnessed a murder, of which the perpetrator was acquitted. Huck wants to get away from everything rather than into adventure. He does take pleasure in some of the new places and people he meets, and above all in being released from the containments of the settlement, but his is a very passive kind of adventuring.

Twain's nearest approach to adventure as we are defining it is to be found in *Life on the Mississippi,* in the description of his own training as a river pilot. He is as ambivalent as ever about most things he describes, but the skill he learns, the pride in that skill, and the sense of Mr. Bixby as a master craftsman, these are solidly in the line of Anglo-Saxon modernist adventure. The pilot is contrasted with both the captain and the mate as being a man of *skill;* and of the three it was a pilot Sam Clemens wanted to be. That central element in his imagination is finally Crusoe-like.

## Biography and Reputation

There were of course other elements in his personality, and they were combined very unstably. The most important thing about Twain as a person, from our point of view, is that he was born the child of the Frontier culture, but grew up to become the favorite writer of the new financier-capitalist culture. He experienced the growth of America in himself—a growth so violent it was like a change of nature.

His childhood was passed in a small settlement, he traveled up and down the river as a youth, and in 1861 went to Carson City, Nevada, and there became a prospector, a silver-miner, and hoax-journalist. *Roughing It* gives a vivid impression of the effect this environment had on him. Henry Nash Smith picks out, as especially revealing, that book's story of a dog ineffectually chasing a coyote, which Twain makes into a fable of the superiority of Frontier values over those of conventional culture; the tenderfoot dog (with a higher self-esteem than he can validate in the West) will always be defeated by the veteran coyote (who looks disreputable but commands the situation). And the imaginative touch which brings the story alive—just because it announces Twain's bedazzlement by Frontier values—is that the coyote seems released from Nature's laws by its extraordinary speed, subtlety, and cunning. He is a Frontier hero, like the Yankee, a hero of invention and practical cunning. So it was straightforwardly, despite the burlesque, the excitement of the Frontier (of Empire) that dazzled Twain.

Frederick Jackson Turner makes some comments on the Frontier mind, which both explain that excitement and can connect Twain again with Defoe and Crusoe. "That coarseness and strength combined with acuteness and inquisitiveness; that practical, inventive turn of mind, quick to find expedients; that masterful grasp of material things, lacking in the artistic but powerful to effect great ends; that dominant individualism, working for good and for evil, and withal that buoyancy and exuberance that comes with freedom . . ."* That is the legend the Frontier created for Anglo-Saxons generally—and a real enough legend, and school of character.[3]

*"The Significance of the American Frontier," in *The Frontier in American History*, p. 37.

The effect of that training in Twain's case was not in any psychological sense democratic. One of the strongest impressions the reader gets from *Roughing It* is of a land peopled by great men, who subject lesser mortals to humiliation all the time. These were boatmen and pilots, in Twain's early years, and then stage coach drivers and division agents; all of them men who need not reply when spoken to, men of brutal social power, that was sometimes physical and even fatal in its manifestations. One of the division agents was the murderer Slade, "A man who awfully avenged all injuries, affronts, insults, or slights, of whatever kind—on the spot if he could . . . a man whose face would light up with a terrible joy when he surprised a foe and had him at a disadvantage" (p. 62). Slade had killed twenty-six men, and the moment when Twain breakfasted with him is in many ways the emotional climax of the book.[4]

It was partly a derivative of this education that Twain hankered —half-humorously—after princely status. Meeting some Austrian royalty in 1898 made him confide to his diary his regret at not being a prince himself. "It is not a new regret but a very old one. I have never been properly and humbly satisfied with my condition. I am a democrat only on principle, not by instinct—nobody is *that.*" But since his culture was capitalist (mercantile) Twain could only play with the idea of aristocracy, as Crusoe played at being Governor. In his later years he was playfully called "the King"; and his millionaire friend, Rogers, was "the Rajah"; both men "held court."

Another derivative of his cultural formation was Twain's self-deprecating and self-destructive attitude to literature. It is worth noting both that his *Innocents Abroad* trip was an act of promotion for a shipping company, and also that 100,000 copies of the book were sold, over two years, door to door, by subscription publishing. "Anything but subscription publication," he said, "is printing for private circulation." But everyone knew that that was the mode of publication of vulgar books, not of literature. Both facts remind us of how intimately Twain associated himself with capitalism in its rawer and more thrusting experiments. He spent a great deal of money and time and energy on get-rich-quick schemes; most notably, and tragically, on the Paige Typesetting Machine. He associated his machine with his novel, *The Connecticut Yankee,* as enterprises (he formed the company the week before he began the novel, and he hoped to have done with both together).

He also promoted a patent food, Plasmon, was director of an Accident Insurance Company, and invented a number of things himself—for instance, Mark Twain's Self-Pasting Scrapbook, and an Adjustable Strap for Garments. And he spent his profits largely, in the manner of other self-made men; for instance, spending $125,000 on his house in Hartford. And making his friends among other great success-figures of capitalism, like William Huddleston Rogers, of Standard Oil. He said of Rogers, "He's a pirate all right, but he owns up to it, and enjoys being a pirate. That's the reason I like him (Kaplan, *Mark Twain and His World*, p. 157). But it was Rogers who saved Twain after his bankruptcy, and Twain could never have saved Rogers; there is a bitter note to what he said to Rogers, "You and I are a team; you are the usefullest man I know, and I am the most ornamental." Rogers, and his secretary, were much involved in Twain's affairs; she had power of attorney, and access to his safety deposit box. Twain was in the power of the millionaires.

In *Mark Twain: God's Fool*, H. Hill says that family, investments, and his literary career were the three strands of Twain's life. Financial schemes were always on his mind, and he was forever suing and suspecting treachery, especially at the end of his life. "Both suspicion and an almost blinding lust for fortune were a part of his nature; he speculated, suffered, and sued as instinctively as he wrote" (p. 80). All this makes him one of the major figures in our literary history, in a sense quite unlike the use of that phrase by literary critics, but a very important sense.

He identified himself with, and participated in, all the fevers of American capitalism in the Gilded Age. He took advantage of none of the opportunities of withdrawal and detachment which "literature," amongst other things, offers to its representatives. It seems a natural consequence that Twain suffered a deep cynicism and depression. "It could probably be shown by facts and figures that there is no distinctively native American criminal class except Congress" (Kaplan, *Mark Twain*, p. 98). And he felt very deeply the corruption that was coming over the country; at times he blamed it on the '48 Gold Rush, which had "introduced the change and begot the lust for money which is the rule of life today, and the hardness and cynicism which is the spirit of today." When the diamond rush began in South Africa, he sent an old Nevada friend called Riley to gather materials there for a book, for he saw that rush as likely to "sweep the world like a besom of destruction." (However others might blind them-selves, Twain saw the likeness between the frontier and the empire.)

More than the other writers we have been studying, therefore, Twain knew that he could not claim to represent literature, or to write for the "discriminating reader." The "discriminating reader," in America even more than in other countries, stood in indignant opposition to other forces of the culture, and Twain had allied him-self to them. He always declared an antipathy to Jane Austen—when he read her, he felt "like a bar-keeper entering the Kingdom of Heaven"—and to George Eliot and to Henry James. And another famous expression of his feelings about literature was the hoax lecture he gave in Boston on December 17, 1898, at a dinner to honor Emerson, Holmes, and Whittier. These men represented literature; but Twain told a story about three tramps using their names, and the trouble they caused in a cabin in the Rockies; which gave him a chance to use the sacred names disrespectfully, and vent his resent-ments in humorous form; only unfortunately those resentments seemed too evident to the audience, who did not laugh. Another famous expression of this was his letter to Andrew Lang in 1890, in which Twain declared that he didn't write for the brain or mind of his society but for the belly and the members.

But it was probably Matthew Arnold who principally represented to Twain the judging and rejecting faculty of literature. And in this confrontation between literature and the adventure writer, we know more about the latter's feelings than we did in the other cases of Defoe, Scott, etc.

Arnold began to criticize America in a way that bore on Twain in particular in the late 1880s. In 1887, he reviewed General Grant's *Memoirs* (published by Twain himself) and complained of their lack of style, and of American boasting and lack of distinction. In 1888 he wrote "Civilization in the United States," in which he said that the country lacked the discipline of awe and respect, and had not solved its human problem. "The glorification of the average man, who is quite a religion with statesmen and publicists there, is against it. The addiction to 'the funny man,' who is a national misfortune there, is against it. Above all, the newspapers are against it" (Kaplan, *Mr. Clemens and Mark Twain*, p. 299).

Twain was bound to apply these criticisms to himself. He was a newspaper humorist, who had come to England as early as 1872, giving funny-man lectures on the Sandwich Islands and the Silver Frontier. (It was in the frontier humorist, one may say, that England first met frontier life, and as we would expect, literature was against it.) Indeed, he was already familiar with the charges. Literary Americans like the popular moralist, Josiah G. Holland, often complained of their humorists' lack of respect. And Twain himself wrote to Mrs. Fairbanks from England in 1873, "God knows, I wish we had some of England's reverence for the old and great." Such criticism often took the form of a cultural threat, moreover, reminding him of his dependence on mere popularity. A literary history of 1888 (published in New York) said that Twain and his ilk "must make hay while the sun shines. Twenty years hence, unless they chance to enshrine their wit in some higher literary achievement, their unknown successors will be the privileged comedians of the republic" (Kaplan, *Mark Twain*, p. 299).

Naturally, Twain had his defenses against such attacks. In May 1886, he wrote in his diary, "My books are water; those of the great geniuses are wine. Everybody drinks water." And he had a position; he didn't care about, didn't believe in, poetry and fiction; he liked history, biography, travel, science—"books with the root of the human matter in them." And he had his allies, powerful voices on the Victorian scene, like Smiles and Macaulay, spokesmen for the modern system. Sydney J. Krause says, "If there was any one writer Twain would rather have been other than himself, I believe it would have been Macaulay. He read and re-read him" (*Mark Twain as Critic*, p. 229). He particularly loved the Macaulay essays on Clive and Hastings, those central documents of Victorian imperialism, and was inspired by them to write a poem, which he published in *Following the Equator*. (It is worth noting that Macaulay's reputation was in decline by the 1880s, and Twain was now defending him. Arnold had called Macaulay "the Prince of Philistines.") Twain and Macaulay (and Lecky, Macaulay's epigone, whose book Twain made so much use of in *Connecticut Yankee*) were writers in defense of the modern system, while Arnold was in attack on it.

Twain declared himself against literary critics as a group, which is to say, literature-as-a-system. On August 24, 1889, he wrote Howells, about *Connecticut Yankee*, "I'm not writing for those parties who miscall themselves critics, and I don't care to have them paw the book at all. It's my swan-song, my retirement from literature permanently, and I wish to pass to the cemetery unclodded" (*Mark Twain-Howells Letters*, II, p. 610). That sounds highly defensive, and we are not surprised to find that there are two years' worth of entries in his notebooks, and a hundred manuscript pages of a projected reply, with the title, "English Criticism on America," which would have been in effect a self-defense against Arnold.

But the only part that got finished was his famous letter to Andrew Lang of 1889, in which he said,

> ". . . the critic has actually imposed upon the world that a painting by Raphael is more valuable to the civilizations of the earth than is a chromo; and the august opera than the hurdy-gurdy and the villagers' singing society . . . and the Latin classics than Kipling's far-reaching bugle-note; and Jonathan Edwards than the Salvation Army; and the Venus de Milo than the plaster-cast peddler; the superstition, in a word, that the vast and awful comet that trails its cold lustre through the vast abysses of space once a century, and interests and instructs a cultivated handful of astronomers, is worth more to the world than the sun which warms and cheers all the nations every day and makes the crops to grow. . . . That mass will never see the Old Masters —that sight is for the few; but the chromo-maker can lift them one step upward toward appreciation of art; . . . they may never even hear of the Latin classics, but they will strike step with Kipling's drum-beat, and they will march. . . . I have always catered for the Belly and the Members, not the Head." (*Mark Twain's Letters*, II, pp. 526–527)

Probably it is some such defense which will always have to be made for the adventure novel and for taking an interest in that as literature. But for whom then *did* Twain write?

If Scott and Cooper were read by the responsible class of their societies (the men of power who also took some serious interest in literature, as distinct from the literary class), then Twain was read, or one feels he was read, by the same class in its irresponsible mood. One says that partly because he was a humorist, and it is the job of humor to give expression to irresponsible feelings. Of course he was in the literal sense read by nearly everyone; but above all by the men of action and the men of power. The question is, in which mood did men say, "He's writing for me," or "That's what I wanted to hear said," or "That's just what I would have said"? Applying that test, I would say that Twain wrote for an irresponsible and certainly an unliterary audience.

From *Innocents Abroad* on, Twain was the spokesman for the practical and innovative man, the pioneer, socially mobile, culturally philistine, emotionally crude. In the *Yankee,* "Raphael was a bird. We had several of his chromos; one was his 'Miraculous Draught of Fishes,' where he puts in a miracle of his own—puts three men into a canoe which wouldn't have held a dog without upsetting. I always admired to study R.'s art, it was so fresh and unconventional" (p. 47). He spoke for that class within America, and for America in that character within the world. And yet his principal heir was an Englishman who wrote for the responsible class par excellence.

In 1889 Kipling came through America on his way from India home to England, to begin his literary career. He came to see Twain, and wrote that he felt the older man's hand on his shoulder as an honor like being invested with the Star of India. It seems likely that that was sincere. Kipling had begun in writing by imitating Bret Harte, and he certainly knew the superiority of Twain to Harte. He was in many ways fascinated by America, and by the Frontier experience and the types of men and expression it had produced. Many English critics, and of the sort most favorable to Kipling, had compared him to Twain very early. Andrew Lang wrote Twain a Jubilee Ode in 1886, and said how he delighted in things under the ban of "culture." Sir Walter Besant, from whom Kipling learned a lot when he was beginning, had written enthusiastically about *Huckleberry Finn* and *The Three Musketeers* and the novel of adventure, in 1898. Bret Harte and Joel Chandler Harris also were popular in England, but Twain in fact became the national favorite, succeeding to the position which Dickens had held. Moreover, Twain returned Kipling's admiration. He admired *Plain Tales from the Hills,* read Kipling's ballads along with Brownings's at public readings, and when he went to India, saw it through Kipling's eyes. (It is because Twain's audience and Kipling's were the same in most ways that we must distinguish them in terms of mood.)


## Owen Wister and Theodore Roosevelt


It is typical of Twain's rather paradoxical relation to the adventure tradition that he, the great writer of the West, played no part in spreading the cowboy myth. That myth is so important a phase in the history of the WASP hero and WASP adventure that we must briefly consider it, and relate it to Twain.

In 1895, Theodore Roosevelt invited Kipling to dine with him in Washington, together with Owen Wister and Frederick Remington. Wister had met Remington two years before at Yellowstone Park, and they were working together on stories about cowboys, which Remington was illustrating. Wister had gone to Wyoming for his health in 1885, when he was twenty-five, after Roosevelt had written to him about how wonderful the West was. Like Parkman, Wister suffered from hysterical headaches, and like Parkman, he sought ideas and practices that would harden both himself and his whole class. Wister was a Philadelphian aristocrat and aesthete who had traveled all over Europe by the time he was twenty-two. He wrote his first story about cowboys in a Philadelphia club in 1891, the night someone said to him that America needed a Kipling of the sagebrush. Thus these men all belonged together; they were collaborating at the task of giving America an adventure hero—one that would satisfy both the democratic and the aristocratic urges of the modern system. They were inventing the cowboy.

For instance, Remington drew a picture which became famous, *The Last Cavalier,* which showed the cowboy as the last variant on the chivalric and cavalier hero throughout the ages. It illustrated Wister's essay, "The Evolution of the Cow-Puncher," in 1895. The essay told the story of a cowboy traveling in the same train with an English peer, and of the instinctive hostility they felt for each other because of the class difference; but the story continued with the peer going to Texas a few years later and adopting the life-style of the cowboy, and revealing himself as fundamentally the same man. "Deep in him lay virtues and vices coarse and elemental as theirs. . . . Directly the English nobleman smelled Texas, the slumbering untamed Saxon awoke in him. . . . Sir Francis Drake was such a one; and Raleigh, the fine essence of Anglo-Saxonism, . . . conqueror, invader, navigator, buccaneer, explorer, colonist, tiger-shooter" (Vorpahl, *My Dear Wister—*, pp. 78–81).

Through the 1870s, cowboys had still been called "herders," and seen as rough, uncouth, barbarous, and violent. Not until the first Wild West Show, in North Platte, Nebraska, in 1882, did the cowboy become a hero; that happened when one of them, called Buck Taylor, caught the eye of a writer, Prentiss Ingraham, who immortalized him in a series of dime novels, beginning 1887. It is he whose work with cowboys is closest to Defoe's with pirates, but his interest in them is less serious. Ingraham first associated cowboys with the semi-Mexican costume so familiar today. Then they were taken over briefly by men of education, above all by Wister.

In 1892 Wister produced *The Virginian*, which redeemed the cowboy both from the dime novel and from the category of uncouthness. Though his Virginian is supposed to get tamed while courting his Bennington schoolteacher, in fact he was a perfect Southern gentleman from the beginning, though one who got up to wild undergraduate pranks. The prefatory note tells the reader that though Wyoming between 1874 and 1890 was very wild, still the Virginian did not speak lewdly to women, and "Newport would have thought him old-fashioned."

The narrator, a civilized man, first sees the other man corralling a pony, and envies the way "he climbed down with the undulations of a tiger, smooth and easy, as if his muscles flowed beneath his skin." The cowboy is a version of the handsome sailor, and is viewed with an even more erotic eye. Then the narrator hears his voice, teasing somebody else, full of lazy charm. And finally he meets the "slim young giant, more beautiful than pictures." At first the cowboy refuses comradeship, because the visitor has been "familiar" with him. Indeed, all the Westerners look askance at the visitor; "Yet I liked the company, and wished that it would like me." In other words, he is on his knees before beautiful young manhood.

But of course the figure we're familiar with from a hundred films, the cowboy who is in a sense Hollywood's major cultural achievement, is not recognizably a knight or a cavalier. Rather like Hawkeye, the Virginian was an attempt to impose a responsible-class profile on an irresponsible-class hero, and the mask fitted only loosely and briefly. Hollywood cut off the literary trappings Wister had attached to the cowboy—though Hollywood has its own gentility.

This is an iconography which has had some curious developments. For instance, it is of some interest that Raymond Chandler said that his private detective, Philip Marlowe, had as antecedents the Virginian and Nick Adams (the Hemingway character). Moreover, when Chandler began writing in 1932 it was for a magazine called *Black Mask*, which then had a masterful editor, Joseph T. Shaw, with a clear idea of his readers. Shaw wrote in 1931 that he pictured the

magazine's reader as "a pretty stalwart, rugged specimen of humanity
—hard as nails, swift of hand and foot, clear-eyed, unprovocative but
ready to tackle anything that gets in the way. . . . [a man who] knows
the song of a bullet, the soft, slithering hiss of a swift-thrown knife,
the feel of hard fists, the call of courage. . . . He is vigorous-minded;
hard, with a square man's hardness; hating unfairness, trickery, injustice, cowardly underhandedness; . . . not squeamish or prudish, but
clean, admiring the good in man and woman." Several readers wrote
in to say that he must have had Theodore Roosevelt in mind, and
they might have added Wister and Remington.

Such was Chandler's original market. And in fact Shaw and Chandler admired each other a lot, and felt in harmony as to their aims
in writing. So the cowboy gave birth to his only rival as culture hero,
the private detective. He too was a responsible-class culture-hero.
Philip Marlowe and the Virginian, Humphrey Bogart and Gary
Cooper, turn out to be cousins. Of course, Hollywood introduced
modulations and inflections, and modernized the characters, by traits
that were, superficially, the reverse of Wister's intentions. The actors
were assertively unaristocratic and unchivalric in style. But these
changes were in style rather than substance.

It was appropriate that it should be Kipling and not Twain at the
Roosevelt dinner. Twain was not in sympathy—as a writer—with this
aristocratic kind of adventure hero. Nor did he notably create heroes
of any kind in his fiction; which is not to say he had none in real life;
but insofar as he drew them (the Yankee is as near as he comes to
a hero) they belong to Defoe's type rather than Scott's. But in his
relation to them, and other matters, Twain has more in common with
Thorstein Veblen, another frontier intellectual and satirist of capitalism, than with Defoe—much less with the well-born Wisters and
Roosevelts.

Veblen was essentially a man of heroes, but his worship of them
was ironic. He devoted his attention first to the financiers or "pecuniary men" of his society. In *Theory of the Leisure Class* (1899) he said
that the ideal pecuniary man was like the ideal delinquent, addicted
to sport and gambling, magic and superstition. That book has often
been called a saga of the doom of the heroes of America's leisure class.
His attitude to them is very similar to that of Norris and Dreiser,
amongst contemporary novelists. But in their novels, and in Veblen's
own writings about financiers, the irony is almost as bitter, as obses-

sive, as doom-laden, as it is in the last part of *Connecticut Yankee*. This cannot be called hero-worship in any ordinary sense, even though the writers brood over this figure they have conjured up with quite as much emotional intensity as real hero-worshipers.

Veblen also reminds us of Twain by an idea like this, from *The Theory of Business Enterprise*, "The ubiquitous presence of the machine, with its spiritual concomitant—workaday ideals and scepticism of what is only conventionally valid—is the unequivocal mark of the western culture of today" (*The Viking Veblen*, p. 348). That could be the Yankee himself; and when Veblen looks at the modernization of Germany, he sees it in terms very like those of Twain's novel. "The case of Germany is unexampled among Western nations both as regards the abruptness, thoroughness and amplitude of its appropriation of this technology, and as regards the archaism of its cultural furniture at the date of this appropriation." And he has a footnote comparing the case of Japan. But that cultural furniture*— being the mythos and ethos of the military castes that ruled those countries—turned out to be more important than he (or Twain) expected. Veblen was also like Twain in that bitterness of alienation that almost strangled his voice with irony.

In later life he somewhat overcame, or turned his back on, that self-destructive irony, and in the early 1920s turned to the engineers; his book *The Engineers*, of 1921, said they were the only men who might create a revolution in America, and that a soviet of engineers should be set up. He in part inspired Howard Scott's Technical Alliance, and Technocracy Inc. (1932). This is something we can well imagine Twain taking up, too—or Defoe. In *Imperial Germany*, Veblen had said that the Englishmen who made the Industrial Revolution atrophied man's earlier bent to impute anthropological qualities to everything; and that free institutions and insubordination go with the machine—and thus are incompatible with the feudal and dynastic state which is superimposed on them in Germany and Japan.

The technocratic hero of Twain and Veblen is thus clearly descended from Defoe and Smiles, and distinct from the gentleman cowboy of Wister and Roosevelt; and yet both types were to be found, in real life, side by side at the helms of power.

---

*\*Imperial Germany and the Industrial Revolution*, p. 83.

## Henry Stanley

A historical hero who combined both sorts of trait (though originally and basically of the first type) was Henry Stanley, whose career is absolutely pivotal in the history of the WASP hero, and who was significantly related to Twain. Stanley is a relevant figure for us to look at in several ways. One is as an Anglo-American. He lived in and worked for both countries, and was a citizen of both. Each felt him at times to be somewhat alien, and to belong to the other, and yet both tried to claim him as their own. The history of his reputation illustrates both the irritated animosity between England and America in the '70s and '80s, and the rapprochement of the 1890s, when there were many calls for a reunion of the two countries on imperialist-racist grounds. At that time Senator Beveridge said, "The American Republic is part of the movement of a race—the most masterful race of history—and race movements are not to be stopped by the hand of man. They are mighty answers to divine commands." And he wrote to his friend, M. E. Ingalls, "Never forget that we are the only people on earth whose farmers buy the adjoining farm before they need it. We are of the blood which furnishes the world with its Daniel Boones, its Francis Drakes, its Cecil Rhodes."* Henry Stanley was another of that company, and the focus of much hero-worship, in England and America.

Frank Hird's authorized life of Stanley, published in 1935, says he was "The last of the great adventurers—to use the word in its best and original meaning. . . . His life story was a romance. From the humblest beginning with every disadvantage against him—absolute poverty, friendlessness, his childhood spent in a workhouse . . . not only an explorer of untiring courage and resource, but a great administrator in the creation and management of the Congo Free State" (pp. 11–12). And Marie von Bunsen (who could have married Stanley, and been 'queen of Africa') described him as "one of the tough Conquistador types with the outward habit of a disgruntled farmer and the phraseology and vocabulary of an American journalist" (Hall, *Stanley: An Adventurer Explored*, p. 275). Not a romance-hero, that is, but an adventurer.

*Quoted in T. F. Gossett, *Race: The History of an Idea in America*, p. 318.

Stanley was born a bastard in Wales in 1841, and brought up in a workhouse until he fought the master and ran away. This conclusion to schooling and opening to adventure we have met before; and in Stanley's story we have reason to suspect some romancing. But it seems to be true that his mother, who lived nearby, denied him love; and that he learned piety, cleanliness, and love of order in the workhouse. So that, whatever details he invented, he was indeed very like the Defoe-style self-made man.

In 1859 he sailed as a ship's boy to New Orleans, where he got himself adopted by an English merchant, Henry Stanley, and took his name; very much like Crusoe. He said that Henry Stanley died in 1861, but it seems that in fact the older man broke off relations with him. In any case, he was effectively an orphan again. During the Civil War he served in both the Northern and Southern armies, and worked as a merchant, a sailor, and a journalist. (This variety of activity and flexibility of temperament must remind us of Defoe's own career.) In the last capacity he reported on the Peace Commission to the Sioux in Montana of 1867 and was much impressed with the Indians' calm and bravery. He recommended the Reservations scheme in the *New York Herald* and the *Chicago Tribune,* as the way to settle their problems. Stanley said later that he learned how to handle African natives from watching and listening to Generals Sherman, Henderson, and Taylor deal with Indians.

It was on this occasion that Stanley made Twain's acquaintance, for Twain also was reporting the Peace Commission. Their careers had been not dissimilar. Like Twain, Stanley had worked in San Francisco, Denver, and Central City, as a printer and as a prospector. He was an expert shot with both rifle and six-shooter, and had known both Wild Bill Hickok and General Custer. Later he, like Twain, had something of a career as a lecturer; he was billed as "The American Traveller," wore a uniform he declared to belong to the Turkish navy, and promised to make the muezzin's call to prayer in Arabic on the lecture platform.

1867 was the year he went to work for James Gordon Bennett of the *New York Herald,* one of the most flamboyant figures in a very flamboyant period of journalism. Bennett was exactly the same age as Stanley, and equally ambitious, and soon became jealous of him. But he sent Stanley to report on the war in Abyssinia, where he achieved a major scoop, by getting reports to his paper before any of the British papers got theirs. He got on badly with the British officers, who called him "Jefferson Brick," after the brash American journalist in *Martin Chuzzlewit*—while he thought them effeminate. This was intercaste jealousy—the mercantile against the aristomilitary. But Stanley was more than a journalist, and he knew it. During the war (swimming under fire, capturing an abandoned ship) he had made himself a hero. And now he had found a profession in which his various abilities could all be combined together.

He had always talked of traveling around the world and having adventures. Like Przhevalsky, he liked to take adolescent boys with him. In 1864 he picked up Lewis Noe, a fifteen-year-old shipmate on the *Minnesota*, who traveled with him in Greece, and who later signed a document releasing Stanley from all claims upon him. Edwin Balch was another boy he tried to take on a world adventure. And later he adopted a page, whom he called Baruti (gunpowder), from a cannibal tribe. As in Przhevalsky's case, we find this fondness for boys matched with a shyness with women. On August 1, 1884, he wrote a friend, "I have lived with men, not women, and it is the man's intense ruggedness, plainness, directness, that I have contracted by sheer force of circumstances. . . . The fact is, I can't talk to women. In their presence I am as much of a hypocrite as any other man, and it galls me that I must act and be affected, and parody myself."

Stanley aimed at heroism early. In 1869, while in Madrid to report on the Spanish Civil War, he wrote to a friend, who urged him to take a holiday, describing his achievement so far, and saying, "How have I done all this? By intense application to duty, by self-denial, which means I have denied myself all pleasures, so that I might do my duty thoroughly, and not exceed it. Such has been my ambition. I am fulfilling it. Pleasure cannot blind me, it cannot lead me astray from the path I have chalked out. I am so much my own master, that I am master over my own passions. . . . It is only by railway celerity that I can live. Away from work, my conscience accuses me of forgetting duty, of wasting time, of forgetting my God. I cannot help that feeling. It makes me feel as though the world were sliding from under my feet." We hear there the voice of the Victorian hero, the conscience-driven conquistador. In the Introduction to his Autobiography, he says, "But I was not sent into the world to be happy, nor to search for happiness. I was sent for a special work."

Bennett commissioned him to find Livingstone, who had disappeared in search of the source of the Nile in 1866. This was of course
a very American thing to do, very offensive to English sensibility, to
make a newspaper stunt out of the great missionary, England's Christian hero of the whole century—and to presume to rescue him, as if
England could not do so, was doubly offensive. Stanley reached
Zanzibar in 1871, set off into Africa and found Livingstone at Ujiji,
established a filial relation with him, and returned to write *How I
Found Livingstone* in 1872.[5]

He turned his adventures into book form immediately, as
Przhevalsky did, and Stanley had much wider circulation; *Through
the Dark Continent,* 1878, was translated into eight languages simul-
taneously. His friend Thomas Wallace Knox made a fictional digest
of it called *Boy Travellers in the Congo.* And Stanley himself in 1874
produced a novel, *My Kalulu: Prince, King, and Slave.* The Preface
says it is written for boys. . . . "Those clever, bright-eyed, intelligent
boys, of all classes . . . boys who have a promising future before
them."[6]

From 1879 to 1884 he worked for King Leopold of the Belgians
in the Congo Free State; the reporter and explorer become nation-
builder. He built a fifty-two-mile road from the lower Congo to
Stanley Pool, which made the Congo navigable as an artery of commerce. There he won the title, Bula Matari, the breaker of stones.
A massive bronze statue of him stood beside Stanley Pool until
demolished in the early 1960s. His two-volume *The Congo and the
Founding of the Free State,* 1885, was followed by editions in seventeen other languages.

In London, he and Twain used to stay at the same hotel, and
Twain persuaded him to sign a lecture contract with his own impre-
sario, "Major" Pond. Twain launched Stanley on his lecture career
in Boston in 1886, saying how his own self-esteem sank when he
compared what he had done in his life with all that Stanley had done.
"When I contrast what I have achieved in my measurably brief life
with what he has achieved in his possibly briefer one, the effect is to
sweep utterly away the ten story edifice of my own self-appreciation
and to leave nothing behind but the cellar" (Farwell, *The Man Who
Presumed,* p. 88).

Twain cited Stanley's indestructible Americanism, too. It was like
a breath of fresh air to see "an untainted American citizen who has

been caressed and complimented by half the crowned heads of Europe. . . . He is a product of institutions which exist in no other country on earth—institutions that bring out all that is best and most heroic in a man" (Hall, *Stanley,* p. 272).

It seems likely that this was genuine hero-worship, of a thoroughly modern-system hero; that Twain saw Stanley as a more effective version of himself—as the man who translated their common values into deeds, not jokes. Twain had by then been interested in the other man for some time. In 1872 he had attended the Royal Geographical Society dinner for Stanley, at which Sir Henry Rawlinson had apologized for the Society's behavior to him over the rescue of Livingstone; Twain described it as a manly and magnificent apology, and the occasion must have been a triumph for all adventurers and all frontiersmen. In 1879 he wrote in his *Notebooks,* "Stanley is almost the only man alive today whose name and work will be familiar a hundred years hence" (p. 304). In 1886 Twain tried to get Stanley to write an autobiography and a boys' adventure novel about Africa for his publishing firm. And in 1891 he was to ask Stanley to write a reply for them to one of the books attacking his most recent African expedition.

In 1887 Stanley had set out to rescue Emin Pasha, a European commanding Egyptian troops in Equatorial Africa, cut off after the defeat of Gordon by the Mahdi in the Sudan. This time he took with him a steel boat, 500 Remingtons, 50 Winchesters, and a Maxim. (When he tested the latter, and found it fired 333 rounds in 30 seconds, he said, "It is a fine weapon, and will be invaluable for subduing the heathen.") He had always been fascinated by new machines, and was an inventor himself; like the Yankee, he overwhelmed a hostile native force at one point by building a wooden tower that floated on three canoes, and out of which came a mysterious voice. But of course what was most notable about this ever-increasing weight of equipment was its death-dealing properties. On this expedition he took 800 men with him, and lost 500 of them. He was much blamed for abandoning a rearguard which got massacred.

The commander of that rearguard, Major Barttelot, was a brutal man, who may have been one of Conrad's inspirations in drawing the figure of Kurtz. (Conrad's trip up the Congo took place in 1890, only two years after these events, and he was, by his own account, thinking about them, and about Stanley.) Barttelot apparently gave floggings of three hundred lashes at a time, and looked on with a wide grin. He buried more than eighty of his carriers in less than a year; and hired a body of cannibals to kill and eat another tribe so that one of his men could record the scene.* A good deal was written about Barttelot and the Stanley expedition as a whole, immediately after.

Stanley and his career were a striking embodiment of those forces of adventure and modernization—of the modern world system— which Twain first celebrated and then accused in *Connecticut Yankee.* The moral disapprobation in which he ended was a much more than personal tragedy.

If we compare Stanley with the great British proconsuls in Africa then, Gordon, Goldie, Lugard, Johnson, we shall see how clearly they all belonged to that upper-class, aristomilitary caste we can associate with Wister and Roosevelt.[7] In such men, the sense of self was supported by an imperialist identity which was not, I think, available to Stanley (or Twain). On the other hand, the latter could of course identify themselves as representing the modern world system. And despite the appalling revelations, and the repudiation of that role, to which some of his late writings bear witness, Twain continued to play that role, and celebrate it in others, up to the end. It was only after his death, in 1910, that some more drastic change imposed itself on writers generally.

---

*Jerry Allen, *The Sea Years of Joseph Conrad.*

# IX

## *Kipling*[1]

DURING Kipling's lifetime the modern system crossed the great divide of 1914–1918, after which everyone assumed that the British empire was dying, and everyone in serious literature was openly hostile to it. We have of course found plenty of evidence that they were hostile before, but most characteristically they had expressed their feeling by ignoring the empire as a literary subject. After 1918 they turned more often to it, in aggression. One of the first examples of such writing was also the finest, E. M. Forster's *Passage to India.*

But partly because of that change in climate, and his consequent disappearance from the literary scene, Kipling's career as an adventure writer can be said to have ended with the outbreak of war. We can restrict our view of him to his work as celebrant of overt imperialism and subverter of literature-as-a-system. For the '90s and the Edwardian years were both the time when England threw off the mercantile mask—the aristomilitary caste moving to the front of the Jubilee processions—and the time when literature nearly accepted alliance with that caste and the empire. Kipling made a gallant effort to mobilize sympathetic men of letters (notably the professors of literature) and to reorganize the literary world's criteria of styles and subjects.

He did not engage in literal intrigue to that end. Kipling's energies went into the act of writing almost exclusively; and insofar as he took a hand in action, it was of a patriotic or political kind, not in matters of culture. His efforts to change literature-as-a-system should be compared with Scott's rather than with Dryden's or Coleridge's. But if he is compared with Twain, he will be seen to have made such efforts, and from inside the system. Because there were differences between England and America, Kipling was more literary than Twain. In the English cultural situation, where the responsible class felt it had political power, its sense of cultural responsibility was more acute. Kipling could hope to ally literature to the responsible class, and he invoked a great deal of literary precedent on his side, against the spiritual rebels of literature. (The powerful sympathy of Kipling and Twain for each other, despite this difference in situation, testifies to the essential identity of their spirits.) But the crucial consequence for this study is that Kipling put great artistic intensity into his work, and we are faced with a closely textured and intricately structured oeuvre, which demands more specifically critical attention than my other authors received.

## *Kim*

In that oeuvre, his only successful full-length narrative was *Kim*. Kipling has much more impressive successes in art than the conduct of a full-length romance; and more impressive successes in meaning than *Kim*, charming as that book is. But we can begin with it.

Clearly Kipling was indebted to *Huckleberry Finn* in designing his story. Twain and Kipling were the two great entertainers of the Anglo-Saxon community in its period of overt imperialism, and they helped each other quite importantly in their work. The two books' major motif alone—the idea of giving the WASP public an Irish orphan hero to focus their feelings on—is quite an important one. It subtilizes the strategy and renews the feeling of the adventure tale. And Kipling also makes Kim a Roman Catholic. And culturally speaking an Indian too. Perhaps we should also credit Twain with the idea of substituting a boy for a man as hero, even though there are several other exemplars of that substitution, and several other pressures on Kipling to make it besides precedent. Nevertheless, if many voices in the situation of the writer of English fiction in the '90s—especially one who wanted to celebrate adventure—if many voices combined to command him, "Write for and about boys," still Twain was the one man of genius to have done it.

Then the relationship between Huck and Jim is strikingly like that between Kim and the Lama; drifting along the River is strikingly like traveling along the Road; the episodic, the picaresque, the picturesque, the humorous—the mixture is the same in both books, and behind both narratives looms the idea of the Frontier and of the Empire. There are of course differences, deriving from differences between Frontier and Empire; for instance, the English novel has no dead bodies and no sordid violence; and Kim is perceptibly more adventurous than Huck—there is less debilitating melancholy in his nature; but the likenesses seem more important. Clearly Kipling took more from Twain than from anyone else, though he combined what he took with ingenious devices of his own; like the Lama's quest, which contrasted and intertwined with Kim's in very clever ways; the Chaucerian or Morrisy charm which he gave to the picturesque cavalcade of his personae and places; and so on.

More important, from our point of view, is the godfather motif; the number of adults who care for Kim and in effect adopt him, the Lama, Mahbub Ali, the Sahiba, Hurree Babu. They in effect compete for his affections. At the end, "The Sahiba is a heart of gold," said the Lama earnestly. "She looks up on him as her son." And Mahbub Ali replies rather sourly, "Hmph! Half Hind seems that way disposed" (p. 283). This is on the first level a device for giving the reader, once he has identified himself with Kim, the luxury of feeling loved —not so very important a meaning. But on a second level, we note that these so adoring godfathers are all Indians, of various kinds— Colonel Creighton, for instance, has a cooler relationship to Kim, less personally affectionate and much less adoring. So what we see—and we see it often in Kipling—is the humble affection offered up to a white boy by potent adult figures representing native races.[2] (Two notable cases are the stories "A Sahib's War" and "A Deal in Cotton.") Is *this* an important meaning? Yes, it is in its own terms very richly and convincingly worked out, however many political objections one has to the idea. And this is a development of a motif in Defoe's novels; Crusoe and Singleton have godfathers in this sense, but the range of meaning Defoe extracts from them is much less. (They are not natives, for instance.)

Another motif is the Great Game, and Kim's secret service work. Hannah Arendt says, "What the dragon-slayer is to the bureaucrat [that is, his myth-world predecessor], the adventurer is to the secret agent" (Arendt, *The Origins of Totalitarianism,* p. 216).[3] The phrase "the Great Game" was used about Anglo-Russian conflicts in Asia from the middle of the nineteenth century on. These conflicts generated anxiety, especially by the end of the century. As Jeffrey Meyers points out in *Fiction and the Colonial Experience,* in 1846 2000 miles separated the English frontier from the Russian in Asia; in 1876, only 500 miles, and those occupied by the unstable Amirate of Kabul; the border between Afghanistan and India was "settled" in 1893, that between Afghanistan and Russia in 1895. But fictionally speaking, of course, Kipling plays on the pun introduced by the fact that Kim is still a child. The Game metaphor is always being demetaphorized by its context in the book—Kim is literally only playing games; though of course it is remetaphorized by the matters of life and death involved; the serious meaning emerges from that interchange—from our sense that men are like boys, and vice versa, that politics is like a game, and vice versa—an insight Kipling is very fond of. The characterization of Mahbub Ali conveys the same feeling, and corroborates the phrase "the Great Game."

A somewhat related idea is that of the training of Kim, which is compared to the way that a colt is trained. Given Kipling's ideology, it is of course a most important matter, this making of a boy into a man. Both those terms are heavily loaded in Kipling's usage, and if "boy" is often all that is wonderful, there is another usage of the word, in contrast with "man," which is contemptuous. And the language for describing the rite of passage is predominantly that of horse training. In *Kim* that language is given mostly to Mahbub Ali, who is a horse dealer, and so it seems special to him; but in fact you find it everywhere in Kipling, and it was, for instance, used by his schoolmaster, Cormell Price, about Kipling himself.[4] What this language brings with it is, one, the idea of breaking the colt's will—the fiercer the will, the better, but it must be broken; two, the idea of the boy as animal, the man as human—or divine—the mature adult lives in a world of remote and alienated wisdom; and three, the idea of the man riding on the boy's back—not to imply any direct sexual excitement, but an intimacy of connection which is in some loose sense erotic. It is only when the Lama is hard on Kim, accidentally, that we are aware there is a significant training relationship going on; in the early parts, when Kim merely likes the Lama, and the Lama merely talks wisdom, the relationship does not feel quite real.

In one way the book is clearly a development from Scott, in that its characterization and even action are so fused with 'cultural' or ethnological observation. To meet someone of a different type, religiously, socially, or racially, is an event in itself, to Kim and to the reader. Kipling is very skillful in making these details, potentially so static and informational, effectively dynamic and narrative; the measure of the gulf between this kind of romance and serious fiction of the Great Tradition kind is that here these "external" details matter so much.

In another way, it is clearly a development from Defoe; in that it is informed by the character's glee at his own cleverness. Only instead of a "do-it-yourself" cleverness, this is a "be-it-yourself" kind, focusing on transcultural disguise. We are told on page 160 that the Hindu child's mind could not temper itself to enter another's soul; "but a demon in Kim woke up and sang with joy as he put on the changing dresses, and changed speech and gesture therewith." Kipling asserted (and John Buchan followed him in this) that it was particularly an Anglo-Saxon gift, to be able to imitate every other race.

The serious fictional meaning of this (for of course Kipling has such meanings, being a great artist) is indicated by the imagery of demons and singing—it is being suggested both seriously and playfully that Kim prefers dissimulation to sincerity—the meaning is in the exchange between "seriously" and "playfully." As in the Great Game metaphor, men and boys exchange identities, and this is doubly exciting because of the difference in status between them, dramatized in the training metaphor.

An interesting example of the social power of Kipling's art is the game played by Kim and the Hindu boy, a competition in noting, remembering, and reciting afterward the jewels on a tray. This training in observation is a part of what Kim learns in preparing to become a Secret Service agent. In Ballantyne's *Coral Island* also there is some stress on "powers of observation," and their value in education, and for adventure. (A related phenomenon is the interest in codes and clues—clues for the central character but also for the reader to pick up and interpret—competitively; this is something you find in Jules Verne, Twain, and of course Conan Doyle; an interest serious fiction eschewed.) But Kipling's description of the Game is not only a good deal more vivid, it had a remarkable social effectiveness. "Kim's Game" became a popular social entertainment—not without its more serious intentions—among the class Kipling wrote for. And that was of course the responsible class—the men of action who also cared about literature. Kipling had recreated that constituency. In the '90s indeed, he had attracted also the men of letters, but they left him by the turn of this century. But Philip Mason tells us that people he met at official dinner parties in India, who declared that they didn't read, would add "except of course *Kim.*"

His audience's loyalty to Kipling was very strong, and its character —because they were not habitual readers—might be called unprecedented. Of the two lines of descent of the adventure novel, he clearly has more in common with Scott than with Defoe, in his interest in culture and in his essentially chivalric heroes. And Scott too had of course a very large and loyal audience. But Kipling is unique because such an artist, unique in the intensity with which he combines material from his audience's most familiar experience—the anecdotes of British India, for example—with large poetic and even mythic preoccupations.

For instance, walking is made into an important moral and indeed cultural activity in *Kim*. It is a significant recommendation of the Lama to Kipling's audience that he is a vigorous walker. And climbing is an intensification of walking; this was strongly felt in late Victorian England, where men like Leslie Stephen made Alpine climbing a big thing. "Day after day they struck deeper into the huddled mountains, and day after day Kim watched the Lama return to a man's strength . . . and where he should have sunk exhausted swung his long draperies about him, drew a double-lungful of the diamond air, and walked as only a hillman can. Kim, plains-bred and plains-fed, sweated and panted, astonished. 'This is *my* country,' said the Lama. 'Beside Suchzen, this is flatter than a rice-field' " (p. 230). And the climbing leads to a sense of geography. "Through the speckled shadow of the great deogar-forests; through oak, feathered and flumed with ferns; birch, ilex, rhododendron and pine, out onto the bare hillsides' slippery sunburnt grass, and back into the woodlands' coolth again, till oak gave way to bamboo and palm of the valley, he swung untiring" (pp. 231, 232). As Kipling handles it, and in this he rediscovered the Elizabethans, and was followed by John Buchan and others, geography became a sort of heraldry of imperialism—every mountain and river evokes the excitement of conquest and possession.[5]

That is surely what the reader felt when Kim "watched the wee cows grazing on the housetops, or threw his soul after his eye across the deep blue gulfs between range and range" (p. 233). What is offered is of course romanticism, but beneath surely lies imperialism. "Thus, after long hours of what would be reckoned very fair mountaineering in civilized countries, they would pant over a saddleback, sidle past a few landslips, drop through forest at an angle of 45 on to the road again. Along their track lay the villages of the hill-folk—mud and earth huts, timbers now and then rudely carved with an axe—clinging like swallows' nests against the steeps, huddled on tiny flats halfway down a 3,000-feet glissade; jammed into a corner between cliffs that funnelled and focused every wandering blast; or, for the sake of summer pasture, cowering down a neck that in winter would be 10 foot deep in snow" (p. 232).

The activity for which Kim is being trained is surveying, which brings together the activities of climbing, observing, native disguise, etc., under the aegis of imperialism. It may seem to the modern reader a euphemism to give this name to the secret service of an imperialist power, but in Kipling's time it was at least a general euphemism. And for his readers the survey had quite exact historical references. Captain T. G. Montgomerie was an engineer in the Great Trigonometrical Survey of India who in 1862 suggested to the Asiatic Society of Bengal that a native could get into Tibet and do survey work there, as a move in the Great Game. He chose men in the Indian Educational Service, and some of them became famous in the closed circles of the Indian administration, like Nain Singh, one of Montgomerie's first batch of eight recruits. They got two years' training in the use of the compass and sextant, and in taking an absolutely regular stride, which they counted on the Buddhist rosaries they carried—an adapted version, with only one hundred beads, and every tenth slightly larger. They carried adapted prayer wheels, with a compass and long strips of paper concealed inside them. Their walking-sticks contained a boiling thermometer, their strong box a sextant, and so on. In 1865 Nain and a companion set off to survey the main road to Lhasa, disguised as Bisahari horse-dealers from

Kashmir; and they returned in 1866 with an excellent map, for which Nain got the Gold Medal of the Royal Geographical Society. It is facts and legends of this sort which *Kim*'s first readers brought to their reading.

The figure of the Lama is both Kipling's triumph and his failure. It is a triumph because Kipling is significantly knowledgeable about lamas, and sympathetic with a renunciatory religion. (It is a related point that Kipling treats the Roman Catholic chaplain with more respect than the Protestant; the Protestant element in the White Anglo-Saxon Protestant formula had begun to lose its potency. Chesterton was selling to a large audience the idea of a Roman Catholic Englishness.) Kipling doesn't offer the insights into such religion that a Dostoevsky offers, but his treatment is—up to a point—dignified. And it is quite a remarkable change in the structure of the romance we have been studying that the Lama should have primacy over Mahbub Ali. The latter is after all a version of the Black Prince— an older Chingachgook for a boy Natty. The Lama is something new; as a hero of passivity, he derives from Twain's Jim, but clearly a major difference of status is involved in giving that figure of practical passivity this dignity of cultural background and spiritual insight.

What happens to the romance genre when this figure replaces Chingachgook or Fergus MacIvor as the hero's major tutor? Not very much happens, and that is Kipling's failure. The Lama's powers are circumscribed by the word "spiritual," which is mutually exclusive with the word "practical." His truths are no use in the world. In the end he is quite simply duped as to who Kim is and what he intends to do with his life; in the end it is Mahbub Ali and Colonel Creighton who have trained Kim; it has been good for Kim to have had the Lama's acquaintance in his childhood, and no doubt he will return to see the Lama on holidays and perhaps in retirement, but that is to say that this acquaintance is for him like a convent schooling for upper-class girls—it adds an irreplaceable polish, the true aristocratic je ne sais quoi. For all Kipling's interest in renunciatory Buddhism, the Lama's only function in Kim's life is to be his Mr. Chips. (Of course Kipling intended something more than that; and achieved something more—otherwise there would be no element of triumph in his depiction of the Lama; but the book expresses a deep ambivalence, betrayed in the quite unsatisfactory and merely tricky ending.)

## *Stalky and Co.*

This is both a more characteristic and a more significant Kipling success than *Kim*, because of the aggressive moral realism of the meaning, and because of the corresponding intricacy of the artistic means. It is an unpleasant and difficult book; but a powerful study of authority. Like many other artists, Kipling often makes his best work difficult and unpleasant—though he *could* simply charm and delight, without compromising, as in the *Just So Stories*.

The introductory poem contains a stanza which reminds us of *Kim*, and indicates the continuity between these two of Kipling's books and most of the others—the concern for how boys are trained to be men and Englishmen.

> Servants of the Staff and chain—
> Mine and fuse and grapnel—
> Some before the face of Kings,
> Stand before the face of Kings;
> Bearing gifts to divers Kings—
> Gifts of case and shrapnel.

The boys were trained to be surveyors, but also to be diplomats and soldiers; to treat with kings or to cannonade them. The stress on kings is very characteristic; it blends an ironic contempt with a deep romantic thrill; which fuse in the feeling "I, as an Englishman, am greater than Kings." This is Kipling's version of the anti-imperialist modern world system feeling in Defoe; and despite Kipling's overt love of Empire (unlike Defoe, his imagination turned to ruling, not trading) and despite this being an imperialist epoch in English history, one meaning of "Kings" as Kipling uses it is anti-imperialist. This is after all one of the meanings of his famous poem "Recessional"; that Englishmen should be on guard against the excitements of success and power—though that warning is suffused and subdued by a surge of precisely those excitements.

The crucial difference between Defoe and Kipling is rather in the different ways in which they treat the theme, and induce the excitement, of "how-to-do-it." Both are devoted to that theme, but in quite different ways. Kipling dazzles the reader with technicalities—wants the reader to be excited about things he hasn't understood. Defoe always genuinely wants the reader to understand—to see how the thing is done. There is an element of insincerity in Kipling's cult of expertise, though not in his cult of the expert. And the skills he does really want to explain to us—Kim's and Stalky's skills—are not really trades but tricks. The tradesmen's skills, which Defoe makes so much of, in Kipling take a rather peripheral position—at least in the prose.

The Stalky poem as a whole is a set of copybook maxims; the boys learned to be each "Keen in his vocation" and "To obey their orders," and were "Set to serve the lands they rule (Save he serve, no man may rule)." It was of course Kipling's fate to deal in copybook maxims; he was an artist in service of his rulers; a fate which brought him his characteristic problems as an artist. If we think of other high priests of the copybook gods, like Samuel Smiles, Horatio Alger, Martin Tupper, we shall better appreciate Kipling's achievement. By his time the system of literature, as we have seen, was driven by a motive of opposition to those gods; the aversion felt by Swift and Coleridge and Arnold had been strengthened by sterner principle. Even the realm of imagination as a whole was inspired by an evasion of those maxims. (Though in most cases the imagination evades the kiss of a culture's truisms only as part of a game in which it finally lets itself get caught.) *Stalky and Co.* is a prime example of how Kipling plays that game. In his verse I think he is less successful. The problem one feels with much of it—the problem T. S. Eliot alluded to in his distinction between verse and poetry—is precisely the difficulty of the flat resonances of copybook maxims. More exactly, Kipling's solutions to that problem, which he solves most typically by indicating "savage" and "primitivist" perspectives behind each maxim, demand more from his command of poetic language than he can give. In his fiction, his language has more factual specificity and his structures more dynamic exchange.[6]

We are told in "An Unsavoury Interlude" that, "Outside his own immediate interests, the boy is as ignorant as the savage he so admires; but he has also the savage's resource." And this is a persistent theme; "tribe" is a word often used. Stalky and Beetle and M'Turk, ". . . spun wildly on their heels, jodelling after the accepted manner of a 'gloat,' which is not unremotely allied to Primitive Man's song of triumph," (p. 27) and are seen on page 38, "learning, at the expense of a fellow-countryman, the lesson of their race, which is to put away all emotion and entrap the alien at the proper time." This they do by deceiving one of the masters, and the point is made by the specificity of the analogy—by the credibility of their behavior and by Kipling's analysis of it. (That's the resource he does not command in his verse.) A final example is the West African war-drum they play, a gift from M'Turk's naval uncle, originally made to signal war across estuaries and deltas. ". . . a deep devastating drone filled the passages as M'Turk and Beetle scientifically rubbed its top. Anon it changed to the blare of trumpets—of savage pursuing trumpets. Then, as M'Turk slapped one side, smooth with the blood of ancient sacrifice, the roar broke into short coughing howls such as the wounded gorilla throws in his native forest" (p. 60). And as Kipling evokes behind the boys this somewhat fanciful picture of primitive man, he evokes before them the more realistic image of the people they will be ruling and fighting in their adult careers. Thus he sets boyhood in an imaginative context radically unlike *Tom Brown's Schooldays*, not to mention *Eric*—even less to mention *The Prelude* or *Emile*—but no less valid, imaginatively.

Kipling's heroes set themselves positively against traditional images of school piety and training—against house honor and cricket and so on. (It is quite comic to see his critics, for instance, who feel themselves to be more skeptical than he of Establishment pieties, yet scolding him for blaspheming against these pieties in *Stalky and Co.*) The boys bring to school life a strong disgust for clichés and for the blatant. The most striking case is in "The Flag of Their Country," when the chauvinist M. P. unfurls a flag before them, and unwittingly drives Stalky to disband his cadet corps. Patriotism has been made disgusting. The major activity of the Cadet Corps had been for the boys to learn each in turn to drill the others, and as a part of the drill to shout insults at them in sergeant-major manner; even more, for each to learn to betray no feeling when thus berated. Thus both halves of the story bear upon silence and restraint of expression. The Flag was "a thing shut up, sacred and apart." They had been training themselves in a devotion to it that was profoundly silent, though superficially loud in blasphemies of various kinds. The success of the story resides in the way its form mirrors the intricacies of the moral paradox involved.[7]

The book's central paradox, around which the others are organized, is that of authority. One of the great lessons the boys learn at school is to obey; and yet the heroes are rebels. This is a serious paradox, for obedience is of the essence of the boys' interrelations— Beetle's obedience to Stalky, for instance; and yet Stalky is a real rebel —Kipling once described Stalky's real-life model as displaying "an unaffected contempt" for all the masters at their school. The paradox is mediated through the mechanism of the Headmaster; he represents true authority, which the boys recognize, and he in effect legitimizes their rebellion against the untrue authority of the other masters.* He implements the paradox by imposing punishments on them which are categorically "unjust." What this does is to give irony a role within a system of piety—to give rebellion a role within a system of authority. Kipling builds a very convincing model of how sincerity—and particularly the sincerity of originality and leadership —can be taught; how a model of aggression and resistance can be built into the teacher-student relationship and not destroy it but energize it. The most elaborate fictionalization of this is the story "A Little Prep," in which Stalky out-maneuvers the Head by revealing the latter's secret heroism to the other boys and organizing an outburst of acclamation which is at the same time disobedience, so that the Head can punish them yet again—the piety is saved from blatancy by being interlaced with impudence and punishment.

In the boys' future stands the life of heroism-in-service, most typically in India, on the North-West frontier. It is represented by the old boys who return to the school, and are just as devoted to the Head as they were as pupils. And by the story in which we hear of Stalky's exploits there, where he has "become a Sikh," but where he behaves exactly as he did at school. (And in fact the real-life "Stalky's" career, as Major-General Dunsterville, did parallel the boy's; long after *Stalky and Co.* was published, in the Great War, he led an irregular force from India into Persia, and camouflaged his cars to look like tanks, and so on.) Thus the picture is essentially a triptych; primitive man, the school, and the Frontier; no panels from what literature calls mature life or civilization, needless to say.[8]

*His authority is ideal and potential—as it were, divine—and so the boys don't rub up against it all the time. The school as a whole actualizes that authority, only imperfectly. And at rare intervals *he* actualizes it perfectly, and then we rejoice, to see the divine power we worship made manifest.

## Biography and Reputation

As for Kipling himself, he was born in 1865 in Bombay, where his father had just become professor of architectural sculpture in the School of Art, and was as such concerned to preserve native Indian arts. He had been designer to a Burslem potter and then worked as a stone mason on the Victoria and Albert Museum. He was a friend of Edward Burne-Jones and William Morris, and part of the arts-and-crafts movement. During Rudyard's holidays in London as a boy he spent many days in the Victoria and Albert Museum, and the other South Kensington museums, and there is a certain similarity between his work and those collections of exotica and ingenuities from all over the world. So he did not inherit warrior traits genealogically, or biologically—by physical or psychical temperament. His vocation as bard of the Empire was always something of an adventure, almost a paradox, a response to an external idea.

His mother belonged to a group of remarkable sisters, one of whom married Burne-Jones, another Edward Poynter, who became President of the Royal Academy, and another the Baldwin whose son became Prime Minister. Mrs. Kipling seems to have been the most sharp-witted and sharp-tongued of all her sisters, and the writer grew up in a highly competitive but very close family. Both his parents were the children of Methodist ministers, but themselves apostates. Alice Kipling is supposed to have thrown into the fire a devoutly preserved lock of Wesley's hair with the remark, "The hair of the dog that bit us." The example of apostasy from religious to artistic spirituality was probably a powerful heritage for the writer. While living with foster parents in Southsea (having been sent home by his parents at the age of six) he spent holidays with the Burne-Joneses, where the arts and ideal values were one—and where he was happy; while at Southsea, where he was very unhappy, the tone was limitedly moral and religious—what he called "evangelical."

When he left school in 1882, he did not go to the university, which would have been the natural place for a boy with his already developed literary and artistic talents, but to India, where he worked as a journalist, and dined at the Club, and entered the world of the Indian services, with their very strong anti-intellectual group loyalties. Martin Fido has suggested that this was a crucial juncture in Kipling's development; that up to that point he might have developed very differently—into a liberal in politics; and in art a more ordinary sort of aesthete.[9]

But he became instead a cub-reporter on the *Civil and Military Review* and *The Pioneer,* under a short-tempered editor, Wheeler, who "licked him into shape."[10] It is perhaps emblematic that in 1883 he wrote a sarcastic review of Morris's socialist poem, "The Day is Coming." He had turned away from his early idealism. He plunged into Indian life from the angle of a reporter, who was sent by his paper to cover princely ceremonies, cholera outbreaks, bridge-openings, divorce and murder trials—he was very excited when one of his soldier friends was convicted of murder. One of his informants was the original of Mahbub Ali. And Kipling in turn was an informant to General Roberts, the Army's Commander-in-Chief, who asked him what the men in the barracks were thinking, in 1889.

By then Kipling, though only twenty-four, was a famous writer in India. His stories and poems, printed in the newspapers, were collected to form the first six volumes of the Indian Railway Library. That year he came back to England and soon found himself famous. *The Times* published a leading article about his work (probably written by Andrew Lang) on March 25, 1890. In the same year, *Lippincott's Magazine* printed his novel, *The Light That Failed* (in the same twelve months, they also published *Dorian Grey* and *Sherlock Holmes*). And also Henley published Kipling's *Barrack Room Ballads* in his *Scots Observer;* one of which, "Danny Deever," caused the professor of literature at Edinburgh University to tell his students, "Here's literature! Here's literature at last!," waving his copy over his head in excitement. The professors generally were enthusiastic; Dowden, Saintsbury, Quiller-Couch, and also the professorial types among men of letters—Gosse, Lang, Whibley.

Kipling had general as well as instantaneous success. Even the fervent liberals and aesthetes were not united against him. In 1892 Henry James wrote to his brother William, "Kipling strikes me personally as the most complete man of genius (as distinct from fine intelligence) that I have ever known." Lafcadio Hearn in 1897 called him, "the greatest of all living English poets, greater than all before him in the line he has taken. As for England, he is her modern Saga-man; skald, scop, whatever you like . . ." (R. L. Green, *Kipling:*

*the Critical Heritage*, p. 173). And C. E. Norton, in *The Atlantic*, for January of the same year, wrote "This splendid continuous fertility of English genius, this unbroken poetic expression of English character and life from Chaucer to Rudyard Kipling, is unparalleled in the moral and intellectual history of any other race. . . . He is one of those poets who have done England service in strengthening the foundations of her influence and of her fame" (Green, *Kipling*, pp. 185, 187).

The man of letters who seems to me to confront Kipling in something of the way Matthew Arnold confronted Twain, and Swift confronted Defoe, is Henry James. James was one of the few guests at Kipling's wedding, and in 1891 wrote a long and enthusiastic Preface to an American collection of Kipling's stories called *Mine Own People*. But he always had reservations, and it wasn't long before they became dominant in his judgment. On Christmas Day, 1897, he wrote Grace Norton that he thought Kipling's talent quite diabolically great, and that as a ballad-writer his future might still be big; but one deplored the fact that in prose Kipling could "make use of so little of life." "Almost nothing civilized save steam and patriotism. . . ." And of course neither of those topics were what James really called civilized. "Almost nothing of the complicated soul or of the female form or of any question of *shades*. . . ." James had once thought Kipling might become an English Balzac, but no longer. After 1900 he lost touch with Kipling and with his work.

Thus Kipling soon began to feel the ideological conflict between himself and other writers; deriving not from his politics—not all conservative writers were boycotted—but from the conflict between his subject matter (adventure) and theirs. In essays like "In Partibus," in poems like his attack on long-haired aesthetes in velvet-collar rolls, and in various stories, he expressed a strong unease. And he was soon attacked; notably by Robert Buchanan in "The Voice of the Hooligan" in the *Contemporary Review*, in 1899, Buchanan described Kipling as giving voice to a hooligan imperialism which was driving the old humanitarianism into retreat; he objected for instance to Kipling's depiction of soldiers, asking, "Is General Gordon forgotten?" that we should see the British army in these vulgar terms. But the crucial dates were those of the Boer War; that experience, and the disillusionment with imperialism it brought, marked the end of the liberal intelligentsia's dealings with Kipling.

During the war he served as a war correspondent in South Africa, where he was already a friend of Rhodes, and wrote propaganda for the war effort. Notably, he wrote a ballad about the British soldier for charity, "The Absent-Minded Beggar," which Sir Arthur Sullivan set to music, and which raised £250,000 in contributions for the soldiers. The dissent of the liberals could be seen within his own family, where Lady Burne-Jones disapproved of the war, refused to read Kipling's dispatches, and refused to celebrate the British victories, drawing popular hostility upon herself. Kipling also started a branch of the Navy League where he lived, and built a drill hall and instituted rifle practice. He was convinced that England needed to prepare for war, as was his friend Baden-Powell, who came to live near him. The Scout motto, "Be prepared," had that military meaning among others. Kipling wrote stories for and about the Scouts, and "The Army of a Dream" about a national militia.

Another of Kipling's critics was Wells, the modern Defoe, but he attacked in the name of politics rather than of literature. Indeed, in his *The New Machiavelli* (1911), which is in part a fictional autobiography, Wells says that Kipling was a very great influence on his generation of young men, and cited as his gifts to them a sense of geography (what we would now call geopolitics) and a sense of discipline and devotion which their own Socialist creed could not give them. He goes on to say—and this is only 1911—"Kipling has since been so mercilessly and exhaustively mocked, criticized and torn to shreds—never was a man so violently exalted and then, himself assisting, so relentlessly hauled down." As far as men of letters went, Kipling was by 1911 already beyond the pale.

During the Great War Kipling was a propagandist, and became a symbol of literature-on-the-side-of-the-war-effort. His publishers put out a Services edition of his works, for men in the trenches. After the war he served on the War Graves Commission, and wrote an official history of the Irish Guards, in which his son had served and died. But in 1919 T. S. Eliot reviewed a new volume of his in the *Athenaeum* (May 1) by saying that no one even read Kipling any more—nobody had even a negative opinion about him. He compared him with Swinburne and contrasted him with Conrad. "Mr. Conrad is very germane to the question, because he is in many ways the antithesis of Mr. Kipling." Eliot called Kipling a poet of ideas, in the same sense as Swinburne was, and a poet of Empire; and he made Conrad the model of everything that is to be admired and preferred—the embodiment of the literary imagination.

Then in 1923 Edmund Blunden reviewed Kipling's regimental history of the Irish Guards, and said it was unconvincing, because Kipling had not understood the pandemonium and nerve-strain of war. Praise of Kipling was gradually restricted to the Kipling Society, where his old school friends "Stalky" and "M'Turk" attended meetings into the late 1930s; where ex-colonels still hoped to convince literary critics that "East is East and West is West" was a good poem because it told the *truth*—that that was exactly what frontier officers felt about the marauding tribes they fought and loved.

It is, I think, important to realize *how* the readers who liked Kipling liked him, *what* they liked in him. Philip Mason, in his book *Kipling,* says that he himself was an idolatrous Kipling fan by the time he was fourteen, having identified himself in turn with Mowgli, Kim, and then Beetle. Then as a young man he came to dislike Kipling strongly. Then he got over that dislike. Such a development bears all the marks of a profound educational experience, shaping a reader's mind more powerfully than serious literature often can. And Mason sums up, "No one has had so deep an influence on a whole generation of a certain class as he did. Here was someone who understood the life they were brought up to, their mistrust of politicians and intellectuals, their inarticulate devotion to a cause, the training they had endured, the tenseness that lay beneath the apparently insensitive outer crust, the tenderness they longed to lavish on dogs and children, their nervous respect for those mysterious creatures, women—so fragile compared with themselves, and yet so firmly authoritarian as nurses and mothers" (p. 307).

C. E. Carrington says in his *Life of Rudyard Kipling,* 1956, that his qualification for writing the biography is one he shared with thousands—that he learned to read with *Just So Stories* and the *Jungle Books;* went to school with *Stalky and Co.,* read history with *Puck of Pook's Hill;* and discovered *Plain Tales From the Hills* as his first adult book. In 1914 he formed his ideas of army life from *Barrack Room Ballads* and "The Brushwood Boy," and the story of a centurion's life in *Puck* "strengthened the nerve of many a young soldier in the dark days of 1915 and 1941" (p. 296). In the Preface, he says, "Looking back, I find no other writer who has seen through the eyes of my generation with such a sharpness of observation. I owe far more

to Kipling than to some of the great classic figures of literature.
. . . There is no other writer, great or small, whose work I knew so
well, and I have been often astonished to find how many others, of
all ages, knew him as well as I did. . . ."

From Carrington we also learn that many of Kipling's stories were
based on newspaper items or current anecdotes. "It was his pride to
record traditional army legends, and he took the liberty of a Scott or
Burns in recording them." For instance, "Gunga Din" is based on
the water carrier of the Guides at the siege of Delhi; "Drums of the
Fore and Aft" on an incident in Orme's *History;* and John Chinn
(in "The Tomb of His Ancestors") on James Outram, the friend of
the Lawrences. Thus if Kipling's audience knew his works very
closely, he knew them and their stories just as well.

Carrington tells us that by the time of Kipling's death in 1936, he
had sold seven million volumes in England and eight million in the
United States, and that he remained a best-seller in the 1950s. The
only sharp falloff in his sales, according to R. L. Green, began in
1919, and that was temporary. His popularity abroad is particularly
striking in the case of Russia. An official estimate of 1958 found that
77 million volumes by British authors had been published there since
1918, of which Dickens had written 10 million, Kipling, Doyle, and
Swift 4.5 million each, Defoe, Galsworthy, Scott, and Shakespeare
3.4 million each. And the same year, Russian professors of English
literature on a visit to England declared themselves surprised to see
the importance given to Lawrence and Joyce, and denied to Kipling
and Galsworthy. (This book sketches a point of view which reconciles
their idea of literature with our own.)

Already at the time of his death Kipling's rejection by England's
literature-as-system was obvious. Of the eight pallbearers who bore
him to Westminster Abbey, none was an important poet or novelist
—which was unprecedented for a writer; his eight included the prime
minister, an admiral, a general, and the master of a college.

Of course he continued to be discovered, by individual critics, by
T. S. Eliot, by Desmond McCarthy, by George Orwell, by C. S.
Lewis. But it is significant that the rediscoveries are often announced
in exactly the same terms—each critic starts by assuming a general
prejudice against Kipling; the previous critic's work has disappeared
each time. Thus Desmond McCarthy discovered that Kipling put his
gifts not at the service of the love story, nor of some adventure in

sensibility, nor of worldly success, but (for the first time in literature) at the service of a man's relation to his work; and that this is the significant thing about Kipling. But a few years later C. S. Lewis "discovered" that imaginative literature in the eighteenth and nineteenth centuries omitted, or thrust into the background, what occupies men most, their work, and that Kipling was the poet of work. Apparently there is something about this obvious truth which makes it keep disappearing. It is not by some temporary or inadvertent blindness that men of letters forget about the world of work; it is by a fundamental law of letters. Literature as a whole is turned away from that view. It is comparatively easy for individual readers to twist themselves around and see something that has been left out; much harder for literature to include it. The system exerts a constant pressure, which keeps squeezing Kipling out. Thus the victory in effect remained with Boris Ford, when he attacked T. S. Eliot for his 1941 *Selection of Kipling's Verse.* Ford, writing in *Scrutiny,* said that Kipling's mind was a very crude instrument; seldom if ever in touch with finer spiritual issues; he was of the '90s and suffered the common disability of an artistic decadence, which is "an atrophy of finer feeling." Ford's is not an impressive essay—it discusses Kipling mainly as a way to attack Eliot, by suggesting a similarity between the two, but it carried more weight than Eliot's essay in the world of criticism.

## Kipling and the Adventure Tale

Be that as it may, within the tradition of adventure tales, Kipling is surely the greatest writer. But it is disconcerting to have to admit that though Kipling is the greatest writer in this tradition, he makes less use of it than any of the others do. The themes of course are there, but the motifs, and the structuring of the motifs into whole forms, are not. He writes very little book-length narrative of adventure; his heroes are not notable for do-it-yourself skills like Robinson Crusoe, or as observer-participants like Waverley, or as atavisms like Kingsley's or Haggard's heroes. And when romance and adventure motifs *are* to be found in his stories from time to time, they cannot be said to shed much light on their location when connected up with the system we have constructed. The fit is not exact enough to give much pleasure or serve much purpose.

On the other hand, it is not to be doubted, on grounds quite distinct from the recurrence of motifs, that Kipling does belong in this sequence of writers. How could one ever discuss imperialism in literature without making Kipling central? And no one more clearly wrote for the responsible class of the empire, as distinct from, and later as opposed to, the literary class. He named his readers as such. In his Foreword to *The Kipling Pageant* of 1897, he talks of his stories as wares, and says to the captain of the ship carrying them— the editor: "The chief part of our business lies with men who are wearied at the end of the day—certain great captains. They will not bring their womenfolk aboard." And when he died, in 1936, General Sir Ian Hamilton wrote, "His death seems to me to place a full stop to the period when war was a romance and the expansion of the Empire a duty." So completely did he symbolize the concerns of the responsible class.

It is of course possible to point out certain alignments between his work and his predecessors', and he did introduce certain developments. One can see that he uses not the figure of the trader put into circulation by Defoe but its replacement, the figure of the engineer; which brought with it an interest in not only machines but the mechanics of political and social life, too. He expresses that interest brilliantly. One can see that in Kipling's work the figure of the solitary adventurer has been replaced by the figure of the solitary administrator—alone in his heart, but at the center of a complex web of powers and information systems. One can see that in his work the figure of the soldier has been assimilated to other modern system heroes, his chivalric and feudal characteristics modernized. One can see that Kipling, following Twain, introduced touches of the sordid and the horrifying into the adventure framework. All these differences obviously reflect the changes we have studied in the nature of civilization and the British empire, and so ratify and corroborate the scheme of development proposed here.

But observing these features of his work does not lead us to the heart of his achievement—does not seem as important in explaining him as the equivalents were in explaining Defoe and Scott. Finally one must admit the fact of Kipling's recalcitrance from a formal point of view, and build an explanation on that. I have already pointed out that Kipling's intensely literary bent, his genius as a craftsman, perhaps exacerbated by his fate of serving the copybook maxims, led him to reject the given in formal terms. In those terms the adventure romance, and indeed its value-bearing subject matter, is much more easily to be found in Conrad. The way Kipling avoided it was above all by dealing in episodes and fragments. The most obvious evidence of that is that he wrote primarily short stories, in a period when extraordinary prestige and reward attached to the full-length novel. But even as short stories, one must be struck by how fragmentary Kipling's anecdotes are, and how often they are told with a stress on their setting, or on their narrative frame, rather than on their subject.

"The Man Who Would Be King" is a good example. The events and the characters are enacted on the stage of an elaborate theater —the newspaper, the editor, etc.—into which we peer from an odd angle. The effect of this is to stress its character as an anecdote. We don't believe that these events occurred, but we believe that they were told. Kipling's method evokes, very fancifully, a whole series of narratives. What is vaguely but powerfully evoked is the social character of British India, where such anecdotes echoed in the background of everyone's imagination, where everyone was, in a consciously fanciful sense, a man who would be king.[11] Though, since the historical figures whom Carnehan and Dravitt caricature are rather Rhodes and Jameson than anyone Indian, it is in fact everyone in the British empire who had half-acknowledged dreams of that sort.

Or take a story like "The Head of the District," in *Life's Handicap,* or "William the Conqueror." Both of them are very brief anecdotes, which leave the reader wanting to know more—about the persons and events involved, but also caring even more about the genre of life; the administration of such a district, with its multiple layers of nationalities and religions, and the relief of such a famine. Or take the more purely literary case; the Paolo and Francesca story in "Through the Fire" or the Antony and Cleopatra story in "Love o' Women," or the story of Keats in "Wireless" or "The Greatest Story in the World." Here you get the fragment of a well-known poem, play, legend, in some sense concealed in alien material, and made evocative precisely by its fragmentariness and its displacement.

Indeed, it is possible to extrapolate out beyond the use of famous specific stories, and to say that Kipling makes evocative use of familiar fragments all the time. Take for instance "Without Benefit of Clergy," which is as complete a treatment of its people and events as you will find anywhere in Kipling. Even there much of the effect derives from the fact that we recognize the figure of Ameera as a sort of Madame Butterfly. We don't need to hear a full realistic account of her. We say to ourselves "there she is again," and that literary commonplaceness is first cousin to the pathos we feel in Ameera's story—the commonplaceness of her fate in the other sense; that it happens so often. That second commonplaceness, moreover, evokes a third sense, of sad familiarity, associated with the social atmosphere of British India as a whole; one *hears* such stories over and over. This too is an anecdote, whose power of evocation comes from the familiarity of its type; again we don't so much believe that it happened as that it was told. (The Madame Butterfly figure of course turns up often in adventure fiction; in Kipling, one can mention "Lispeth" and "Georgie Porgy.")[12]

Whatever one thinks of that explanation, it is undeniable that Kipling was a hugely successful propagator of the imperial idea and imperial fiction, in England, and abroad. French and Italian critics, before 1914 but also after, often said that England did not appreciate him.[13] In 1934 André Maurois said France could not be expected to get excited about Shaw, having had a Voltaire of their own, but she had had no Kiplings; and told how he had read Kipling when he was sixteen or seventeen, and how *Kim* had affected him more than any other book he read had given him an heroic idea of life.

## Rhodes and Imperialism

The most important historical hero of the British imperialism which Kipling celebrated, of course, was Cecil Rhodes, and a significant relation developed between the two men. It was in 1898 that they became friends (at the same time, Kipling forged an alliance with Alfred Milner, another of the great political imperialists of the time). He became Rhodes's wordsmith. "After the idea had been presented —and one had to know his code for it—he [Rhodes] would say: 'What am I trying to express? Say it, *say* it.' So I would say it, and if the phrase suited not, he would work it over, chin a little down, till it satisfied him."* Rhodes designated a house on his estate to be a writers' residence, and it went first to Kipling, who spent several winters in South Africa as Rhodes's guest. Reciprocally, Kipling received inspiration from Rhodes. He said of Rhodes that his personality revealed the spirit of the age; and wrote to him confidentially, "England is a stuffy little place, mentally, morally, and physically." They both criticized men and countries by adventurer criteria. When Rhodes died, it was Kipling who wrote his epitaph, and he was a trustee of the Rhodes Scholarships.

At the same time, it is important to note that Kipling never drew a figure like Rhodes in his fiction. (Perhaps as near as he came to it was the caricature figure of Daniel Dravitt.) Of course, British imperialism in India, which Kipling knew first and best, was quite different from imperialism in Africa; in India, England administered a highly structured and civilized society, and the cultural image of the Englishman there was Roman and proconsular—the weary but selfless administrator, who preserves the peace and the law for the benefit of ungrateful aliens. In Africa England had instead the sense of uninhabited country, and fortunes to be made, and a free hand for speculators, pioneers, farmers—the empire was half a frontier. But almost certainly not this difference but Kipling's artistic conscience warned him away from Rhodes as a fictional subject. In fact, Rhodes was made a character in a good many contemporary novels, as well as innumerable essays and articles and poems, but none that would have satisfied Kipling's artistic taste.[14]

Cecil Rhodes was born in 1853, the son of a clergyman, and one of seven brothers, most of whom went to Eton or Winchester and then to Oxford, but Cecil did not (a link with Kipling). He was a frail, dreamy, introverted boy, bookish and falsetto-voiced and weakhearted. Like Kipling, he responded to the public idea of Empire rather than to an inherited family identification with it. In 1870, because of his health, he was sent to South Africa to join his brother Herbert. The two involved themselves in gun-running schemes almost immediately, but at the same time, Cecil was working on his exams to enter Oxford, the idea of which he was in love with. He was always fascinated by machinery and gadgets, and by scientific methods, and when the big rush began, he was the first man to use a

---

*Quoted in C. E. Carrington, *The Life of Rudyard Kipling*, p. 212.

watchmaker's glass to examine diamonds. And there were other such Crusoe motifs to his personality.

He made money immediately and in 1873 entered Oxford, though he had to leave it before taking a degree, to look after his diamond-mine interests. But while there he made friends who were later his allies in African politics—for instance, Sidney Shippard, who became administrator of Bechuanaland when that was acquired in 1884. He was also inspired by Ruskin's lectures celebrating the Empire.[15]

The lectures were what Oxford gave Rhodes in the way of inspiration, but it also gave him a certain leverage in the social prestige of an Oxford gentleman, which he used in his dealings with other South African diamond merchants. And the institution of the Rhodes Scholarships in some sense combined all these aspects of Oxford.

Rhodes drew up his first will in 1877, leaving the fortune he meant to make to the colonial secretary, to fund a secret society (at Oxford he had become a Mason—another link with Kipling). This society was to colonize Africa, the Holy Land, the Euphrates, and South America; to recover the United States, and to set up an imperial parliament. These were the ideas which were gradually modified into the Rhodes Scholarships. In 1893 he founded the Society of the Elect, with W. T. Stead, naming the Jesuits as his models, and with Lords Rothschild and Milner as his associates. The final arrangement was to provide scholarships to Oxford for sixty men from the colonies, one hundred from America, and fifteen Germans (to be selected by the kaiser) each year; men qualified by criteria which combined scholarship with sportsmanship and manliness and moral force. They were to be "the best men for the world's fight."

Rhodes's general ideas were crudely Nietzschean and Darwinist, in accordance with the atavism and saga imagery of his phase of imperialism. "I am a barbarian. I believe with Ruskin that all healthy men love to fight, and all women love to hear of such fighting. . . . I love the big and simple." And, "Expansion is everything. . . . These stars . . . these vast worlds which we can never reach. I would annex the planets if I could" (Millin, *Rhodes*, p. 138). For him, Rome had a positive image, was an inspiration and model for England to follow. He read Marcus Aurelius and Gibbon, compared his own profile to that of Emperor Titus, and for six years kept twenty classical scholars at work translating Gibbon's sources; which cost him £50,000 and ran to hundreds of volumes. He read biographies of Napoleon and hung a portrait of Bismarck in his bedroom. He both participated in the excitement of Empire and spread the excitement—far beyond the limits of England.[16]

In America, Grover Cleveland said, "America would pay $300,-000,000 for Cecil Rhodes" (Gross, *Rhodes of Africa*, p. 417). And Twain, in *Following the Equator* II, called Rhodes ". . . the most imposing figure in the British Empire outside of England. When he stands on the Cape, his shadow falls to the Zambesi. . . . That he is an extraordinary man, and not an accident of fortune, not even his dearest South African enemies were willing to deny, so far as I heard them testify. The whole South African world seemed to stand in a kind of shuddering awe. . . . yet there he stands, to this day, upon his dizzying summit under the dome of the sky, an apparent permanency, the marvel of the time, the mystery of an age, an Archangel with wings to half the world, Satan with tail to the other half" (pp. 376–377).

Rhodes and Kipling were of course figures in the history of the idea of imperialism, as well as in that of the British Empire.[17] We cannot afford the space to study the history of that idea, but it is worth pointing out that their phase of imperialism links up rather strikingly with Carlyle's, though separated by a gap of forty years and more. (During which the quite different meaning of the word we associate with J. R. Seeley had developed. For that matter, Ruskin's idea, Disraeli's idea, Dilke's idea, do not remind us of Kipling half so much as does Carlyle's.) In "Chartism," Carlyle says, "The stream of World-History has altered its complexion; Romans are dead out, Englishmen are come in. The red broad mark of Romanhood, stamped ineffaceably on that Cast of Time, has disappeared from the present, and belongs only to the past. England plays its part . . . and out of Hengst's leather boats what Wellingtons, Washingtons, Shakespeares, Miltons, Watts, Arkwrights, William Pitts and Davy Crocketts had to issue. . . ." (Bodelson, *Studies in Mid-Victorian Imperialism*, p. 28). This is the idea we associate with Kipling and Rhodes; it only needed the politicians' stamp of approval to turn this imperialism into the overt kind. Bodelson points out that Carlyle celebrated the strong man as hero, and the Englishman's great empire of silence, long before Kipling. The saga influence developed gradually, and overbore the mercantile idea. In a sense, all England changed caste

—more exactly, key representatives took on warrior-caste traits. But in fact the changes at the end of the nineteenth century only gave free play to caste-characteristics long culturally suppressed.

## Caste

Kipling described *Westward Ho!* as a military-caste school,[18] and it is clear how important an effect it had on him, to be educated in such an establishment and then in the Indian Services environment he went on to. Many of the differences between his fictional sensibility and Twain's—for instance, his idea that Americans were in some sense culturally adolescent—can be traced to that education. What he met in India obviously reinforced that tendency; not so much Indian social formations as the social stratification and caste pride which the English in India had developed there. Literarily, moreover, he found Indian culture a help to expressing that sensibility. Thus in "The Eyes of Asia" he has a Rajput write home from London, "It is not true there is no caste in England. . . . The high castes are forbidden to show curiosity, appetite, or fear in public places. In this respect they resemble troops on parade. Their male children are beaten from their 12th year to their 17th year, by men with sticks. Their women are counted equal with their men. The nature of the young men of high caste is as the nature of us Rajputs. They do not use opium, but they delight in horses, and sport and women, and are perpetually in debt to the moneylender. . . . They belittle their own and the achievements of their friend, so long as that friend faces them. In his absence they extol his deeds" (*The War and the Fleet in Being,* p. 150). The Hindu categories are there only as an indirect means to celebrating the English aristocracy.

Caste thinking is also reflected in Kipling's preference for Muslims over Hindus. This preference was becoming general among Englishmen in India in his lifetime. There were political reasons for this (by making an alliance with this powerful minority, the English split the forces of Indian nationalism) but it was just as much an expression of their spontaneous caste-feeling that Muslims were Kshattriyas (the warrior caste), fiery, proud, gallant. As England came to identify its own interests more and more with its soldiers, it came to value the military caste in other countries too.[19]

It is therefore worth an effort to realize, in terms other than Kipling's own, and on evidence somewhat other, what the characteristics of that caste in England were, and even more—because of the difficulties of the literary reader—what its attractions were. These men (all castes are masculine, but this was a masculine caste) were spirited, commanding, enterprising, simple; above all, commanding. James Morris says, in *Pax Britannica,* page 46, ". . . at that moment of her history, [1897] Britain was settled in the habit of authority—authority in the family in the church, in social affairs, even in politics. It was the last heyday of the patricians . . . the English posture abroad was habitually one of command. To the educated Englishman responsibility came naturally. No other power had been so strong so long. . . ." And it is important to notice there the mixture of political and psychological fact, for that mixture is the essence of caste.

The ideas will best be conveyed by examples. I might begin with a citation from J. A. Froude's *Oceana,* in which he describes enthusiastically Sir George Grey, whom he met in New Zealand. Grey's life, he declares, has been a romance; he began as an officer in the Engineers, then became an explorer in Australia, was at thirty governor of South Australia, then governor at the Cape (and collector of rare books), then governor of New Zealand. There he led the last war against the Maoris—but he is now their beloved white father, their protector, and has collected a volume of their songs and ballads. Grey lived, when Froude met him, on an island he owned, formerly a nest of pirates, now inhabited by people who are his "lieges" and "feudatories." There finally we see how Scott's legends bore on the facts of Empire. "They feel for him what the sons of Ivor felt for Fergus" (p. 311). Grey's is the life of an empire aristocrat, but perhaps too externally described to make clear the psychology of caste.

Winston Churchill's dispatches as a war correspondent, collected by R. Woods as *Young Winston's Wars,* give us a somewhat more personal insight into this temperament. Churchill wrote always enthusiastically about the enemy, and felt all the tragedy of war, even while delighting in the "fine adventures" to be made out of all this misery and ugliness. The note Churchill strikes is developed more fully in this entry by his contemporary, Richard Meinertzhagen.

When war broke out in 1914, this professional soldier who played an important part in developing England's secret service—and who had killed many men—wrote, "I love the naked raw life, bereft of all the trappings and tomfoolery of modern civilization. Wide horizons in thought and vision, freedom and always more freedom, fresh air and exercise and a contempt for Death—that is what I love. Those are the conditions I understand. Must I leave all that behind and without mercy work night and day to kill my fellow men? Must I take part in unrestrained murder?" (Lord, *Duty, Honor, Empire*, p. 281). It is important to grasp the distinctions between different kinds of killing, to do justice to this caste and its role in the national life.

In explaining Meinertzhagen, his biographer quotes a passage from Richard Burton, about returning to the desert, which combines chivalric and atavistic feelings. "At last once more it is my fate to escape the prison life of civilized Europe, and to refresh body and mind by studying Nature in her noblest and most admirable form—the nude. Again I am to enjoy a glimpse of the glorious desert, to inhale the sweet, pure breath of translucent skies that show the red stars burning upon the very edge and verge of the horizon and to strengthen myself by a short visit to the wild man and his home" (Lord, *Duty*, p. 338). Burton, I think, gives one some real insight into the form of manhood which Kipling so admired, and of which England in his time specially made use, needed, and rewarded.

Richard F. Burton (1821–1890) was the son of an Irish colonel who gave him no regular education; when sent down from Oxford in 1842 he set out for India with his bulldog; learned to speak Hindi and Gujerati in Baroda, then moved to Sindh, and got leave to wander the country for three years, learning Arabic, Sanskrit, Pushtu, and native ways of life—an older Kim. He is a prime example of that often-met love of Islam as the culture best suited to the chivalric temperament. Burton wrote a *History of Sindh* in 1851, also a book on falconry, 1852, and another on bayonet exercises, 1853. In 1853 he made a trip to Mecca, disguised first as a Persian mirza, then as a dervish, then as a Pathan. He took an Arab name, which he ever after signed himself by. And this was the story he told in *Narrative of a Pilgrimage to Meccah and Medinah*, published in 1855.

He took the trip as an investigation for the Royal Geographical Society, he says; but also because he was weary of progress and civilization. He is free with his scorn for Hindus, for all educated

Babus, and with his love of all wild races, who are ready to fight. He translates this into American Frontier terms on occasion. "The free trapper combines, in the eye of an [American] Indian girl, all that is dashing and heroic in a warrior of her own race, whose gait and garb and bravery he emulates, with all that is gallant and glorious in the white man" (p. 30). His narrative, and his (implicit) characterization of himself, is very knockabout and even bloodthirsty, against the Victorian convention. He tells us a lot about a "boy Mohammed" he picked up who could have suggested Kim; being volatile and astute, with an acute sense of honor, selfish and affectionate. We are reminded also of Kipling's novel by Burton's eye for racial, religious, etc., types. And by a kind of cosmopolitanism very like Kipling's. Burton often mocks England by comparing its manners and morals to the Orient.

The most striking thing is his evocation and praise of the desert, the natural habitat of Islam and chivalry.

> In the Desert, even more than upon the ocean, there is present death. . . . In such circumstances, the mind is influenced through the body. Though your mouth glows, and your skin is parched, yet you feel no langour, the effect of humid heat; your lungs are lightened, your sight brightens, your memory recovers its tone, and your spirits become exuberant; your fancy and imagination are powerfully aroused, and the wildness and sublimity of the scenes around you stir up all the energies of your soul—whether for exertion, danger, or strife. Your morale improves; you become frank and cordial, hospitable and single-minded; the hypocritical politeness and the slavery of civilization are left behind you in the city. Your senses are quickened; they require no stimulants but air and exercise—in the Desert spirituous liquors excite only disgust. (p. 104)

This is a landscape of threnodic militarism, like Haggard's.

What Burton must remind us of also is T. E. Lawrence, and there is indeed a similarity, though Lawrence was of a type which included other elements. But it is striking to find how many of the elements of Lawrence's story, which we shall consider in the next chapter, are also to be found in Burton; the glamour of the black tents, the natural aristocracy of the desert, the evil Turkish beys; and the hard and unsentimental friendships between men.

In 1880 Burton translated Camoens's *The Lusiads*, the sixteenth-century Portuguese poem in celebration of Vasco de Gama and of exploration in Portugal's Golden Age. Burton saw himself as another Camöens, and loved the memory of the romantic age of discovery.

In 1883 he published *The Book of the Sword,* a three-volume study of *l'arme blanche.* And in 1885–1888, a fifteen-volume translation of *The Arabian Nights,* famous for its pornographic explicitness of sensuality.

Burton evokes as completely as anyone the strain of Victorian feeling opposite to the missionary, the liberal, and the man of conscience—the opposite to what Haggard called "the children of light." He creates a voice and an image for the Kshattriya type, unrepresented in Victorian literature, and to be rediscovered in the twentieth century by literary rebels like Evelyn Waugh. But there were in Victorian England many men like Richard Burton, and many more who wanted to be, and among them men of mind and talent. They were the men Kipling expressed and served.[20]

One of the most prominent examples was Colonel Richard Meinertzhagen. Meinertzhagen (1878–1967) was the son of one of the Potter sisters, a nephew to Beatrice Webb, and so born into a ruling caste. Beatrice Webb says in her autobiography, "As life unfolded itself, I became aware that I belonged to a class of persons who habitually gave orders, but who seldom, if ever, executed the orders of other people." This is one aspect of caste, and noted in a very caste manner.

While a boy, Meinertzhagen played the War Game, as did most children of middle- and upper-class families at the end of the century; soldiers, fort blocks, etc., were often permanently set up in a barn, and tactical games of some complexity were played, training the imagination for war; in 1913 H. G. Wells wrote a monograph about this phenomenon. (One might contrast that with the shop-keeping games that merchant-caste children played.) At Harrow, one of his teachers was that Bosworth-Smith whose life of Lord Lawrence I have quoted. He also heard Stanley lecture at Harrow, and met him at his own home, where Stanley said, "If you ever travel in Africa, rule your men with an iron discipline, share starvation and hardship, and never give in." He also met Rhodes, who invited him to South Africa, but his father did not allow him to go. Richard only gradually won permission to make his career in the army, for the Meinertzhagens and Potters had no military traditions. Richard's struggle to follow his vocation was another example of that militarization of English culture at the end of the nineteenth century.

Meinertzhagen was a fine ornithologist, and in love with Nature generally, although above all a hunter, or, as he himself put it, "obsessed with blood-lust." That was one of the interests he combined with his military duties in Africa. He began his intelligence work on the Nandi, a war-like tribe like the Masai, in Kenya. From that he passed to playing *Kim*-like tricks upon the Germans in intelligence work, and spying on Russian forts in the Crimea. Like adventure-heroes in fiction, Meinertzhagen was often in trouble with his superiors in the British army (just like Stalky); at a farewell dinner in Nairobi, the officers staged a roughhouse afterward as usual, but two men with grudges set upon him in earnest, whereupon he broke both their noses with his knee. At the same time, he was a man of great sensitiveness and self-doubt.

It is important in considering the literature of the time to remember that silent world of soldiers, in which insubordination and violent hoaxing were often marks of the truest talent and the truest vocation, and where there was much of the finest intelligence and sensitivity also. (It is the world Evelyn Waugh tried to enter in the Second World War.) That world had its readers too. Edward Creasy's *15 Decisive Battles of the World*, 1851, had thirty-eight reprints by 1894; it was followed by Malleson's *Decisive Battles of India*, 1883, Colonel Whitton's *Decisive Battles of Modern Times*, 1922, and so on.

Finally, as an example of caste temperament, and caste categories of thought and feeling, let us look at Leonard Woolf, who at twenty-eight had 1000 square miles to rule in Ceylon and 100,000 subjects. Woolf was not a soldier, and indeed belonged to the political and cultural party opposite to Kipling's, but I think he plainly shared certain caste-traits with Kipling's heroes. He presents himself in *Growing* (published 1961) as melancholy, fond of solitude, fond of animals, strongly sexed, hot-tempered, a strong administrator who was complained of but respected by the natives. He competed fiercely but didn't want to succeed as an officer of the empire. At the end of his seven years there, in 1911, he was ready, if Virginia Stephen had not accepted his proposal, to return there, marry a Singhalese, and bury himself in Hambantola, as a permanent but lower-rank ruler. These are the traits of a Kipling hero.

What makes this doubly interesting is that he shows us something of conscious choice and effort in this caste personality. He felt himself very unlike the Anglo-Indians he worked with. When he first went to Ceylon, he took his fox terrier with him, like Burton two generations earlier, but also a ninety-volume edition of Voltaire. (The first saved him, in the eyes of the Anglo-Indians, from the opprobrium earned by the second.) On the ship going out he learned to improve the social facade behind which he hid his intelligence, and to deal with Ceylon civil servants, and planters. "The process is what is popularly known as 'making a man of him.' It made, let us say, finally a man of me, though the man was, and has remained, three-quarters sham" (p. 37). His real self, he felt, expressed itself only in his letters to Lytton Strachey. But he was made a man, and more deeply than he suggests there.

For in a story he tells about a police magistrate he lived with, called Dutton, one meets the manly Woolf, the aristo-military Woolf, and it is just as striking a presence as the Strachey side of his personality, the Voltairean intellectual from Bloomsbury. Dutton had been described to him in advance as "a bloody unwashed Board School buggar, who doesn't know one end of a woman from another," and "it must be admitted that there was some truth in the portrait" (p. 63). In fact, the portrait Woolf draws is essentially the same. Dutton reminded him of Leonard Bast, in *Howard's End:* and with good reason, for Forster drew exactly the same figure. Dutton read cheap editions of great books, wrote poetry himself—about "fays"—and played the piano badly. His talk of women and love made Woolf "feel slightly sick."

Given a job in England with the post office or the inland revenue, Dutton would have been happy, Woolf says. Because there his colleagues would have been small timid men like himself. "In Ceylon he lived the life of a minnow in a shoal of pike. The basis of his character was timidity, which, as so often, was compensated underneath by boundless self-conceit" (p. 65). He had been a scholarship boy, and had risen above his parents' station in life. "Unfortunately this meant that he was given the kind of education which completely addled his fairly good brain and destroyed every chance of his becoming a rational person. . . . Literature, art, music, poetry, history, mathematics, science, were pitchforked into his mind in chaotic incomprehensibility. . . ." (p. 66). He was denatured by ". . . the undigested, sticky mess of 'culture' which they provided for him. His roots began and ended in Peckham, while his mind was full of Keats" (p. 66). He married a missionary, Miss Beeching, who later complained to Woolf of her husband's impotence.

This is a very Kiplingesque story; this man and Leonard Bast, and Septimus Smith in *Mrs. Dalloway*, are all descended from Kipling's Cockney clerks, like the man in "The Greatest Story." They are drawn the way Kipling drew and saw that figure. The anecdote is full of caste feeling; what little men like this lack is the caste element of temperamental fire and form; they are, to use Hindu terms, Banias trying to be Kshattriyas. Lacking that element of style, that feeling for form, they should never have been given access to the world of the imagination.

Woolf pays tribute to Kipling as the poet of Anglo-Indian society, but grudgingly, and in a way that denies him any insight into men like himself. He says he could never decide whether Kipling had copied colonial society exactly or whether his social world in Ceylon was copying Kipling. "In Kipling's stories and our conversations there was the same incongruous mixture of public-school toughness, sentimentality, and melancholy" (p. 46). But the real Woolf, he implies, did not take part in those conversations. All seven years in Ceylon, Woolf felt he was acting a part; he couldn't really have become an imperialist—"a white ruler of our Asiatic empire."

Woolf could only use Kipling's categories ironically, and yet he could not escape from them. He belonged to Kipling's world, psychologically as well as by situation, and to deny that was in effect to lie. And that seems to be typical of the failure of the English intellectual response to Kipling.[21]

# X

## *Conrad*

C ONRAD'S reputation as a great modernist began after World
War I, after the modern system had entered into its period of self-
doubt and general disrepute. The British empire in particular was
then accused by enemies both outside and inside the system, and
amongst the latter "literature" proved itself one of the most bitter.
It is paradoxical, in more than one way, that Conrad should be
associated with this process of accusation, but the historical facts are
indisputable—he was and is so associated. His critical reputation and
literary interpretation have been inseparable from the anti-imperialist
ideas general after 1918. Indeed, the critics' interpretations are much
more separable from the books Conrad wrote than from those political ideas. But there is another aspect to his importance for us.

From our present point of view, Conrad is a subject of rather
similar interest to Tolstoy. First of all because he represents Poland,
a country on the periphery of the modern world system, where the
sequence and development of that system's ideas was markedly out
of phase with England's. And secondly because, like Tolstoy, Conrad
used adventure material in fiction and yet identified himself with the
most serious ideas of his time; claimed to stand at the very center of
literature as a system; and consequently moved the adventure material he used somewhat from its peripheral position in the serious
imagination. (Though in Conrad's case what happened was as much
that he combined quite crude material of that kind with a mood

antagonistic to adventure—so he did not redeem the adventure form
—he did not refine the adventure mood itself and separate out what
was potentially valuable within.)

I cannot, myself, believe Conrad to have been an intelligence or
a talent comparable with Tolstoy. But he was treated as such; he was
given an extraordinarily reverential response by the men of letters of
his own time and since; and the reason for that misjudgment bears
very interestingly upon our argument. It was just because Conrad
seemed to bring the adventure tradition to an end by transvaluing it
—and because his actual ambiguity could be read as a subtly profound
strategy—that literature acclaimed him its champion and in his name
triumphed over imperialism and the forces allied to it in English
culture. The Empire went into rapid decline after 1918, and England
lost its lion's share in the modern world system. Serious literature, so
long in resistance, and the children of light generally, felt that they
were winning the cultural battle. And Conrad, of all people, was
decked out in general's uniform and set to lead the victory parade;
though he was at best the Pétain of a literary Vichy.

He was born in 1857, eight years before Kipling, but he was the
opposite of precocious; he began life as an author after Kipling, and
in his wake. He designed his first books in some sense to fit into an
imaginative space defined by Kipling; at least that is what is suggested
by something in the Author's Note to his first novel, *Almayer's Folly*,
1895. He says that a woman reader has dismissed books like his,
adventure tales of the tropics, etc., by calling them "decivilized"—
the standard attack on adventure material. Conrad replies that this
is a feminine judgment; in fact the events he tells about are fully real
and the characters are men and women like ourselves—"though
admittedly they are not the graceful and charming phantoms that
move about in our mud and smoke, all refinement and no heart."
Such images imply a great deal of Kipling's scheme of ideas; for
instance his imaginative geography, with its distribution of reality and
unreality, between London and the frontier, between the core countries and the periphery.

Conrad grew up in Poland, where his father was a poet and a
patriot, who had suffered exile for conspiring against Russia, the
imperial oppressor. The boy grew up in a tradition of political idealism and patriotic indignation, of an aristomilitary kind. Poland in the
nineteenth century was obsessed with its loss of sovereignty. Many

Poles, including an uncle of Conrad's, had fought in Napoleon's armies against Russia, and so had taken part in that enormous romance.

Poland became a constitutional monarchy in the sixteenth century; the nobles rose to power, and the peasants were reduced to serfdom, at the same time. Also "the discovery of America paved the way to the second feudal system in Poland, made poor by the imports of gold and silver from the American continent. In contrast, the same era led to the establishment of modern manufacturing plants and industrial enterprises in western Europe, ushering in the period of early capitalism." This is the account of the *Encyclopaedia Britannica*, and it makes Poland a case of Wallerstein's theory of the semiperiphery.

The same is true in political history. The nineteenth century, or the period from 1795 to 1914, is known as Poland's "captivity," after it was divided between Russia, Prussia, and Austria. Throughout the century, Poland had individual exile-patriots, and volunteer legions, fighting against these three countries, or against imperialist tyrants elsewhere.

The first such legion, fighting under Napoleon against Russia, won back Poland's reputation as one of the great military nations. And there were also unexiled patriots, rebelling at home, and often severely punished for doing so, as Conrad's father was. This patriotism was heavily stamped with the character of the aristomilitary caste, which provided most of its leaders, and its expression in literature, which was important to its self-consciousness, was correspondingly romantic, though Christian-Romantic. The literary vocation that Conrad entered was characterized by Scott and not by Defoe.

When the first of the large-scale military risings failed, in 1831, there was a "Great Migration" of Poles to Paris; in which various men of letters played a large part, notably the three poets, Mickiewicz, Slowacki, and Krasinski. Literature (and music) was unusually important in the culture of nineteenth-century Poland, because closely allied to patriotism and rebellion. These three poets taught a messianism according to which the Poles were a Chosen People, called to suffer crucifixion, like Christ, because they had stood for Human Freedom; they must rise again, and when they did, their rising would usher in the reign of justice, liberty, and love. Mickiewicz, in his *Books of the Polish Nation and the Polish Pilgrimation* (1832) had passages like this: "And the nations forgot that they all stem from one

Father, And the Englishman said: my Father is the Ship, and my Mother, Steam. The Frenchman said, My Father is the Land, my Mother the Bourse . . . [But] In proportion as you enlarge and perfect your souls, by so much will you improve your laws and enlarge your frontiers. . . . Do not, therefore, excessively admire the nations which grow fat in prosperity, or which concern themselves mainly with difficult husbandry, or with disciplined organization. . . . The Polish Pilgrim says "Who so would follow Freedom, let him leave his country, and hazard his life" (*Poland,* Schmitt (Ed.), p. 336).

This patriotic and chivalric Romanticism was an important element in Conrad's situation as a writer. It set a standard of extreme idealism, and a model of heroic temperament, to which he responded but against which he also reacted. Of course he was not the first writer to do so, and there were other elements in the Polish literary situation.

We can glimpse his alternatives, and generally the conditions of Conrad's early life through the biography of a slightly older Polish novelist, Henryk Sienkewicz, 1846–1916, who made his career in Polish literature but like Conrad found an international audience. As a boy Sienkewicz read Polish history and biographies of Napoleon, and also *Robinson Crusoe* and *The Swiss Family Robinson;* and dreamed of finding an uninhabited island for himself. Later, he read Scott and Dumas. And then, as a student at Warsaw University, 1865–1871, he read the serious writers of the century, the children of light, Comte, Mill, Darwin, Spencer. This is the paradigm of nineteenth-century education in Europe; a layer of adventure images, upon which in higher education a layer of almost opposite ideas was laid.

In 1863 came another of the great Polish uprisings, and the patriots—especially those in the Great Migration, which clustered in Paris and London, hoped that the liberal powers, England and France, would intervene on their behalf. When they did not, many young people became disillusioned with politics altogether, and even with patriotism, of the old romantic-chivalric kind.

They began to see the Polish past as a shameful story of serfdom, intolerance, and class privilege, and set to work instead for the modernization and rationalization of their nation's life—worked to bring about its entry into the modern world system. This movement is clearly related to Defoe's ideology and sensibility, and versions of it developed in several semiperipheral countries. The Polish version was called "Organic Work." And a natural complement to that was the dream of starting life afresh, in Crusoe-fashion, in the wilderness. Sienkewicz was a friend of the famous actress Modjeska, and her circle, who in 1875 conceived the idea of going to live in America. Sienkewicz's enthusiasm provoked one of the others to exclaim, "Let us all go. We will kill beasts, build huts, make our own garments of skin, and live as our fathers lived" (Giergielewicz, *Henryk Sienkiewicz*, p. 25). They wanted to seek adventures in the jungles of virgin land of the United States, Modjeska tells us in her *Memoirs*, 1910. She saw herself bleaching linen at the brook, as the maidens did in the *Iliad*. Her son wanted to work on the Panama Canal, and that seemed a natural corollary of her vision.

Sienkewicz actually did go to California, and wrote back to the others in 1876, "My attire consists of a flannel shirt, red pants, and a sombrero costing $1. The climate does not require anything else. . . . I got rid of my nerves, my catarrh, my toothache. I sleep like a king. . . . Until now the hardship of this Cossack life only strengthens me. . . . I am as healthy as a bull, much stronger than my red brothers, cheerful and happy. Every morning when I wake up, I remind myself where I am, and I can't restrain a smile of sincere satisfaction." (p. 28.) He lived out those Defoe fantasies and found the experience very strengthening as an adult, but he returned to be a writer in Poland.

As a novelist, he wrote a Scott-like trilogy on Polish history, beginning with *With Fire and Sword* in 1884; and in 1896 published his best-known book outside Poland, *Quo Vadis?*, which had 250 printings in France alone; and in 1905 he won a Nobel Prize. In 1910 he helped introduce the Boy Scouts into Poland; and in 1912 wrote a children's adventure tale that was very successful, and was translated into English as *In Desert and Wilderness*. This is a version of the English adventure, and the literary heir of his American experience. It tells of the adventures of a Polish boy and an English girl in the Sudan and equatorial Africa. Stas Tarkowski, who is fourteen, is fiery, proud, and an expert rifle shot, swimmer, rider, and linguist. Nell Rawlinson, who is eight, is dainty, babyish, with long, golden hair, adored by the natives, and by her black nurse Dinah. Their fathers are both widower engineers working on the Suez Canal; the Pole had fought in the 1863 rising against Russia, been imprisoned in Siberia, and escaped. England is presented as punishing slave dealers all over the world. Gordon is in Khartoum, besieged by the Mahdi, and the children are kidnapped by the latter's agents. They press Stas, with brutal menaces, to renounce Christianity and become a Moslem, but he stands firm. Soon he finds a chance to shoot a lion and his two captors, and the children are free. They wander, lost, through Africa, with their dog, Saba. They pick up Kali, a Black Prince who has been enslaved and who becomes devoted to them. They also free the King, an elephant they find trapped in a ravine, blasting a way out for him by explosives. Then Stas unmasks a fetish man and wins a war for Kali's tribe.

The story is thus a bricolage of motifs from the English adventure novel of the eighteenth and nineteenth centuries, and its interest for us is to show the wholesale way that material was taken over in 1912 by a literature on the periphery of the system. Indeed, that is one interest of Sienkewicz's career as a whole, though the other is the light it throws on Conrad. The latter did not write Crusoe stories or live out Crusoe fantasies or engage in Organic Work; his imagination was too deeply romantic for that; but he was nevertheless influenced by English ideas, and above all by the idea of England.

Conrad had read the literature of France and England as a boy, as well as Polish books. At eleven he declared that all his favorite books were Cooper novels about Natty Bumppo. After that he turned to reading the lives of explorers, from Columbus to Livingstone. The kind of childhood reading he makes particular mention of, in his late essays, is of geography books. He says that Mungo Park and James Bruce were "the first friends I made when I began to take notice—I mean geographical notice—of the continents of the world into which I was born" (*Last Essays*, p. 19). He described himself as a contemporary of the Great Lakes of Africa, in the sense that he could have heard of their discovery in his cradle, and in the later '60s he did his first bit of map-drawing by transferring the outline of the new country of Tanganyika onto a blank map. His idea of Africa was mixed up with images of Mungo Park, Dr. Barth, and above all, Dr. Livingstone—"the most venerated perhaps of all the objects of my early geographical enthusiasm."

This enthusiasm was to lead to a very significant disillusionment when Conrad finally got to Stanley Falls, because that part of the world then could evoke no "shadowy friend or great haunting memory" (Livingstone) but "the unholy recollection of a prosaic newspaper 'stunt' (Stanley) and the distasteful knowledge of the vilest scramble for loot that ever disfigured the history of human conscience" (the Scramble for Africa). The occasion was moreover Conrad's trip up the Congo in 1890, which so disillusioned him with Belgian imperialism, and led to *Heart of Darkness.* That is the curve of Conrad's engagement with the idea of adventure, from boyhood enthusiasm to mature disillusionment. And though one can explain the dynamic of that curve in terms other than the political history of Empire—Conrad's temperament was predisposed to disillusionment on other grounds—still that political history did correspond to and justify his development. Conrad represented and identified with the European conscience as a whole, in that curve.

But like Kipling, Conrad was very conscious of the history of adventure, and its heroes of the past, and often evoked them, in his fiction and elsewhere. In a letter of December 26, 1903, to his friend Cunninghame Graham, he tells of the horrors of the Congo, and says he would like to bury himself in an account of the original Spanish conquistadors, "If only to forget our modern Conquistadores. Their achievement is monstrous enough in all conscience—but not as a great human force let loose, but rather like that of a gigantic and obscene beast. Leopold is their Pizarro, Thys their Cortes, and their 'lances' are recruited . . . of all sorts on the pavements of Brussels and Antwerp" (*Joseph Conrad's Letters to R. B. Cunninghame Graham,* C. T. Watts [ed.] pp. 148–149). But if the Belgians are sordid, the Spaniards must have been romantic, to make Conrad's point. As this suggests, Conrad's imagination was dominated by romance, as distinct from adventure, in all its major categories; even though the idea of modern system values and the corresponding temperament was very important to him, as we shall see.

At the age of seventeen, he told the uncle with whom he lived that he wanted to be a sailor. This not only meant a life of adventure, but a life far from Poland. And in 1874 he entered the French marine service in Marseilles, and socially entered a circle of political conspirators, who promoted the cause of royalty in France and in Spain. In 1878, after either a duel or a suicide attempt, he left France and became a seaman in the English merchant marine, which seems to have always presented itself to him as "unromantic." England and her merchant navy presented themselves in Defoe-like terms to Conrad; as useful, effective, sober, solid, devoted to duty and not to honor;

*Conrad*

to service and not to glory. This was an ideal which had been recommended to him (though not as specifically English) by his uncle, and it clearly promised him a stability, by being midway between the two extreme conditions toward which Conrad was drawn—romantic excitement and black pessimism.

Of course England also meant to Conrad a quite romantic kind of adventure-heroism, of which the representative most important to him personally was James Brooke, the White Rajah of Sarawak. Brooke was born in 1803, and so belonged to that early nineteenth-century England which Conrad, writing of Marryat, called a fabulous period of vigorous romance. Romance is always a category in the eye of the beholder, whatever the facts of a particular case, and it is likely that if Conrad had visited Brooke's Borneo as a contemporary, he would have been as disillusioned as he was by the Congo. But as a legend Brooke was very important to him.[1]

On June 15, 1920, Conrad wrote to a Brooke descendant about the Great Rajah, as he called him, "The first Rajah Brooke has been one of my boyish admirations, a feeling I have kept to this day, strengthened by the better understanding of the greatness of his character and the unstained rectitude of his purpose." His correspondent had written to praise *Lord Jim* as the best book ever written about the East Indies, and Conrad continued, "The book which has found favour in your eyes has been inspired in great measure by the history of the first Rajah's enterprise."*

In some sense, the story of the White Rajahs of Sarawak begins with Alexander Hare. (So we gather from Steven Runciman's *The White Rajahs,* Cambridge, 1960.) Alexander Hare was a merchant of Malacca, who worked with the imperialist statesman, Stamford Raffles, from 1811 on, to get Borneo from the Dutch for the British. (At that time, Holland, the imperial power in the East Indies, was nominally the ally of Napoleon and thus the enemy of Britain.) Hare got a private estate of 1,400 square miles assigned him, of which he was sovereign prince, where he kept a palace and a harem. One of the adventurers who joined him there was John Clunies-Ross, a Scots adventurer, who afterward became hereditary prince of the Cocos Islands. Thus Borneo was a happy hunting ground for men who would be kings, from before Brooke's day, and until long after.

*Quoted in Robert Payne's *The White Rajahs of Sarawak.*

304

In 1815 Java was given back to Holland, and Raffles had to concentrate his schemes on Singapore—and Hare lost his estate soon after. But Brooke read Raffles's essays about British power in the East, and was much influenced by them. He had been born in Benares, where his father was judge of the High Court. Like Clive and Burton, Brooke was rebellious at school, and only found himself when he got to lead some volunteer horse in the First Burmese War in 1825. (Admiral Austen, Jane Austen's brother, who played a part in that war, later played a part in the history of Sarawak, coming there in 1851 to suppress pirates for Brooke.) Brooke criticized the East India Company, and had to resign. He inherited a fortune of £30,000 in 1835, and immediately began preparations to acquire a kingdom in the East. He issued a prospectus, describing Borneo, in 1838, and the next year, arrived there, and gave his help to the Rajah in putting down a rebellion.

In 1841 he was made governor of the province of Sarawak, and in 1846 he published his first book describing what he had done. It had three editions, and made him a national hero in England; but aroused the hostility of Liberals like Cobden and Gladstone, and Radicals like Joseph Hume. (Except for the group around Wakefield and Durham, whose radicalism owed something to French Revolution principles, the Radicals were then anti-imperialist.) A lot of controversy centered around the question of certain pirates, whom Brooke claimed British help in suppressing (on the Rajah's behalf) and of whom the Liberals doubted either the existence or the piracy. (They were wrong about this, it seems, though in general they were right to suspect Brooke of personal imperialism.) Finally, however, Brooke established himself as Rajah of Sarawak, and his nephews and heirs were given the exotic titles of the Tuan Besar, the Tuan Muda, and the Tuan Bongsu. This was one of the great Victorian stories of a Man Who Would Be King, and Conrad embraced the myth enthusiastically.

But because of his divided temperament, with its reversals of sympathy, he relied even more on the unromantic British heroism described before. Moreover he continued to believe in this British style, even during and after his disillusionment with imperialism and romance. We find an essay, "Well Done," of 1918 in which he says "I venture to affirm that the main characteristic of the British men spread all over the world, is not the spirit of adventure so much as the spirit of service. I think that this could be demonstrated from the history of great voyages and the general activity of the race. . . . Yes, there is nothing more futile than an adventurer, but nobody can say that the adventurous activities of the British race are stamped with the futility of a chase after mere emotions. The successive generations that went out to sea from these Isles went out to toil desperately in adventurous conditions. A man is a worker. If he is not that, he is nothing."*

Thus Conrad was really much more old-fashioned than Kipling, closer to both Scott and Defoe, in his understanding of England and her role in the modern world system. While Kipling was describing the transition to Empire, and the rise of the military caste and decline of the mercantile, Conrad celebrated the old-Defoe-style virtues. And his romanticism is closer to Scott than to the saga-atavism that came in after Carlyle, which adapted the chivalric hero to the newer needs of the imperial imagination. Of course, Conrad *had* modern elements to his imagination, but they stood in antagonism to every kind of adventure and political enterprise in general, and left his idea of the British Empire in particular quite old-fashioned and consoling to the general English reader.

## The East Indian Trilogy

Conrad began writing fiction by speculating about a man called Almayer or Olmeyer, whom he had met in the East Indies; a failed adventurer. This man was, one might say, the antithesis to Rajah Brooke, and it is significant that the counterpart was the one who really engaged Conrad's creative imagination.

It took him some years to write *Almayer's Folly*, during which time, he says, he was always haunted by the image of that man, and by his social and geographical setting in the Eastern Archipelago. Then his second novel, *Outcast of the Islands*, also has Almayer as a character, and a third novel (not finished until much later), *The Rescue*, has the same general setting, the same themes, and as hero

*In *Notes on Life and Letters*, pp. 189, 190.

Tom Lingard, who is a minor character in the first two. The three books therefore constitute a sort of triology, and a considerable body of work—perhaps Conrad's most sustained engagement with a subject. Lingard (also a character drawn from real life) was a successful adventurer; known as the Rajah-Laut, the King of the Sea, or King Tom (Conrad followed Kipling with his play upon the idea of kingship). Almayer (and later Willems in the second novel) is a failure. And it is highly characteristic of Conrad and the writers who followed him that it was the second type that fixed and fascinated their attention.

The British books of this kind had not examined the failures of empire, and one may say that Almayer struck Conrad with the force of a new idea—or of a revolution in ideas. (Kipling's shady men, Carnehan and Dravott, were after all romantically large.) The force naturally came from Conrad's expectations and desires of failure, which had always been there, though hitherto differently named. Conrad saw—and this is why subsequent writers chose him as their godfather—that the Empire was a stage strewn with extraordinary failures, as well as with extraordinary successes. His books are full of examples of human seediness and villainy—Gentleman Brown in *Lord Jim,* Gentleman Jones in *Victory.* These are adventure-villains, the obverse of adventure-heroes, and Conrad delights in them, artistically, with much less equivocation than he does in the heroes.

Almayer marries a Malay girl who had been adopted by Lingard. He does so to win the latter's favor and become his heir. He has a half-caste daughter, Nina, whom he educates as white, but who chooses to be Malay instead and rejects him for being a white adventurer. So in Conrad the themes of adventure and empire are entangled with sex and miscegenation. This complex of themes was only touched on by Kipling, and hardly even that by writers before him, but literature was increasingly under the influence of the erotic movement; and the growing importance of racial theory within the imperialist idea made it a natural development for Conrad to pursue. A further extension of the idea is that Almayer has "gone native"; a phrase which was to inform a good deal of fiction, like Somerset Maugham's, over the next thirty or forty years. Almayer dreams of retiring back to Holland with his wealth, and seeing his daughter triumph in white society, but he gradually slips downhill out of white identity entirely. And in the second novel, this happens to Willems even more dramatically. He too marries to gain favor with a rich man; he too meets his fate in a proud native beauty; but she—her name is Aissa—enslaves him; he does physical work at her bidding, so that his racial identity is really parodied and trampled in the dirt. In various ways like that, Conrad depicts the Empire as a place inhabited by dreams of making it, but by facts of not just failure but total self-destruction.

But besides the character of Almayer, the East Indies islands where he lives are themselves important. (Each area of the empire has an elective affinity for a certain kind of story; Kipling's stories about the imperialism of India are quite unlike Haggard's stories about the imperialism of Africa; and Conrad's affinity is for the East and West Indies.)[2] Archipelagoes are always a favorite site for piracy, and consequently for a many-layered structure of power. In this story of Borneo, for instance, there are Dyaks of various kinds, and tribes subordinate to them, over whom rule Malays (the Rajah Lakamba and Babalatchi); over whom, in some sense, are the Arabs (Abdullah and his nephew Rashid); over whom are the Dutch (including, precariously, Almayer); and then there are the English and the Chinese. These layers do not lie neatly one above the other, moreover, but interweave; and the sense of such complex political situations is one of Conrad's strengths—one sees it again in *Nostromo;* he knew how to put political complexity into fiction, though in static rather than dynamic terms.

The plot is set in motion when Dain Baroda, the Rajah's son from Bali, comes to Almayer and persuades him to sell gunpowder, to make it possible for him to make war against the Dutch. Almayer puts gunpowder into the hands of blacks to use against whites. That is, he sells his white soul. Dain Baroda is a Black Prince, except that he is not subordinate to, or much related to, a white man. His loyalty is to Nina Almayer, and his splendor is erotic rather than political. Nina, who chooses passion and epic in him, is in other ways like Kingsley's Ayancora. The significant new element is Almayer's futile and fumbling betrayal of his race and himself; that is what Conrad and the reader pay most attention to.

Conrad's imaginative mode is much closer to Scott's than to Defoe's. It is highly operatic; people are presented in striking postures and gestures that are held unchanging over several pages, and were very theatrical to begin with. Scenery and costume are given in great detail, and often the action is static, or if it moves, then, as in Cooper, the scene expands sideways, changed by the arrival of more and more characters, rather than by moving forward. In the climactic scene Dain is joined in his hiding place by—one after another—Nina, then Almayer, then Babalatchi, then the Dutch and Taminah. One feels that the central characters, who embody the story, are paralyzed; they ought to move, but they can't; and one feels that about Conrad often.

The new characters he is interested in, figures of decadence and villainy, had been treated by American writers, and in American legend. Conrad in fact treats the Empire as if it were a Frontier in this regard—in the focus of his perceptual interest. Almayer and Willems are not too different from the King and the Dauphin in *Huckleberry Finn;* Gentleman Brown and Gentleman Jones might have turned up in the stories about Davy Crockett and Mike Fink. But aesthetically Conrad was an old-fashioned romantic and had no sympathy (while Kipling had a great deal) for the American and Frontier modes of narrative and characterization; e.g., the use of dialect. So he relies on English-novel techniques—typically Dickensian—for rendering, say, Cornelius in *Lord Jim,* even though those techniques somewhat subvert his purposes by their playful exaggerations.

In these early novels, there is a dream of treasure, in gold and diamonds. There is a sinister hag, Mrs. Almayer. There is a naked corpse, of Dain. There is an explosion, on Dain's brig, while the Dutch are aboard, so that they are killed (Conrad often makes use of such explosions). There is a chest full of the money which Dain paid Mrs. Almayer for Nina. And so on; that is enough to show how lavishly Conrad used the motifs of the adventure-romance; and he continued to do so throughout his writing career.

*The Rescue,* the third novel of the series, was not published until 1920. The Author's Note says that it was half written in 1898, but put aside because first *The Nigger of the Narcissus,* then *Youth,* then *Lord Jim,* demanded to be written. He says that it was writing the first of these three that gave him the consciousness of mastery first. And it is true that his work then takes an artistic leap forward. But these early and comparatively neglected books are nevertheless interesting, in their own right, and even more from our point of view. The third of them is a failure artistically, but the reasons for its failure are interesting.

In *The Rescue*, Tom Lingard is young, and is presented as a romantic hero; he is explicitly compared with James Brooke, the White Rajah. Conrad says Lingard lacked Brooke's advantages of birth, position, and intelligence, but shared his sympathy for the people of the forests and the sea.[3] This could be a formula for a version of Daniel Boone or Davy Crockett. But in fact Conrad's treatment is theatrical-romantic. Lingard is given a well-shaped head, a beard that burns gold in the sunlight, and a narrow waist. He is engaged in winning a kingdom for a Malay prince and princess when the story opens. Prince Hassim has saved Lingard's life on a previous occasion, and they have formed a Natty-Chingachgook relationship. But their plot is foiled when the schooner of a rich English politician runs aground near their secret meeting-place, and Lingard falls in love with the politician's wife, a Gwendolen Grandcourt-figure. Because of her, he sacrifices everything else, and sails away embittered. All that second half of the book is badly done, but its place in the design of the whole is important from the adventure-myth point of view. Its message is that there are possibilities of heroism, romantic friendship, greatness, out on the seas, which are ruined by the intrusion of representatives of London and civilization.

The whole story is made up from motifs important to the adventure-romance. There is, for instance, a ring that is passed to and fro between Lingard and Hassim, as there is in *Lord Jim*. The Malay princess, Immada, is in love with King Tom, but stands no chance against the English beauty Mrs. Travers, with whom she is often contrasted. This is Madame Butterfly again; the sexual pathos of the inferior race, the triumphalism of the superior. And the heroic heritage of the modern system is invoked often: "Did you follow with your ghostly eyes the quest of this obscure adventurer of yesterday, you shades of forgotten adventurers who, in leather jerkins and sweating under steel helmets, attacked with long rapiers . . ." (p. 96). The triology, being apprentice work, is more in the adventure tradition than the rest of Conrad's fiction. But the later novels work with that tradition's motifs, even as they resist and undermine the spirit of adventure.

## Conrad's Later Books

In *The Nigger of the Narcissus* (1897) Conrad introduced a character who was to be important to the further development of adventure. This is Donkin, the evil-spirited man, the nay-sayer; he alone
sees through James Wait, the fraudulent Nigger of the title, and he
is favored therefore by Wait, and in a sense by Conrad. The author
shows himself fascinated by such men, who insistently deny, betray,
and sneer at the values other men agree to live by.[4] Melville had
been similarly fascinated, and the characters of that kind which the
two writers create are a clue to the larger similarity between the
latter—that they are both so ambivalent about adventure and heroism. They both affirm and deny those values. Since the surface of
their books, the stories they were in a sense commissioned to write,
celebrated adventure, we feel that more profoundly they were hostile to it. But it is probably more accurate to say they were ambivalent.

For Conrad's *Youth* (1898) has the ring of conviction, and is
an entirely romantic story, entirely affirmative about adventure
values. At the end, Conrad/Marlow says, "There was all the East
before me, and all life . . . And I thought of men of old, who,
centuries ago, went that road in ships that sailed no better, to the
land of palms and spices, and yellow sands, and of brown nations
ruled by kings more cruel than Nero the Roman, and more splendid than Solomon the Jew" (p. 107). The whole story offers both
adventure and romance, strengthening the latter with the former.
The unimaginative, unromantic Captain Beard braces the system
of shipboard life, the system of the merchant marine, with his integrity, and so safeguards the highly imaginative Marlow (and, we
may add, Conrad) against the excesses and collapses that threaten
him. (The excesses and collapses later attributed to Kurtz in
*Heart of Darkness.*)

And *Typhoon* tells the same fable, in much exaggerated—though
wholly successful—terms. The universe throws every horror it has at
Captain McWhirr, who represents British ordinariness, and he with-
stands them. All the metaphysical grotesqueness of life rears up (there
are wonderful scenes with the Chinese rolling to and fro, fighting for

their dollars while the typhoon is at its worst) but the captain ignores and so masters it. And Jukes, who represents imagination, and Conrad, and the reader, are deeply impressed and grateful. These are, Marvin Mudrick says and I agree, the best of Conrad's work. Mudrick says that that best work was all written in novella form, and all produced in six years. The later and longer novels, so lengthily expounded by the critics, are badly flawed.

The other two fine pieces of that kind are *Outpost of Progress* and *Heart of Darkness.* In the latter, Marlow's first vision of the station, and his walk along the river, his "two hundred mile tramp," are both superb. And indeed the idea of Kurtz is a compelling one; at least it is now, after so many fine critics have lavished their imagination upon him. But it is not at all a realized idea.[5]

And it is still necessary to insist that Conrad, far from attacking English imperialism in the opening pages of this story, is assertively glorifying it.

> The old river in its broad reach rested unruffled at the decline of day, after ages of good service done to the race that peopled its banks, spread out in the tranquil dignity of a waterway leading to the utmost ends of the earth. . . . It had known and served all the men of whom the nation is proud—from Sir Francis Drake to Sir John Franklin, knights all, titled and untitled—the knights-errant of the sea. It had borne all the ships whose names are like jewels flashing in the night of time, from the *Golden Hind.* . . . Hunters for gold or pursuers of fame, they all had gone out on that stream, bearing the sword, and often the torch, messengers of the might within the land, bearers of a spark from the sacred fire. What greatness had not floated on the ebb of that river into the mystery of an unknown earth! . . . The dreams of men, the seed of commonwealths, the germs of empire (p. 2).

So when Marlow says, "And this also has been one of the dark places on the earth" (which comes immediately after and is the starting point of the story), the meaning is clearly contrastive and depends on the reader feeling unequivocally how great England has become and still is.

We are told that "The conquest of the earth is not a pretty thing when you look into it too much," but that means that "What redeems it is the idea only." Of course, the idea must not be a "sentimental pretense"; it must not be such ideas as Kurtz has and other non-Englishmen who try to imitate British imperialism; this is Conrad's equivalent for Kipling's "lesser breeds without the law." The saving idea, the English idea, is a tough realism, almost a non-idea, an intellectual silence, like Stalky's silence about the flag; in this story that dour pragmatism is represented by Marlow's rivets. "What more did I want? What I really wanted was rivets, by heavens! Rivets. To get on with the work—to stop the hole. . . . I don't like work—no man does—but I like what is in the work—the chance to find yourself" (p. 23). This element in British adventure—the Defoean element—is symbolized in Towson's book of directions in seamanship. "Not a very enthralling book; but at the first glance you could see there a singleness of intention, an honest concern for the right way of going to work, which made these humble pages, thought out so many years ago, luminous with another than a professional light" (p. 31). This is the ghost of Defoe and Smiles, the spirit of the modern system past. Conrad felt himself very distant, in psychological and historical time, from that spirit, but still celebrated it.[6]

*Lord Jim* (1900) is, as Mudrick says, and as Conrad's account of the writing makes plain, an overblown short story. It demonstrates the effort it cost Conrad to make a full-scale, full-weight artistic form for his adventure material, which could contain all his ambivalence about it. The story is very like Kipling in its glorification of the English boy; but it is different because Conrad shows his ambivalence. Indeed he makes much of that ambivalence, though he also muffles it in ambiguity. And what spoils Jim as an adventure hero saves him as a modern fiction character.

But he *is* an adventure hero. Like Conrad himself, Jim found his vocation for the sea after a course of adventure reading.

> On the lower deck in the babel of two hundred voices he would forget himself, and beforehand live in his mind the sea-life of light literature. He saw himself saving people from sinking ships, cutting away masts in a hurricane, swimming through a surf with a line; or as a lonely castaway, barefooted and half naked, walking on uncovered reefs in search of shellfish to stave off starvation. He confronted savages on tropical shores, quelled mutinies on the high seas, and in a small boat upon the ocean kept up the hearts of despairing men—always an example of devotion to duty, and as unflinching as a hero in a book (p. 5).

He apprenticed himself to all the heroes we have been studying, from Robinson Crusoe on; he affiliated his soul to the genre.

Conrad of course offers us an ironic view of that genre. But he affirms its value. His own affirmations—though the critics have made a big mystery of them—are surely represented by Stein's remarks. "A man that is born falls into a dream like a man who falls into the sea. . . . The way is to the destructive element submit yourself, and with the exertions of your hands and feet in the water make the deep, deep, sea keep you up" (p. 130). This is not a warning against illusion, but against the opposite. One must accept illusion, including the illusion of adventure, one must live in it, interact with it, in order to keep going, to keep afloat. England represented that method in action; Stein might philosophize it, but Captain Beard and Captain McWhirr enacted it. So this is an endorsement of adventure. The adventure idea may seem to us (men of letters) to have betrayed Jim, because it incited him to a heroism he could not achieve, and then to a savage self-punishment. But Conrad meant rather that Jim betrayed it; after all, when he tried harder, or better, with his second leap, the idea yielded itself to him. He became a hero of exactly that kind.

Amongst Conrad's later, larger fictions, *Nostromo* (1904) has received most praise. It has indeed a powerful, Cooper-like sense of geography and history, plus a grasp of politics in places like South America, on the periphery of the system, which no other English novelist could offer.[7] A plot-summary can make the book sound wonderful. Unfortunately Conrad, again Cooper-like, can't make such a plot move forward. These novelists were alike in being profoundly ill at ease with the conventions of their genre.

The story is of a doomed rising, like the story of *Waverley*, but this book is, even sentimentally, on the side of the conservatives. The Negro liberals, the insurrectionary party, are to him quite grotesque. And this is symptomatic of a general alienation from liberalism and from the adventure material, which makes him handle it all clumsily. Also after the Scott model are the operatic heroines, Antonia and Dona Emilia; indeed, they are very close to Waverley's Flora and Rose, but handled clumsily enough to seem more like Cooper's heroines. The best thing is the most modern, the figure of Nostromo, just because that figure expresses Conrad's sense of alienation. Nostromo is the man whose identity it is to belong to the English, to be "our man," their man. This idea sums up all the bitterness of the colonial—the absorption of even virtue by the English. But, as in the case of Kurtz, the idea of the character is quite distinguishable from, and far superior to, its realization.

Despite his alienation, moreover, Conrad was still an imperialist. The confrontation between Captain Mitchell, another of Conrad's comic English captains (comic but better than tragic) and Colonel Sotillo, a caricature of Latin volatility and pretentiousness and pretence, reinforces all the racist stereotypes of imperialism. When Sotillo sees Mitchell's gold watch, he "became so interested that for an instant he forgot his precious prisoner" (p. 269). He had never seen anything so fine, and his officers closed in and craned their necks behind his back. "There is always something childish in the rapacity of the passionate, clear-minded, Southern races, wanting in the misty idealism of the Northerners, who at the smallest encouragement dream of nothing less than the conquest of the earth. Sotillo was fond of jewels, gold trinkets, of personal adornment" (p. 269). So he tries to steal the watch. And everything he does is a racist caricature. He advances one leg, and puts his arms akimbo; he points at his prisoner with a long, almond-shaped nail; he has coal-black ringlets and moustache. Meanwhile, against him, the English Mitchell is absolutely solid.

The novel is made up of adventure-romance motifs. It has treasure —indeed, stolen and buried treasure; it has love—indeed, forbidden love; it has a revolution, a dramatic landscape, a colorful cast, and so on. It is clearly a Scott romance. There is the modern, postimperial bitterness, embodied in Nostromo, of course. That bitterness is spoken out by Martin Decoud, whose pessimistic comments on the hopes that inspire other people are gradually born out by the plot. But it is important to note that Decoud has been completely undermined as an authority, from his first introduction. Despite his pretensions to historical insight, we hear, Decoud "was an idle boulevardier, in touch with some smart journalists, made free of a few newspaper offices, and welcomed in the pleasure haunts of pressmen. This life, whose dreary superficiality is covered by the glitter of the universal blague, like the stupid clowning of a harlequin by the spangles of a motley costume, induced in him a Frenchified—but most un-French —cosmopolitanism, in reality a mere barren indifferentism posing as intellectual superiority" (p. 130). Here again Conrad puts himself firmly on the side of the traditional values and temperament style, British adventure values and styles. So the reader's responsive mood of ruthless irony is again undercut and shattered.

And finally *Victory* (1915) which conveys a strong sense of the ending of the great adventure of the modern system. As in *Nostromo*, an island plays a part, as a place of disaster, where again it is shown —though by a different event—that a man *cannot* live alone. Thus there is a reversal of the *Robinson Crusoe* pattern, with its happy island motif. When islands are places of disaster, adventure is dying, and self-confidence in general is failing. The hero's last words are "Woe to the man whose heart has not learned while young to hope, to love—and to put its trust in life." That affirms adventure, in a yearning and hopeless fashion. But the burden of the book is quite opposite—that salvation lies in the denial of appetite and illusion— though of course salvation does not mean success. "It is not the clear-sighted who lead the world. Great achievements are accomplished in a blessed, warm mental fog . . ." (p. 92). But here, as elsewhere, that scheme of ideas is masked by another, which is almost its opposite. Conrad set the two sides of his temperament fighting, and backed them both equally.

Mudrick says of Conrad that ". . . those of his works which most successfully challenge the nullifying blast of his temperament are tales of the sea" (Mudrick, *Joseph Conrad: Twentieth Century Views*, p. 3). (Tales of the sea being one of the main energizing myths of the modern system.) There Mudrick identifies Conrad's temperament wholly with its impulses to negate. But it seems clear that Conrad felt his division that way himself (set temperament in opposition to faith and duty) and used England and its naval traditions consciously to strengthen his more positive side. In his essay, "Well Done," he says, "The mere love of adventure is no saving grace. It is no grace at all. It lays a man under no obligation to faithfulness to an idea and even to his own self. . . . There is nothing in the world to prevent a mere lover or pursuer of adventure from running at any moment. . . . You find them in mysterious nooks of islands and continents, mostly red-nosed and watery-eyed, and not even amusingly boastful. There is nothing more futile. . . . Adventure by itself is but a phantom, a dubious shape without a heart" (Conrad, *Notes*, pp. 189 and 190). He says adventure but he means romance, and he denies it in the name of modern system values. At other times, as the critics are quite right to insist, he denies the latter quite devastatingly. His ambivalence is total.

## Conrad and Criticism

Aesthetically speaking, the really striking thing about Conrad's use of the motifs we have been studying is the clumsy lavishness of that use, the wholesaleness of his acceptance of the form, compared with the discriminations and transformations Kipling imposed upon it. And Conrad's skepticism about the spirit of adventure makes his use of the form more gross and strident. But you would never guess that, reading the critics.

Of course Conrad, like every other writer, made a selection from among those motifs, which made them in some ways his own. But by and large, he followed Scott's selection, especially in his treatment of women; though he introduced, again often in connection with women, motifs and meanings from the modernist imagination, such as those of the erotic movement.[8] And then there is an element of grotesque exaggeration in his writing, which seems to derive from Dickens and other post-Scott rhetoricians. Conrad probably avoided following and learning from Kipling, the real formal innovator in adventure. He seized the opportunity, during the Boer War, to separate himself from Kipling politically, and ever after spoke of the latter as a Patriot—and himself as an Artist. And Henry James, who had repudiated Kipling, embraced Conrad, received him on behalf of literature.

In 1919, as we have seen, T. S. Eliot also embraced him, distinguishing him from Kipling as the sheep are to be distinguished from the goats on Judgment Day; "He is, for one thing, the antithesis of Empire (as well as of democracy); his characters are the denial of Empire, of Nation, of Race almost; they are fearfully alone in the Wilderness." Conrad is great because he is the embodiment of negation. Unlike Kipling, "Mr. Conrad has no Ideas, but he has a point of view, a world." This, clearly, is what makes a serious writer. And modern critics, notably F. R. Leavis in England, have followed Eliot.

Indeed, there is no repudiation by the serious critics for us to discuss. Literature-as-a-system welcomed Conrad, unlike the other novelists in this sequence. This is very understandable; due as it was to the implicit and by no means dishonorable ideology of serious literature. But it was still a fatal error. (This book's approach to literature makes such mistakes less likely; and that is perhaps its main recommendation from a literary-critical point of view.) Conrad is certainly rich in political and psychological insight into the sins and follies of imperialism; insights that open metaphysical depths beneath the adventurer and the reader. But he is not the master of those insights. He equivocates, and often denies them; partly out of artistic clumsiness, partly out of philosophical uncertainty, but also out of genuine ambivalence. Thus the critical enthusiasm for Conrad, like the enthusiasm against Kipling, is not to the credit of the generations that entertained it. Intellectually and aesthetically it was a kind of stupidity or perversity; and judged more generally and ideologically, while one cannot fail to sympathize with the motives behind it, those were surely familiar enough to have been understood and controlled. The failure to do this was especially fatal for Englishmen. Intellectually and aesthetically, England's readers and writers after 1918 were nearly all the children of Kipling, as Eliot and Orwell came to acknowledge, and to deny him in the name of Conrad was in some ways only a fit of pique.

For Americans it was not such a crucial issue. Hemingway acknowledged his debt to Kipling, and that acknowledgment is related to a kind of strength in him which the English writers failed in. Hemingway has heroes; he carries on the development of the WASP adventure; the English writers chose Conrad and rejected Kipling just because the former announced the death of that hero. Indeed, Hemingway's debt was to the imperialist adventure writers, generally. His hero figures, for instance Wilson in "The Short Happy Life of Francis Macomber," owe as much to Edgar Wallace as to Kipling. Wallace's Sanders, who appears in *Sanders of the River,* and other collections, is the same short, sandy-haired man, with the brusque manner and the harsh voice, uneasy with women but sentimental about men. Perhaps via Hemingway, something of Kipling seems to have reached Norman Mailer also in the flamboyant structural and stylistic devices of his journalism. Certainly Mailer's *Why Are We in Vietnam?* is the most distinguished novel using primarily adventure motifs, of modern times; though it follows American and not British models of adventure.

It was above all the love of the male hero which British literature lost or gave up, and which American literature won, after 1918, when

the United States took over the cultural leadership. And along with the male hero, we lost a whole range of modes of moral seriousness. That is what the consecration of Conrad has meant. Mailer's novel uses adventure in a critical analysis of imperialism, without losing faith in adventure itself, in a way that British writers have not been able to manage.

# XI

# *In the Trough of the Wave of Imperialism: Adventure Images after 1918*

After the Great War, and after Conrad, the adventure form persisted; both as a narrative genre and a style in heroism—its presence permeated English culture after 1918. But the persistence of the form of adventure was no more marked than the resistance to its spirit. At least in the world of literature one can say flatly that England after 1918 was unadventurous; men as serious as Defoe and Scott could no longer write adventures; and the men who could felt the moral support of their audience progressively withdrawn, so that the adventures grew more and more immoral, from Bulldog Drummond to James Bond.

The most typical formal result of combining persistent form with resistant spirit must always be satire; and much satiric or ironic adventure was written, by new writers like Evelyn Waugh or Graham Greene. (However, terms like form and spirit being so slippery, those satires in their way endorsed the spirit of adventure.) And outside literature one can say that the moral and social basis of adventure, its constituency, narrowed. The exploits of a Lawrence of Arabia, and the rhetoric of a Winston Churchill, seemed more the property of a single class than had the heroism of their Victorian predecessors. This too is a matter of persistence and resistance combined.

## The Change

The idea of a serious literature of adventure was much expounded by responsible critics at the time of World War I. Arthur Waugh said, "When a people has found its soul, its literature has always found a voice";* and it was in times of war that it found its soul. Of course, in wartime such things are said more easily even by responsible critics. But Leslie Stephen (who died in 1904) "knew many of Mr. Rudyard Kipling's ballads by heart, and shouted Henry Newbolt's 'Admirals All' [about Drake, Nelson, etc.] at the top of his voice as he went about the house or walked in Kew Gardens, to the surprise of the nursemaids and the parkkeepers." And Stephen was a central figure in the system of literature, a serious intellectual and literary critic. But this anecdote reminds us of the change impending at the time of his death. His biographer included the anecdote in his *Life and Letters,* and said it was given him by one of Stephen's daughters—either Virginia Woolf or Vanessa Bell, who did not recite Kipling or Newbolt. Stephen was a man of letters, but he was also a member of the responsible class, and his reading partook of both characters. But his daughters and their readers belonged by intention at least only to the former, and adventure was not their kind of literature.

The change was particularly clear-cut because at the very end of the nineteenth century, and particularly after the scandal about Oscar Wilde and aestheticism, there had been the move to reunite

*In *The Fortnightly,* November 1917.

the two reading publics; it was professors of literature who welcomed Kipling, as we saw, and writers like Chesterton offered to please both publics, with his ballads and his critical essays. (This is the mood John Gross has described and documented in *Decline and Fall of the Man of Letters.*) The split between Defoe and Swift, or between Scott and Coleridge, was declared to be merely local and temporary, not profoundly meaningful. There was a stress upon the Elizabethan age as paradigmatic for literary history, because then the literary class was just as excited and active and brilliant as the military and economic classes. Saintsbury said that when one looked at Elizabethan history, "it must appear that it would have been more odd if Elizabethan literature had not been great than surprising that it was."

I have quoted these comments from *The Literature and Art of the Empire,* which is Vol. XI of a twelve-volume *The British Empire,* edited by Hugh Gunn, which came out in London in 1924. The authors of this volume, Edward Salmon and Major A. A. Longden, say that a literary harvest followed the Armada and another followed Waterloo, and they confidently expect another to follow the Great War. But in fact there was to be no equivalent to Shakespeare and Scott, because the imperialist confidence in England had failed. The fiction that got written in the next decades, including the adventure fiction, expressed revulsion against Empire.

In the 1920s and 1930s, however, the standard poet promoted in schools across England was John Masefield; it was his poems about ships and islands and pirates (and de la Mare's) which English children learned by heart. ("Sea Fever" was the first poem I learned at school.) This was a continuation of late-Victorian literary imperialism. Between 1885 and 1905 ten major biographies of Nelson appeared. (All stressed his dying words, "Thank God I have done my duty.") In 1895–1896, Sir Arthur Quiller-Couch, professor of English literature at Cambridge, brought out his two-volume *Story of the Sea,* full of the old legends: for instance, of the Armada, and the Protestant wind that came up to defeat it and save England in 1588. The same myth of the sea, and ships, and sailing, was taught in the 1920s, in perhaps more conscious and desperate propaganda for the WASP hero than ever before.

And in prose, after Kipling came John Buchan; who was also a tremendously popular writer, and in terms of talent similar to Stevenson; that is, a man of great deftness, and craftsman-talent, but dedicated to adventure and soon repudiated by literature-as-a-system. T. E. Lawrence said that Buchan's books were like athletes racing; "so clean-limbed, speedy, breathless. For our age they mean nothing; they are sport only; but will a century hence disinter them and proclaim him the great romancer of our blind and undeserving generation?"* Lawrence himself, in *Revolt in the Desert,* and in his translation of Homer, and even more in his career, embodied the same idea as Buchan put into fiction. Indeed, it is pretty clear that Lawrence is the man from whom Buchan drew the hero of *Greenmantle.* And, in schools and elsewhere, Lawrence was promoted as England's twentieth-century adventurer, in the 1920s and 1930s. Buchan and Lawrence were the Kipling and Rhodes of postwar England. But in the unsympathetic air of '20s and '30s seriousness, they lacked the power to convince and dominate.

For after 1918, as Lawrence's remark indicated, their idea met stiff resistance, especially in literary men. When Q. D. Leavis compiled her questionnaires for *Fiction and the Reading Public,* asking among other things who leading authors thought their readers were, P. C. Wren (the author of *Beau Geste,* a very popular adventure-romance) wrote, "The bulk of my readers are the cleanly-minded, virile, outdoor sort of people of both sexes, and the books are widely read in the Army, the Navy, and the Public Schools, and the Clubs. . . . Although I now make a good many thousands a year, I still am not a 'professional novelist,' nor a long-haired literary cove. I prefer the short-haired executive type."† By then, such a declaration was much more suicidal for a writer than the equivalent remarks by Scott and Cooper. The responsible class who read the latter two authors, and some part of whom presumably read Marryat and Kingsley, were not to be counted on in the 1930s to swallow that tone, or—except as merest pastime—to read that kind of adventure. So even if Wren had chosen his words better, his declaration would still have meant that he was not trying to please a literate audience at all. The adventure of imperialism had lost intellectual and moral credibility, as it had not done in the nineteenth century, and so Wren's audience, however large in numbers, was essentially a minority.

The end of the war had brought a general revulsion against imperialism. The fifth of President Wilson's Fourteen Points was a demand

---

*Quoted in Colin Watson, *Snobbery with Violence,* p. 43.
†Watson, p. 222.

for "A free, open-minded and absolutely impartial adjustment of colonial claims." And in close succession came the activities of the Sinn Fein in Ireland, the Bolshevik Revolution in Russia, the foundation of the League of Nations, and the publication of Lenin's *Imperialism*. In India, 1919 saw the first Government of India Act, and then the Amritsar Massacre.*

The men of letters joined in a literary movement in sympathy with this revulsion, whether they were liberals or conservatives politically. The liberal Forster attacked Lord Cromer, one of the heroes of Victorian imperialism, in *The Government of Egypt*, 1921. But the conservative T. S. Eliot, in his 1919 essay, attacked Kipling, and sharply distinguished Conrad from him, as anti-imperialist; indicating the way in which criticism of Conrad, and of literature generally, would go for two generations. Eliot was followed notably by F. R. Leavis—notably and mistakenly, as I have argued. The interest of the mistakenness is that it testifies to the strength of the drive behind it, the drive to find a hero of anti-imperialism who was also a hero of modernism in literature.

The novelists of the next generation continued to write about the Empire, but from an ironic point of view. Besides Forster's great novel, we have Maugham's series of stories, from the group who had begun publishing before the war. And from those who began their literary careers after it, we can pick out George Orwell and Joyce Cary, Evelyn Waugh and Graham Greene, among those who used the imperial setting, and to a considerable extent the adventure genre, but sardonically.

Cary is an interesting case biographically. He went to Nigeria just before the war, and was put in charge of emirates that covered an area as large as Wales. He had been one of six selected from sixty-four candidates for the Administrative Grade of the Civil Service. But he left the Service in 1920, and began writing in the '30s, much influenced by Conrad, and his point of view is anti-imperialist. *Aissa Saved*, 1932, is about the disintegrating effect that Christianity has upon pagan religions; *African Witch*, 1936, is rather like *Passage to India*.

Orwell's *Burmese Days*, 1934, also owes a lot to *Passage to India*, of which it is practically an episode. Orwell served in the Imperial

*Jeffrey Meyers brings these facts suggestively together in his *Fiction and the Colonial Experience*.

Police in Burma 1921–1928. Greene and Waugh didn't follow Forster; they knew the empire as travelers and journalists, not as civil servants or conscientious liberals. Nor did they aim at writing great novels; both of them make less use of Conrad than, by ironic reversal, of the Buchan-Mason-Henty pattern of adventure narrative and description. They may be said to have written antiadventures—though one should not confuse that form with Mailer's *Why Are We In Vietnam?*, in which the antagonism is to Empire, not to adventure.

## The Persistence

But of course such large changes of mood and image did not occur all together or all at once. There was much conscious resistance to the swing away from adventure and Empire, and much more blind continuance in old paths. For instance, the White Rajahs of Sarawak continued to perform their Lilliputian imperialism until after the Second World War. A Brooke dynasty had been established, and there was as much palace intrigue and unhappiness about inheritance as if it were Rome. The original Brooke disinherited his oldest nephew in favor of the second, Charles; he, who began to reign in 1868, distrusted his oldest son, Vyner, and wanted the next son, Bertram, to be his heir. Vyner in turn disinherited his natural heir, his nephew Anthony, in 1939. The empire might be miniature, but its imperialism was life-size. There was a great deal of excitement about the selection of and the discipline of the young men who went out to serve as officials under the Rajah. And there were always rival adventurers to deal with—Claude Moses and Baron von Overbeck in the second half of the nineteenth century, and in the twentieth century Gerald MacBryan, who became the Rajah's private secretary, and seemed about to inherit the throne. He, in 1935, having married a Malay bride, made a pilgrimage to Mecca as a Moslem, and proposed to become international leader of the Moslems of the East, with Sarawak as his headquarters. (Again we see the attraction of Islam for the military-caste adventurer at the end of our period.) But in 1946 the Brookes finally handed their kingdom back to Borneo, as the British empire in general disintegrated.

MacBryan's trip to Mecca must remind us of England's then most famous adventurer, Lawrence of Arabia. Lawrence's vision of himself as hero had affinities with Conrad's vision of heroism—with Lord Jim, for instance. But Lawrence's youthful reading was dominated not by sea-adventures, but by medieval romances, especially the French ones—the *romans d'aventure* of the twelfth century, like those by Chrétien de Troyes. And he told Liddell Hart, "I also read nearly every manual of chivalry"; plus Morris and Tennyson's romances and sagas; and he carried a copy of Malory throughout the Arabian campaign. Morris's work was particularly attractive to him —as it was to the young Kipling. Lawrence loved *Sigurd the Volsung,* and in his mind related the saga people it described to the Arabs he was working with.[1]

He told Hart that as a boy he had dreamed of leading a crusade. "Naturally, it would be a crusade in the modern form—the freeing of a race from bondage" (Hart, *T. E. Lawrence,* p. 80). But when he first got out to the Middle East it was to work on archaeology, though his job had some connections with the British Secret Service. The Arab boy Dahoud became his Friday—to whom he later dedicated *Seven Pillars of Wisdom*—and Prince Feisal became his Black Prince. But though we use terms first associated with Defoe, Lawrence's feeling for these men is like Scott's or Conrad's—much more romantic. He saw Feisal as representing an older, harder, fiercer mode of being, deeply alien to his own. Like Kim, and Burton, Lawrence loved to adopt Arab dress and Arab personality, and to use them to manipulate his allies and his enemies.

He found the Bedouins "a people of primary colours, or rather of black and white, who saw the world always in contour. They were a dogmatic people, despising doubt, our modern crown of thorns."[*] As a modern system man, he lacked something, which he found in the Bedouins. That makes it clear how chivalric-romantic his vision was —much more romantic than Scott's—even though he sometimes denies that. "The epic mode was alien to me, as to my generation. Memory gave me no clue to the heroic, so that I could not feel such men as Auda in myself. He seemed fantastic as the hills of Rumm, old as Malory."[†] He denies any feeling for the epic and heroic, but obviously in doing so asserts it.[2]

He loved the epic language he could attribute to them, and

*Quoted in Paul Zweig, *The Adventurer,* p. 237.
†Quoted in Zweig, *Adventurer,* p. 235.

could himself use in talking of them. In the Epilogue to *Seven Pillars,* \* "There was left to me ambition, the wish to quicken history in the East, as the great adventurers of old had done. I fancied to sum up in my own life that new Asia which inexorable time was slowly bringing upon us. The Arabs made a chivalrous appeal to my young interest, and when still at the High School at Oxford already I thought to remake them into a nation, client and fellow of the British Empire." This is that overexcited language—it arouses the instinctive distrust of the literary reader—which is equivalent to Lord Jim's romantic fantasies. "I meant to make a new nation, to restore a lost influence, to give 20 millions of Semites the foundation on which to build an inspired dream-palace of their national thoughts." Alongside this rhetoric, as in Conrad's Jim, and in Buchan heroes, ran the *Boys' Own Paper* jargon of this letter to a friend, written in the middle of the Rising, "I hope this sounds the fun it is. The only pity is the sweat to work them up, and the wild scramble while it lasts. It's the most amateurish, Buffalo Billy sort of performance, and the only people who do it well are the Bedouin. Only you will think it heaven, because there aren't any returns, or orders, or superiors, or inferiors; no doctors, no accounts, no meals, and no drinks" (Mack, *Prince,* p. 155).

Back at All Souls, Oxford, after the war, Lawrence engaged in undergraduate pranks, while he was made into a national hero by Lowell Thomas, and by Winston Churchill and John Buchan. He was a reincarnation of the WASP adventurer, appearing just when it seemed that hero was vanishing, that option was being denied to Englishmen. Buchan said about him, "I would have followed Lawrence over the edge of the world. I loved him for himself and also because there seemed to be reborn in him all the lost friends of my youth."†

Lawrence responded vividly to his admirers' sense of him. He was the spirit of youth. In a page of his introduction to *Seven Pillars,* subsequently canceled, he wrote, "Yet when we had achieved and the new world dawned, the old men came out again and took our victory to remake in the likeness of the former world they knew." He began to translate the *Odyssey* in 1927. But the tormenting sense of self-betrayal led him to throw away the hero-identity he had so brilliantly built up, by entering the Air Force under an assumed name.

*Quoted by John Mack, *A Prince of Our Disorder,* p. 191.
†From John Buchan, *Memory, Hold-the-Door,* p. 229.

## In the Trough of the Wave of Imperialism

Herbert Read said, in reviewing *Seven Pillars,* that Lawrence was not a hero because he was self-conscious. That term means a badly controlled self-consciousness, one that betrays him, by betraying how he shapes himself to suit the expectations of those he presents himself to. That is certainly true of Lawrence, and constitutes one link between him and Conrad's Lord Jim; it is no doubt connected to the self-doubt in both of them; but one must also think of the self-doubt of the epoch as a whole, the resistance of the culture.

Through most of his life he was a figure of romance—a figure out of Scott or at least Conrad, and not out of Defoe or the more interesting side of Kipling. But at the end of his life he became excited about machinery and mechanics. It was now aircraft, and after them speedboats and motorcycles, that absorbed him; and he loved the company of mechanics—because "to them their work alone is real." He was turning away from the personalism of romance. He wrote to another airman, "For thousands of years nature has held this mastery of the last element in her lap, patiently waiting for our generation, and you and I are of the holy ones chosen" (*The Letters of T. E. Lawrence,* p. 725). And to Robert Graves, on February 4, 1935, "I have convinced myself that progress today is made not by the single genius, but by the common effort. To me it is the multitude of rough transport drivers, filling all the roads of England every night, who make this the mechanical age. And it is the airmen, the mechanics, who are overcoming the air" (Mack, *Prince,* p. 331). That was like Defoe's and Smiles's feeling for mechanics and their machines. At that moment—the last in his life, for he died in the following year —Lawrence was reuniting the modernist elements in the heroic sensibility he exemplified.

Finally it is worth considering a woman writer of Lawrence's generation who wrote some acute studies of the epic and heroic landscape which people of his type—and her own—have again and again sought out to support their self-stylization. Her approach was basically aesthetic, but what she says may be associated particularly with the military caste. I am referring to Isak Dinesen, and her two books, *Out of Africa* (published 1938 in the United States), and *Shadows on the Grass* (1961 in the United States). Her father had been an officer in the Danish army (also for a time an adventurer in the States) and she saw her relations to her servants on the model of his to his soldiers. She lived in some sense on a frontier, in Kenya, though her social situation was more that of the plantation South in America; Europeans re-creating for themselves an agrarian aristocracy. She describes her life on her 6000-acre farm, twelve miles from Nairobi, where the views were immensely wide, with great cultural nostalgia. "Everything that you saw made for greatness and freedom, and unequalled nobility" (*Out of Africa,* p. 4). And it was the human landscape she was concerned with as much as the natural. The natives were her servants, but in some sense her superiors. They lived "in life itself, within their own element, such as we can never be" (p. 19). She told her servant, Kamante, tales from the *Odyssey,* and he took them as natural.

And beyond the servants, who were Somalis—a handsome and haughty people—and the agricultural Kikuyu, there were the Masai, a fighting race prevented from fighting, and her portrait of them is one of the most vivid parts of her book. She describes them on page 131 as "a dying lion with his claws clipped, a castrated nation." And on page 135, "They have, to the utmost extent, that particular form of intelligence which we call chic; daring, and wildly fantastical as they seem, they are still unswervingly true to their own nature, and to an immanent ideal. Their style is not an assumed manner. . . . The Masai carriage of the head, with the chin stretched forward, as if he were presenting you his sullen arrogant face upon a tray . . . his bearing makes of him . . . an object for contemplation, such as a statue is, a figure which is to be seen, but which itself does not see . . . faces sleek and swollen . . . neck muscles swell in a sinister fashion, like a cobra, leopard, or bull, a thickness so plainly an indication of virility that is a declaration of war to all the world." This is the Richard Burton sensibility again, the warrior caste of Europe recognizing its equivalent on another continent.

And the English friends she made there, before the First World War, were adventurer figures, from the caste we have studied. Berkeley Cole was a Restoration figure—he had to have champagne sent out to him in the forest, and served in the best crystal, at 11:00 every morning; Denys Finch-Hatton was an Elizabethan—he took her up in his plane. They loved the Masai as she did. The old settlers were untamed, being younger sons of old English families, she tells us. They often formed Hawkeye-Chingachgook relationships with some dark, untamed nomad or hunter; and hunting itself is a love affair with the hunted—for her, most notably, with the lion. Isak Dinesen is a heroine out of John Buchan, a sister to T. E. Lawrence.

In the later book, she describes her servant Farah, "a cheetah noiselessly following me about at a distance of five feet, or a falcon holding on to my finger with strong talons and turning his head right and left" (*Shadows on the Grass*, p. 20). She and her servants made up a unity together, Master and Servants. All Africans, she says, are precocious but cease developing early, so the men are like European boys of thirteen to seventeen. This is the best age. "In such young Europeans, too, the code of honour, the deadly devotion to the grand phrase and the grand gesture is the passion urging them on to heroic deeds and heroic self-sacrifice. . . ." They are like the heroes of the Icelandic sagas. "The same ravenous ambition to distinguish themselves before all others and at any cost to immortalize themselves through a word or gesture, lies deep in the heart of the sons of the desert as it did in the hearts of the untamed, salty young seafarers of the Northern Seas" (p. 13). Everything in those sentences is defiantly in the chivalric mode of the military caste; nothing conciliates the mercantile caste and its sensibility. She compares her feelings for "my people" with her father's feeling for his soldiers. He had written, "The love of war is a passion like another, you love soldiers as you love young women-folk—to madness, and the one love does not exclude the other, as the girls know. But the love of women can include only one at a time, and the love for your soldiers comprehends the whole regiment, which you would like enlarged if it were possible." It was the same thing with the natives and her, Dinesen comments (*Out of Africa*, p. 18).

But such sweeping gestures of self-affirmation as hers and Lawrence's were rare in twentieth-century Britain; they were also self-consciously romantic—less in accord with realities in the sphere of politics than the equivalent had been in the nineteenth century. And in the sphere of the arts the dominant mood was ironic or gloomy, dandy frivolous or prophetic grim.

But that mood of negation—negation both of Empire and of the modern system as a whole—dominated all the humanities, in the widest sense of that term. It is symptomatic that anthropology, the study of the primitive peoples on whom empire was imposed, became a field of study central to all modern seriousness. The work of Malinovski and Radcliffe-Brown in England began a movement of thought which both sprang from and strengthened this revulsion.

*In the Trough of the Wave of Imperialism*

Gradually British sociologists and anthropologists, and those of other countries, ceased to reconstruct the prehistory of civilization, or of the laws of social evolution, in the way which led to self-congratulation by the advanced countries.* Malinovski was strongly influenced by Conrad, in matters of style, and that usually means a temperamental affinity.

## After the Second World War

And since 1945 anthropology has been influenced above all by Claude Lévi-Strauss, whose orientation is very antimodern, and whose major points of reference are very close to those of this book. He says, "I have little sympathy for the century in which we are living, for the total ascendancy of man over nature, and of certain forms of humanity over others. My temperament and tastes carry me towards more modest periods when there was a certain balance between man and nature, the diverse and multiple forms of life."† A tribe that eats roots and spiders and wears no clothes may have solved its problems of social organization better than we. Lévi-Strauss dislikes and distrusts the modern world system, made up as it is of progressive-acquisitive-inventive societies, hot and mobile and thermodynamic, like the steam engine. He says we must go back to before Socrates and seize mind before it became our mind; the golden age was the neolithic, before men invented writing and cities. Indeed he is antihumanist. "The world began without the human race, and will end without it." He regards change as proof of impermanence and imperfection, not of energy.

This is clearly the reverse of Defoe's ideology, and announces a complete redirection of sympathies. And other intellectuals have taken up Lévi-Strauss's attitudes. Octavio Paz says mortality is the mediator between culture and nature. It is death that condemns us to culture; an idea which Norman O. Brown has developed at length. And when, in *The Savage Mind*, Lévi-Strauss said, "The ultimate goal of the human sciences is not to constitute, but to dissolve

*See J. W. Burrow, *Evolution and Society.*
†Quoted in *Claude Lévi-Strauss: The Anthropologist as Hero*, N. Hayes (Ed.), M.I.T., 1970, p. 10.

331

man . . . ," that clue was followed by other Paris structuralists.

He has made anthropologists the intellectual heroes (wounded heroes) of our time. He describes them as mutilated men—men in revolt against their own society. They go elsewhere to find what is lacking at home; the Golden Age, where sorrows were dissolved by festivities, and men could converse with the Powers. Only by finding and recording that Golden Age can they be reconciled to themselves. (His own life and character were thus reconciled by his practice of anthropology, says Edmund Leach in his essay in *Claude Lévi-Strauss: The Anthropologist as Hero.*)

Thus the anthropologists represent and lead the poets, the pure scientists, and the whole modern movement of silent resistance, within and against Western culture. Lévi-Strauss says, in *Tristes Tropiques*, that law and medicine students are noisy, aggressive, right-wing, while "an arts and science student is characterized by an attitude of refusal towards the demands of the group" (p. 46). For him, teaching and research are "a refuge or a mission," not a training for a profession. And anthropology is the most extreme form of those studies.

In the same book he describes the beginning of his career, in February 1934, when he sailed to Brazil, with a vivid consciousness of following in Columbus's path, but with the hope and meaning of the journey reversed. From Dakar they reached "the fateful latitude 7 north, where in 1498, during his third voyage, Columbus, who was heading in the right direction for the discovery of Brazil, changed course towards the north-west, and so managed, by some miracle, to arrive two weeks later at Trinidad and the coast of Venezuela" (p. 67). (He was then on the edge of El Dorado, which V. S. Naipaul too has been writing about at the same time and in the same mood as Lévi-Strauss; these are the crucial places and journeys for our imagination, now again as they were so long ago.)

Lévi-Strauss describes the Doldrums as "the last mystical barrier between two regions so diametrically opposed to each other through their different conditions that the first people to become aware of the fact could not believe that they were both equally human. A continent barely touched by man lay exposed to men whose greed could no longer be satisfied by their own continent. Everything would be called into question by this second sin; God, morality, and law. In simultaneous yet contradictory fashion, everything would be verified in practice and revoked in principle; the Garden of Eden, the Fountain of Youth, Atlantis, the Hesperides, the Islands of the Blessed, would be found to be true; but revelation, salvation, customs and law would be challenged . . ." (p. 68). The old myths ceased to be energizing—became literary—Crusoe and his epigones displaced them. This chapter, "The Doldrums," is all about Columbus, and about the damage done by the world-wide spread of the modern system.

And, though less authoritative than Lévi-Strauss, England had its prophets of anti-imperialism. Of course World War II brought a revival of the old adventure heroics, which persisted for a few years, and at lower levels of culture. In a book called *British Adventure* (1947) Nigel Tangye says, "It can hardly, however, be disputed that these islands have bred more men and women of adventuresome spirit in relation to population, than any island or continent we may choose." And in a little volume about Gandhi of about this date, Reginald Reynolds introduces him to British boys by describing the port of Porbandar—where Gandhi was born—in terms used by Stevenson or Masefield.

But at the level of significant statement, the writers of England were producing books like Strachey's *End of Empire*, 1960, or Philip Mason's *Prospero's Magic*, 1962.[3] Mason's book is one of a group that take *The Tempest* as a myth of imperialism, and analyze its implications. (Others include Leslie Fiedler's *The Stranger in Shakespeare*, 1972, and D. O. Mannoni's *Prospero and Caliban*—1956 in the U.S.) Mason spent his career in India as an administrator and magistrate (when he returned to England he was shocked to find that Englishmen cheated too) and he analyzes a Prospero complex in himself. It was something he grew up with. His father had been a doctor in the north of England, no grandee, and yet he grew up to regard servants as belonging to another race. He says that before 1914 people would have been shocked to see a maid coming out of the lavatory they used, and the class feeling was reciprocated. Even in the village he grew up in, there were parts where boys of his class were liable to have stones thrown at them. Such racist and class hostility was greatest between 1880 and 1920, he says, because power was being transferred away from the upper class.

But it was his whole culture that was being transformed, including his literature. He says that his boyhood was full of tales of islands, like

333

*Peter Pan,* and *Treasure Island,* and *Robinson Crusoe,* and *The Tempest.* But now he can't enjoy such tales. The literary critics of his youth, like Quiller-Couch, loved *The Tempest,* and could see nothing in it to offend; because the men of his generation accepted authority—accepted it as theirs. Now we don't. Until recently, Mason says, we all assumed that civilization justified imperialism; the writings of Voltaire atoned for the wrongs done (by the Roman empire) to Vercingetorix. But now we don't. His book is all about the giving up of power, by his country and his class.

The Stracheys had figured at the very top levels of the Indian administration. Sir John was finance minister under Lord Lytton, 1876–1880, Sir Richard presided over the Famine Commission, 1876–1878, and so on. John Strachey's *The End of Empire,* setting out to consider England's relation to the world, now that her empire is being dissolved, professes political hope but expresses historical bitterness. He quotes Engels in *Anti-Dühring,* "Without slavery, no Greek state, no Greek art and science; without slavery, no Roman empire; it is very easy to inveigh against slavery and similar things in general terms, and to give vent to high moral indignation at such infamies. Unfortunately, all this conveys is what everyone knows, namely that these institutions of antiquity are no longer in accord with our present conditions and sentiments." That bitterness about civilization as a whole is inevitably a substratum of the mood in England in this historical moment.

But we are concerned primarily with literature, and with narrative. The form of adventure lived on after the spirit of adventure had died. Sometimes, indeed, the spirit reversed itself, and yet continued to use the old patterns and motifs. Some of the most characteristic fiction of the 1930s in England were the antiadventures of Evelyn Waugh and Graham Greene, in which the Empire and the adventurer were both mocked. (The fact that both writers were also anti-Protestant, and Waugh at least was antidemocratic, is no coincidence.) Like other ironical writings, of course, these books' message was ambiguous. Their form subverted their spirit, and Waugh's adventurer, Basil Seal, though stamped with official disapproval, remained the most vivid and impressive figure in his stories. Waugh never accepted, at the deepest level, England's loss of Empire. He invoked the exemplary heroism of T.E. Lawrence and Winston Churchill in *Put Out More Flags,* and Gerald MacBryan is a putative model for Basil Seal.

Books of that kind still came out in England in the 1950s and 1960s, when Anthony Burgess joined the earlier writers. And we have seen even later than that how the adventure form subverts quite passionately radical intentions, in Pontecorvo's film, *Burn*. In this story of a slave revolt on a West Indian sugar island in the nineteenth century, we find a Black Prince, a romantic landscape (photographed with sadomasochistic sensuousness), and a white adventurer, played by Marlon Brando. Brando is bad but complex, the Black Prince is good but simple; naturally the audience's identification is overwhelmingly with the former. The adventure form carries its own imperialist message, despite the individual artist's intentions.

We are still, in the late 1970s, in the postimperial and anti-imperialist age, but fictional modes are changing away from the simple antiadventure that Greene and Waugh wrote. Amongst the significant new writers there are three names to mention, Doris Lessing, Paul Scott, and V. S. Naipaul. They have accepted the loss of the Empire, as an ideal and as a fact, in ways that Waugh and Greene never did. That loss is their starting point. It is no accident that Lessing and Naipaul are both Empire-born, and their postimperialist and anti-imperialist vision of England is a large part of their intellectual dowry. They have come back to England, to London, part of the huge immigrant movement, as the frontiers of Empire curled up and rolled back. But they have a moral advantage over English writers, by having lived on that frontier, so long veiled from English view. It is significant that they include no element of adventure, and in fact Lessing so avoids the Black Prince figure that she has practically no native characters at all.

In *Guerillas, Guerillas,* Naipaul does use elements of adventure, but steeped in an ultra-Conradian irony, an acid which quite neutralizes their mythic potential. This technique gives him as many artistic problems as it gave Conrad, and Naipaul nowadays is most interesting for "what he wants to say," and so for his nonfiction. In *The Loss of El-Dorado* (1969) he says that, in the Trinidad he grew up in, history was an imperialist fairy tale about Columbus, Raleigh, and the Indians—not about slavery but the abolition of slavery. He tells the story of El Dorado, down into the nineteenth century, in Conradian style, as a sardonic grotesque comedy. But Naipaul has gone far beyond ordinary anti-imperialism; in this story he is sympathetic above all to Raleigh, who "might have been king of the Indians."

## In the Trough of the Wave of Imperialism

Raleigh is his hero, as he was Defoe's. Raleigh's book about Guinea, "suggests mines and gold, spaciousness, enamelled forests, a world in which the senses, needs, life itself, can be extended. The book is part of the world's romance" (p. 86). But what is important in Naipaul, always, is not his affirmation or his argument, but the field of his perception, which is truly prophetic. He tells the story of a Robinson Crusoe figure who arrived in Trinidad in 1593, having spent fourteen months on St. Helena; and he comments that thus Trinidad links the two great fantasies of the New World, Crusoe and El Dorado, Crusoe and Cortes.

Naipaul presents himself as bitterly antiromantic, but nowadays he seems rather bitterly romantic; for his skepticism directs itself above all to all *alternatives* to the modern system. In his most recent book, *India: A Wounded Civilization,* he describes his family memories of Indian life as "a trap door into a bottomless past," and warns everyone against following Gandhi down through that trapdoor. The premodern culture is a form of death in life. Naipaul's vision is still Wellsian, as it was in *A House for Mr. Biswas,* but in reading his last books we think less of *Tono-Bungay* than of *Mind at the End of Its Tether.* The Wellsian vision comes close to madness when what it rests on so denies all its hopes, when technology seems destruction, and Defoe's dream becomes a nightmare.

Paul Scott's *Twilight of the Raj* can be seen as an attempt by the English literary mind to return to the point at which it severed connections with Kipling. For it is not only the setting of his novels which remind us of the earlier writer; it is the thematic subject-matter, the nature of authority and the workings of justice, in a huge empire. His characters—unlike most modern-novel characters—are known essentially in their work, and their relation to that work. But this subject-matter is combined with other things, which derive from the anti-Kipling interregnum, and belong to it in mood; notably, the plot element of an unjust punishment of an Indian who enters into social relations with the English, so like the plot of Forster's *Passage to India,* and the post-Proustian form, with its reverbatory action and reflective analysis, so like Powell's *Music of Time.* Scott may be said to attempt, in fiction, what Orwell attempted in the essay, a reconciliation of Kipling's imagination of responsibility (imagining what power and authority feel like) with anti-imperialist and anti-ruling-class feelings. He re-associates the officer class with a moral seriousness which in post-1918 England has been ascribed instead to the non-officer class. This effort at reconciliation and bringing together is perhaps reflected in the massive size of his novel-series. His form is essentially synthetic, and that is his weakness as well as his strength.

Doris Lessing is a more major figure than either of the two men; largely because she has affiliated herself to the great tradition of the serious novel in English, and tried to give it its modern adaptation. She belongs to a group of writers whose hour has just struck, the women born in the empire, who rebelled against its male ethos as well as against its imperialism and made their fiction out of that rebellion. They were usually daughters of fathers who had failed as adventurers, and mothers who had, in consequence, played a masculine role. In this generation there are Jean Rhys and Elspeth Huxley; in an earlier one, Olive Schreiner and (to some extent) Katherine Mansfield. But Lessing's most important novel for our purposes is not one set in the empire at all, but *Memoirs of a Survivor* (1974) because it is such a dramatic reversal of *Robinson Crusoe* in form. There is no sign of that reversal being conscious, but the writer appeals to anti-Defoe sympathies in her audience. The narrator is a middle-aged woman who looks after a child called Emily Cartwright during a future period when London is breaking down. Machines, services, transport, energy sources, all collapse, fail, vanish. Trade returns to the condition of barter. Primitive skills revive but cannibalism does, too. Emily becomes girlfriend to Gerald, who leads a tribe of boys who live on the street; but he is defeated by a gang of savage kids who grew up in the Underground. If we put the story beside Defoe's, we notice a number of reversals: the survivor replaces the entrepreneur; the sense of an ending replaces the sense of a beginning; a woman replaces a man; staying home replaces going abroad; running down replaces winding up; a disintegrating London replaces Moll Flanders' intensifying London; an empire-originating novelist replaces an empire-oriented novelist. No story could more decisively announce the death of adventure, and the message has been accepted without a murmur, as something everyone agrees to.

# Conclusion

I HAVE not been arguing that imperialism is foolish, dangerous, and wrong; and I shall not do so now, though that of course is what I believe. I have argued only that imperialism has penetrated the fabric of our culture, and infected our imagination, more deeply than we usually realize. I thought that the field of literature offered particularly telling examples of this infection, because there, at least in serious literature and serious discussion of literature, we usually feel ourselves remote from imperialism and its influence. In fact, I have tried to show it is rather that we are resistant to that influence, and remote only in the willful sense. All of which takes imperialism for granted, and ignores its political character.

But I do want to point to the background of politics, of practical action. We all, like Marx, want to pass from explaining the world to changing it. First I want to point to the likenesses and differences between that serious-literature, high-culture, resistance to Empire, and other kinds; notably Gandhi's and Tolstoy's more powerful, political and religious resistance. The moral realism and moral scruple, the aversion and recoil from imperialism in all its phases, which work at the motor root of serious literature, work at the root of Gandhi's and Tolstoy's teaching too. But in that teaching they are developed gigantically. Literature turns away from that subject matter and that mode of action, to create in effect an alternative world —often alternative in theme and motif, always in psychic substance —though still a world whose colors are the meanings of this one. Gandhi and Tolstoy began to build with bricks made out of the same materials as the Empire-builders themselves use, trying to take up the same psychic and cultural space as the house we actually live in, trying to displace that house.

Their work is something I shall discuss in the next book in this series, but it connects with some things in this one, because it is related to the literary-cultural resistance, though largely by negation. Tolstoy's Christian anarchism derives some of its interest and authority for us from his participation, as writer, soldier, and citizen, in Russian imperialism; and from his later investment in domestic life and the domestic novel, those standard liberal alternatives to active imperialism, which came to seem to him criminally inadequate. Gandhi was never a novelist, and so does not figure in this book at all. But it was a substantial paradox in Gandhi's anti-imperialism that he invoked the greatness of India's past, and the pride of Indians in their culture—which was of course an imperialist culture. He offered to make India great again, and Indians proud. He even urged them to be violent—in order to fit themselves to renounce violence. (It is not clear to me that he is to be condemned for that paradox. Perhaps he is rather to be admired. Just because practically every kind of political energy can be called imperialist to some degree, we should perhaps *demand* some combination of imperialism with its opposite, and reject only the wrong kinds.)

The life examples of Gandhi and Tolstoy, in that book, will suggest, more powerfully than any arguments I could frame, how imperialism can be resisted passionately, splendidly, tragically. But is there anything to be done less extreme than that, but more vigorous than the mere continuance of traditional culture; any practical and contemporary application of the ideas developed historically and theoretically in this book? What I want to suggest in this last chapter is that there is.

Now that the Empire is definitely dismembered, and England no longer has the lion's share (but something more like a jackal's share) in the world system, it must surely be possible for at least Englishmen to look at the adventure tale differently, to get beyond the persistence and resistance described in the last chapter. It must be possible for them to see it in a different relation to literature-as-a-system, and to see that system in a different relation to culture as a whole. In the more purely speculative sense of "to see" that argument has already been made in the previous chapters, as far as scholarship and theory go, and in the practical criticism of Kipling and Conrad. I have tried to build a new imaginative framework for the adventure tale; and that must remain my book's principal and substantive aim. But I had also a further aim, reaching beyond the limits of scholarship, to provide a platform for a new approach to English literature as a subject of

study—as a part of the national education—something to be substituted for the implicit system I was taught by. That substitution
would be what one could do in the field of literature-in-education
towards a larger cultural change. To promise such a change, even
completely to plan it, I must leave to men like Marx, but anyone may
work toward it.

It is not a question of weaning oneself away from any enthusiasm
for imperialism. That job has been done, as far as humanists are
concerned. The system of literature was always in some sense hostile
to adventure, as we have seen, and after 1918, however the form
persisted, there was a general moral resistance to the spirit. What is
needed, odd though it may seem, is almost the reverse; a general
turning toward adventure in ready appreciation, an unprejudiced
curiosity about and respect for its strengths, an acknowledgment of
our heritage. The way to achieve that—as far as institutional means
go—is to teach the adventure novel in schools and colleges.

I must foresee the objection that to teach these books would mean
not teaching others, and that those, for instance the novels of the
Great Tradition, are of higher literary value. That is true, according
to the traditional—and perfectly valid—meaning of the word "literary." But there are other ideas of literature, and culture, and value.
The adventure novel has one large advantage in seriousness, in that
it deals with that body of historical fact which Simone Weil called
"force." In her essay, "The Iliad or the Poem of Force," she said,
"Only he who has measured the dominion of force, and knows how
to respect it, is capable of love and justice." So the vision of love and
justice of those who turn away from force—as the serious novel does
—is ultimately inauthentic. She studied the *Iliad* in the context of
the German conquest of France, and she chose that poem because
it was about that body of historical fact. Well, so are adventure
novels. They measure its dominion only in the mode of romance, but
that is more than the courtship novel does. That makes them a
satisfactory object of study.

It will be obvious that this argument assigns a large scope to the
critic and teacher; since in themselves, or as usually read, adventures
don't make us think seriously about the dominion of force. But the
critic and scholar took a large scope in presenting the domestic novel
to us too—the seriousness we find in those novels is largely, though
legitimately, due to the serious work done by them. They made

discriminations in them and between them, and brought historical contexts to bear upon them, of great intensity and scope. The difference is just that the adventure novel cannot even seem to have the same *sort* of seriousness as the critics'. The two are on different wavelengths. But Defoe and Scott were of course serious men; and if Jane Austen and George Eliot were more so (which I would dispute anyway) this is clearly not a matter of more or less. It is a matter of the adventure novel's spirit—in all its dispositions of seriousness and lightness—seeming hostile to the critics' spirit. And that hostility can be overcome, I believe, if the critics think about literature—think about the adventures—in a new way.

I need hardly say that the domestic novel should continue to be studied, by students who specialize in the history of the novel. When looked at in connection with the history of Empire and the myth of adventure, that novel will be seen to have new aspects of interest. Take for example Jane Austen's use in *Persuasion* of the contemporary culture-hero Frederick Wentworth, that embodiment of English-navy virtues and charms. Jane Austen had two well-loved brothers in the navy, one of whom played a prominent part in the addition of Burma to the Empire, and the naval officer was her model of manliness. As it happens, Fanny Burney also had such a brother; thus we see one typical relation of the courtship novel (its writers *and* its readers) to the adventurous and imperialist half of England. It was the sisters of the heroes of Empire who wrote and read the serious courtship novel; and whatever their judgments on imperialism, they remained on good terms with their brothers and men like them— even good imaginative terms, as *Persuasion* shows. At the same time, they offered in their novels an alternative to the imaginative world of adventure—something independent of that half of England; while later writers offered a reaction against it. So how to define that novel's relation to Empire is a challenging problem. Thus the study of the courtship novel too can receive a new impetus from this connection. But as for its more general appreciation, its strictly cultural function, one can let people find their own ways to it.

But I mustn't claim that the adventures won't be inferior in certain literary ways. That is unfortunate, but the prize is so large that the price is worth paying; and it means mainly that we must alter the way we teach. These books should not be taught as English Literature, but as what we might call British Studies, by analogy with American

Studies. That is, we should give more attention to each book's cultural function, its circumstances of publication, its readership, its career, and the rewards it brought its author, and *his* career. Defoe, Scott, Twain, Kipling, all participated in so much of the history of their times that they may be said to have embodied it. And then it will make sense, once the adventure novel is at the center of our curriculum, to study the whole phenomenon of publishing, and libraries, and the teaching of literature. Though that has often been proposed over the last fifty years, by critics with a sense of political responsibility, it has never made sense when combined with their sense of literary value, which was apotheosized in Jane Austen. *Her* publishing history had nothing to do with the mass market or the macrophenomena of literature. But replace Austen with Scott, and that sociological background leaps into relevance. For me, a great deal leaps into quite personal relevance.

In the course of my reading for this present book, I came across a sentence that struck me very personally, in Parker T. Moon's *Imperialism and World Politics.* In his book's second paragraph, Moon says, "Every man, woman, and child in Great Britain has ten colonial subjects, black, brown, and yellow." That struck me personally because the book was published in 1926, and I was born in 1927. I was born in the back of a London sweetshop, which had never even known a cleaning woman; but still, *really,* I was born one of those suburban sultans—suburban White Rajahs, Wells and Kipling equally my cradle-sponsors. Of course I had no consciousness of having "coloured" subjects, even in my moments of most serious moral or political reflection. In fact, the more serious I got (as I grew up) the less likely I was to arrive at that consciousness. Who, after all, might have taught me—who, in literature, was saying such things? Kipling—that was precisely the legend beneath his cartoon of the white child adored by native servants. But of course I didn't read Kipling; as it happened, I literally didn't read a word of his in my youth, but even if I had, it would have been in a nonserious way. Seriousness meant, in terms of authors, T. S. Eliot, D. H. Lawrence, F. R. Leavis; in terms of ideas, it meant not dwelling on such thoughts as that I had ten subjects, black, brown, and yellow.

There was of course Orwell, who did want me to cultivate what we might call a Kipling-consciousness, given an anti-imperialist slant. But, at least if we think of the novel, *Burmese Days,* rather than of

Orwell's essays, we must say that even Orwell's effective message was that the whole consciousness of Empire was something infected and pustulent, not something to linger on. This was an effect of the system of literature, which deflected the individual novelist's aim.

Not to dwell on such thoughts seems to me a fair enough cartoon-description of the message of all serious literature on the matter. What Eliot and Lawrence and Leavis told me was to think about other things—highly specified and deeply interesting things; but to do so meant, in effect, to ignore the Empire. It meant to think about the story of the sisters and their marriages, from *Religious Courtship* to *Women in Love* (not to mention *The Three Sisters*, Richardson, Austen, James, Flaubert, and Tolstoy). And not to think about the brothers and their adventures, from *Captain Singleton* to *Captains Courageous* (not to mention *The Three Musketeers*, Scott, Kingsley, Cooper, and Karl May).

In intellectual discussion we often assume that to ignore anything is a sin of irresponsibility; but in the context of action, ignorance can be a very positive and constructive policy—to turn away from $x$ and concentrate on $y$ is perhaps the most effective way of enforcing your judgment of the two. What literature told me (obliquely) was "concentrate your mind and your will on this material; identify yourself with it, embody it, become its representative and champion; that other material is for the minds of another type of person, who will be, in certain ways and at certain moments, your enemy." That was an effective and valuable policy, for the culture and for the individual.

Even in secondary school, I got good marks and high praise for knowing what kind of person Emma Woodhouse was, and why Mr. Knightly was the right man for her to marry. I was valued for having that kind of insight, that kind of knowledge; and as I didn't feel valued for much else, I was grateful for that, and still am. And even if my personal situation had been more favorable, I should still have concentrated myself in obedience upon that psychic material. It was my cultural fate. And I don't and couldn't regret anything so central to everything I have been.

But of course ignorance cannot ever be wholly satisfactory. And now, when we have to *see* it as ignorance, its positive message too familiar any longer to dazzle us, we must look around for some alternative. And we find that historical conditions have changed in such a way that an alternative is available. We are now fifty years away from 1927; nearly fifty from 1930, which George Woodcock tells us was the moment when the Empire—though already on the defensive—achieved its greatest geographical spread.

(We should not let such paradoxes bother us. John Strachey says that it was in the 1950s that England finally found the El Dorado it had been four hundred years in search of—the oil in its Middle East sheikhdoms—much more profitable than India or the West Indies had ever been. Nevertheless the Empire was dead by the 1950s, even if the money still rolled in. That money was not the fruit and flowering of English enterprise, as the golden guineas Defoe handled were—though it was more real, more moral, than the North Sea oil money will be. Sterling was meager and ignoble stuff by the 1950s, good only for consolation, because English culture had shrunk.)

The half century of my lifetime has been a period of national shrinkage and crumbling. If we take my parents' lifetime, the change is even more dramatic. Both were born in 1890, and remember the Diamond Jubilee of 1897, when the Empire included forty-seven separate governments, the navy had three hundred and fifty ships (the next biggest, the French, had only ninety-five) and Englishmen were individually bigger and fitter than other Europeans, according to army recruit measurements—and five members of the Cabinet were over six feet tall, the conventional measurement of great size. Nowadays we don't think of ourselves in such terms.

But that shrinkage and crumbling has affected civilization more directly than culture, the dominant strains in Englishness more than the recessive, the men of Empire more than the men of letters. The balance of power between the two has shifted in favor of literature. And so there is no need for the old defensiveness, the old ignorance. There is no longer need to turn away from the Empire, in that purposive way. It no longer has that power to seduce the young, the glamour of that enormous animal vitality. We can look at it directly, because it's only a moon now, not a sun. We can look up into the heavens, and study it, as a burned-out star, or rather a splendid constellation of stars. We can think about the brothers' story and all it means.

# Notes

## Chapter I

1. In the first book of this series, *The Challenge of the Mahatmas,* I compared *The Tempest* with *Robinson Crusoe,* and argued for the superior interest of the latter from the present point of view. The two stories have a lot in common, as many scholars have noted, but Defoe's version is what I call an energizing myth; its primary effect on readers is to make them want to go out and do likewise; Shakespeare's story is not energizing in that sense. (John Seelye has made a similar argument, in "Some Green Thoughts on a Green Theme," *Tri-Quarterly,* 1972.)

2. Defoe says, in *A Plan of the English Commerce* (1728), page 53, "I am not at all fond of that modern assum'd style, by which some authors think they do us an Honour, when they call the extended scattered Colonies and Dominions of the English or British Nation the English Empire . . . it is no honour, 'tis enough the King has the opulence of an Emperor, without affecting the title." But on page 113, he says, "the English Nation swelled into an Empire of Nations," under the protection of its navy.

3. When the core countries grew rich, their wealth had a peculiarly virtuous character—the whole nation, or so it seemed to those who loved the modern system, grew rich. In *The Chimera* (1720) Defoe says that in England the people are rich, the government poor; in France it is the other way round. *The Chimera* is a pamphlet on the French economy and John Law's attempts to solve its problems. Frenchmen were eager to sell their public bills and buy into Law's Mississippi Company, Defoe tells us, because those bills ran at a discount of 60 to 63 percent. It is because Englishmen would never do that, Defoe says—because our funds have been made sacrosanct by Parliament—that England will always be in debt, but the English will always be wealthy.

4. Voltaire said in 1735 that the French were the whipped cream of Europe, while England excelled in the more masculine virtues. That was an image Defoe himself had used before, but it is more striking to see it adopted by the disobliged party to the comparison. And if France, so close to being a core nation itself, felt herself at such a disadvantage, one can guess how strong feelings were on the periphery and beyond.

5. Iron, as we see as late as Kipling, was the emblematic metal of the modern world system. As late as 1750 England passed an Iron Act, forbidding colonies to build rolling mills, forges, and processing plants of their own. Iron was to belong to the imperial country. But the attachment had a moral and imaginative character, as well as a prudent and acquisitive one. We put our trust in iron—and we took our pleasure in gold.

And hence gilding was a principal form and emblem of art and luxury, in seventeenth-century Europe as a whole. Braudel has some interesting remarks about baroque art (in his *The Mediterranean*) describing it as an art of propaganda for the Counter-Reformation, created from on top by the friars, for whom Rubens, Caracciolo, Ribera, Zurbaran, Murillo merely executed the paintings. That art too was marked by a profusion of gilding, often of iron. Defoe's writing has an aesthetic character almost opposite to baroque painting, and yet his taste in luxury (that is, his society's taste, in which he participated) has something in common with theirs. What that something is, it seems to me, is shown in the gilded iron of gateways and doors and church ornaments, and the various kinds of inlaid wood and precious stones you can associate with that.

6. Mumford suggests also (on page 70 of *Technics and Civilization*) that the mine

and its industries are the concrete models of the conceptual world built up by seventeenth-century physics. This is doubly interesting because of the influence which that conceptual model had over the rest of science, and, through that means, over European philosophy. One might point to Hobbes, for instance, as a political philosopher strongly influenced by mechanistic physics; and Hobbes was close to Defoe in several points of doctrine.

7. Saltpeter is potassium nitrate, which occurs in long crystals with a salty taste, and is used in pickling and in pyrotechnic explosions. It occurs naturally, often called niter, as an incrustation on the soil of hot countries like India or Iran, where nitrifying bacteria convert sewage into nitrates. This process has been imitated artificially in Europe. Beds are prepared from humus, dung, animal refuse, wood ashes, and lime, exposed to the air, and moistened with urine and stable runnings. A white film will then crystallize on the windboard side of the beds, and can be scraped off.

8. "Art," in the intenser meanings of that term, is not wholly to be identified with the Brahmin caste, any more than imagination is to be identified with conscience, or religion with morality. In Hindu caste terms, it is the sadhu who seems more analogous with the artist (if we stipulate, again, that we mean the most intense and spiritual kind of artist). Sadhus and Brahmins are two different kinds of holy man, often at cross purposes, and yet also parallel in tendency.

9. Genres that Defoe distrusted—in just the way his whole caste distrusted them —include romance and theater. His attitude to romance, which he believed to be a literary equivalent of Roman Catholicism, will be discussed later in the chapter. Theater I will say just a word about here.

In his *Review* for 1709 he has two essays, one dated August 30 and another September 1, against playhouses and plays. He declares them to be always immodest, bawdy, and blasphemous. He blames the gentry for the tendency of the plays, and proposes to pension off all the players, at the rate of the best salary they ever earned while on the stage, and to raise the money by voluntary contribution. It is evident that he counts on the sympathy of rich merchants, because they are hostile to theater.

10. One can illustrate the distrust the merchant caste felt for the aristocracy from the very early history of the East India Company. While the government was negotiating with the merchants about their charter, it suggested that Sir Edward Michelbourne should sail on their expedition. The merchants objected that they had "resolved not to employ any *gentlemen* in their place of charge"; and requested that they might be "allowed to sort their business with men of their own qualitye, lest suspicion of employment of *gentlemen* being taken hold upon by the generalitie, do dryve a number of the adventurers to withdraw their contributions." (Found by James Mill among the "Minutes of a General Court of Adventurers," and quoted by Reginald Reynolds in *White Sahibs in India*, page 3 of the 3rd edition, London, 1946.)

11. There are of course other definitions of adventure. Paul Zweig, in *The Adventurer*, gives one quite unlike mine. He says that adventurers always flee women, and reinvent themselves as men, in order to find wholly male pleasures; he cites Achilles and Patroclus, Quixote and Panza, as pattern examples. While in our own, domestically inclined, culture, the adventurer has been rejected as a "demonic, half-human personage." This began to happen in the sixteenth century, when romance became precious and frivolous. Robinson Crusoe, Zweig says, is not really an adventurer at all. While Conrad's Lord Jim could become a character in serious literature only because he failed to become an adventure hero—because of his cowardice on the *Patna;* it is Jim's stream of compulsive talk, and the secrets behind that stream, which make him an interesting figure for our culture.

My own point of view is different. I think Crusoe *is* an adventure hero, of modernist adventure—the kind appropriate to the modern world system. About the phenomenon of *Lord Jim*, I must of course agree, but I attribute the phenomenon to a different cause; it is not our culture as a whole which is domestic, but our serious literature. And that split within culture, that specialization of seriousness, is a weakness. Serious culture has to live by reaction against civilization, just as conscience has to live by reaction against the appetitive ego, but the first two must not build themselves private worlds which exclude the second two. As Thomas Mann says, the *Bildungsroman* (he is speaking of *The Magic Mountain*) is the sublimation and spiritualization of the novel of adventure. Insofar as serious writers have turned away from the adventure tale, and its subject matter, the frontier and the empire, they have turned away from an essential part of modern history. I think that turning away has weakened the character of their seriousness.

12. In 1695 Defoe became manager-trustee of a public lottery, of which the prize was £50,000, and in which every ticket was called an adventure.

13. Of course this hostility between military adventure and high culture is not exclusively Western. You find the same thing in India; notably, in the literary interpretations of Krishna and Rama, which make them spiritual heroes, and their battles metaphorical. But then India too was something of an empire-and-not-an-empire, its dominant caste Brahmins.

14. Cortes promised his men fame, or glory, and compared them to the Romans. Even Bernal Diaz, the least romantic of the Conquistadors, boasted of his nobility; he said that he had fought in 119 battles, twice as many as Caesar; and that he, like Caesar, wrote in order that his descendants might know of his exploits. And of course this chivalric style fits Prescott's sense—our sense—of the social fate of the Spanish nobility, and their need for military adventures. Wallerstein says it was noticed at the time that the Reconquista had been giving the nobles employment for many years, and that only the attack on North Africa, and then on Mexico, saved them from unemployment.

In other words, the psychological and sociological facts are in accord with the romance Prescott made out of them. Isabella became queen in 1474, Aragon and Castile were united in 1479, the Inquisition was founded in 1480, and the last Moors were driven off the peninsula in 1492. In that adventure of nationalization, the Spanish military caste played a dominant role. (Indeed, a not insignificant part was played by the military caste from other countries, in the form of knights errant, going on adventures.) When that ended, they were at a loss. The discovery of the New World, at just that moment, brought them a less solid glory (America rewarded merchants better than soldiers) but a more solid wealth.

Seville was then the center of the New World trade, and de Madariaga describes it as "teeming with the most glorious pageant that history had ever seen. The incoming caravels, radiant with the light of the New World; captains, pilots, adventurers, monks, soldiers of fortune, Indian caciques, now stark naked, now dressed in exotic attire with golden rings and headdresses of silver and plumes; slaves, men, women, children, shivering and hungry; gold, gold, gold, . . . the discoverer himself, passing through the streets of Seville at the head of one of his carefully organized processions, richly decorated with popinjays, glittering with golden chains and golden masks of strange design and profile; or perhaps, by contrast, clad in the dark brown frock of a penitent monk of St. Francis, or even, in iron chains, as a proud, shipwrecked, sullen prisoner; waves upon waves of excitement; new lands; banks of pearls; islands to be had for the asking."* How well we recognize that excitement, in the speaker, but also in the thing described, even if we are familiar only with English or American literature. That is

*Quoted in Jon White, *Cortes and the Downfall of the Aztec Empire*, pp. 43, 44.

the excitement of empire, of the frontier, the excitement of the windfall and the boom.

15. We might take Defoe's account, from his *A History of the Principal Discoveries and Improvements in the Several Arts and Sciences,* (1727) page 273. "From hence Ferdinand Cortez, with at most four hundred foot and four hundred horse, landed on the great continent of America, near La Vera Cruz, marched up sixty miles into the country; fought and beat an army of nearly forty thousand Tlascallans, and after that another of one hundred thousand . . . This handful of men, then extending every way, carried on the Spanish conquests for above two thousand leagues . . ."

16. It is especially interesting to note such slogans in the mouths of those to whom those stories meant fear, not pride. Thus the Mogul emperor, Jahangir, is supposed to have said to the English ambassador, Roe, that one Englishman could beat three Portuguese, and one Portuguese three Hindus. And three centuries later a Chinese mandarin, a governor in Manchuria, told the Russian explorer Przhevalsky (the Russian Stanley) that every Russian was worth twelve Chinese in a fight, and hence there could be no war between the two countries.

17. This story would seem to be archetypical in a loose sense; in that it corresponds to a structure of feelings that recur in many times and places. We shall meet it in Russian literature about the conquest of the Caucasus, for instance, by Pushkin and Tolstoy. The story turns up, in fiction but also perhaps in fact, whenever thoughts of conquest stir men's minds. In 1528 in Florida, John Ortiz, a soldier of Narvaez, was rescued by a chief's daughter; and that is John Smith's story about Pocahontas in 1608. Though in his *Generall Historie* of 1624, Smith claimed to have been rescued by lovely ladies in France also, in Turkey, and in Tartary, which sounds more like fiction.

18. The story has many other motifs important in adventure fiction, of which two must be mentioned. One is the hideous temples of human sacrifice, and their grinning idols—which Cortes' men rolled down the temples' innumerable steps to destruction —and the black-garbed priests running to and fro overhead during the battles. That motif is used often by, for instance, Rider Haggard. The other is the Aztec legend of Quetzalcoatl's return from the ocean, and their duty to yield their empire to him— the legend which worked to the Spaniards' advantage. Fair-skinned men with flowing beards were expected, and they came. Primarily, of course, it was the Aztecs who were deceived by this myth, but there may be a case for saying that the Spaniards and Europeans generally were more largely deceived. There is an unmistakable undertone of gratification in the voices of historians who repeat the story; for the Europeans *were,* after all, in that situation, gods.

Take, for instance, Prescott's perfectly realistic glorification of Spanish arms, when Cortes displayed his troops on a beach before an Aztec chieftain. "The bold and rapid movements of the troops, as they went through their military exercises; the apparent ease with which they managed the fiery animals on which they mounted; the glancing of their weapons and the shrill cry of the trumpet, all filled the spectators with astonishment; but when they heard the thunders of the cannon, which Cortes ordered to be fired at the same time, and witnessed the volumes of smoke and flame issuing from these terrible engines . . . " (Vol. I, p. 189) that finished them off. That is always the mythic moment, when we fire the guns, and the natives flee, or fling themselves flat on their faces. But it is none the less factual for being mythical.

We are dealing with several different kinds of myth; the particular superstition about Quetzalcoatl; the more generally mythic attitude of the Aztecs, who, as Octavio Paz says, experienced all historical events as rites, and the Conquest as a last rite; and then—*our* myth—the extraordinarily evocative spectacle of Spaniard confronting Aztec as contemporary Europeans saw it; which is, I think, the way it must be felt by us today, with much the same intensity of feeling, however differently we value it.

When Braudel says that Mexico and Peru were cultures, not civilizations, and that they were immature, their potentials unachieved, their growths unconsolidated, he is seeing what Cortes saw. So is Parry, when he describes their religion as the sad acquiescent faith of the last great Stone Age culture; or White, saying that they were in the grip of a deep cultural psychosis, their over-ritualized religion the expression of deep fears. We cannot escape from the feelings of that myth ourselves.

19. Macaulay's claim that "everyone knows who strangled Atahualpa" (while they don't know about Surajah Dowlah) may sound exaggerated now, but there is some evidence that the stories of Cortes and Pizarro were circulating in at least eighteenth-century England. For instance, W. H. Dilworth, whose schoolbooks were used extensively, published a *History of the Conquest of Mexico* in 1759, describing it as "for the improvement of the British youth." In the same year he also published *The Conquest of Peru by Pizarro and Voyages of Adventure in Florida, especially those of de Soto.* And in 1799 John Britton, later a famous antiquary, published *The Enterprising Adventures of Pizarro.*

20. The cavalry was, in most European armies, dominated by the aristocratic caste, and so out of sympathy with modernist ideology—was, in fact, still chivalric. Of course, that caste supplied the officers to the infantry too. But the latter was part of the modern system, its self-image shaped by that ideology and by its iron, almost mechanical, discipline. Though that was combined, in great soldiers, with a bold inventiveness, independence, and indiscipline; qualities often linked to the aristocratic temperament. One sees that combination at work in the great triumphs of modernist armies like Clive's and Cortes's.

When those two virtues, discipline and indiscipline, were distributed between two modern system opponents, the issue became uncertain. When the rock-like British infantry met sharp-shooters with individual initiative, they were often defeated, as in the American War of Independence, and the Boer War. But as long as a British army (or that of any other European power) faced an enemy from outside the system, they could display amazing courage, devotion, and energy, and defeat immensely larger forces.

Of course, if the enemy did not belong to the modern system, he almost certainly was inferior in military technology. But the victories of the Europeans are not all to be attributed to that technology; and some of the power that technology had seems to have been spiritual. See for instance the paltry number and quality of muskets Cortes took with him, and the immense effect he made with them.

It is interesting to reflect on the very different success which England and Spain met with, when fighting armies belonging to the core states of the modern system. Soon after Cortes's fabulous success against Mexico, Spain struggled in vain against the Dutch provinces for many years, though there she had great advantages in numbers of troops and supplies. And just after Clive's fabulous success against India, England struggled in vain to subdue her American colonies, with again great advantages in numbers and equipment; instead of, as in India, great disadvantages. These differences, whether or not formulated and focused by the mind, worked powerfully on the imagination of all concerned.

21. His purpose is "to consider Britain's relation to the world now that her empire is being dissolved." He calls Clive in India a better example of what empire in general has been than Cortes in Mexico, "because the work of the latter was lost." In any case, the Spanish were antimercantile in style, and would have led the world back to the servile imperialism of antiquity. (Venice and Portugal first established a mercantile imperialism—and out of that grew the capitalist imperialism of England.)

# *Notes*

## Chapter II

1. The event that the modern system in England recognized as epic, as its foundation myth, like Marathon for Athens or the Great Trek for the Boers, was the defeat of the Armada—the defeat of Catholic Imperial Spain—in 1588. And it is perhaps significant that it was a sea event. Sea fights, especially defensive ones, are easier for nonempires to celebrate than territorial aggressions, like Henry V's invasion of France. (Though Raleigh's report on the Armada, to be found in Hakluyt's *Voyages,* will remind us how bloodthirsty and chauvinist defensive sea fights can be.) This is the story that was being retold by Kingsley and Kipling right up to the twentieth century. Shakespeare, in this as in so many matters, was not centrally of the tradition.

It is worth noting that Shakespeare, and for that matter Marlowe, had neither knights nor merchants among his main characters. He represents neither the military nor the merchant castes. Sidney and Raleigh styled themselves as knights, but in a rather fanciful way; while the sea dogs of Devon, Drake, Hawkins, Grenville, etc., were powerful incarnations of a cross between the two castes. But Elizabethan literature did not respond to that, or only in an idealizing and romanticizing way.

2. J. W. Hunt, in *Forms of Glory,* analyzes the *Aeneid* pictorially, finding three panels in it, each consisting of four books. The first panel, predominantly dark in color, deals with Dido and the fall of Troy. The second, predominantly bright, describes games and troop reviews, visions of Roman glory, and of Augustus. And the third is again about Troy, and the horrors of war. As a whole, therefore, the *Aeneid* brings together conflicting feelings about Rome and empire, to reconcile them in a steadier version.

3. *Henry V* is the climax of Shakespeare's history plays, and there is some reason to suppose that most Elizabethan writers saw that king's story in epic terms. Samuel Daniel, in his poem, *Civil War,* written a few years before Shakespeare's play, says,

> O what eternal matter here is found
> Whence new immortal Iliads might proceed.

And Raleigh said of the English kings, "None of them went to work like a Conquerour, save only King Henry the fifth."

Moreover the play is a sequence of historical tableaux, with a Chorus, prologues, and an epilogue. And it clearly sets out to do what Sidney said epic poetry should do: arouse admiration, inflame the mind, encourage imitation. (It was probably first performed in 1599, while Essex was in Ireland, establishing British empire there.) In other words, this is Shakespeare's structurally imperialist work, as its content confirms.

The play is full of ideas which recur in imperial writing through the centuries to follow. For instance, in Act I, Scene 2, when Ely and Canterbury speak, Ely says that

> . . . my thrice-puissant liege
> Is in the very May-morn of his youth,
> Ripe for exploits and mighty enterprises.

That celebration of the powers of young men runs all through the adventure tales, from Defoe to Kipling. And Canterbury talks of a beehive as a model for the state;

> The singing masons building roofs of gold,
> The civil citizens kneading up the honey, . . .

You will find the same language, as well as the same idea of civilized greatness, in Kipling's "The Mother-Hive."

And the talk about English manliness, especially in war, is very similar to the talk we shall meet in Defoe. The French are made to say that the English are bastards of the Normans, engendered upon a wild and savage stock: their climate is foggy, raw, and dull, and so are they; but this all redounds to their credit. They have no imagination, but great courage. Henry says that when his troops were in health, "I thought upon one pair of English legs, Did march three Frenchmen." But he must not brag; the English style is plain in everything, as we see in his wooing of the French princess.

The play's endorsement of war and militarism is unequivocal. In his speech in Act III, Scene 1, Henry says,

> But when the blast of war sounds in our ears,
> Then imitate the action of the tiger;
> Stiffen the sinews, summon up the blood,
> Disguise fair nature with hard-favoured rage . . .
> Now set the teeth and stretch the nostril wide,
> Hold hard the breath and bend up every spirit
> To his full height. . . .

It is no doubt this militarism and the equally unequivocal patriotism which account for the unpopularity of the history plays with men of letters. The Elizabethan audiences were enthusiastic about them, but when Shakespeare's literary reputation revived (among men of letters) at the end of the seventeenth century, the history plays were neglected. It is true that in modern times they have been played more often, but the interest in them has been of a political theory, or history-of-ideas, kind. From a literary-moral point of view they are still largely deplored. Tillyard and Mark Van Doren complain of *Henry V*'s inferiority, and Traversi talks of its pessimism and growing coldness.

4. An interesting example of another social order and the literary form that corresponded to it, is given in Aldous Huxley's *Grey Eminence*. This is the churchman's crusade poem; alternative to both the merchants' adventure and the knights' romance, but closer to the latter. Huxley is talking about Père Joseph, the adviser to Cardinal Richelieu, who in fact tried to launch a real crusade, and more than once; in 1615 with the Duc de Nevers at its head, and later with Wallenstein. His literary form was the epic poem in Latin hexameters. He composed a *Turciad* in 4,637 lines, which was praised by Pope Urban VIII as a Christian Aeneid, but apparently only two copies were ever printed. That is a very poor record to compare with the innumerable editions of *Robinson Crusoe*, and clearly Père Joseph backed the losing horse, literarily and culturally speaking. The Roman Catholic Church, and Latin hexameter poems, were both doomed to defeat by the modern world system. But it is worth remembering that in terms of immediate political effectiveness, he was one of the most powerful men in Europe in his lifetime—which was in the same century as Defoe's. Anyway, Huxley says, "In an age when there were no Westerns or detective stories, the most exciting reading matter an imaginative boy could get hold of was probably to be found in the chronicles of the crusades. To a child of François du Tremblay's times [Père Joseph's natal name was du Tremblay], the infidels occupied the place reserved in the minds of a more recent generation of schoolboys for the Indians. Most men, as they grew up, forgot about the infidels, just as they now forget about the Redskins. Not so François du Tremblay" (page 134).

Huxley gives us a very long cultural perspective there. For by the seventeenth century the Crusades were very old and almost purely legendary, just as the Redskins were by Huxley's time; Redskin stories began in Defoe's time (he was the originator of the twin genre, pirate stories); thus we now stand in the same relation to those stories, so long the energizing myth of the modern system, as Père Joseph stood to the Crusade stories which energized the medieval system. He wrote a new Crusade-poem, and tried to start a new Crusade. I think it more appropriate, as a response to our

# Notes

situation, to try to reconsider the dying genre, rather than to revitalize it. But of course I'm a literary critic, not a practical statesman like Père Joseph, who had power at his disposal.

5. I am not suggesting that only, or mainly, knights read these romances; nor that other social orders simply adored or even admired knighthood and chivalry. No doubt much of their reading was purely literary or purely escapist. And the same could be said of the other half of my analogy, the adventure tales that served the merchant caste. The nonmerchant readers did not literally sit dreaming that they were merchants. What seems to be true, in both cases, is that a considerable body of literature was written, tied to one social order, and was read by something like a general reading public. Then what seems probable, what one must assume, is that that reading carried with it something like a general imaginative fealty to, in the one case chivalry, in the other mercantilism, even when the readers' conscious thinking was highly critical of that idea.

6. Lévi-Strauss's account of the Caduveo people in *Tristes Tropiques* suggests that this form of romance, and its connection with a military caste, is not limited to European culture. The Caduveo nobles had paintings stenciled on to their bodies, like our playing cards, and Lévi-Strauss calls them so many Davids, Caesars, Alexanders, and Charlemagnes. They were "like characters in some romance of chivalry, absorbed in their cruel games of prestige and domination . . ." (page 193). The girls among them sometimes followed a warrior, as his page or his mistress. The women often aborted or killed their children, and adopted others. Extravagantly "noble" in their attitude to life, he says, they produced nothing, relying on others for their upkeep, and living out ideas of courage and magnanimity.

7. Mather's life of Phips is cited by Sacvan Bercovitch in *The Puritan Origins of the American Self,* as deserving to win for Mather the title of "father of the American success story." I give a hint of Phips's story in the next chapter. He was the first governor of Massachusetts under the new Charter of 1692.

8. Protestantism was certainly a very important value to Defoe, and though he inclined to minimize sectarian differences between Anglican and Dissenter, or between Presbyterian and Congregationalist, he had no such feelings about the differences between Protestant and Catholic. Catholicism stood to him for superstition, tyranny, inauthenticity, in religion; and it was inseparable from tyranny, licentiousness, laziness, in the rest of life. And that feeling remained surprisingly strong and constant throughout the life-span of the modern system, at least among its proponents. To take a rather random instance, J. R. Seeley, the most dispassionate and scholarly of imperialists, called the papacy "the burning heart of all human discord," and cherished a life-long passion for Milton as "the Protestant poet"—this in the late nineteenth century. (Seeley's father brought out a pamphlet, "The Pope an Impostor," in 1850, which went into ten editions.) Seeley's was a Broad Church Protestantism, following Coleridge and Thomas Arnold, though more ethical and naturalistic than theirs; it would have been quite congenial to Defoe. (See John Gross's introduction to Seeley's *The Expansion of England.*)

9. This book was quite successful. It had eight editions in five years, and was reprinted many times in the eighteenth and nineteenth centuries, in America as well as England. It was used in the education of the children of George I (Paul Dottin, *The Life and Strange and Surprising Adventures of Daniel Defoe*).

10. Thus one of Hannah More's most famous *Cheap Repository Tracts* was "The Two Shoemakers," about two apprentices, good James Stock and bad John Brown. The *Cheap Repository Tracts,* which contained each a story, a sermon, and some short poems, were written for the sunday schools begun in the 1790s by Robert Raikes.

Three a month were issued between 1792 and 1795, and they sold in tens of thousands. Then the stories were collected and published separately. The most famous was "The Shepherd of Salisbury Plain," about a shepherd with a crippled wife and five children, all of whom accept their misfortunes with exemplary patience. The religious moral had some antirevolutionary bearing, and another tract by More was said at the time to have saved England from a French revolution. Both the stories I summarized are to be found in *Religious Courtship;* which shows again how powerful, how long-lasting, were the currents of thought with which Defoe identified himself. I am tracing only the patterns of one subgenre of his fiction; but the wide sweep of his work as a whole is also relevant.

11. Lewis Feuer's book on the history of science *(The Scientific Intellectual)* in which he argues that science derived from the Epicurean rather than the Puritan tradition of thought, assembles the facts of what I have called the antithesis. The Epicurean tradition clearly *was* very important; and clearly *did* constitute an opposite to Puritanism; and yet out of that opposition between the two emerged a cooperation —science was born, and born bearing the traits of both parents.

12. Edmund S. Morgan, in *The Puritan Family* (New York, 1966) says that the Puritan preachers' favorite figure of speech, for describing God's relation to man and His church—the closest comparison they could find—was always marriage. While Levin L. Schücking, in *The Puritan Family* (1970), reminds us that domestic asceticism was not something new; that eighteenth-century family piety was very close to that prescribed by Richard Baxter in the seventeenth century, and even to the sobriety prescribed by Thomas Brecon (1512–1567). The latter says, in his Catechism of 1560, "to live soberly, should seem to be so purely, discretely, modestly, temperately, and sagely to institute our life, that our consciousness should never accuse us of any evil but testify with us, that we live and do all things godly." (Quoted in Schücking, p. 7.) New Year resolutions were entered into family Bibles, and then re-examined at the year's end. Women were often portrayed as the apostles of gentleness, and later of culture, to men. Mercy in *Pilgrim's Progress,* Schücking suggests, was a first sketch for Pamela.

Schücking says that Elizabethan Puritans were unlike the Baptist communists (whom Troeltsch mistakenly took to be the typical sectaries of that time) just in the importance they gave to the family. Elizabeth did not supply enough preachers to the Anglican churches, and from the 1560s on the conventicles were suppressed, so that Puritans had to make the family the Christian temple. Children were taught by their parents; taught to despise all riches and display, and all idleness and vanity, and all pride and boastfulness. (One recalls Clarissa's motto, "Rather useful than glaring," and the contrast between her and Lovelace in this regard.) Baxter said in *Christian Doctrine* "So that it is an evident truth, that most of the mischiefs that now infest or seize upon mankind throughout the earth, consist in, or are caused by, the disorders or ill-governedness of families." (Quoted in Schücking, p. 56.) And in the eighteenth century this Puritan tradition developed into something more feminist. Fordyce's 1766 *Sermons to Young Women* assigned women the work of missionaries to men, working especially in culture and literature. Goldsmith, in his 1767 *Poems for Young Ladies,* said he had included "such pieces as innocence can read without a blush." And Bowdler brought out his *Family Shakespeare* in 1807. The movement apparently went hand in hand with a feminizing and genteelizing of culture.

13. A passage by Larzer Ziff will explain how Puritanism expressed itself expansively, in colonization and generally on a national and international scale. "A culture of expansion, distrustful of volume as mere resistance, Puritanism asserts a remarkable capacity to reduce the abstract meanings of volume to the precisions of the word and

to reduce the physical existence of the dimension of space—be it represented by an alien psyche, a wilderness, or outer space itself—to the two-dimensional plane of its technology. Created in response to the expansion of population, trade, and self-mastery in the post-medieval world, it suited the new world superlatively well and will retain its suitability, it is to be presumed, until such time as expansion itself no longer suffices and stasis must be contemplated." (*Puritanism in America*, p. 311.) This shows us the extrovert counterpart to that intense measurement of the minutiae of class, sex, and decorum, which we find in the Puritan novels.

14. Watts was suckled on the steps of a jail in which his father was imprisoned, and at his dissenting Academy heard Cromwell's former chaplain, John Howe, preach. He was in touch with the old Puritanism, and was essentially a man of religion. At the same time, his own career was as chaplain to Sir Thomas Abney, a rich merchant who became lord mayor of London, and one of his paraphrases of the Psalms appeared in *The Spectator*. So he was also a man of the eighteenth century and a man of letters. He is at his most interesting from our point of view when he unites the two identities; in certain hymn stanzas which we can apply to Clarissa, and which help us to understand the spiritual and even religious aura which still clung to stories like hers.

> On earth the usurpers reign,
> Exert their baneful power;
> O'er the poor fallen souls of men
> They tyrannize their hour.
>
> Into a world of ruffians sent,
> I walk on hostile ground;
> While human bears on slaughter bent
> And ravening wolves surround.

15. I have limited myself to the themes of the domestic novel, but more formal characteristics could be related to this set of ideas, if there were space enough. Ian Watt has pointed out, in *The Rise of The Novel*, that Defoe and Richardson were the first great writers to present plots not taken from the literary-mythical heritage; and has explained the implications, that Nature was not completed and unchanging. Their novels implied a growing, changing, progressive universe.

Defoe disapproved of epic, and classical literature, and indeed of myth. Homer, he said, had sung "the Wars of the Greeks . . . from a Reality, into a meer Fiction." (Watt, p. 242.) While Richardson spoke of "the fierce, fighting Iliad," and its responsibility for the militarism of his own times. Indeed, all Watt has to say about formal realism is relevant to this discussion.

I will restrict myself to his quotation from Mrs. Barbauld that Richardson has "the accuracy of finish of a Dutch painter," with the concomitant contrast that Reynolds preferred the great and general ideas of Italian painting to the "literal truth and . . . minute exactness in the detail of nature modified by accident" of the Dutch. This is exactly like the contrast between Richardson and Fielding in serious fiction, and it has quite large implications for the taste that preferred one or the other. Let me point out also that the Dutchness of those Dutch paintings is not irrelevant. Those paintings are the great expression of the modern world system in artistic terms by the Dutch of that period. They correspond to the English novels (which came a little later, just as English supremacy did) and it is worth noting that these painters were not patronized by the rich Dutch of their own time (who preferred classicizing French art), just as the ruling class of England originally despised the novels of Defoe and Richardson.

16. Samuel Smiles, in *Self-Help*, page 300, speaks of Agar's perfect prayer, "Give

me neither poverty nor riches; feed me with food convenient for me," and connects this with the virtue of living in the middle station, unobserved, not to be seen of men. Clarissa was the heroine of the modern system's persistent moral scheme.

While Lovelace was brought up by his mother to "bear no control." His tutors were told he must not know what contradiction or disappointment were. He naturally grew up very wild and gay; "a young man." He is often described as young, unbroken, his passions unsubdued. He quotes Milton's Satan, and compares himself. And his friends are young men with aristocratic names—Belford, Belton, Tourville, Mawbray. Richardson saw the world in terms of the Puritan drama.

17. Smiles says, in *Self-Help*, p. 233, that Wellington was a far greater man than Napoleon because "Napoleon's aim was Glory; Wellington's watchword, like Nelson's, was 'Duty'. The former word, it is said, does not occur once in his despatches; the latter often, but never accompanied by any high-sounding profession."

## Chapter III

1. It was around 1680, just as Defoe was coming of age, that the modern business world was born, J. Sutherland tells us in his *Defoe* (New York, 1958). Fortunes were made overnight on the 'Change which would have taken forty years of prudent trading and hoarding. Tradesmen set up coaches, and entertained with silver plate and footmen. Stockjobbing, lotteries, and speculation began; coffee houses, the penny post, and newspapers which appeared two or three times a week, helped all this. Imports rose from seven millions' worth in 1662 to eleven and a half millions' worth in 1688. Defoe was so much a part of all this that Sutherland speculates he may have aimed, in the early part of his life, at becoming lord mayor of London.

2. In *Memoirs of a Cavalier*, the narrator speaks of "the Blackness of those Days, when Law and Justice was under the Feet of Power; the Army ruled the Parliament, the private Officers their Generals, the common soldiers their Officers, and Confusion was in every Part of the Government." (p. 270 of the edition by James Boulton.)

3. It is interesting to study how the Dutch gradually lost their modern system energy in proportion as they lost their primacy within that system to England. This is even more striking in the Dutch abroad than in those who remained at home. Hannah Arendt points out in *Origins of Totalitarianism* that the Boers were the first Europeans to lose their pride in living in a world created and fabricated by man. "They agreed to vegetate on essentially the same level as the black tribes . . ." (p. 194). They employed large numbers of slaves, but their economy was unprogressive, and they hated the *Uitlanders* above all because they would make South Africa a productive economy. They had retreated from a thrifty and intensive cultivation to become herdsmen and hunters. Indeed, there is a retreat—though not in the same direction —in the New York Dutch whom Cooper depicts in his Littlepage novels.

## Appendix to "Defoe and His England"

4. England in Defoe's day, and London more strikingly than any other part, was newly prosperous. Braudel says that London in 1700 supported 100,000 people out of trade, but another 100,000 lived off the work done by and for administrative officers, and for the nobility and gentry who settled around the government.

# Notes

It was during these years that such expressions as "Al at Lloyds" became current, lasting in most European languages for two hundred and fifty years, and a clue to much. The firm of Lloyds were underwriters (named after Ned Lloyd's coffee house, established under Charles II) who examined and classified ships and cargoes, and insured them. There was also a growing sector of investors, grouped around the Stock Exchange, while at the other end of the social scale, the East End was already artisan, marine, and semicriminal in its population.

Another clue to that period in England is given by Keynes in his *Treatise On Money* (1930) when he wonders how much Elizabethan England owed to Francis Drake, and Augustan England owed to William Phips. Both these men found and brought to England frontier windfalls once removed. Drake's *Golden Hind* returned from a voyage in 1580 with between £300,000 and £1,500,000, a return to his financial promoters of 4700 percent on their investments, Webb calculates. Queen Elizabeth paid off England's foreign debts with her share, and had enough left over to invest £42,000 in the Levant Company; the profits from which company in turn launched the East India Company. Keynes says that that booty was "the foundation and origin of British Foreign Investment." While William Phips found sunken Spanish treasure off Hispaniola a hundred years later that brought to his stockholders a return of 10,000 percent and much strengthened William III's position on the throne. The boom which began with that windfall ended only with the establishment of the Bank of England, of the Stock Exchange in 1694, and in the following year, the reform of the currency by Locke and Newton.

Among the principal founders of the bank was William Paterson, a friend and associate of Defoe, who was also the parent of the Darien company, an important episode in the history of capitalism and also that in of the Union of Scotland and England. In 1695 Paterson convinced the Scots parliament to launch a company to colonize and trade on the Isthmus of Darien, near Panama, in the general area of El Dorado. The first expedition sailed in 1698, but the company met with determined obstruction by English rivals as well as by Spanish, and so failed, with much loss of life and also of the investments of merchants at home. This caused much bitterness in Scotland. The union was, or included, an act of reparation by England, financially; it set up an equivalent fund of nearly £400,000, of which over half went to pay Darien investors, and the rest went to pay off the Scots' national debt. The failure of Darien also convinced Scottish investors that they could only get their share of trading profits from such schemes by merging Scotland with England. Thus the union was entered into in part as a means to joint mercantile imperialism. There are many such anecdotes, each embodying another aspect of the complex subject, and in most of them Defoe could be named.

We could in fact take our sense of Defoe's England from his own works; and first of all from his *Whole Tour of the Island of Great Britain,* published 1724–1726. As Pat Rogers says in his introduction to the Penguin edition, this is a deeply imaginative book, employing all Defoe's skills as chronicler, polemicist, and creative writer, as well as encyclopaedist. Rogers quotes Christopher Morris saying of this period, "The English were becoming highly immodest about their own political discoveries, their own great men or 'worthies', their own architecture or landscape, and, above all, their own prosperity." Defoe was very well suited to celebrate this new prosperity, and he worked out a literary formula (the tour of the country) which proved highly successful, for other writers as well as for himself. It was the nearest thing to a British epic; verse epics were projected in this period, with titles like *The Brutiad* and *Boadicea,* to rival Virgil or at least Tasso, and some were even written; but more successful was the crop of topographical and historical works, by Camden, Leland, and Drayton, among others. And of these, Defoe's *Tour* was the flowering. Defoe had found the right form, and later writers imitated him.

This was a genre more congenial than epic to the merchant caste, being factual not romantic, and commercial not military. And this specimen, the most successful of the genus, went through nine editions, of which the last appeared in 1779. Samuel Richardson was the publisher of the second and third, and the editor of at least the third. Walter Scott used one of them in writing *Rob Roy*.

In the Preface to Volume I, Defoe says, "This [England] is the most flourishing and opulent country in the world . . ." He exults in the new houses—"and gentlemen's houses"—to be seen everywhere. He gives much detail about the docks and gunyard at Woolwich, and about Rochester, the navy's chief arsenal. He describes with imaginative zest the warehouses and storehouses; "the rope-walk for making cables, and the forges for anchors and other iron-work, bear a proportion to the rest; as also a wet-dock for keeping masts, and yards of the greatest size, where they lye sunk in the water to preserve them, the boat-yard, the anchor-yard . . . the sails, the rigging, ammunition, guns, great and small-shot . . ." (p. 105). His mere lists of material wealth are full of excitement.

Defoe's imagination was vivid but unromantic. When he got to Land's End, he rode his horse into the water, to feel the moment when England stopped; and described the rocks of Cornwall as being cemented together by the ores they contained, to make England strong against the waves. This is his kind of imagination. But he says, in Letter 3, "I shall sing you no songs here of the river Thames in the first person of a water-nymph, a goddess, (and I know not what) according to the humour of the ancient poets. . . . but I shall speak of the river as occasion presents, as it is really made glorious by the splendour of its shores, gilded with noble palaces, strong fortifications, large hospitals, and publick buildings; with the greatest bridge, and the greatest city in the world, made famous by the opulence of its merchants, the encrease and extensiveness of its commerce; its invincible navies, and by the innumerable fleets of ships sailing upon it, to and from all parts of the world" (p. 173). This, he says, will be a "more masculine" manner of speaking. But full of glee, nevertheless.

There is always something new, in England, he exclaims. "New foundations are always laying, new buildings always raising, highways repairing . . . so that as long as England is a trading, improving nation, no perfect description . . . can be given." And in London, "New squares, and new streets rising up every day to such a prodigy of buildings, that nothing in the world does, or ever did, equal it, except old Rome in Trajan's time" (p. 332). (At such moments one sees that Defoe, not Pope, was the true Augustan; and one of his last pamphlets was about London and entitled *Augusta Triumphans*.) "Some have said that there is not less than 100 million of stock transferred backwards or forwards from one hand to another every year."

At the same time he deplores the assemblies, newly in fashion, because they always end in intrigue. In Vol. II, page 231, he says, "They are a plan laid for the ruin of the nation's morals, and which, in time, threaten us with too much success that way." For Defoe, though deeply excited about progress, was full of qualms about luxury. He wanted England to put its trust in iron, not gold (though of course she, and he, would always *take* the latter, too).

In the section on Scotland, he says, "I hope it is no reflection upon Scotland to say they are where we were, I mean as to the improvement of their country and commerce; and they may be where we are" (Vol. II, p. 280). If stock and implements are supplied to the Scots, and if their husbandry is changed, all that is needed is that they stay home and work. But work means enterprise, capitalist enterprise, as emerges in this comment. "I believe they are very good Christians at Kirkenby, for they are in the very

*Notes*

letter of it, they obey the text, and are contented with such things as they have. They have all the materials for trade, but no genius to it; all the opportunities for trade, but no inclination to it. In a word, they have no notion of being rich and populous, and thriving by commerce . . . it is to me the wonder of all the towns of North Britain . . . they have the Indies at their door, and will not dip into the wealth of them; a gold mine at their door, and will not dig it" (Vol. II, p. 323). It's a measure of the distance between the two nations in development that Defoe has to say he does not use "merchant" in the Scots sense, to mean a shopkeeper, but in the English sense, "merchant-adventurers who trade to foreign parts, and employ a considerable number of ships" (Vol. II, p. 315).

*A Plan of the English Commerce* (1728) has an interesting Preface, in which Defoe justifies his book by an imaginative description of the web of commerce as a whole. "The clothier sorts his Wool, dyes and mixes the Colours; the Comb, the Card, the Wheel, the Loom, are all set on Work by his Direction, and he is call'd a Master of his Art, and he is so; but ask him where his Cloths are sold, by whom bought, to what Part of the World they are shift, and who are the last Consumers of them, he knows nothing of the Matter. . . ." (p. vii). This is the imagination of the new society, excited to the point of affirming itself in heraldic images. "The Commerce of the World, especially as it is now carried on, is an unbounded Ocean of Business; Trackless and unknown, like the Seas it is managed upon; the Merchant is no more to be followed in his Adventures, than a Maze or Labyrinth is to be trac'd out without a Clue" (p. ix).

For Defoe, English commerce was primarily the cloth industry, as we shall see, and it is no accident that this was the first trade to be industrialized in England. It is while exploring Defoe's world that the modern reader first becomes aware of his own native landscape, of the factories missing from the England of Shakespeare and Chaucer, and of the driving force of change and progress within Defoe's landscape.

Defoe often urged his countrymen on to imperial and colonial efforts. "There are New Countries, and new Nations, who may be so planted, so improved, and the People so managed, as to create a new Commerce; and millions of people shall call for our Manufacture, who never called for it before" (p. xi). Despised Portugal is taking advantage of this. Five times the amount of European goods that used to go to Portugal's colonies abroad, thirty years ago, are now sent there. But England's trading genius and adventuring temper needs to be revived. We have very few subjects in America, to buy our goods, while "the decayed and indolent Portuguese and Spaniards have many."

Defoe had a very strong sense of national identities, following the cultural plan of the modern world system. Thus the Portuguese (on the semiperiphery now) are decayed and indolent, while the Turks (always outside the system) are enemies to trade, and discourage industry and improvement, and even dispeople the world. "The Mahometans abhor Business and Labour, and despise Industry, and they starve accordingly." And again, "View their condition; they are miserably poor . . . idle, indolent, and starving, . . . and all for want of Trade" (p. 11). And in Russia (on the periphery) workmen hack up a whole tree to get a plank, and sell it no dearer than do Swedes who, by means of saws, get three or four planks from a tree.

At the center of the system, in England, people are at their most shrewd and solid and vigorous. English workmen do more work, and eat and drink more than others. Our workmen's work is strong and substantial in everything they do. But this is not genetic but ethical racism. Defoe says England was not always a center of trade. It had made itself so by effort.

This idea is connected with the gospel of work, the work ethic. ". . . the diligent trading manufacturing World work chearfully, live comfortably. . . . Whereas the unemploy'd World groan out their Souls in Anguish and Sorrow . . . and sink under the weight of their Idleness and Sloth . . ." (p. 29). And this gospel derives from and applies to specifically modern conditions. Defoe tells us that in the past people were divided into Master and Servant, or Lord and Vassal; but now it is Landlord and Tenant—and even in war the long purse is now more effective than the long sword. The merchant caste has triumphed over the military.

England only came to life under those commercial princes, the Tudors. Henry VII set us to manufacture our own wool. Then Elizabeth, "that glorious princess," encouraged her navigators to range the seas "searching the Globe for discoveries, planting Colonies, and settling Factories in all Parts of the World" (p. 99). She "opened all these Doors, she sent out all these adventurers, she planted all those Colonies" (p. 101). Hence developed that English sturdiness, which Defoe describes in terms quite like Shakespeare's in *Henry V.* But the stress on English cloth is Defoe's special contribution, and he makes rich metaphorical use of it.

French cloths look good and deceive the inexperienced buyer, but they lack substance, compared with ours. "But when they came to wear, the consumer presently found the advantage; as the English cloth weighed 20–30–40 lb. a bale more than the French at the scale; so, in the wearing, there was no comparison; the French were like drugget, rough and woolly; the English like velvet, smooth and solid; the French wore nappy and coarse; the English wore soft and fine; the French wore into rags, and wore out; the English wore firm and lasting, even to the thread; . . ." (*Compleat English Tradesman,* Vol. II, p. 100). Other nations also characterize themselves by their textiles, including the world beyond the modern system. Silks and muslins, for instance, are characteristic of India; exquisite but fragile, luxurious and a touch immoral, as befits an eastern empire. While native tribes show how primitive they are by not weaving at all, but wearing bark or palm-leaf garments.

Thus English broadcloth *is* English character; and the French cloths are an example of the "superficial performances of that nation . . . the real intrinsic Worth of the Goods is found in the English cloths, and in them only. The Czar, the Grand Seignor, the Sophy, and the Mogul, all wear English cloth . . . not too thin for the frozen Laplander, nor too thick for the scorch'd Americans, not too gay for the Men, not too grave for the Ladies."[*]

This master metaphor, of cloths, weaving, and moral substance, runs all through Defoe. Peter Earle quotes a passage, written in 1713, in which he says the French have "very bright and quick fancy in contriving fashions, figures, and fancies." (Earle, *The World of Defoe,* p. 91.) They are said to be, "whip't cream, froth and surface." Their lack of real prosperity is seen in the wooden shoes they wear. (The English wear leather shoes, and leather is morally like cloth, flexible but durable, expensive but sober.) And the Spanish are proud, the Italians licentious, the Portuguese cringing—all sins against the modern system ethic.

The philosophy of history this leads to is unstable in its evaluation of national "greatness"—of empire. Defoe often compared England with Rome, but his approval of a similarity between them varied. In the *Tour* he hoped that the roads of England might be restored to the perfection they had when the Romans ruled this island. But he also saw a likeness between Rome and France, and that was something he disapproved.

---

[*]It is perhaps of interest that in an English pamphlet of 1650, it was said that Dutch cloths will not fail color or be threadbare in seven years' wearing, while the English dressed and dyed their cloth basely (W. J. Webb, p. 134). By Defoe's time, the English were more sure of themselves.

# Notes

In contemporary Europe, France and Versailles were Defoe's measure of magnificence, and he quite often invoked it to praise England. But he always condemned the source of that sort of magnificence; Louis XIV was "the august tyrant," and Defoe's hero was Marlborough, our man against Louis. He came to see Rome and France as both military countries—hence empires—and then he saw England as blessedly unlike both.

In *History of the Principal Discoveries, etc.* (1727) Defoe devotes a lot of attention to Rome's enemy, Carthage, and to the Carthaginians' subtlety of wit, and their address in commerce, business, and colonization, which was like the English. Chapter VII is entitled, "Of the encrease of commerce and navigation under the Carthaginian empire, and the check given to useful discoveries, by the success of the Romans against them. Also some probable account, of the first peopling of America by the Carthaginians." They are described as "a people wholly addicted to a search after new discoveries, and boldly venturing into all parts of the world for them" (p. 76). The Romans, on the other hand, were a nation inspired with glory of arms, and puffed up with innumerable triumphs over others, but not at all addicted to the glories of peace, the improvements of the industrious, etc. (p. 124). One begins to sense there his connection of Rome with France, and on the preceding page he had said that the "industrious trading part of the nation has always been beggared and impoverished by the violence and fury of arms. . . ." and "the soldier has always been the plunderer of the industrious merchant. . . ." England had soldiers, and was proud of them; but it was not—and France was—a soldier's country. England (like Carthage) was a merchant's country. (Frenchmen agreed; Bishop Huet a few years later described England and Holland as mercantile countries, and urged France to imitate them therefore.) Thus Defoe was able to define his country and the modern system almost explicitly in the language of caste.

Defoe's journalism was a good deal concerned with French militarism. His *Review* was originally entitled a *Review of the Affairs of France.* On May 31, 1705, for instance, we find him attributing to the French the design of universal monarchy, of empire, and on April 19, 1709, he identified France with Glory, and Louis with arbitrary power. Louis's prodigious designs threatened the whole world.

When Louis was rumored dead, in 1712, Defoe wrote a panegyric on him as God's Scourge upon the world, which is an interesting example of the sort of language used in tribute to heroes one disapproves of; imaginative tribute, moral disapproval. In his *Review*, viii, page 586, "a head capable of the deepest councils; a temper fiery, haughty, magnificent, and to his own subjects dreadful; qualified to reduce the nobility to an abject submission, and the commons to the most profound slavery . . ." That is the language of Milton about Satan, Prescott about Cortes, or Scott about Napoleon. (Quoted by Earle, p. 74.) In *Review*, 111, Defoe wrote "May Lewis XIV be a Memento Mori to men of pride, and show them the emptiness of human glory. Where now are the equestrian statues, the title of august and invincible? Why should one man think to mate the world? Men may say, 'Tis no equal match. But why then has he set himself up a match for the whole world? That pride is punished here—and God has smote him—let us wait, and He will bring him down; for all His works are perfect, and this blow cannot end here." Defoe was one of the first men to use the term and the concept, "balance of power."* His is the voice of the modern world system in

---

*This, and Defoe's fondness for mechanical analogies for politics (see the machine fable about the Constitution in *The Consolidator*) remind one of Hobbes. Hobbes is often said to have invented the phrase "the balance of power," and the subtitle of *Leviathan* is "The Matter, Form and Power of a Commonwealth." The dynamics of government, the balance of trade, and the circulation of wealth, were ideas the two international politics, and we can find the same attitude in Scott against Napoleon, and in Buchan against the Kaiser.

Whereas in contrast with France he set Holland above all. In the *Review* for Jan. third, 1706, we read "In nations and empires 'tis the same; what infinite crowds of people flock to Holland; cities without number, and towns thick like the houses in other countries, that the whole country seems to be one populous city; people in such multitude that all the land in the country can't find butter and cheese for them, much less maintain them. All this attend upon trade; by trade they possess the world." But trade means objects of real use and value, not luxuries. In 1713 Defoe complained that English trade is much declined from thirty years before, because in place of the cloth manufacturers we used to see in London, we have coffee, tea, drugs, china, and gilded-leather shops, which he considers the same as no-shops.

In *The Compleat English Tradesman* he rejoiced in the fact that 30,000 people are always at work underground in Newcastle to supply London with coal. At the same time, "It is very hard, and a melancholy reflection, to think that wickedness should have got such a root in this nation, and should be so effectually fixed, that it cannot be removed, but at the expense of some part of our trade. . . . It is next to incredible, what a share the luxury of the age has, in the employment of families . . . the greatest empires have always fallen from luxury" (Vol. II, p. 225).

In *The Poor Man's Plea* of 1698 he had talked in more Puritan style, of how luxury got its footing in England under James I; while Charles I established Wickedness by a Law. (He means the Book of Sports, which declared recreation lawful on Sundays after church.) Under Charles II lewdness and debauchery had arrived at a meridian. Now William and Mary were fighting it, by means of the Society for the Reformation of Manners, etc. In Defoe's late work also his tone was less heartily complacent and worldly. In *Augusta Triumphans* (subtitle, "The Way to Make London the Most Flourishing City in the Universe") we read on page 3, "We have been a brave and learned people, and are insensibly dwindling into an effeminate superficial race." He demanded strengthening the watch, and clearing the streets of strumpets, forbidding gaming tables and Sabbath debauches.

But more important for our purposes are the midlife attitudes he expresses in, for instance, the *Essay Upon Projects*, of 1697. He says there that the projecting humor began in 1680, as the monster it now is (though in origin it goes back to Noah's Ark). But it was then (that is, in his own youth) that the joint stock companies for founding colonies began, and they begat stockjobbing; which he describes as a "trade managed with the greatest intrigue, artifice, and trick, ever." These attitudes could be described as ambivalent, but it seems clear that the gleeful component is dominant. At this essay's date he still considers the Romans "the pattern of the whole world for improvement and increase of arts and learning, civilizing and methodizing nations and countries conquered by their valour" (p. 72).

Thus Defoe's nonfiction names the modern world system with great analytical acuteness, though considerable moral ambivalence, and gives a framework to his novels which relates them to the history we are discussing.

5. Vol. I (published 1598) was dedicated to Lord Charles Howard, the admiral. Vols. II and III (published 1599 and 1600) were dedicated to William Cecil, Lord Burleigh, Elizabeth's great statesman. Hakluyt also had dealings with Walsingham, and generally stands midway between the sailors themselves and the bureaucrats. In

---

men both regarded as of central importance. Hannah Arendt called Hobbes the greatest philosopher of bourgeois politics; of its basis in property, its antitraditionalism, and its process of expanding wealth.

1589 he was one of the nineteen to whom Raleigh assigned rights in the Virginia Colony. In 1597 he was one of those Cecil consulted about the idea of colonizing Guinea—Raleigh's El Dorado. And he helped to organize the East India Company, which in turn put a copy of his *Voyages* into every one of their ships as ships' stores.

6. It is worth noting that Defoe's attitude to "savages" or "natives" (and the attitude of most adventure writers) swings between this one and the opposite, according to which they are devils, bloodthirsty, obscene, and depraved. What is most striking is not either attitude in itself, but the loose swinging between them. In *Captain Singleton*, as the English pass from one village in Madagascar to another, they pass from a community of angels to one of devils. It is obvious that the natives are seen primarily as "the other," as projections of either the Englishmen's fears or their hopes. But it is worth stressing, in Defoe's case, the willingness to see them in ideal terms. In *Madagascar, or Robert Drury's Journal* (1729) he says "Wherever people have not been corrupted by Europeans, they are innocent, humane, and moral. Men in the state of nature, and considering God as the author of the universe, form no other notions of him, but what are consistent with justice, wisdom, and goodness . . ." (p. 34). Hobbists see men everywhere fighting each other. But there are women and children as well as men; fondness for them is the true state of nature. "From hence arise benign dispositions, softness of temper, and friendships . . ." *Madagascar* is a book whose authorship has not been clearly attributed, but Arthur W. Secord, the Defoe scholar, thinks that the natural philosophy passages are likely to be by Defoe.

7. If the Spaniards cared, this convenient captive tells us on page 403, they would have miners and engineers there, who would find enough gold to enrich the world. "So this land, so fruitful, pleasant, and agreeable, any nation in Europe is free to settle in, for anything we can do to prevent them. We have only the Pope's grant of it. We don't cultivate it."

8. One of the sharpest commentaries on that aspect of the book is to be found in Lewis Mumford's *Technics and Civilization*. His section on "Social Regimentation" has a paragraph on page 42; "The ideal man of the new order was Robinson Crusoe. No wonder he indoctrinated children with his virtues for two centuries . . . [the story] . . . combining in a single setting the element of catastrophe and adventure with the necessity for invention . . . [In the new order Crusoe introduced] . . . Invention took the place of image-making and ritual; experiment took the place of contemplation; demonstration took the place of deductive logic and authority." Despite the geniality of his tone, of course, Mumford is indicting this new order. His book came out in 1934, and is one of those diagnoses of the modern system that were to become increasingly frequent; writers like Mumford too had to turn back to Crusoe, as much as the celebrants of that system.

9. What is at work there is a passion to explain, which is the dominant passion in the book, and controls whatever else Defoe does and intends, and how we react. Insofar as Defoe fails as a novelist, here and elsewhere, fails to interest us in his characters' emotions, and in his characters, it is because of this. It is a possessive and reductive passion, which reduces everything else to backdrop and stage scenery.

10. That may seem rather sweeping, but this does seem to me a case where the ingenuity of scholars has led them astray. The truth about *Crusoe* is so clear, but still so exciting, because so important, that it is merely perverse to turn away toward something less certain. That truth has been discovered time and time again, by all sorts of people. For instance, in 1912, James Joyce, in his lecture, "Daniel Defoe," given in Italian in Trieste, said he had read every line of Defoe, and the only other authors of whom that was true were Flaubert, Ibsen, and Ben Jonson. He called Defoe the first author with English characters and stories. "His women have the indecency of

beasts; his men are strong and silent as trees. English feminism and English imperialism already lurk in these souls which are just emerging from the animal kingdom. The African pro-consul Cecil Rhodes descends in a direct line from Captain Singleton . . ." and *Robinson Crusoe* reveals more than any other book, "The way and heroic instinct of the rational animal, and the prophecy of empire . . . The true symbol of the British conquest is in Robinson Crusoe . . . as Friday is the symbol of the subject races. The whole Anglo-Saxon spirit is in Crusoe; the manly independence; the unconscious cruelty; the persistence; the slow yet efficient intelligence; the sexual apathy; the practical, well-balanced, religiousness; the calculating taciturnity."

At the other extreme of literary sophistication we have Henry B. Jackson's *Robinson Crusoe—Social Engineer* which tells how his discovery of the novel solved, for the author, the whole problem of labor, and opened the path to industrial peace. Jackson says, "Robinson Crusoe is typically Anglo-Saxon in his patient acceptance of fate, and his effort to make the best of it. Crusoe's gospel is the same as that of Kipling. It is the gospel of work and the gospel of courage." Jackson finds in the book, as a blueprint for the future, exactly what Joyce found in it, as an explanation of the past. And he quotes the Victorian, Frederick Harrison; "*Robinson Crusoe* contains, not for boys, but for men, more religion, more philosophy, more political economy, more anthropology, than are found in many elaborate treatises on these special subjects." And that indeed is true understanding the economics, etc., to be of the modern system kind.

Indeed, Lukacs makes the same point very well, from the Marxist point of view, in *Studies in European Realism,* with the help of the following quotation from Hegel about the epic form and ancient culture. "What man requires for his external life, house and home, tent, chair, bed, sword and spear, the ship with which he crosses the ocean, the chariot which carries him into battle, boiling and roasting, slaughtering, eating and drinking—nothing of all this must have become merely a dead means to an end for him; he must feel alive in all these with his whole sense and self, in order that what is in itself merely external be given a humanly inspired individual character by such close connection to the human individual. Our present machinery and factories, together with the products they turn out and in general our means of satisfying our external needs, would in this respect—exactly like the modern state organization —be out of tune with the background of life which the original epic requires" (p. 155). Lukacs goes on to say that this is indeed the problem facing the modern bourgeois novel, and to allow that Defoe solved it. But he insists that Defoe's was "exceptional good fortune" and "an isolated, unrepeatable instance." In fact, of course, it has been repeated innumerable times—at least, that is the argument of this book. But Lukacs was looking for a continuance within his favorite authors, like Scott, Balzac, and Tolstoy, where it is naturally far to seek. (Except in Scott, if you read him in the rather special way I suggest.)

11. He says in this essay that he had intended to write an encomium on money, "as the sum and substance of all human arts, common industry, and the end of life as to this world," but decided it was not necessary. Everyone civilized—even the Americans—realize that gold and silver are the valuable species.

12. The gold and silver lace-man alone provided work for many lesser tradesmen; for instance, wire-drawers, button-makers, thread-spinners, embroiderers, makers of spangles, bugles, fringes, frogs, and tassels; each of which had his own workshop. (This subject is elaborated in R. Campbell's *The London Tradesman,* 1747, pp. 147–154, according to Peter Earle.)

13. In *The Farther Adventures of Robinson Crusoe,* we find a passage that recalls that one, on p. 91. ". . . the echo's rattling from one side another, and the fowls rising from all parts, screaming and making every sort, and several sort of, noise, according

*Notes*

to their kind, just as it was when I fired the first gun that perhaps was ever shot off in that place since it was an island."

I think this makes it clear that Defoe knew and intended the symbolic effect of the original passage; at the same time that effect is artistically naive, compared with similar passages in "literature." Just because it is less under his control, however, it transmits the natural symbolism of the subject more immediately. I want to suggest that that happens quite often in the adventure tales, and that is the sort of aesthetic pleasure they can give, and the sort of aesthetic theory that suits them.

14. Peter Earle points out that Defoe's heroes explore all the land masses left unoccupied by the core states, with the exception of North America—that was left for Cooper. When they venture into the other civilizations of the arena, as Robinson Crusoe does in *Farther Adventures*, his attitude, for instance to China, is fundamentally philistine. It is, incidentally, of symbolic interest to us that Singleton's journey across Africa is more or less the route Stanley was to take in the mid-nineteenth century. Defoe's fantasy was acted out by Stanley over a century later—an example of the history of the modern system.

15. Essentially the same view, with the same distribution of sympathies, was held by the antagonists, the groups opposed to the modern system. Thus Isaiah Berlin describes Russians' sense of Westerners as people "enviably self-restrained, clever, calculating, and fenced in, without capacity for large views or generous emotions." (*Russian Thinkers*, New York, 1978, p. 181.) This is how Crusoe and Singleton and all the white captains emerge, even from Defoe's pen; and the projected counterpart is a Black Prince, passionate, disorderly, and generous.

16. If then Swift established himself at the center of literature-as-a-system, surely this contradicts my earlier theory that literature as a whole allied itself to the merchant caste? There is indeed a contradiction here, but it is in the historical facts themselves. Swift personally was a living paradox and his whole group was "reactionary," and such men and such groups, living contradictions of their society, are often central to literature. Serious literature lives as a (conscious or not) contradiction to the dominant strains in the larger culture, and to the compulsions those strains impose upon writers. So in Defoe's time literature as a whole was allied to the dominant caste, even though its most brilliant and authoritative representatives were in opposition—and were generally praised for being so opposed.

17. W. L. Payne points out, in *Mr. Review* (New York, 1947) that between 1704 and 1713, the years of Defoe's *Review*, Pope and Swift published *The Rape of the Lock, A Tale of a Tub, The Essay on Criticism*, and *An Argument Against Abolishing Christianity*. And yet the *Review* mentioned no living authors by name. Defoe mentioned only five authors more than once, and his comments on them were standard.

18. Limits-to-growth, and steady-state-economy, have always been the implicit economics and energetics of serious literature. It has not participated in the expansive moods of the culture, and this has been manifest in matters of style as well as of statement. (One of the things meant by "journalist" or other phrases for non-serious writers is that they do so participate.) This is true of both the classical and the romantic phases of serious literature; both are forms of withdrawal, whether—as in the first case—the withdrawal is ironic, contemplative, or aesthetic, or—as in the second—it is nature-worshipping, Christianly compassionate, or erotic. These last alternatives (represented by Wordsworth, George Eliot, D. H. Lawrence) are expansive and assertive in their own way, but it is a way in opposition to the society's. (The last is the most interesting case, because fertility, and so in a sense growth, is one of its values; but still it is self-evident that Lawrence—and Tolstoy, and Hardy—imply a steady-state economics.)

364

19. The ambiguity derives from lack of specificity. If one is speaking of eighteenth-century literature, then its spirit is Swiftian; if of eighteenth-century culture as a whole, then it is Defoean. The literature reacted against the culture, as is its wont—this is its strength and its weakness. In *Kangaroo,* D. H. Lawrence's representative feels ashamed of himself, in his conflicts with a political leader because he, the man of letters, is so fretful, spiteful, reactive, against the other man's "simple and steady loveliness of spirit."

It is also necessary to be specific about nationalities. In France, eighteenth-century literature—at least the encyclopaedists—expressed less reaction against the mercantile spirit than literature in England. The encyclopaedists found their enemies in the military caste and its ecclesiastical allies. (In many ways they were better heirs to Defoe —they made more of his heritage, intellectually and literarily—than anyone in England.) That was no doubt because the mercantile caste did not dominate French culture as it did English, and so did not need reacting against.

20. Smiles takes his examples from the working class, while Defoe is concerned with the middle class; but both are primarily concerned to dissociate the gentleman-idea from the actual aristocracy. Smiles says the tone of living in England has got altogether too high. Boys are given a taste for dress, style, luxuries, and amusements. We see "gingerbread young gentlemen thrown upon the world, who remind one of the abandoned hulls sometimes picked up at sea, with only a monkey on board" (*Self-Help,* p. 290). This is the voice of the merchant caste, mocking the aristomilitary style, and those who affect it.

Defoe's message was essentially the same, though he put more stress on education in the conventional sense. The well-bred are to be envied and emulated, not the wellborn. The oldest sons of well-to-do families are often kept at home, not sent to school or university, and consequently remain big babies.

Defoe also has an eloquent passage on education which illustrates the connection he sees between that and adventure. The reading man "may travel by land with the historian, by sea with the navigators. He may go round the globe with Dampier and Rogers, and know a thousand times more in doing it than all those illiterate sailors. . . . He may measure the latitudes and distances of places by the labours and charts of those who have surveyed them, and know the strengths of towns and cities by the descriptions of those who have stormed and taken them . . . he marches with Hannibal over the Alps into Italy, and with Caesar into Gaul, and into Britain, with Belisarius into Africa, and with the Emperor Honorius into Persia . . . he discovers America with Columbus, conquers it with the great Cortes, and replunders it with Sir Francis Drake . . ." (*Compleat English Gentleman,* p. 226). This is an idea of education in full alliance with adventure; it is notable that it is military as much as mercantile.

## Chapter IV

1. Hugh McDiarmid makes the same judgment, with the opposite evaluation. "Scott's novels are the great source of the paralysing ideology of defeatism in Scotland, the spread of which is responsible at once for the acceptance of the Union and the low standard of 19th century Scots literature" (C.M. Grieve, *Lucky Poet,* p. 202).

2. He followed the course of the peninsular war eagerly, unable to sleep when things went ill for England, and was deeply shocked when Jeffrey wrote an article critical of the British action.

3. I use "operatic" to mean the most extreme form of "theatrical." In an anony-

mous review of his own work, Scott observed that he had derived his narrative methods from the theater. And in his comments on *Quentin Durward,* he says that he gave the character Charles of Burgundy the trick of half-drawing his sword because that is a stage tradition in the characterization of Richard III. In fact the characterization and the plots of all his novels move very largely by means of such stage devices. This is another sign of how different romance is from adventure, for there was an antagonism between the mercantile sensibility and theater. Of course, several of Scott's villains have connections with the theater; Scott was something of a Puritan himself. And of course Richardson, a Puritan novelist, made much use of theater traditions. But Scott was theatrical, and Richardson was not, in the sense of inviting the reader to see the grease paint and the prompter.

## Appendix to *"Waverley"*

4. There are a few more of the Waverley novels it is worth touching on, in order to amplify points so far only sketched in. For instance, the Introductory to *The Fair Maid of Perth* (1828) shows us Scott's skepticism about, and impulse to mock, the legends he loves. He tells of a Cockney visitor being shown the indelible stains left by Darnley's blood on the floor where he was murdered in Holyrood House. "Two hundred and fifty years, ma'am, and nothing take it away?" the visitor said to the housekeeper showing him around, "Why, if it had been five hundred, I have something in my pocket will fetch it out in five minutes . . ." And he produced some patented Scouring Drops from his pocket. Scott tells us that the housekeeper screamed as loudly as Mary herself on the night of the murder. The whole anecdote is pure modernism, and could come out of *The Connecticut Yankee,* though Scott then turns around and argues that the bloodstains probably *are* genuine.

In *Old Mortality* Scott depicts the Presbyterian and fanatic, as opposed to the chivalric, side of Scottish life. He was accused by some critics of being prejudiced against the Presbyterians, and certainly he makes their fanaticism particularly terrifying in the scenes of war; in Habbakuk Mucklewrath, the mad preacher, and in John Burnley of Balfour, who murders Archbishop Sharp. Their opponent, Graham of Claverhouse, is a soldier in the grand style, and Scott's very sharp sense of genre distinctions—the very different diction and psychology, etc., can be attributed to different social orders—gives Claverhouse every advantage. Clearly, in the novel, as in life, Scott was hostile to moral and religious intensity; he avoided parsons and preachers socially. When Old Mortality says about the Cameronian sect, "We are the only true Whigs. Carnal men have assumed that triumphant appellation, following him whose kingdom is of this world," Scott appreciates the picturesque effect, but his deeper reaction is one of alarm.

*The Pirate* is a novel which draws on Defoe for its basic anecdote (and Kipling tells of *his* family acting it out when he was a child). It is set on Zetland in 1724–1725, and the Scots in it have the English role; they are modernist reformers, trying to change the islanders' agricultural methods with a new coulter, spade, and harrow. The islanders themselves belong to a remoter past; they plunder wrecks and give no help to drowning sailors; there is much chanting of Norse runes, and talk of Berserkers, sea-kings, sorcerers, giants, and dwarves. When Clement Cleveland, a pirate, is wrecked there, Minna Troil, a romantic Zetlander, thinks him a sea-king, because he has fought the English. "One of an oppressed race, my father is a Zetlander, or rather a Norwegian," she tells him, "who will not care whether you fought against the

Spanish, who are the tyrants of the New World, or against the Dutch or English, who have succeeded to their usurped domain" (p. 234). And in fact Cleveland grew up on Tortuga, his father being a buccaneer, and he wears flamboyant piratical clothes. But he himself has to warn Minna: "Think not of such visions. Denmark has been cut down into a second rate kingdom, incapable of exchanging a single broadside with England; Norway is a starving wilderness" (p. 235). It is the same lesson of realism, but the historical scope is different, and closer to Defoe's.

*Redgauntlet* is a novel very close to *Waverley* in pattern, being about a Jacobite revolt. In the Introduction, Scott says that the Jacobite enthusiasm of the eighteenth century is the finest theme imaginable for fiction. The Highlanders were an ancient and high-spirited race, "their character turning upon points more adapted to poetry than to the prose of real life." Their rebellion naturally melts away at the end, when General Campbell brings a pardon from the Hanoverian king to the last group of would-be rebels. Only the fierce Redgauntlet goes into exile with the prince, and he tells his nephew (our representative) that the fatal doom will pass from their house now, because he, the nephew, has chosen the winning side. The family had been "unlucky," everything had gone wrong for it, because it was Jacobite. Now its young heir has sincerely and spontaneously chosen the Hanoverian cause, everything will go right. The moral for Scotland is clear. In the Introduction, Scott says it was Walpole who defeated the rebels—Walpole the representative of Hanoverian commercial realism at its most antiheroic. But Scott is on the Hanoverian side. He says that the great martyr of the Jacobite movement, Dr. Cameron, was in truth a dangerous conspirator.

A basic narrative device in *Redgauntlet* is the division of the narrative center between two young men, Alan Fairford, and Darsie Latimer, who represent Sense and Sensibility. To monitor the events through exchanges between these points of view is of course an eighteenth-century serious-fiction device, perfected by Jane Austen. (The exchanges in *Redgauntlet* are epistolary, another of those devices, but a less relevant one here.) Scott learned a lot from that tradition, and, one guesses, from Jane Austen in particular. Sense, after all, was the moral voice of the modern system; sensibility could be the voice of its alternatives—and would then be dangerous. Colonel Talbot, as a character, and as a function in the plot of *Waverley*, is Austen-like and one of the best done things in that novel.

But Scott also made a considerable contribution to nineteenth-century serious fiction, in *The Heart of Midlothian*. Effie and Jeanie Deans, the contrast between them, and particularly the characterization of Jeanie, are very important models for subsequent novelists. Effie, who takes the wrong turning, and thereafter must hide a broken heart behind a gay facade, is the model for *Bleak House*'s Lady Dedlock, and many other such, while Jeanie must be one of the models for Esther Summerson, the heroine of the same Dickens novel. The characterization of Jeanie translates the Puritanism of her forebears into the kind of virtue suitable to the Victorian novel— as the figure of Clarissa did for the eighteenth-century novel. The theology, the piety, the religious practices dissolve into this decent, quiet, tidy, little figure, strong in feeling but antipassionate, antihedonist, antierotic. Her influence is visible in George Eliot heroines like Mary Garth in *Middlemarch*. And perhaps she may be said to stand halfway between Fanny Price and Jane Eyre; Jeanie introduces the feature of sturdiness so important to the better Victorian heroines. In a similar way, Effie's seducer, Staunton, stands halfway between Lovelace and Rochester. Like Lovelace, he had been overindulged as a boy (his mother was a Creole) and he is associated, like several of Scott's villains, with the stage. In this novel, as in Defoe's *Religious Courtship*, we get a glimpse of the road not taken, the road of serious fiction. Though in fact both Defoe and Scott did contribute significantly to the development of the domestic novel.

But we must concentrate on the adventure novel, and its association with the themes of empire and frontier.

*Quentin Durward* treats the material of chivalry in unusually analytic fashion. The Introduction says that in the fifteenth century egotism "was now for the first time openly avowed as a professed principle of action." The feudal system, and the spirit of chivalry "by which, as if by a vivifying soul, that system was animated," began to be abandoned, and the modern system began. Louis XI, who represents the new spirit in the novel, is described thus: "Base enough for any and every useful and political purpose, Louis had not a spark of that romantic ardour, or of the pride generally associated with it, which fought on for the point of honour, when the point of utility had been long gained." That sentence is of course perfectly ambivalent.

And though Louis is compared with Goethe's Mephistopheles, we are also told that he stood, in his antichivalric fashion, for peace, strength, and national unity. In the opening scene, Louis appears incognito, in mechanic-bourgeois dress, and Quentin, the young hero, tells him that were he king, he would throw down the defensive walls and *live*, with breaking of lances and gallant tournaments and feasting with nobles, and dancing with ladies (p. 22). But the progress of the plot, and especially the contrast between Louis and his opponent, Charles the Bold, of Burgundy, makes it clear that the true wisdom is Louis's. (In *The Fortunes of Nigel*, a character like Louis, James I, is drawn with similar care and affection, which rings a good truer than Scott's tributes to flamboyant romance heroines like Elizabeth or Mary Queen of Scots.) The modern system is justified.

*A Legend of Montrose* has some very striking symbolic contrasts of the old with the new. There is much talk of the purse-proud English, and their new luxury. The silver candlesticks of their domestic dining tables are contrasted with the Scots equivalent, which is a gigantic Highlander standing behind the chair of each guest, holding a drawn sword in his right hand and a flaming torch of bog pine in his left. The claims of the old ways against the new never found a more splendid symbol. The hero, Monteith, has a dash of "the old heroic times' generous romantic chivalry," unlike "the sordid, calculating and selfish modern character" (p. 319). But he retires at the end to a life of privacy, like Waverley, happy in public regard and domestic affection. He accepts the new world. The old world is represented by gigantic Allan M'Aulay, gifted with second sight, cursed with a hatred of the English; he is the son of a woman who was scared out of her wits when her brother's head was set on the table by his murderers; and he is driven by bursts of murderous madness. The contrast clearly teaches the reader to adapt to the modern world.

And finally, *Rob Roy* (1817). The Introduction to the novel says, on page 3, "Rob Roy owed his fame in a great measure to his residing on the very verge of the Highlands and playing such pranks in the 18th century as are usually ascribed to Robin Hood in the Middle Ages. . . . Thus a character like his, blending the wild virtues, the subtle policy, and unrestrained license of an American Indian, was flourishing in Scotland during the days of the Augustan Age, of Queen Anne and George I. Addison, it is probable, or Pope, would have been considerably surprised if they had known that there existed in the same island with them a personage of Rob Roy's peculiar habits and profession." (Defoe, having the same interests as Scott, did know about Rob Roy, in fact wrote about him.) He hated the Union with England. "His ideas were those of an Arab Chief, being such as naturally arose out of his wild education" (p. 18). And Scott also mentions that marriage operations like the rape of the Sabines were then common in the Highlands and in Ireland.

What is notable there is how Scott defines his characters' interest by making comparisons between them and primitive life. The same is true in other novels; a character in *The Pirate* is compared with an Obi woman, and Highlanders in *Waverley* are compared with American Indians. They are conceived with reference to a world-historical contrast between the modern life-mode and its various alternatives. But the imaginative act does not get past a gesture or a hint at that larger meaning.

*Rob Roy*'s hero, Frank Osbaldistone, is another Waverley. His father is a London businessman and a Presbyterian—who disapproves of poetry and theater and Oxford, and everything else feudal or chivalric or romantic. He is, we may say, of Defoe's party. But he is an adventurer, in his modern system way. "Impetuous in his schemes, as well as skillful and daring, each new adventure, when successful, became at once the incentive, and furnished the means, for farther speculation. It seemed to be necessary to him, as to an ambitious conqueror, to push on from achievement to achievement, without stopping to secure, far less to enjoy, the acquisitions which he made" (p. 59). Frank is, in the matter of sensibility, a rebel; interested in literature, he has translated *Orlando Furioso*. So he is ready to be attracted to the romantic alternative represented by his Roman Catholic and Jacobite cousins; one of whom describes Frank's father scornfully as "loving and honouring the King as a sort of Lord Mayor to the empire, or chief of the board of trade." But Mr. Osbaldistone, and Nicol Jarvie, his associate in Glasgow, are on the winning side in the novel; and as usual with Scott, the two senses of winning go together; Frank is brought to see that they are in the right, emotionally, too. Chivalric and feudal values are reconciled with more modern ones, but by means of being subordinated to them.

On page 57, Jarvie says, "But I maun hear naething about honour—we ken naething here but about credit. Honour is a homicide and a blood-spiller, that gangs about making forays in the street; but Credit is a decent honest man, that sits at home and makes the pat play." The way Scott involves Jarvie in adventure despite this philosophy; and the way he makes us like him; were direct models for John Buchan in *Huntingtower*. They were also, more indirectly, modeled on Defoe; in the rough sense that both are comic celebrations of mercantile adventurers—though Scott (and Buchan even more) gives us an aristomilitary perspective on the merchant, which Defoe doesn't. But elements of William, and Moll Flanders, and others, may have entered into the conception of Jarvie. He and Jeanie Deans, in *Midlothian*, are perhaps realizations of the fictional idea that is potential in William—the figure of religious seriousness so designed that the novel-reader can feel sentimentally and humorously fond of it.

5. In "Such, Such Were the Joys," George Orwell says that his prep school, and the slice of English upper-class culture it served, made a cult of things Scottish; ostensibly in the name of the Scots' "plain living and high thinking"; really because holidays in Scotland were the prerogative of wealth. This was the final fate of Scott's imaginative legacy—the mythos and ethos he created for the English ruling class. Not that that mythos in its early period was *radically* different in character, but it was less banal. Other writers of Orwell's generation satirize that Scots piety of the English upper class—Nancy Mitford, Cyril Connolly, and Evelyn Waugh.

6. Scott was born in 1771, and lived through a period in which Scotland enjoyed the sort of industrial development which Defoe had promised her at the time of the Union. Her production of linen doubled during Scott's first thirty years. Cotton boomed, so that Glasgow outgrew Edinburgh. In 1799, when he was twenty-eight, the Carson iron works was founded, which produced the light cannon England used in the Napoleonic wars. Scott welcomed the new prosperity—no man more—but he feared the new class of industrial proletariat, because he wanted to preserve old values (aristocratic but also peasant values, which he wanted the dominant merchant caste to adopt or accept) and he saw revolution as the worst of dangers. At the end of his

life in 1831, at the polls at Jedburgh, he was reviled by the party that was demanding reforms.

A precocious child, with a phenomenal memory, and a great entertainer, he did not get on with his older siblings, but was fond of his younger brothers, Tom and Daniel; both of whom failed in life rather dramatically. The latter, who went out to the West Indies, showed fear in a moment of stress, and was disgraced. Scott refused to wear mourning when he died a couple of years later. Tom merely went bankrupt, much less of a crime by the gentleman's code, and Scott was not so bitter about it—though of course he lived by the merchant's code too. He felt, late in life, that his touch had been blighting—that no one close to him could flourish.

Scott entered adult life as a lawyer, and David Daiches tells us that the legal profession in Scotland then was the guardian of Scots antiquities. Like other men of his class and profession, Scott saw the Scots law and the Scots church as the last bastions of his country's cultural independence left standing by the Union. It was, Daiches implies, the feeling of the whole legal profession then, that the memory of the old life, the heroic life, should be preserved in documentary and literary trophy-form, since it could not be continued in political form. Certainly Abbotsford, the mock-feudal house on which Scott lavished so much money, was a museum of antiquities and relics; and he tried to establish with his servants there a patriarchal relationship.

He was always a man who played a part. He had an intended personality, even in the most private relationships, which was genial, blunt, hedonistic, lazy. In his *Journal*, in 1829, he commends Lawrence's portrait of him, because it "conveys the idea of the stout blunt carle that cares for few things and fears nothing." But Scott was in fact a slave to his work; and much of his behavior bears the stamp of an anxious and obstinate, sly and secretive man; notably his relations with the Ballantyne brothers, whom he involved in his own ruin, not very honorably. There was a fund of cynicism and pessimism at the bottom of his nature.

He says in his *Journal* (p. 121) that until he was eighteen he felt a passion for solitude and fancy; and having stuffed his head with nonsensical trash, he was undervalued for a time in society. "As I grew from boyhood to manhood I saw this would not do and that to gain a place in men's esteem I must mix and bustle with them. Pride and an excitation of spirits supplied the real pleasure which others seemed to feel in society. . . ." (p. 50). He still really prefers solitude, he says, but accepts worldly values. He admires, for instance, the young, strong, and handsome. "I have perhaps all my life set an undue value on these gifts. Yet it does appear to me that high and independent feelings are largely though not uniformly or inseparably connected with bodily advantages. Strong men are usually good-humoured. . . ." (p. 21).

His literary work, and his literary taste, surely show a clear parallel to this psychological effort, which must of course carry with it a certain insincerity. He said he liked Goldsmith because he "contrives so well to reconcile us to human nature." Earlier in 1829 his Journal contains an entry "In fact, I have very little respect for that dear Publicum whom I am doomed to amuse . . ."; he knows "no publick worth caring for or capable of distinguishing the nice beauties of composition." And in 1831 he declares he is sure mere fear keeps most people from suicide.

Like Byron, Scott denied the sincerity of his own work; Lockhart says he considered literary achievement *far* below practical achievement. To hold this was in effect to deny his own best self, and it is therefore no surprise to find him imitating the world and the aristocracy. He was snobbish about dukes and kings, and the state visit George IV paid to Scotland in 1822 was his great triumph. Of course, this had some advantages for his work. Like Defoe and Twain, Scott refused to withdraw from the world morally, as most writers withdraw. He imitated and participated in his culture's fever of appetite; for instance, the fever of financial credit; in 1825 he failed financially for between £70,000 and £80,000, and though he devoted his remaining years to redoubled writing in order to earn money, he still owed £22,000 when he died in 1832. And if this story begins to remind us of Twain, we can remember also that both men played the king with their families and friends, held court, reigned.

7. Brooks Adams wrote, in *The Law of Civilization and Decay;* "Very soon after Plassey, the Bengal plunder began to arrive in London, and the effect appears to have been instantaneous, for all authorities agree that the 'industrial revolution,' the event which has divided the 19th century from all antecedent time, began with the year 1760 . . ." (Quoted on page 17 of Reginald Reynolds, *White Sahibs in India*). The money also had political effects. In 1767 Lord Chesterfield tried to buy his son a seat in Parliament for £2,500, but found they had all been secured by East or West Indians, for £3,000 or £4,000. Clive's income was estimated to be £40,000 a year by Sir John Malcolm, who wanted, as Macaulay said, to make it out as low as possible (Reynolds, p. 64). Burke said, "Animated with all the avarice of age, and all the impetuosity of youth, they roll in one after another, wave after wave, and there is nothing before the eyes of the native but an endless, hopeless prospect of new flights of birds of prey and passage, with appetites continually renewing for a food that is continually wasting" (Reynolds, p. 10).

8. The alliance of Evangelicals and Utilitarians in Indian policy was typical of much that was happening in 19th century England, which bore on imperialism. Grant and Wilberforce won Parliament over to an Evangelical policy—that England should take responsibility for the morality and religion of India. Wilberforce told Parliament in 1813 that the Hindu divinities were monsters of lust, injustice, wickedness, and cruelty. The Evangelicals had always fought against Enlightenment tolerance and rationalism, and had blamed the French Revolution on the spread of those doctrines. See, for instance, Hannah More, John Thornton, and John Newton.

James Mill, the Utilitarian, also attacked Voltaire's "silly, sentimental infatuation with Eastern despotism." It was in 1819 that Mill's *History of British India* reached Calcutta, and in the same year that he was hired by India House; so we can count his influence as strong from then on. When Lord Bentinck went out to be Governor General, in 1828, he said to Mill, "It is you that will be Governor General."

As a result of these twin pressures, English policy in India altered very considerably. Charles Trevelyan wrote a pamphlet in 1834, justifying the abolition of Fort William, where Oriental Studies had been pursued and employees of the Company been trained, in the spirit of Enlightenment tolerance. It was to Haileybury College in England—a creation of Charles Grant—that trainees were to be sent henceforth, for a more English and Christian preparation. And in 1835 Macaulay wrote his Minute, recommending that education in India be given in the English language, and with reference to English literature. (In religious matters, Alexander Duff was Macaulay's counterpart; he tried to convert the Bengal intellectuals to Evangelical Christianity.)

This concern for education brought together the Dissenters, the Evangelicals, and the Utilitarians—in Indian policy and in other matters. This alliance was in effect the conscience of England throughout the nineteenth century, and it is important to note in how many ways it was a revival of the combination of Puritan and rational interests for which Defoe spoke at the end of the seventeenth century. Grant's concern for continuous self-examination, private religious exercises, and good works, and his sense of life's precariousness, all were clearly Puritan. And this interest, while itself moral, was clearly allied to the merchant and not to the military caste. Thus the dialectic discussed before, as operating at the beginning of the eighteenth century, and affecting

# *Notes*

the history of the novel, was renewed at the beginning of the nineteenth. This was one of the pressures forcing the adventure novel, in both the Defoe and the Scott periods, out toward the periphery of literature—since both the old and the new Puritanisms were antiadventurous.

9. This movement continued. In 1790 two-thirds of America's population of 3.9 million lived within fifty miles of the Atlantic; in the next fifty years 4.5 million crossed the Appalachians; one of history's great migrations, as Michael Paul Rogin says in *Fathers and Children*. In the chapter on Tolstoy and Russia, I shall have occasion to discuss the corresponding migration—eastward—there. It seems likely that the nations that engage in such migrations of conquest and expansion (as opposed to the migrations of misery and slavery such as those caused by Hitler and Stalin) want to hear adventure narratives. All migrations on that scale, whatever their emotional character, are bound to be epic events.

10. Avrom Fleishman says the historical novel began with Scott because "the tension between tradition and modernity first achieved definitive terms in Scotland" (*The English Historical Novel*, p. 38). He is talking about the Scottish school of speculative history, to which Scott belonged. Fleishman reads the Waverley novels as one long sustained history of social institutions.

11. A related development was taking place in the science of man. In the 1840s ethnological societies were founded in most of the capitals of Western Europe and in New York City. They hoped to advise statesmen and administrators, because the modern world system was establishing its power over native populations all over the world, and political, social, and moral problems were arising. In the 1860s, there followed a generation of anthropological societies. At the same time, theories of imperialism and racism were being developed. In France such theories were formulated by Michelet, Thierry, Renan, de Gobineau. Michelet said the French were a free people because of their Gaelic nature, but by the same token needed severe preceptors. De Gobineau was an aristocrat by faith, and feared the degenerative effects of miscegenation. His *Essay on the Inequality of Human Races* (1853) set up divisions between the yellow, the white, and the black. Renan's *Poésie des Races Celtiques* (1854)—its ideas taken up by Matthew Arnold in 1866—allowed the Celts no aptitude for politics. They are all sensibility, individuality, and dream; they are romantic and feminine, worshipers of women and love. English commentators on the Irish, like Kingsley, were more brutal. Charles Dilke, in *Greater Britain*, one of the founding documents of British imperialism, declared that there was a struggle and antipathy between the Anglo-Saxon and the Celt; and he believed "The gradual extinction of inferior races is not only a law of nature but a blessing to mankind" (Vol. I, p. 209). He saw the English as a race of officers, captains, whose destiny it was to command other races. Hannah Arendt says that race and bureaucracy were two ideas discovered in the first two decades of imperialism.

## Chapter V

1. In those serious courtship novels, of course, the threatening force, sexual and social, was embodied in aristocrats, not in Indians. That Cooper could ever have written *that* story is hard to imagine. Whenever there was a conflict between Puritans and aristocrats—and Cooper often encountered and imagined such conflicts—he felt himself on the side of the latter.

2. When told to cut down a tree, the brothers stand around it, assertively indolent

and inert. Then one steps forward and buries his axe in the trunk, pauses, and finally brings it down. Only then do the others begin to act, and strip off the branches with showy efficiency. And this sullenness extends to their family relations also. Asa, we are told, had spread a spirit of insubordination among his brothers. And this painfully reminded his father of how *he*, in his youth, had cast off his aged and failing parents.

3. This question of size is clearly symbolic and related to the advancing frontier. In *The Spy* there is a gigantic Virginian, Trooper Lawton. Later there will be gigantic Kentuckians, and then, in other authors, gigantic Texans, and then Californians. While to Englishmen, Americans in general seemed big; also Australians and Canadians. I think it fair to assume that, besides a difference in literal size, certain gestures which claimed size—which extended the literal lines of the body—were practiced by the frontier culture; and were accentuated in loci of confrontation, as for instance when frontiersmen came to the city.

The Frontier was a mythical place; take Boone's Kentucky as an example. Arthur K. Moore, in *The Frontier Mind*, says that Kentucky was the last rumored Paradise to fill large numbers with serious expectation. It was referred to as "the garden of the United States," or (by Moses Austin, in 1797) as the Promised Land, the Goodly Inheritance, the Land of Milk and Honey.

The frontiersmen of Kentucky were typically from Ulster. Of 200,000 people who arrived in the English colonies between 1717 and 1775, one-third were Ulstermen. J. R. Commons has said that these men formed the Western type, which gradually became the American type, in politics and industry. They preferred the small towns inland to the coastal settlements, and soon regressed to a more primitive life-style there. For instance, the men often gave up wearing breeches and took to the Indian breechclout. One of their culture heroes was Simon Kenton, a greater fighter and Indian-killer than Boone, who scalped Indians and stole their horses, in the same way they stole the Americans'. He was put into a novel, *Simon Kenton*, by James Weir, in 1852; but his legend was typically oral and not literary; literature was allied to gentility, and if Daniel Boone was a good deal less genteel than Natty Bummpo, then Simon Kenton was a good deal further out than Boone.

## Appendix to "Cooper's Books"

4. Two of Cooper's sea-novels illustrate how much closer he comes to Defoe when he treats of this subject matter. First of all, *The Crater* (1847) which was in fact yet another adaptation of *Robinson Crusoe*—indeed, one of the best—and translated into French as *Le Robinson Américain*. In this nineteenth-century version, Crusoe's island becomes so fertile under his management that it is rapidly colonized, and soon has 379 colonists, with 500 Kanakas to do the manual work. Mark Woolston, the central character, who represents Cooper, becomes governor halfway through the story; but prosperity brings corruption (in the form, notably, of newspapers and demagoguery at the polls) so that Woolston retires in disgust. He soon finds his judgment endorsed by the Almighty, for a convulsion of the ocean bed swallows up the island and its unworthy population. Cooper's story so accelerates and extrapolates Defoe's that it could be read as a nineteenth-century satire on eighteenth-century innocence. But the first half is clearly a romance, in the general spirit of Defoe—though without the striking similarity of tone that we find in the other books to Scott.

The second is *The Sea-Lions* (1849), which was clearly inspired by Franklin's contemporary explorations of the Arctic, and which includes a passage on how climate is affected by the inclination of the earth's axis to the plane of its orbit (pp. 347–351). The heroine couldn't understand the hero's reference to this, so Cooper himself explains it to the reader, showing a passion for science and explanation which is very much in Defoe's line. But even in this book we find him commenting on his characters in aristocratic style. "As for the self-respect, and the feelings of caste, which prevent a gentleman from practising any of those tradesman's tricks, the deacon knew nothing of them" (p. 24).

Thus even in his sea-novels, Cooper spoke with the voice of Scott rather than of Defoe. But we cannot confidently attribute the lower interest of those novels to this one author's caste loyalty, for the sea-novel in general has not been a high genre. (Melville and Conrad, it is true, mated sea material with metaphysical and spiritual profundity, but they did so by crossing genres, and so produced an infertile offspring.) Why the sea material, so closely linked as it was to modern system ideology, did not shape itself—at the high culture level—into the system's central myths, is a question full of interest. That in fact it was Defoe and not Smollett who wrote the great modernist story, and that Cooper's forest novels were more mythic than his sea-stories, deserves discussion.

Cooper's first sea-story, *The Red Rover,* used fictional devices like kidnapings, birthmarks, recognition scenes, which derive from his reading of romances. But he also knew the subliterary sea-stories and sailor legends of England in the eighteenth century, when the sea was the country's great pride, sailors the national heroes, the sailor's life something of a frontier life. Popular sentiment then identified England with the navy, and sailors with liberty of various kinds. Nevertheless, this sentiment was not well represented in fiction or at any high level of culture. It was expressed above all in popular songs, dances, entertainments, operettas, like Charles Dibdin's and Isaac Bickerstaff's—for instance, the latter's *Sailor's Return,* 1760. (Charles Dibdin wrote seventy dramatic pieces, and altogether nine hundred songs, mostly about sailors and the sea. *The Dictionary of National Biography* quotes the remark, "He brought more men into the navy in war time than all the press gangs could.")

There was a gap between all that and literature, except that in fiction there was Smollett; his novels were what nautical fiction meant to Cooper when he began. But Cooper was (together with Marryatt) a significant innovator. Smollett's *Roderick Random* (1748) does indeed carry the motifs of *Robinson Crusoe*, and of other modern world system stories, but its spirit is different. It is an adventure tale, but not modernist adventure. Smollett was basically a picaresque writer, who worked within the limits of a genre, itself clearly fixed within the system of literature. His subversive energy was all spent in satire and "realism"—the harsh, grim, and disillusioning details which are contained by the genre, in its negation of romance. That sets him much further from Defoe than Scott or Cooper were to be. Smollett offers us only a dark-shaded report on experience. *Roderick Random,* for instance, has very little sea adventure, and its sailors are mostly eccentrics; they don't represent their vocation in any ennobling way; the sea episodes take place in a man-of-war, and lack the excitements of individual enterprise; the ship is practically a government institution, to be rendered in the same terms as a prison. And the sea merely a place of dangers.

Prescott praised Cooper* for having animated the ocean with a living soul, unlike Smollett; also because Cooper's ships were small, light, graceful, feminine. He compared Cooper with Byron, who was then usually credited with having made the ocean romantic, as opposed to Smollett, but still real, as opposed to the semifantastic ocean of the romances and of *The Tempest.* Cooper and Marryatt, who between them founded nineteenth-century sea fiction, were, like Smollett, interested in the man-of-

---

*In *North American Review,* 1832.

Notes

war situation, with all its institutional aspects, its incarnation of discipline, but they did not treat it with satirical realism. They—most strikingly, Cooper—treated it in the mode of modernist romance.

In Cooper's novels, the ships are always beautiful, and the sailors are always handsome. Tom Tiller in *The Water-Witch* has "the reckless air and manly attitudes of so fine a specimen of a seaman that he attracted a knot of admirers on the sea-front —with his firm and resolute step, he resembled some fancied sea-god." This handsome sailor, who attracts admirers around him as soon as he steps ashore, reappears in Dana and Melville, and is a very clear example of how modernist adventure could serve the modern world system as propaganda. He puts into the minds of readers the idea of a personal power, a more than ordinary intensity of being, to be attained by becoming a sailor. (That is, I think, how we should understand the eroticism of such portraits, which are strikingly frequent in sea fiction, and strikingly infrequent outside that; this is not "homosexuality," but eroticization as a mode of intensification.)

The sea was the home of freedom within the modern world system, for several reasons. The new trade and the new techniques had first been developed at sea; the new enterprise was essentially oceanic; England, the leading country of the system, was an island; ships and sailors were free of the land, with all its feudal ties. And since freedom was so big a part of the modern system ideology, the ocean was a big part of the modern landscape. And Cooper's America felt it was born to outdo England, in freedom, in seamanship, in adventure, and everything else.

It was quite generally believed that America's destiny lay on the ocean—that she was to continue England's destiny there too, of course supplanting her. In 1813 an American magazine declared that "the glorious successes of our navy have kindled a new and holy spirit of nationality, and enabled the humblest citizen among us boldly to say to the world that he too has a country." And America's part in the defeat of the pirates of the Caribbean and those of the Barbary shore were popular triumphs. By the 1840s, the U. S. dominated the passenger trade between New York and Europe, and its whaling fleet amounted to three-quarters of the world's total. By 1850 the tonnage of the shipping fleet was five times what it had been in 1815. And up to this date it was possible for Americans to see the ocean as their domain in the same sense as the frontier was after that. In 1835 de Tocqueville still prophesied sea power for the U. S. He said that Americans "are born to rule the seas, as the Romans were to conquer the world." And Cooper's *Notions of the Americans* (1828) is full of maritime nationalism. He says the sea is America's manifest destiny—that she is not an agricultural nation. "The great outlet for the rest of the world, the path of adventure, and the only, at least the principal, theatre for military achievements open to the people of this country, is on the ocean" (Vol. II, p. 86).

He puts a stress on adventure. In America the laboring class reads more of adventure than it does anywhere else, and "this is an inducement that stimulates the restlessness of moral excitement . . . which tempt men to quit the land for the water" (Vol. I, p. 337). And sea adventure was naturally linked to nationalism. Cooper's novel *Homeward Bound* and his *History of the American Navy* argued for a big navy, and his novels *Mercedes of Castille* (1840) and *The Two Admirals* (1842) were outgrowths of the *History.* Forest adventure was linked to territorial expansion, and imperialism—uncomfortable thoughts for Cooper. He wanted to see America sailing, and he wanted to write about America sailing. It was events that forced him to enter the forest and deal with all the problems it contained. He tried to deal with them in a sea-captain-like way—insofar as the different myth of the forest permitted that.

One might say that Cooper tried to make linked alternates out of his forest and sea-tales, and the very different heroes he found for each. In the sea-tales, for instance

375

# *Notes*

*Miles Wallingford* and *The Crater,* he has military caste heroes and relationships; as
also in his Littlepage and Effingham society novels; all are full of young men's strong
feelings for other young men of the same caste. The heroes are courageous, commanding, adventurous, sexually ardent (though Cooper can give us only the most
conventional account of that ardor) and essentially idle. All this is not true of the
forest-tales. Natty Bumppo is precisely not a military caste hero, and this accounts for
Cooper's clumsiness in handling him. But when Natty grows old and dies, in *The
Prairie,* the caste hero, Captain Middleton, is his heir. (At least, he divides the heritage
with the clownish Paul Hover.) And the caste hero and heroine, Oliver Effingham and
Elizabeth Temple, are Natty's heirs in *The Pioneers.* In these ways, Cooper tried to
assimilate the forest-democracy to the sea-aristocracy; or at least to provide a mechanism of transition from frontier anarchy to rule by hereditary captains.

But Cooper had not the gifts for such a heroic feat of myth-making. The sea
material, it seems, would not be allied to the serious mind of the culture, or reward
the efforts of the serious artists. Only light reading resulted. The forest material,
though immediately more recalcitrant, especially to a writer with Cooper's purposes
and loyalties, ultimately yielded more significant fiction.

5. In the Preface to *The Pilot,* page xi, Cooper says about flogging, "With several
hundred rude beings confined within the narrow limits of a vessel, men of all nations
and of the lowest habits, it would be to the last degree indiscreet, to commence their
reformation by relaxing the bonds of discipline, under the mistaken impulses of a false
philanthropy. . . ."

6. He was of course a historian himself in his novels—and in a more systematic
sense than at first appears. Like Scott, and indeed Dumas, Cooper covered a large area
of history in a fairly consistent way. This is the argument of John P. McWilliams, Jr.,
in *Political Justice in a Republic.* He says that Columbus appears in *Mercedes of
Castile* and that each generation thereafter, from 1675 to 1850, is dealt with in one
novel each.

7. In *Montcalm and Wolfe,* Parkman said about Pitt, "The middle class, as yet
almost voiceless, looked to him as its champion; but he was not the champion of a
class. His patriotism was as comprehensive as it was haughty and unbending. He lived
for England, loved her with intense devotion, knew her, believed in her, and made her
greatness his own; or, rather, he was England incarnate" (Levin, p. 50). And "England
sprang into fresh life under the kindling influence of a great man, like Nature reviving
at the touch of the sun."

8. He referred to his malady as The Enemy, and made war on it, triumphing over
his body. Though his father was a minister, he referred to the clergy habitually as
vermin, for his allegiance was not to the Brahmins but to the aristomilitary caste. He
said in 1884 that democracy had still to prove that it could give "the world a civilization
as mature and pregnant, ideas as energetic and vitalizing, and types of manhood as
lofty and strong, as any of the systems it boasts to supplant." He had made an effort
to do that himself in 1846, and in the Civil War, he and Motley made such a hero
out of Oliver Wendell Holmes, Jr. Later Motley made such a hero out of General
Grant, and later still out of Bismarck.

Those heroes were of the WASP race—the race to which the historians themselves
belonged—and after the rise of Germany to power they extended the idea to include
all Teutons.

## Appendix to "Historians"

9. The Spain Prescott described was in the vanguard of political and geographical progress, and exalted by the religious fervor of Queen Isabella. He said that his Spain had set new standards of national unity, royal justice, and efficiency (Levin, p. 32); while Ferdinand defeated the "self-indulgent" Moors, and "stood firm" against the Pope. We hear about Spanish *liberty;* the seaboard was the natural seat of Spanish liberty—though the mountains were too. The Italians were in those days the decadent and over-refined race (Macaulay said the Spanish then were Roman to the Italians' Greekishness).

For Motley, writing about a slightly later period, "Spain still personified . . . chivalry, loyalty, piety; but its chivalry, loyalty, and piety were now in a corrupted condition. The form was hollow and the sacred spark had fled" (Levin, p. 4). Whereas in Holland and England intelligent enterprise had not yet degenerated into mere greed for material prosperity. It still included the love of danger, the thirst for adventure, the thrilling sense of personal responsibility; which "led those bold Dutch and English rovers to circumnavigate the world in cockleshells, and to beard the most potent monarch on the earth, both at home and abroad, with a handful of volunteers" (Levin, p. 4). The Dutch were trained to liberty by their experience of the ocean. They carried with them over the world the seed of religious freedom and the spirit of commerce, industry, and self-reliance.

These national differences are crystallized in, for instance, ship design. The Spanish galleon was "about as clumsy and amphibious a production as could be hoped of human perverseness. High where it should be low—exposed, flat and fragile where elevation and strength were indispensable—encumbered and top-heavy where it should be level and compact, weak in the waist, broad in the stem and stern . . ." (Levin, p. 34). And so on, all of it suggesting that the galleon, and the Spaniards, were not manly. This is typical modern system rhetoric.

Motley was the most blatant of the four, and a glance at the Preface to his book on the Dutch Republic will sum up what I have said so far. That republic was "an organized protest against ecclesiastical tyranny and universal empire"; the Roman Catholic Church was the type of tyranny, while "the splendid empire of Charles V was erected on the grave of liberty." William the Silent was the Washington of the sixteenth century, and his republic instructed the world in "that great science of political equilibrium which must always become more and more important"—the balance of power, to preserve which was, from Defoe on, a prime international concern of the middle class in the core states of the system. "The maintenance of the right by Holland in the 16th century, by Holland and England united in the 17th, and by the U. S. A. in the 18th, forms but a single chapter in the great volume of human fate; for the so-called revolutions of Holland, England, and America, are all links of one chain."

But the chain of progress and modernization was now declared to depend on the character of one race, the Anglo-Saxons. "To all who speak the English language," said Motley, "the history of the great agony through which the Republic of Holland was ushered into life must have peculiar interest, for it is a portion of the record of the Anglo-Saxon race—essentially the same, whether in Friesland, England, or Massachusetts" (Levin, p. 74).

Prescott saw the Spaniards as Visigoths, while Bancroft and Motley found the germs of modern liberty in Teutonic tribal organization. They wrote of the "Germanic" nations that had accelerated the upward march of history. Both studied in Germany, and were sent there on diplomatic missions. Both were friends and admirers of

Bismarck, and Bancroft of Von Moltke, too. The 1874 volume (No. X) of Bancroft's *History* had two long chapters on Germany and the American colonies. Motley divided the Dutch race between the Celtic Belgae and the German Nervii. The former were inflammable and audacious and vast—" the gigantic Gaul derided the Roman soldiers as a band of pigmies." But they could not sustain a battle as the Germans could. The Nervii were simple, stern, and chaste; while of the Friesians he said, "Those violent little commonwealths had blood in their veins. They were compact of proud, self-helping, muscular vigor." Parkman said the Anglo-Saxon race was "peculiarly masculine . . . peculiarly fitted for self-government." Free institutions would not suit the French, who are excited by opposition, carried away by impulse and passion, running to extremes and to abstractions.

This nationalism and racism constituted a new direction in history-writing. Hume had called the Anglo-Saxons "a rude, uncultivated people, ignorant of letters, unskilled in mechanical arts, untamed to submission under law and government, addicted to intemperance, riot and disorder," who did not deserve "a particular narrative." Much of that phrasing, notably the word "untamed," suggests Hume's general opposition to adventure.

10. The system of political ideas in America corresponded, at some points, to its system of literature. Thus in *Virgin Land,* Henry Nash Smith tells us that there were two main conceptions embodied in the early visions of Empire; the first was essentially a command of the sea, the second a population of the continent. This was a conflict of a mercantilist against an agrarian conception, and in terms of images, a passage to India versus a garden of the world. It was a political issue, and there was a party to promote each image. The leader of the former party was Thomas Hart Benton, who had served under Jackson and saw himself as the heir of Jefferson. The latter party was made up of New Englanders. Politically, this corresponded to the literary division in Cooper, between the novels of the forest and those of the ocean. Both divisions express a deeper agony of decision for America.

But by the middle of the nineteenth century, the end of Cooper's life, the decision was taken. The idea of American empire was aimed at the development of the continent. One of the crucial developments was the railroad. In 1845, Asa Whitney asked Congress for a tract of land sixty miles wide, on which to build a railroad from Lake Michigan to the Pacific. Benton supported him, and began to talk of the Garden of the World, and to see in vision cities rising across the continent, like the Ruins of Empire in reverse. This was an important aspect of the exhilarating American idea— that history could be reversed. In Europe and Asia, one saw the sites of former cities and palaces; here one saw the sites of future such. Benton talked about the great Roman roads, describing his Central National Road; and with the same exhilaration as Kipling showed in describing his Great Trunk Road in *Kim.* A land empire—even if it called itself a frontier—was bound to mean an imperialist ideology. And that took a virulent form in America.

For paradoxically, the crucial difference between the American experience of Frontier and the European experience of Empire, in the first half of the nineteenth century, was that the former became the more imperialist. This change manifested itself in the realm of politics, and the new American politicians were quite different from the old ones. As Richard Yoder says, in "The first Romantics and the last Revolution," between 1810 and 1828 American politics gained a reputation for unsavoriness, and men like John Adams and John Quincy Adams, and even more their admirers, turned away from politics towards literature. The New England account of American history became conservative, not expansivist. The Adamses treated the American Revolution as the achievement of national *unity,* above all, and John Quincy at least preferred to praise the Constitution rather than the Revolution. The Romantic writers and artists (Cooper, Irving, Allston, Bryant, Dana, the Channings) came of Federalist families, and were uneasy with Revolutionary themes. Thus Allston refused to paint the battle pieces in the Capitol Rotunda, and Hawthorne, in *The Grandfather's Chair* (1840) stressed the natural lawfulness rather than the revolutionary fervor of Massachusetts in Revolutionary times. These men found the Adamses more congenial than the new Adams as cultural sponsors. If we try to compare and contrast English experience, we might say that Palmerston had some traits (of imperialist expansion) in common with Jackson as a political leader. But Palmerston worked *with* men like Peel, Russell, Bright, Gladstone, men who belong with Adams—men who were very unlike Jackson. Similarly, the hero of empire contemporary with Boone on the frontier is perhaps James Brooke, the White Rajah of Sarawak. The differences are enormous; that Brooke was born into the military and land-owning caste, and that his exploits took place so far from England and so out of its range, are just two. The effect of these differences, from a literary point of view, was that there was no difficulty for a romance-writer in using the material of Brooke's career, as Conrad in fact did. Brooke fitted perfectly into the categories of romantic adventurer.

11. Everything to do with the battle was enveloped in ideas which associated Jackson with Nature and virtue. Addressing the citizens of New Orleans beforehand, Jackson said, "Inhabitants of an opulent and commercial town, you have by a spontaneous effort shaken off the habits, which are created by wealth, and shown that you are resolved to deserve the blessings of fortune by bravely defending them." He and his followers often spoke of the sudden wealth which had arisen in America since the Revolution, and of the voluptuousness and effeminacy it brought. His troops wore no uniforms, their hair and beards were long, and they observed no external discipline. They fought in Indian style, in small groups, harassing the English.

## Appendix to "The American Hero"

12. Boone is of importance to this study above all because he was another incarnation of the same idea as Robinson Crusoe, so that we can learn more about that idea, and what Defoe made of it, by studying Boone and the other American folk heroes.

Boone was born in 1734 to Quaker parents, and in 1742 Count Zinzendorf held a Synod of the Moravians near his house, where Delaware converts to Christianity preached peace to their brethren. (Thus there were in his heritage elements of the same conflict as Cooper dramatized in Natty.) Moreover, according to John Bakeless's *Daniel Boone*, Indians visited the Boone home as friendly neighbors during his childhood; from conversing with them Daniel learned how to think like an Indian— so that when leading other whites against them as an adult, he always knew in advance what the Indians would do. (This idea should remind us of *Kim*, and point up the similarity of Frontier and Empire.) For he grew up a man of war; as a kinsman said he was "ever unpracticed in the business of farming, but grew up a woodsman and hunter" (Bakeless, p. 10). He both changed caste and reverted socially—which helped make him a typical frontier hero. He was the only notably bad speller among the forty-five grandchildren of George Boone. He left school early, after he knocked down the teacher who tried to discipline him. (This story was told of many heroes of empire —for instance, Stanley—and also heroes of romances—for instance, Roderick Random.)

Boone's great fame was earned when he led the settlers into the new land of

Kentucky. This was land that the English government had reserved to the Indians by the Proclamation of 1763, and so he was involved in many battles against Indians and was captured by them. In fact, he was adopted by the Shawnees as Sheltowee, Big Turtle; his hair was plucked out, all but the scalp-lock, and he was scrubbed by squaws in the river, and painted, and renamed—given an Indian identity. He was sometimes said to be a white Indian. But he escaped, as soon as he could, returned to his countrymen, and led them to drive the Indians out of their land. Still, he was very uneasy with the machinery of white civilization, notably the law; and declared he never wanted to live within 100 miles of a damn Yankee. So when the Spanish governor general of Mississippi, Zenon Trudeau, invited him to move again and settle there in 1795, he was interested. It was a time when Spain was trying to revive her dying empire by inviting in new white settlers, notably disaffected colonists from English or French realms. Many followed Boone to the Spanish Territory, for he was extremely famous as a guide; and there he died in 1820.

His story was told many times in print, and in a way that testifies to innumerable tellings orally. Some of these versions of his character differ significantly from what Cooper (and other responsible-class writers) tried to make out of Boone. In 1832 came John A. McClung's *Sketches of Western Adventure* (Maysville, Ky.). This depicted the West as full of violent adventure, and rejected Eastern versions of Boone as too genteel. McClung even criticized Boone himself for giving too literary and philosophical an account of himself. (In 1818 Boone had told John M. Peek that he had been "a creature of Providence, ordained by Heaven as a pioneer in the wilderness, to advance the civilization and the extension of his country.") *(Sons of Leatherstocking)* The truth, said McClung, was that Boone loved hunting, solitude, and excitement, and was not ordained by Providence or anything else to advance civilization. There were, Richard Slotkin tells us, nine editions of McClung's book, in Cincinnati first, and as late as 1844 (Slotkin, *Regeneration Through Violence*).

Davy Crockett was famous for killing, and for boasting that he had killed when he hadn't. In his autobiographies he describes a shooting-match scene, which he won by putting a spent bullet into the hole left by his first shot, and claiming a perfect double bull's-eye; "Swaggering," he says, "will answer a good purpose at times." But his story is also more full of real violence, and a taste for violence, than Boone's—as for instance the description of the savage fight with a cougar. In Crockett we see the WASP hero as killer. His image was more antigenteel than Boone's—harder to assimilate to Natty Bumppo. Of Irish descent, he grew up on the frontier. His grandparents were murdered by Creek Indians, and a deaf-and-dumb uncle was captured by them, and lived eighteen years in Indian captivity. Davy ran away from home, and spent very little time at school; at fifteen he was still illiterate. He fought alongside Andrew Jackson in 1813, but made his political career in opposition to him; in fact, Crockett's fame was in some sense a publicity invention of the Whigs, who needed a Western man to attract some of the Western vote away from Jackson and the Democrats. He played the role of frontier hero, and played it to the gallery.

His books are full of hints that he may become President, which remind us of the startling new links then being forged in America, between cultural irresponsibility and political power. Crockett became a magistrate first, and in his account of his work one can hear the populism of all his politics. "My judgements were never appealed from, and if they had been, they would have stuck like wax, as I gave my decisions on the basis of common justice and honesty between man and man, and relied on natural-born sense, and no law-learning to guide; for I never read a page in a law book all my life." Elected in 1827, as "the wild man from the West," his speeches, as he reports them, were all style and no content, politically. He refers to Jackson as "the government,"

"King Andrew," or "the old Roman," though he keeps his real bitterness for Van Buren, the vice-president.

13. These innumerable dime novels—a tremendous force, at a low cultural level—relay the image begun by Defoe in *Robinson Crusoe*. *Buffalo Bill* (1881) begins with a list of "the strange heroes who loved the trackless wilds . . . who stood as a barrier between civilization and savagery, risking his own life to save the lives of others . . ." It does not name Crusoe—only Crockett, Carson, Boone, and the other Americans; but we have shown ample reason why that line points in the direction of the shipwrecked Englishman. At the level of formula, therefore, the irresponsible class was being given the same idea as the responsible. Of course, other literary elements, in style, incident, characterization, made the total meaning different.

14. This was an American modification that loaded quicker, hit harder, and more exactly, and kept clean longer. Stories about rifles go back a long way. In 1775 the *Virginia Gazette* reported Captain Crescap's 130 riflemen, who could perform incredible feats of marksmanship. One of them could hit a dollar-sized piece of paper on a board 5″ x 7″, held between his brother's knees at a distance of sixty yards.

15. Since I have made narrowly specific allusions to the connection between the American folk hero and Natty Bumppo, I should recall also the broader scope of the former's influence, out beyond America altogether. In Germany, Karl May's version of Natty, Old Shatterhand, with his Indian comrade Winnetou, had enormous influence on German youth at the end of the nineteenth century, as we shall see. In France there was Gabriel Ferry's *Coureur des Bois*, in seven volumes, 1853, which was very popular; and Gustave Aimard's fifty novels of that kind. And in Britain Stevenson says that to him in his youth, "America was to be a promised land," because he had read Aimard's *Loyal Heart, or the Trappers of Arkansas, The Pirates of the Prairies,* and *The Gold Seekers.* Ohio was the favorite haunt of Stevenson's imagination, and he says an Englishman thought of America as a young man brought up in an old and rigid circle, and taught to distrust his own instincts, thinks of a family of cousins, all his own age, who keep house together, far from restraint and tradition. This sums up neatly for us the fascination the Frontier hero exerted on the citizen of the Empire.

Finally, let me quote Webb on the frontiersman. "It was his aloneness and the passivity and impersonality of the force against which he moved that explains so much that we in the U. S. have called American. Fundamentally his aloneness meant that man was at last really on his own. He could do in this new environment anything he wanted to do and as much of it as he wanted to do without human opposition. For example, if he wanted to cut down trees, kill game, or navigate streams, he could cut, kill, and navigate without seeking a permit or running afoul of a policeman. . . ." (*The Great Frontier*, p. 34). The hazards he ran were of a different kind—his opponents were the impersonal laws of nature; the risk that the tree might fall on him, for instance. "The fact that this man found his own rewards and punishments and complete self-responsibility for his fortunes, did things to his psychology." The interest of that description is that as well as unifying our folk heroes and Natty, by defining what they have in common, it also points back to perhaps the purest of all embodiments of that idea in Robinson Crusoe. This is the WASP hero in one of his most potent incarnations, the man alone on his island. Webb was not thinking of Defoe, but his remarks make it clear how perfectly that book trained the imaginations of its readers for the tasks which the frontier as well as the empire held ready for them.

*Notes*

## Chapter VI

1. This boomerang effect, and Britain's exemption from it, was discussed by Sir Halford Mackinder (1861–1941) the founder of geopolitics, and theorist of British imperialism. "The separation of the tropical Empire from the European island, although perhaps a source of weakness from the military point of view, has had the extreme advantage, that on the one hand imperial rule in the dependencies has not corrupted freedom at home, and on the other hand those who exercise that rule, go out generation after generation with the spirit of justice and trusteeship ever renewed from their free homes and schools." This quotation, attributed to 1924, is to be found in Bernard Semmel, *Imperialism and Social Reform* (p. 176).

An example of the difference between political conditions in the home country and those in the empire is given by George Dangerfield in *The Damnable Question*. Ireland had a police system, he says, while England itself had justices of the peace (the "gentlemen of the parish"). And while Englishmen *thought* of police systems as something characteristic of European despotisms—of czarist Russia, for instance. Another example is given in Mark Twain's *Following the Equator:* he says that in Australia and Tasmania convicts got fifty lashes for quite small offenses, though England had just repealed the law which allowed up to twenty-five.

2. The idea of importing technical experts from the West into Russia goes back even further than that, and there had even been some practice of it, on a smaller scale. Ivan the Terrible had tried, but met the opposition of the Poles, Swedes, and Lithuanians. In 1547 a hundred and twenty four such experts were turned back at Lübeck, while on their way to Russia. And Sigismund August of Poland wrote to Elizabeth of England in 1567, warning her against strengthening Russia's power by such means. "One supplies them with munitions of war, with arms the use of which they did not know, and what appears most dangerous to me, one procures to them adroit engineers" (John Bowle, *The Imperial Achievement*, p. 18).

3. Nicholas saw the brilliant charge of the Life Guards at Austerlitz, but also the tragic consequences; and the contrast between the two is one of the novel's dominant chords. ". . . of all that mass of huge and handsome men, of all those brilliant, rich youths, officers, and cadets, who had galloped past him on their thousand ruble horses, only eighteen were left after the charge" (p. 304). The dead lay like heaps of manure on the ploughed land.

4. And the occasion, in *The Cossacks*, is the discovery of a dangerous-looking footprint, which is likely to remind us also of Crusoe. Tolstoy had of course read *Robinson Crusoe*. As a boy, and as a father, with his own children, he played games derived from that story. (He also read, and reread, Dumas's historical romances. And he mentions, as an important influence in his early reading, Prescott's *Conquest of Mexico*.)

5. The Russian Formalist, Victor Shklovsky, wrote a book on Tolstoy in 1928, in which he analyzed *War and Peace* as the product of two forces, ultimately irreconcilable, Tolstoy's caste-identity and the novel-form's inherent liberalism. He says Tolstoy intended to glorify the Russian nobility, and to canonize the legend of its heroism during the Napoleonic invasion, but that the tendencies of the novel-genre undermined his intention, and made the meaning of the book more democratic. I see support there both for my interpretation of Tolstoy, and for my theory of genre. Serious fiction was allied to liberalism, as adventure was allied to modernist imperialism.

6. In *The Russian Levites: Parish Clergy in the 18th Century* (Harvard University Press, 1977) Gregory L. Freeze says that the Russian clergy developed a "castelike structure" during the eighteenth century, "as medieval Muscovy became modern

Notes

Imperial Russia." He himself hesitates to name it bluntly a caste, though he says that was the general term in mid-nineteenth-century Russia. The official term was *soslovie,* usually translated as estate, and Freeze combines that with caste. He says that the formation of such *soslovia,* out of the medieval social groups called *chiny,* was "a process unique to Imperial Russia; while other European countries were beginning to break apart the traditional estate structure, Russia began to build just such an order of closed social estates" (p. 218). The clergy was the most hereditary and the most separate in juridical status, but the nobility and the merchants were something like castes—and became so in modern times. This is important for us to bear in mind when considering the challenge of Tolstoy's caste-thinking, and caste-thinking in general.

7. In his *Reminiscences,* written near the end of his life, Tolstoy attributed insincerity to his early works, *Boyhood* and *Youth,* on the grounds that they implied a "democratic tendency," which he says he didn't really feel at the time of writing them. That is an example of the sort of insincerity of which he accused Turgenev and the others.

8. It is worth noting that Tolstoy's brother Sergei bought a gypsy girl, and lived with her the rest of his life, having several children by her; that his brother Dmitri bought a prostitute from a brothel and made her his common-law wife; that their father, when sixteen, had a bastard son who became a postilion and who, after the father's death, came begging from his half-brothers (Tolstoy remembered his embarrassment, because the bastard brother looked much more like their father than they did). And finally that Tolstoy himself had a bastard son in 1858, who grew up to be a coachman who worked nearby.

9. On the whole, the Cossacks are much more like American frontiersmen than servants of the British Empire. But one can recognize something Cossack-like in the men John Buchan describes meeting in South Africa. "They were the true adventurer type—long, thin, hollow-eyed, tough as whipcord . . . I took off my hat in spirit to the advance-guard of our people, the men who know much and fear little . . . You can readily whistle them back to the defense of some portion of the Empire or gather them for the maintenance of some single frontier; but when the work is done they retire again to their own places, with their eyes steadfastly to the wilds but their ears always open for the whistle to call them back once more" (*The African Colony,* p. 161).

10. Braudel points out the larger background to the Caucasian wars; that the danger to civilization has always come from either mountain people, like the Caucasians, or the nomads of the deserts and the steppes; the horse and camel people, like the Tatars or the Bedouins. Such men were the war-makers and meat-eaters. They jeered at the men of the settlements, who were often (in Russia, for instance) vegetarian. Islam never securely converted her nomads, the Berbers of North Africa or the Kurds of Central Asia. While sorcery, witchcraft, and vendettas—all such social forms flourished on the mountain tops, in Corsica and Sardinia, and so on. Civilization had to choose, either to excommunicate their mountain enclaves, as China and India did, or to domesticate them by force, as Europe tried to do.

## Chapter VII

1. According to Smith, scores of newspaper articles and periodicals and sermons also pointed out the likeness between Lawrence and Cromwell; both men cared naught for appearances, spoke freely, swept obstacles from their paths, worked like heroes, and made others work.

2. Two more examples of this kind of adventure tale are Michael Scott's *Tom Cringle's Log* (Paris, 1836) and E. H. Trelawney's *Adventures of a Younger Son* (London, 1831). The first, though vigorous and stirring, is formally enchained to Smollett. The second is Romantic; as Byron said, Trelawney was "the personification of my *Corsair*. He sleeps with the poem under his pillow and all his past adventures and present manners aim at his personification" (Quoted in the Introduction to the Oxford English Novels edition of *Adventures.*). One point of interest is Trelawney's masculinism; in this, as in many other ways, he usefully exaggerates tendencies implicit in the adventure and romance forms. He wanted to call the book *A Man's Life,* and when Mary Shelley told him that women would not read the manuscript he showed her, he replied, "My life . . . is not written for the amusement of women . . . it is to men I write, and my first three volumes are principally adapted to sailors. England is a nautical nation . . ." (Introduction, *Adventures*).

3. Max Müller, in his memorial Preface to *The Roman and The Teuton,* described Kingsley as the ideal man. He recalled those ". . . features which Death had rendered calm, grand, sublime . . . How children delighted in him! How young, wild men believed in him, and obeyed him too! How women were captivated by his chivalry!" His funeral in 1875 collected men of all sorts, gypsies and farm-laborers, sailors, bishops, and governors. He will be missed "wherever Saxon speech and Saxon thought is understood."

4. In that message Kingsley was of course very unlike Macaulay and James Mill and the Utilitarians. But his view of India was not so remote from theirs. James Mill's *History of British India* gives a very Hobbesian idea of the state's origin, says J. W. Burrow, in his *Evolution and Society.* The state is seen as a machine, and the civil philosophy is as demonstrable as geometry is. His Books II and III try to determine the stage of civilization reached by native India. His criterion is as follows: "Exactly in proportion as Utility is the object of every pursuit may we regard a nation as civilized." (Quoted in Burrows, p. 45.) In India, of course, he found that many pursuits did not have Utility as their object. So Mill blamed the Orientalist scholars (like Sir William Jones) for inducing the West to overrate Indian culture, which was really very backward. "By conversing with the Hindus of today we in some manner converse with the Chaldeans and Babylonians." Mill, Macaulay, and the Whigs of the *Edinburgh Review*, were very rough in their judgments on the East in general—in conscious dissent from the eighteenth-century high-culture fondness for the exotic. Their line of thought may be associated with merchant-caste low culture—the cultural tendency to which Defoe belonged.

5. Indeed, Dumas's portrait of Richelieu is like Defoe's. Both portraits are composed of phrases like "exquisite subtlety" and "finished art." In the second issue of his *Review,* Defoe described Richelieu as "the most exquisite master of politics, Cardinal Richelieu, whose life and management may hereafter take up a considerable part of these papers . . . the most refined statesman in the world." And writing to Harley, Defoe recommended to the English statesman Richelieu's arrangement of having a series of three offices, each one more secret than the one before, and the third so private that no one was admitted except in the dark (Defoe, *The Letters,* p. 39). Another letter to Harley makes it clear how personally fascinated Defoe was; for he compares himself in Edinburgh, hiring people to betray their friends, with Richelieu. Richelieu was for Defoe what Macchiavelli was for the Elizabethans; and the fascination continued throughout the life of the modern system, as Dumas's success makes plain.

6. That book is credited with beginning the "ethnographic novels" which filled the

penny dreadfuls after 1874. (See Brian V. Street, *The Savage in Literature*.) It is also the book in which Henty describes his trip up river with Stanley.

7. Ballantyne is an interesting figure, in a number of ways. He was son and nephew to the Ballantyne brothers who were close friends of Scott. They printed *The Waverley Novels,* and even copied the manuscripts out so that their employees should not see and recognize Scott's handwriting. Thus he was brought up in the Waverley cult, and was much influenced by it. But at sixteen he was sent out to work in the Hudson's Bay Company, and stayed there six years, 1841–1847. His first book, published in 1848, was entitled *Hudson's Bay;* while his first fiction, published in 1856, *The Young Fur Traders,* had the same setting. Thus he embodied two of the major ideas of Scotland, from our point of view; and from 1856 to 1894 he poured out a stream of very popular boys' fiction, which combined the two, and carried the message of adventure.

8. And this became stronger during his second period, according to Huet's classification. Between 1878 and 1897 his stories were mostly about colonization, and not about the adventures of colonizers but about native rebellions against them. He wrote about the Greek insurrection of 1826, the French-Canadian insurrection of 1837, the Indian Mutiny of 1857, the Bulgarian independence movement, and so on. His work became more literary, and made more reference to Scott. According to Jean Chesneaux *(Une Lecture Politique de Jules Verne),* there are three main strands to Verne's liberalism. He was in the tradition of 1848; that shows itself in Captain Nemo's gallery of heroes, in *20,000 Leagues Under the Sea,* which included Kosciusko, Botzaris, O'Connell, Washington, Lincoln and Brown. (Compare Defoe's list of Protestant heroes, and Smiles's.) But he was also a utopian socialist, whose heroes work for a scientific and fraternal exploitation of the earth. And he was finally an anarchic libertarian—against the police and for outlaws in general; his books show a strong interest in mutinies, and in islands which are *milieux libres*—alternatives to society.

In the third period, 1898 to 1905, according to Huet, he returned to the subject of voyages, but the mood of his work was much grimmer. *L'Etonnante Aventure de la Mission Barsac,* not published until 1914, tells of Henry Killer's wonderfully efficient settlement in Africa called Blackland, which makes use of ingenious ideas devised by the scientist Marcel Camaret, but works by slave labor. This is a dystopia, and all the enthusiasm for science of the earlier books has gone sour.

Of these three periods, the most important from our point of view is the first. Besides the titles already cited, it is worth mentioning *Les Enfants du Capitaine Grant,* 1867–1868, a three-volume odyssey about those children in search of their captain-father, who was shipwrecked while founding a Scots colony in Patagonia. The theme must remind us of Defoe, and it is worth noting also the fondness of Verne for captains. After Captain Singleton and Captain Roberts, we have to wait until Verne began writing to meet such a concentration on this figure in fiction. The story of Captain Nemo, 1870, owes more to Dumas in the revenge motif, and is more politically motivated. Nemo is an Indian prince in disguise, and he sinks a British cruiser as part of his revenge. But *L'Ile Mystérieuse* (1873) is closer to the Crusoe pattern; an engineer, a journalist, a seaman, and a child are wrecked together, and are saved by the expertise of the engineer. He is an American called Cyrus Smith, who has as much skill of hand as ingenuity of mind, and they name the place Lincoln Island. It is, Chesneaux says, an Anglo-Saxon parable, a hymn to work.

9. Take for instance Andrew Lang, who played a large literary role, as the friend of Twain, Kipling, and Haggard, and who edited the Border Edition of Scott. In his introduction to *Ivanhoe,* 1894, Lang defended Scott thus—against Ruskin: "Perhaps

# Notes

Mr. Ruskin was never a boy. Scott, like Thackeray, had been a boy, and never forgot that happy company of knights, ladies, dragons, enchanters, all the world of Ariosto . . ." Lang's identification of boyhood with chivalry was of the first importance in the history of children's literature. So was his identification of romance with self-indulgence, in opposition to intelligence and criticism. He continues, "We cannot all be old and melancholy . . . There shall be cakes and ale, though all the critics be virtuous, and recommend stuff 'rich in heart-break'. Still shall the greenwood trees be green . . ." That pouting whimsy was so often employed by Scots writers that it comes to seem inherently Scottish.

## Chapter VIII

1. Justin Kaplan has pointed out how many features *Connecticut Yankee* shares with that standard adventure-romance of the period, *King Solomon's Mines;* a wicked shaman, an eclipse, a love affair, a climactic battle, and a clash of cultures. (Kaplan, *Mark Twain and His World*, p. 146.)

2. In 1877 he wrote about Germany, "What clean clothes, what good faces, what tranquil contentment, what prosperity, what genuine freedom, what superb government!" The Germans seemed to be applying modern system values to life, under Bismarck, and it was a natural corollary that they should appreciate Twain's humor so enthusiastically. His works were brought out there in six volumes between 1874 and 1878, and he was a favorite German author. It was known that the Kaiser himself loved *Life on the Mississippi.*

3. There were many sides to that character, and several of them ugly. There was a Frontier racism, which one hears sometimes in Twain; in, for instance, this sentence from *Roughing It.* "The Bushmen and our Goshoots are manifestly descended from the self-same gorilla, or kangaroo, or Norway rat, whichever animal-Adam the Darwinians trace them to" (p. 132). And some of Twain's animus against Cooper was his Frontiersman's contempt for the Noble Red Man image which Cooper had carved in the service of the responsible culture of America.

It may be relevant, in this connection, to point out that the road and the ride West Twain describes in *Roughing It* are very like the road and the ride (from Charlestown to Johannesburg in South Africa) which Gandhi describes in his *Autobiography.* It was on this journey that Gandhi came up against brutal racism, and received his decisive call to political action. He was humiliated for being an Indian by a coach-driver who was a "man of power" exactly like those Twain celebrates. The road to Johannesburg was one of the Great Transport Roads of South Africa. "It was all Romance, the first form of Romance," says a 1914 description, *The Old Transport Road,* by Stanley Portal Hyatt. Johannesburg, which had a population of 40,000 in 1893, but 160,000 by 1904, was (like some California cities) called "the central sin-spot of civilization." (See Hamilton Fyfe, *South Africa Today,* 1911.) Gandhi himself remembered its citizens as always running, never walking, and everyone as being obsessed with gold. It was therefore a typical mining and bonanza town, just like those Twain knew; among the street names were Gold, Quartz, Banker, Claim, and Nugget. (Gandhi called the Transvaal the El Dorado of the Western world.)

The similarity between Frontier and Empire comes out in an American's description of Pretoria, where Gandhi spent a year (Poultney Bigelow, *White Man's Africa*). "It was about noon; the sun was broiling down as it does in Texas; the broad, dusty streets reminded me of an average prairie town west of the Mississippi, and this impression was further heightened by noting great freight wagons drawn by sixteen oxen, and scrawny mustangs galloping about, with sunburnt, shaggy Boers astride them" (Quoted in C. D. S. Devanesan's *The Making of the Mahatma,* p. 248). This was Twain's environment, including incidents like that in which Gandhi was involved. Twain saw, and indeed described, many such incidents. But he identified—not unambivalently, of course—with the drivers, not with the insulted and injured.

4. Twain asks his readers to share his own humiliation before these figures of violence—his own doubt of "civilized" values when in their presence—and it is notable how clearly American Studies still mirrors that doubt and embarrassment. I don't (any longer) think that simply a weakness in American Studies. I now think the self-confidence of critics who do not embody these doubts unreal. But there is no doubt that it considerably hampers work in that field. I can take a couple of examples of the embarrassment I mean from Henry Nash Smith's tributes to Twain. First from his introduction to *Mark Twain: 20th Century Views.* "This is the kind of veneration that railway conductors and gifted Irishmen in bars might feel for generals or prizefighters; it is not their usual attitude towards men of letters. The fact is that in the popular conception Mark Twain was not a man of letters . . ." (p. 2). The second from *Mark Twain: the development of a writer,* where he says that the humorists' diction contrasted with that "considered appropriate for the upper ranges of literature," just as vernacular values contrasted with those of "accredited spokesmen for American society." All kinds of unprinted quotation marks flutter around the phrasing of those passages, announcing an embarrassment about "men of letters" and "American society," and for that matter "the people"; an embarrassment which debilitates the argument, since those are the crucial concepts it employs.

5. The serious mind of England was furious. The Royal Geographical Association, which had been preparing an expedition with the same purpose, said Stanley's story was all lies. The Brighton meeting of the British Association in 1872 invited Stanley to speak, but openly disbelieved what he said.

The English response shows how how staid the English mind had become; how completely the puritan-merchant mind had subdued itself in its alliance with the aristocracy; had formed an establishment. But it is important to note that Americans didn't believe Stanley either, though their disbelief was less disapproving. Even in New York, such was the atmosphere of journalism then, it was confidently asserted that Stanley was writing his reports, locked up in a hotel room somewhere in the city; and for a long time no one really believed them. "Dr. Livingstone, I presume?" was a broad joke from the beginning, at the popular as well as more sophisticated levels of culture. The whole affair, but especially the contempt of the English establishment, deeply upset Stanley. It is a vivid case of Anglo-American mutual hostility.

Ill-feeling continued. When his dispatches were published, a year later, the *Saturday Review* said that Stanley described bloodshed with relish; and accused him of carrying too far "the American method of treating savages." (Here we see Empire dissociating itself from Frontier.)

But public opinion changed toward Stanley. In 1873 he reported the Ashanti war, in Africa, and made friends with G. A. Henty in the course of it. The latter commemorated their travels together in his popular *By Sheer Pluck.* When Livingstone died, Stanley was commissioned by the London *Telegraph* to continue exploring the lakes which the former had been investigating, in search of the source of the Nile. The disreputable newspaperman became the famous explorer. In 1875 he persuaded the King of Buganda to let Christian missionaries into his territory; and that was the first step in the process which resulted in the addition of Kenya and Uganda to the British Empire.

# Notes

About this time, the other kind of complaint about him began to get louder. By his own account, his expedition in Buganda killed thirty-three natives and wounded one hundred—Stanley himself shot fifteen. He began to be called the modern Pizarro. Sir John Kirk, the British consul at Zanzibar, said that Stanley had kicked a man to death. It was also a cause of scandal that Stanley made alliance with Arab slave traders. The latter went west across Africa in his footsteps. In 1889 one of their raids destroyed a hundred villages and killed thirty thousand people. Being an explorer did not mean a career in pure science, or pure adventure; it meant conquest and often war.

6. The novel is dedicated to those suppressing slavery, but its interest is part adventurous, part (innocently) pornographic. The story is about Selim, a white-skinned Arab lad from Zanzibar, slender and girlishly beautiful, who is awakened from childishness to boyishness by the challenge of the American consul's son. "Nazarene lads are bolder and more manly than we," he says; much to his audience's gratification. So he gets a rifle, and goes to Africa, with his two slaves, to find adventure. There he himself gets enslaved by blacks, and often flogged, until he is befriended by Kalulu, prince of the Watuta. The latter is a "type to make the marble forms of Phidias blush; body, arms, and limbs were unmistakably magnificent in shape . . . a perfect youthful Apollo . . . [with] surpassing grace of movement and manly beauty" (p. 137). Selim's skin, on the other hand, is soft and smooth, and he has lustrous orbs, and quite often his clothes are taken off. The two become fast friends, and Stanley compares them with David and Jonathan. "What boy, of any nation, in any public school, has not some friend who is as dear to him as a born brother?" (It was of course predictable that one aspect of so large a cult as that of "the boy" in nineteenth-century England should bear this sexual character; a general judgment must be that that character makes itself felt quite rarely.)

7. Gordon was the most remarkable of these proconsuls, and as a personality he cannot be said to be typical of anything, with his religious mysticism and unworldliness. But his career was typical, in some ideal-type sense, of British imperialism then; as a troubleshooter, first in China, then on the Danube, in the Sudan, in India, in South Africa, in Palestine, and again in the Sudan; where he finally died, to become one of England's great military martyrs.

More typical is Sir George Goldie (1846–1925). He was born into a wealthy aristocratic family, ran away from Woolwich Military Academy to Egypt, and lived three years in the Sudan with an Arab mistress (and was always interested in the idea of rebuilding a Sudanese empire). Having come back to England, he again eloped, this time with the family's governess, to Paris in 1870, and married her reluctantly in 1871. He was a domineering presence, an atheist who read Ibsen and Wagner. In his own words, "All achievement begins with a dream. My dream, as a young child, was to colour the map red. In 1877 I left England (largely to escape from personal entanglements) to explore the interior of Nigeria. On the journey back I conceived the ambition of adding the region of the Niger to the British Empire." He had first gone there in 1875, to look after the interests of a firm which belonged to his family. In 1879 he took over the other English firms that traded there, and in 1886 got a royal charter to develop Nigeria, and led wars against the Nupe and Iloria in 1896. Frederick Lugard and Mary Kingsley, the explorer, were his allies in imperial politics.

Lugard was born in India in 1858, where his father was an Evangelical missionary. He acquired Uganda and organized Nigeria for the empire, and actually became governor of Hong Kong, and then of Nigeria. His biographer, Margery Perham, says of his caste identity, "It was a double sense of caste in that he felt himself to belong to a class within his nation and to a nation within Africa, both of which he believed, had the code of noblesse oblige." Back in England, he always dressed for dinner, even in those last years of his life when that was an old joke. She says he was "the supreme type of that imperialism which had long been the pride of his country and was now judged, by the major part of humanity, as something very near a crime."

Finally, Sir Harry Johnston, 1858–1927, known as the Prancing Proconsul, because of his oddity and gaiety. He was very small and young-looking and vivacious, a gifted artist, linguist, botanist, and zoologist. But he set up the new country of Uganda in 1899. He fought his battles under a huge white umbrella, and dressed his Sikh constabulary in white, yellow, and black, and put the same colors on his notepaper.

These heroes had a less Carlylean style in heroism than the Lawrence brothers, and the Indian army men generally—as embodied in them, the Empire is perceptibly more modern. But they were all men whose sense of self was supported by an aristocratic caste identity.

## Chapter IX

1. Kipling is an obvious subject for any study of imperialism in literature, or of the great popular novelist, or of the WASP hero, or of caste psychology. Nevertheless, in coming to Kipling I face a double challenge, both aspects deriving from his being more purely and intensely an artist of literature than the other writers we have considered; being quite possibly, as T. S. Eliot said, the greatest man of letters of his generation. This means on the one hand that he is very inventive and "original," so that his work doesn't fit simply into the patterns I have been drawing; on the other it means that he deserves and demands a quantity of exposition and analysis which, within the limits of this book, I can't afford to give him.

The impulse to give him that is also strong because he, much more than the other adventure novelists, has been badly treated by critics. I am not thinking of the hostile essays—there are plenty of acts of repentance, too—the significant bad treatment is silent and general, is manifested as much in neglect as in anything else, is the work of an inhibiting prejudice in the mind of nearly every literary reader.

There is a resistance to Kipling which is an extreme example of the hostility to literature and the adventure tale that we have been studying; extreme because of Kipling's politics. The feeling against him is the by-product of reasoned convictions which I would never call prejudices in themselves; but their by-product is a disturbance of literary judgment. You may decide that that prejudice is a small price to pay for valuable convictions—and certainly I have small hope of undoing the prejudice by an argument—but ideally it must be possible to both cherish one's political convictions and see Kipling as a great writer about imperialism.

2. Of course Kim was in effect a native boy too, and one element in the English audience's fondness for him was that Kipling evoked their memories of such boys on his behalf. They said, "I knew a boy just like Kim." Independently of Kipling, they had focused their fondness for India on nimble, impudent, mischievous Indian boys of that kind—as opposed to Indian girls or adults. This bias was not felt merely with "natives"; it was a striking feature of late Victorian culture, that its emotional focus was on boys. We have seen that children's literature turned to the service of boys, in the middle of the nineteenth century, and that serious writers devoted their talents to that kind of writing. And something similar could be seen happening in other features of the culture, besides literature. At no other time could a play like *Peter Pan* have had the extraordinary success it had in London. This aspect of *Kim* is another example of Kipling's gift for taking material from the

# Notes

very surface of his audience's mind, and fitting it to his serious artistic purposes.

3. Hannah Arendt has several perceptive and sympathetic things to say about Kipling in her *Origins of Totalitarianism.* "The author of the imperial legend is Rudyard Kipling, its topic is the British Empire, its result the imperialist character . . . and chivalry, nobility, bravery, answered the legend's call "And" Imperialism was a chance to escape a society in which a man had to forget his youth if he wanted to grow up" (pp. 208 and 210).

4. He told him, "You needed a tight hand in those days," and Kipling goes on to speak (in *Something of Myself*) of "the necessary wrench on the curb, that fetches up a too-flippant colt." While later, in India, his newspaper "chief" "took him in hand and broke him." Kipling says, "For three years or so I loathed him," but does not even need to add that later he valued the discipline he had received. And in *The Complete Stalky and Co.* there is a poem, "The Centaurs," which is about the training of young colts by Chiron, their stern preceptor.

5. The word "great," the capitalization of nouns like Road and River, and Mountain and House, and the use of phrasing evocative of the Bible or Shakespeare, and a whole corpus of such devices, Buchan inherited from Kipling. For instance, in *The African Colony,* there is a chapter about the Cape–Cairo Road, entitled "The Great North Road"; in which we read of the romance inseparable from all roads, and of a river that "pours a stately flood through the low coastlands to the sea" (p. 161). Buchan was very skillful at this sort of thing. Toward the climax of *Prester John,* the hero writes, "Behind me was heathendom and the black fever flats. In front were the cool mountains and the bright streams and the guns of my own folk." (He has escaped from territory held by insurgent blacks.) He goes on to quote "Night's candles are burned out." It would be impossible to evoke in fewer and simpler words the major sanctions of his high culture—Shakespeare, the Bible, *Pilgrim's Progress,* hill-climbing in Scotland; or to ally those ideals to the facts of imperialism—as represented by "the guns of my own folk"—more tactfully.

6. Also in essays. During the Great War, Kipling gave some remarkable talks of that kind, one to the Guards Cadet Corps in 1917, called "The Magic Square," on the primitive origins of military drill, and another to junior naval officers in 1918, called "The First Sailor," on the primitive origins of ships and sailing. (Both are to be found in *A Book of Words.*)

The idea of primitivism had definite political affiliations. Liberals believed that man had developed past his primitive ways, and should be *ashamed* of any traces of them in his mind. For instance, J. A. Hobson says in his *Imperialism* (1902), "Imperialism is a depraved choice of national life, imposed by self-seeking interests which appeal to the lusts of quantitative acquisitiveness and of forceful domination, surviving in a nation from early centuries of animal struggle for existence. Its adoption as a policy implies a deliberate renunciation of that cultivation of the higher inner qualities . . . etc." (p. 368). This book is a very important context in which to find such a declaration. Hobson's interpretation of imperialism, based on the history of South Africa and the Boer War, began the theoretical development of that concept which was taken up by the Left everywhere. Lenin, Luxemburg, and Kautsky, all made use of Hobson.

He said that the diamond merchants of the Rand had caused the Boer War, and the military imperialism was capitalism's natural mode of expansion; and that such imperialism was essentially like the Roman kind, and would create servitude and license, overcentralization and parasitism, even in England. His theory, arriving in the context of the general moral revulsion against the British part in the Boer War and the Belgian part in the Congo, carried a lot of conviction against Kipling's party. And

*Notes*

it is important to note how the idea of primitivism belonged to that conflict. Gandhi, for instance, developed Hobson's idea; literature—at least, the ideology of the great writers, like Eliot, Pound, and Lawrence—unconsciously followed Kipling.

In Kipling's party, or in alliance with him, we must put Karl Pearson and his "science" of eugenics. Pearson was a socialist; but he wanted a "warrior-chieftain" to lead his socialist state. He and Francis Galton proposed a Jihad (to be conducted by means of eugenic controls) against customs and prejudices that impaired the physical and moral qualities of the English race. Women should be sexually free, but politically confined to the kitchen and the nursery. And it is important to remember that both Shaw and Wells were eugenists for a time.

7. We can measure the effect of Kipling's fictionalization of this theme if we look at his essay on the same subject, "An English School," of 1893. (In *Land and Sea Tales*.) The school motto was "Fear God and Honour the King" and the hymn sung on the last Sunday of every term was "Onward Christian Soldiers"—the favorite stanza being, "We are not divided, All one body we, One in hope and doctrine, One in charity." There we glimpse the United Services College as more ordinary celebrants of its virtues would have described it. And of course he saw it that way, too. He quotes the poem the school sent to the Queen (written by himself, though he doesn't say so).

> Such greetings as should come from those
> Whose fathers faced the Sepoy hordes
> Or served you in the Russian snows
> And, dying, left their sons their swords.
> For we are bred to do your will
> By land and sea, wherever flies
> The Flag, to fight and follow still,
> And work your Empire's destinies."

Those are the copybook maxims that echo behind the slang and the cynicism of *Stalky and Co.*, and whose resonance makes it an extraordinary book.

## Appendix to *"STALKY and Co."*

8. Most of Kipling's works deliver the message, "harness your imagination in the service of your society," and not all are intricately structured. Some deliver that imperative as crudely as you might think—reading literary critics—Kipling always wrote. But even those books are pungently flavored and full of literary interest. Let me cite a few cases.

In *Letters of Travel, 1892–1927*, we find an early essay, "Captains Courageous," which says on page 83, "There's a man in Yokohama who in a previous life burned galleons with Drake. He is a gentleman adventurer of the largest and most resourceful —by instinct a carver of kingdoms, a ruler of men on the high seas, and an inveterate gambler against death. . . ." There we see how Kipling (like Twain) would put his imagination at the service of the successful businessmen he met—his splendidly historical and poetic imagination.

On page 90 of the same book, he says, "A man who has *lived* . . . has heard the Arabian Nights retold and knows the inward kernel of that romance which some little folk say is vanished. Here they lie in their false teeth, for Cortes is not dead, nor Drake, and Sir Philip Sidney dies every few months if you knew where to look. The adventurers and captains courageous of old have only changed their dress a little and altered their employment to suit the world in which they move. Clive came down from

# Notes

Lobengula's country a few months ago protesting that there was an empire there, and finding very few that believed. Hastings studied a map of South Africa in a corrugated iron hut in Johannesburg ten years ago . . ." There we might say that Kipling is serving the politicians, if one calls Rhodes a politician. "The others, big men all and not very much afraid of responsibility, are selling horses, breaking rails, drinking sangaree, running railways beyond the timber-line, swimming rivers, blowing up tree trunks, and making cities . . ."

Thematically, therefore, Kipling wrote about and for adventure. And his writing had a more aggressive edge against other themes and values than previous adventure writers. Thus he wrote in an essay about and from Canada in 1908, "A People At Home" (pp. 141–142), "I wonder sometimes whether any eminent novelist, philosopher, dramatist or divine of today has to exercise half the pure imagination, not to mention insight, endurance, and self-restraint, which is accepted without comment in what is called 'the material exploitation' of a new country" *(Letter of Travel).*

A somewhat similar idea is expressed in a story, "A Conference of the Powers," of 1890, in *Many Inventions,* in which a group of young subalterns meet the great novelist, Eustace Cleever—who may be a partial portrait of Henry James. When this man of letters looks at these men of action, Kipling notes that, "The line of the chin-strap, that still showed white and untanned on cheekbone and jaw, the steadfast young eyes puckered at the corners of the lids with much staring through red-hot sunshine, the slow, untroubled breathing, and the curious, crisp, curt speech, seemed to puzzle him utterly (p. 28)." "Him" being the Jamesian novelist, whom we may take to represent literature. "To me," the latter said softly, "The whole idea of warfare seems so foreign and unnatural, so essentially vulgar, if I may say so, that I can hardly appreciate your sensations" (p. 29). When one of them, called "The Infant," tells him about Burmese dacoits who crucify their victims—Cleever "could not realize that the Cross still existed." These young subalterns deal with such facts daily; they have all killed enemies, all enjoy fighting, and all like their enemies. The novelist's mind is "stretched" by them and his soul "over-awed." When the Infant says modestly that he has only seen Burma, Cleever adds, "And dead men, and war, and power, and responsibility." After the encounter he says that no one would sing (that is, write novels) if he could kiss (that is, fight wars).

(I haven't meant to imply, even by silence, that Kipling was not occasionally vulgar —in the way that last quotation shows. But I think readers often find him vulgar when it is his subject matter that embarrasses them, and it is their own ideological squeamishness that is at fault.)

The poem "To the True Romance," in the same volume, says,

> Thou art the Voice to kingly boys
> To lift them through the fight,
> And Comfortress of Unsuccess
> To give the Dead good-night.

(The language is, as in Kipling generally, chivalric-romantic, rather than Defoe-plain. There are plenty of facts in Kipling, but they are subsumed in mythic patterns.)

This kingly-boy side of Kipling's work receives one of its most full-scale treatments in "The Brushwood Boy," 1895, interesting also as a simpler kind of failure than is at all common in Kipling. George Cotter is the perfect English upper-caste boy, responsible for the tone of his school; where the "wise and temperate" Head has led him to see how men and boys are "all of a piece," and that he who can handle the one will control the other. When he joined his regiment, "he bore with him from school a character worth much fine gold . . ." (*A Kipling Pageant,* p. 350). ". . . his training had set the public school mark upon his face, and had taught him how many were the 'things no fellow can do.' By virtue of the same training he kept his pores open and his mouth shut." He boxed his men into obedience and devotion to him. One sees here something Kipling usually conceals, or expresses more discreetly, his love of young Englishmen of "the right type." It was indeed a social passion of the time, which you meet in many writers, and which often seems quite cannibal in its relish of their physical charm. Kipling usually avoided describing his hero directly; for instance, in "A Sahib's War," we hear the narrative of a Sikh servant about his young master—who is dead before the story begins—and our sense of the young Englishman's beauty is suggested only by the ugliness of the three Boers whom the Sikh fiercely sacrifices to his memory—a fanatical preacher, his fat wife, and his idiot son.

George Cotter is, one may say, a prince of the copybook maxims. Kipling for once has tried to introduce no reactive moral realism, no unpleasantness. He is what English mothers then wanted their boys to be. The other element in this characterization is yet more romantic—that he dreams, and in his dream life roams an entirely different country from the banal one of every day. Sexless in real life—when his mother tucks him up for the night, she can tell he's never been kissed—his destiny is to meet a girl who dreams of the same world he does. Thus their eroticism can all take place in that dream world, and in this world they are just Girl and Boy, which is how they address each other. This is Kipling-as-Barrie, and the vision of England, embodied in George's home, is equally as golden and unreal as the characterization. It is all rose gardens and white peacocks and "the shadow of the old house lay long across the wonderful English foliage, which is the only living green in the world. 'Perfect! By Jove, it's perfect.' Georgie was looking at the round-bosomed woods beyond the home paddock, where the white pheasant boxes were ranged; and the golden air was full of a hundred scents and sounds" (*A Kipling Pageant*, p. 364). The same sense of England's beauty, as something rich and perfect, valuable and vulnerable, can be found in "They," 1904, and "An Habitation Enforced," 1905. In the first, the house is built of weather-worn stone, with mullioned windows and rose-red tile roofs, yew topiary, and "a great still lawn." There is a great rose-grown gate and a heavy oak door sunk deep in the thickness of the wall. (Heavy, deep, and thick are often key words in this kind of writing.) In the second, some Americans buy an old house and learn how to live in it, and thereupon they get over their nervous problems and are able to have a child. (This suggests the connections the culture felt between this kind of expensive beauty and a therapy for exasperated nerves and impaired fertility.)

The ineptitudes of "The Brushwood Boy" are embarrassing rather than interesting. But *The Naulahka*, the novel Kipling wrote with his American brother-in-law, is interesting, even though not very successful. It combines material from the Frontier (from Twain's world) with material from the Empire. The story opens with Nick Tarvin and Kate Sheriff in Topaz, Colorado. She is the daughter of a railway engineer, but was converted to religion and social work at school, and wants to go to India to help Indian women, who are nothing but their men's chattels. He is a real estate and insurance agent, who "believes" only in Topaz, a man who habitually lies and tricks his competitors, but who has surrendered his conscience to Kate, and is willing to obey what she says are its laws (p. 21).

> The Law whereby my Lady moves
> Was never Law to me
> But 'tis enough that she approve
> Whatever Law it be.
> For in that Law and by that Law
> My constant sourse I'll steer;

# Notes

> Not that I heed or deem it deed
> But that she holds it dear.

Kipling tells us that "men to whom life is a joke find comfort in women to whom it is a prayer." (p. 21.) Nick is a "nervous, bony, loose-hung man, with a kind, clever, aggressive eye, and a masterful chin" (p. 23). Elected to the state legislature, he tells the other legislators dry and laconic anecdotes in Abraham Lincoln fashion.

Kate goes to India as a medical missionary, and Nick follows her to the court of an opium-addict maharajah. There he dams a river, trains the maharajah's son to be manly, and makes the maharajah laugh. Another Connecticut Yankee, he dominates the splendid and jeweled court by his gunplay and his skill in horse-breaking. "It made him tired to see the fixedness, the apathy and lifelessness of this rich and populous world, which should be up and stirring by rights—trading, organizing, inventing, building new towns, making the old ones keep up with the procession, laying new railroads, going in for new enterprises, and keeping things humming" (p. 121). He has a putative romance with Sitabhai, the most beautiful of the maharajah's wives, a Morgan le Fay character, who says, "If you were a king and I a queen, we would hold Hindustan between our two hands" (p. 277). She throws a knife at him and he responds with a kiss upon her lips. Here the story works out some of the implications of *Connecticut Yankee* which Twain turned away from. Kipling wrote a poem on the same theme.

> Strangers drawn from the ends of the earth, jewelled and plumed were we
> I was the Lord of the Inca Race, and she was the Queen of the Sea.
> Under the stars beyond our stars, where the veinless meteors glow,
> Hotly we stormed Valhalla, a million years ago.

This is the same vein of feeling as Haggard's *She* develops—the Anglo-Saxon hero's feeling that for a man like him there must be something better waiting than an Anglo-Saxon woman.

Kipling felt a generous, though not uncomplicated, admiration for America and the Americans; a much more romantic feeling than he had about Englishmen. He felt that America was still boyish, and shirked discipline, shirked moral realism and responsibility. So in *Something of Myself* he wrote, "I never got over the wonder of a people who, having extirpated the aboriginals of their continent more completely than any modern race had ever done, honestly believed that they were a godly little New England community, setting an example to brutal mankind" (p. 441). But in *From Sea to Sea*, he says, "Wait till the Anglo-American-German-Jew—the Man of the Future—is properly equipped. He'll have just the least little kink in his hair now and again; he'll carry the English lungs above the Teuton feet that can walk forever; and he will wave long, thin, bony, Yankee hands, with the big blue veins on the wrist, from one end of the earth to the other. He'll be the finest writer . . . etc." (p. 109). Americans were for him an intensified version of Australians or Canadians, and almost citizens of the Empire.

On the whole, Kipling's attitude toward America was very similar to Stevenson's, who said in *From Scotland to Silverado* that an Englishman thinks of America with envy; that there is a hostility between them, because tomorrow belongs to the Americans—"for us, England and yesterday." This was, I think, a very widespread feeling in England at the end of the nineteenth century, and it could be connected with the split we have discussed between Empire and Frontier. (It is worth noting, also, some striking parallels between Kipling and Stevenson, biographically and literarily; that they both married American women, older than themselves, and somewhat managing and maternal; that their books were family enterprises—Kipling's father providing illustrations to his books, Stevenson's son-in-law doing the same for his—; that they sprinkled verses, that looked like quotations, through their narratives, as part of a way to bring literature into forced alliance with adventure; and so on.)

Whereas Kipling's tone about Englishmen at home tends to be this of *Letters on Leave*, "A Death in the Camp." "Above that they seem to be, most curiously and beyond the right of ordinary people, divorced from the knowledge of the fear of death . . . because they have everything done for them they know how everything ought to be done . . . little trifles like colonial administration, the wants of the Army, municipal sewage, housing of the poor, and so forth. Every third common need of average men is, in their mouths, a tendency or a movement or a federation affecting the world" (p. 184). On the next page he complains of a man who "knows all about the aggressive militarism of you and your friends; he isn't quite sure of the necessity of an Army; he is certain that colonial expansion is nonsense; and he is more than certain that the whole step of all our Empire ought to be regulated by the knowledge and foresight of the working man . . . (p. 185) . . . You mustn't treat any man like a machine in this country, but you can't get any work out of a man until he has learned to work like a machine . . . (p. 197) . . . I honestly believe that the average Englishman would faint if you told him it was lawful to use up human life for any purpose whatever. He believes that it has to be developed and made beautiful for the possessor" (p. 190).

This vein of thought, Kipling's most interesting but most shocking, is again expressed in "Drums of the Fore and Aft," 1888, his story about a green regiment that broke under fire, and how two drummer boys rallied it by playing "The British Grenadiers." ". . . wherefore the soldier, and the soldier of today more particularly, should not be blamed for falling back. He should be shot or hanged afterwards—to encourage the others—but he should not be vilified in newspapers, for that is want of tact and waste of space . . . (*A Kipling Pageant*, p. 101). . . . Speaking roughly, you must employ either blackguards or gentlemen, or, best of all, blackguards commanded by gentlemen, to do butchers' work with efficiency and dispatch . . . and God has arranged that a clean-run youth of the British middle class shall, in the matter of backbone, brains, and bowels, surpass all other youths. For this reason, a child of 18 will stand up, doing nothing, with a tin sword in his hand and joy in his heart until he is dropped" (p. 103).

If this were an evaluative account of Kipling's work, I should spend a long time on stories like "The Bridgebuilders," 1905, which is a very remarkable confrontation of the myths of India with the antimyths of the modern world system. The Hindu gods have caused the Ganges to flood and beat against the great bridge which Findlayson has just built. The burden of the story is the question whether the white man's gods are merely another embodiment of the multiform Indian gods, or whether they represent something new in the world; and there is some real strength of feeling and sharpness of sight on both sides.

But I have space for nothing more than *Puck of Pook's Hill*, 1905, and its continuation, *Rewards and Fairies*, 1910. These are retellings and dramatizations of key episodes in English history, narrated by Puck to two modern children of the age of Kipling's own. Kipling had often been reproached—by Chesterton, for example—with writing about England as if he were a foreigner, without knowing it from inside. In serious fiction, this was the age of Hardy, dominated by a powerful mood honoring English ruralism, and these stories are in some sense Kipling's contribution; nonimperialist, nonindustrial, nonmechanical; quietist, cyclical, fertility-oriented. Kipling accommodates his older, somewhat opposite interests to these, and the two make a rich mixture. Here the primitive origins of modern customs are much more gently evoked

—though "The Knife and the Naked Chalk" and "Cold Iron" do that very beautifully —and it is the historical origins which interest him.

Most important from our point of view are the stories about the Roman centurions and the Saxon and the Norman brothers-in-knighthood. These are important because of the powerful use Kipling makes of a motif we noted in Dumas; the confrontation between young men—here a pair each time—and an older man who represents a cold and in some ways sinister wisdom. Sir Hugh and Sir Richard face deAquila, small and crooked-nosed, bitter and wise and responsible. Parnesius and Pertinax face Maximus, the great Roman general, who offers the former greatness in return for a cruel but politic deed. (The implicit identification of England with Rome is an important step in the development of that theme—since as late as Kingsley the identification was fought off as sinister. It is negotiated by stressing the frontier character of the Roman settlements—the Great Wall is, as Kipling describes it, a frontier town—and that of course implies an identification with America too.) The young men love each other, fight and compete against each other; the old man is spiritually alone and rather sinister, but imposes his will upon them, the will of civilization; it is an implicitly emotional, in some sense an erotic, transaction, but much more metaphorically so than the equivalent in *Kim.*

Kipling was a great metaphorician, a great artist of allusion. This is to be noted particularly in his language, which alludes to various areas of experience and expertise. One direction is indicated by the language of the Bible and the sagas; another is the language of trades and crafts; another is the language of sports and military affairs. But the allusion is not only a matter of vocabulary, it is also a matter of concept and factual detail, description and characterization, all of which are likely to be extremely compressed, complex, and suggestive. In *Puck* the allusion is predominantly historical and literary in direction, and the book is a triumph of vivid and richly intricate evocation of the English past. In this aspect of his work Kipling is quite worthy to be put beside Scott and Shakespeare. These stories are in fact Kipling's Foundation Epic; except of course that these are short stories and at an opposite extreme from the epic poem in most formal terms; that paradox—the fragmentariness of Kipling's form, combined with the monumentality of his themes—is something I must return to.

The motif of iron runs through *Puck of Pook's Hill;* it is introduced in the first story, of Weland's sword, which is given to Hugh the Saxon. "Knights of the Joyous Venture," an adventure tale which uses most of the motifs we have been following, describes how Hugh and Richard sell iron in Africa, and get gold and ivory in return. "A Centurion of the 30th" also has lots about iron. And *Rewards and Fairies* begins with "Cold Iron"; a story in which a fairy child becomes human, at the age of sixteen, when he finds a slave-ring of iron, and fastens it round his own neck. Thus one of the most important motifs in the modern imagination received careful literary treatment, at the climactic moment of the system's career.

9. He went to the United Services College, the school depicted in *Stalky and Co.* In *Something of Myself* he describes it as a caste school, meaning the military caste. Seventy-five percent of the boys, he says, were born outside England, and hoped to follow their fathers into the army. In "An English School" he says, "and so the men she made went out to Boerland and Zululand and India and Burma and Cyprus and Hong Kong, and lived and died as gentlemen and officers" (*Land and Sea Tales*, p. 562). And indeed, in 1914, of his schoolmates, Godby was commanding the New Zealand forces, Maclaglan led a brigade of Australians, Rimington was chief engineer in Mesopotamia, and Dunsterville (the original of Stalky) was to lead an expedition into North Persia. (Carrington, *Life of Rudyard Kipling.*)

10. In a talk given to a naval club, in 1908, he said, "One is influenced forever by

one's first commission, and mine threw me among disciplined men of action—the Indian services—where men were required to live under authority and act under orders." And in *Something of Myself* he said that at the club in India he met, "none but picked men at their definite work."

11. This theme of kingship, and this way of playing with it, runs through all the adventure genre. In *A General History of the Pyrates*, 1724, Defoe says the Madagascar pirates had slaves and seraglios, and came out to meet Woodes Rogers, "attended like Princes; and since they actually are Kings de facto, which is a kind of Right, we ought to speak of them as such." But their clothes were worn out; "their Majesties were extremely out at the elbows"; and he left them in "a great deal of dirty State and Royalty . . . and if Ambition be the darling Passion of Men, no doubt they were happy. One of these great Princes had formerly been a Waterman upon the Thames . . ." (pp. 61–62).

That is the satiric-realistic stress, such as we find in Twain's "The Duke and the Dauphin." It is really quite continuous with the more romantic stress we can hear in this passage from John Buchan's *Salute to Adventurers* (1915), a romance which sums up an unusual number of these motifs. Andrew Garvald, a Scots merchant, has helped an Indian find his kingdom in Virginia in the 1680s, and so this king, Shahlah, urges Garvald to ride west with him, and give up trade for kingship. "While the blood is strong in the veins shall we ride westward in the path of a king?" Garvald reflects, "I might be a king over a proud people, carving a fair kingdom out of the wilderness, and ruling it justly in the fear of God. These western Indians were the stuff of a great nation. I, Andrew Garvald, might yet find that empire of which the old adventurers dreamed." But in fact he chooses the quieter destiny, the white man's way, marriage, and trade.

12. I have argued in another essay, "Our Turn to Cliché," that English literature after 1918 is characterized by a marked preference for quotation, allusion, and cliché. I cite Virginia Woolf and Graham Greene as particularly notable among novelists for the importance of this device in their work. (The essay is to be found in my *Trans-Atlantic Patterns*.) It now seems to me that they learned this art—though they are not so expert at it as he—from Kipling. If so, this unacknowledged debt is a neat example of the general ingratitude of modern English literature; they have claimed Conrad as father while owing more to Kipling—for this seems to me a very significant debt, establishing the important terms of reference for all criticism.

13. The other European countries had followed England in adding territory during these years. Hannah Arendt says that in two decades the British added 4.5 million square miles and 66 million people; the French 3.5 million square miles and 26 million people; Germany 1 million square miles and 13 million people; Belgium 900,000 square miles and 8.5 million people. Such countries needed stories of Defoe's or Kipling's kind.

In the decade before 1914 there were French novelists who wrote about Algeria with some of Kipling's ideas and techniques; for instance, Robert Randau (*Colons*, 1907, and *Explorations*, 1909), who depicted France as a land of ideas, Algeria a land of action, and made much of the regenerative effects of close contact with the soil. There was also Louis Bertrand, who compared the English with the Romans, the French with the Carthaginians, turning Defoe's idea to France's advantage. In those years, Barrès, Maurras, and Seillière were all saying that France had become overcivilized and needed more force and violence, which she could find in colonization. Pierre Mille (1865–1960), who had lived in London and admired the English, and translated Kipling, wrote stories around a character, Barnavaux, who was like Kipling's Irish soldier, Mulvaney.

# Notes

In Germany the colonies promised an escape from the pressures expressed in Willkomm's *Die Europamüden,* of 1838, says Hugh Ridley, in "Germany in the Mirror of Its Colonial Lit." (*German Life and Letters,* July 1975.) The colonies felt free from the pressures of class that troubled Germany, a freedom which attracted the army but also the civil service and the peasant farmers. Frenssen's *Peter Moors Fahrt Nach Südwest* was very popular. Hans Grimm (1875–1960), who had lived in England and South Africa, wrote *Volk Ohne Raum,* 1926, which sold 750,000 copies, and became an officer of the Colonial Service. Mille also was an authority on French colonial matters, and both followed Kipling's naturalist-aesthete line, though Mille's landscapes are lyrical, while Grimm's are utopian; but Mille approved miscegenation (and native culture) while Grimm repudiated it. Germany also had some women writers about colonial life; Frieda Von Bulow, in love with Carl Peters, in *Tropenkoller,* depicted colonial life as making every German an aristocrat. And in *Ludwig v. Rosen,* 1892, she showed that colonial life offered a hardness, passion and archaic quality that would redeem even effete aristocrats. Frieda Kraze's *Heim Neuland* had a heroine who sought sexual liberation until she found, in the colonies, that that would reduce her to the level of the natives.

It may be appropriate here to describe the phenomenon of Karl May, also. He bore no known relation to Kipling, but he belonged to Kipling's era, and bore a very important relation to the Anglo-Saxon adventure hero. Karl May (1842–1912) wrote forty volumes of Western adventures, translated as a whole into twenty other languages; 24 million volumes by him have been sold in Germany, and 2.5 million of *Winnetou* alone. Winnetou is the son of the chief of the Mescalescou Apaches, who becomes the blood brother of Old Shatterhand, a German adventurer on the American frontier with a blond beard, etc., who could fell both man and beast with a blow of his fist.

May wrote in the first person, and was photographed wearing Shatterhand's costume—fringed leggings and hunting jacket, two revolvers and a bowie knife, a gun on his back and one in his hands. In various ways May encouraged his readers to believe that he *was* Old Shatterhand; he built himself a Villa Shatterhand with his profits. (He was in prison for fraud and theft—on other charges—early in his career.) He had at one point earned a living writing soft-core pornography, and these books are full of idealized homosexuality. But there is a surface ideology of Christian knighthood—Shatterhand converts Winnetou.

But May's interest lies in his success. *Der Spiegel* called him recently a Praeceptor Germaniae, and the greatest influence on German youth between Goethe and Mann; there is an annual Karl May Festival at Bad Segeburg. Hitler recommended him to his general staff, and Einstein and Schweitzer both acknowledged his moral influence. Georg Grosz wrote in his autobiography "The reading of these books awakened in the youngster a yearning—that secretly exists in practically every German—for distant lands and exotic adventures. (These books could well have been the result of the ardent propaganda of the time for German colonial expansion.) Yes, indeed, we certainly had a warm place in our hearts for our great, blond, German-American hero, Old Shatterhand, who with one blow of a clenched fist could lay low a horse, not to mention a contemptible traitor. . . . Winnetou was one of the ideals of the German youth of my day. He actually became a national hero, even more famous than his renowned colleagues, Uncas and Chingachgook, because there was something 'German' about him." This is a particularly vivid case of a general phenomenon, the infection of other core countries with the virus of Anglo-Saxon adventure.

14. Amongst novels about Rhodes, we can mention Gilbert Parker, *The Judgement House,* 1913. Sarah Gertrude Millin, *The Jordans,* 1923. Morley Roberts, *The Colos-*

*sus*, 1899. Antony Hope, *The God in the Car*. G. Skeleton, *Dominion*, 1925. F. B. Young, *City of Gold*, 1937–1939. And Stuart Cloete's trilogy, beginning with *Turning Wheels*, 1939.

15. Ruskin said "There is a destiny now possible to us, the highest ever set before a nation to be accepted or refused. We are still an undegenerate race; a race mingled of the best northern blood. We are not yet dissolute in temper, but still have the firmness to govern, and the grace to obey . . . will you, youths of England, make your country again a royal throne of kings? . . . And this is what England either must do, or perish: she must found colonies as fast and as far as she is able, formed of her most energetic and worthiest men . . . if we can get men, for little pay, to cast themselves against cannon-mouths for love of England, we may find men also who will plough and sow for her, and who will behave kindly and righteously for her, and will bring up their children to love her" (R.A. Huttenback, *The British Imperial Achievement*, p. 101).

16. At the same time he much admired the Boers for their pastoralism, and thought of himself as in some ideal sense a farmer. He worked hard for Anglo-Boer unity, and admired Kruger. His plans might have succeeded but for the discovery of gold in the Transvaal, which led indirectly to the Jameson Raid in 1895.

In relation to black Africa, on the other hand, he was simply expansionist. In 1888 he signed a treaty with Lobengula, which gave the latter £100 a month, 1,000 Martini rifles, 100,000 rounds of ammunition, and a gunboat. The Aborigines' Protection Society had warned Lobengula, but he thought he was signing away a mine, not a country. The charter was delivered to him by a contingent of Royal Horse Guards, who galloped up to the kraal in silver breastplates and plumed helmets, escorting a coach emblazoned with V. R. (Victoria Regina) and drawn by eight silver-caparisoned mules. In 1889 the British South African Company was chartered—on the rumor of the discovery of King Solomon's mines in Mashonaland. In 1890 his 186 Pioneers (some of them Boer) began their march north there and to Matabeleland, using dynamite and naval searchlights to strike terror into the Zulus. Each of the Pioneers was promised 3,000 acres and 115 gold claims. Rhodes told them, "You have the proud satisfaction of knowing that you are civilizing a new part of the world. Those who fall in that creation fall sooner than they would in an ordinary life, but their lives are better and grander" (Huttenback, p. 112).

17. In fact, Lenin, in his *Imperialism* (1916), quotes from a speech of Rhodes of 1895. "I was in the East End of London yesterday and attended a meeting of the unemployed. I listened to the wild speeches . . . in order to save the 40,000,000 inhabitants of the United Kingdom from a bloody civil war, we colonial statesmen must acquire new lands to settle the surplus population, to provide new markets for the goods produced by them in factories and mines . . . If you want to avoid civil war you must become imperialists."

18. Many public schools had some connection with the army. In 1830, 12 percent of the boys leaving Harrow and Rugby joined the forces; in 1850, 27 percent; though it fell off later—in 1880 it was only 14 percent, but it is worth noting that nearly all of those reached the rank of colonel or above. And some schools had very strong military traditions. Cheltenham sent out 4,237 boys between 1841 and 1910, and 1,896 served in the forces; while Clifton had much the same record (Ellis, *The Social History of the Machine Gun*, p. 101).

19. The link with the aristocracy, and the social career of the military caste, can be traced to some degree in Army Lists. In France the Revolution drove aristocrats out of the army, but they returned after 1815. The more they were pushed out of the economic and political life of nineteenth-century France, the more they took over the

# Notes

army—and later on, the empire. (Their other field was diplomacy, where aristocrats could serve their country while hating their government, hating the French state.) In 1875, out of the 365 cadets at the military academy of St. Cyr, 102 had "de" before their name. In Germany at about the same time, 65 percent had "von" before theirs. That proportion sank, but in 1914 it was 53 percent for officers above the rank of colonel. In England, in 1875, 50 percent were from the aristocracy-plus-the-gentry. (I take all these estimates from "Officers and Gentlemen" in Ellis, *The Social History of the Machine Gun.*) And Army Regulations breathed the spirit of chivalry—with a concommitant hostility to technology. The French regulations, according to Ellis, said the army must always take the offensive, must always charge, and cavalry must be the army's real strength. And there was a cult of the well-bred horse. The British Cavalry Training Manual of 1907 said, "It must be accepted as a principle that the rifle, effective as it is, cannot replace the effect produced by the speed of the horse, the magnetism of the charge, and the terror of cold steel."

20. Hannah Arendt points out in *Origins of Totalitarianism* that imperialism gave a new lease on life to social structures which would otherwise have collapsed; and we might add, psychological structures. She says that the educated classes everywhere welcomed it, for that reason, though governments often fought against it. All the parliamentary parties, in England, France, and Germany, collaborated in imperialist programs sooner or later; and it was Englishmen in the colonies, or thinking about the colonies, who were the most patriotic-militant. The effect of all this on psychological structures—mediated via school, notably—was to promote the development of leaders, commanders, captains. This is how the Kshattriya caste, to which Kipling belonged, and for whom he wrote, was propagated. In India itself, that caste almost certainly owes its origin to a similar imperialist situation.

21. This is the idea I hinted at in the first footnote to p. 285. The Bloomsbury sensibility (and in this it was only typical of most kinds of English sensibility after 1918) declared itself the very opposite of Kipling's, in feeling for words and for personality, in taste in letters and in life generally, as well as in politics. And yet the only significant writer who owed nothing to Kipling, or practically nothing, was D. H. Lawrence. I say "practically nothing" because Lawrence's primitivism, and its political corollaries, are not totally unlike Kipling's. But on the whole, Lawrence did indeed choose Hardy and not Kipling as his godfather. But his colleagues did not. This is immensely important for understanding the cultural conflicts of England over the last fifty years.

## Chapter X

1. Brooke was important to adventure enthusiasts generally. I have already mentioned his appearance in the dedication to *Westward Ho!*. And when Borrow said it was a crown of glory to carry the blessings of civilization and religion to the barbarous, he asked, "But who has done so in these times?" and answered himself, "Only Rajah Brooke." And A. P. Wallace said the Dyaks looked up to Brooke as to a supernatural king.

2. One of the likenesses between the two locations is indicated by the legends of treasure. In *Almayer's Folly* we are told, "The coast population of Borneo believes implicitly in diamonds of fabulous value, in gold mines of enormous richness in the interior. And all those imaginings are heightened by the difficulty of penetrating far inland, especially on the north-east coast, where the Malays and the river tribes of

Dyaks, or Head-hunters, are eternally quarrelling." This is very similar to the situation in Costaguana, in *Nostromo,* and in the historical Guinea, where European adventurers (like Raleigh) were drawn further and further on by such stories among the native population. There is no reason to declare that Conrad was drawing an analogy by this coincidence. A safer conclusion to draw is that in fact Europeans' imaginations all over the world were set aflame by contact with the already burning sparks of adventure and ambition of native imperialism.

3. On page 1, Brooke is described as being "a true adventurer in his devotion to his impulse—a man of high mind and of pure heart." Conrad's language blends adventure with romance. Brooke, we are told, "recognized chivalrously the claims of the conquered; he was a disinterested adventurer, and the reward of his noble instincts is in the veneration with which a strange and faithful race cherish his memory."

4. *Victory* (1915) presents adventurers as villains. The main villain, Gentleman Jones, is a sort of Gilbert Osmond of adventurer, while the hero, Axel Heyst, is in retreat from the world, and is the opposite of an adventurer. Conrad's sympathies lie with him, though they are, as ever, ironic. Reflection is a pernicious habit, as Stein had said in *Lord Jim,* and Axel is too reflective and clear-sighted.

5. Jeffrey Meyers, in *Fiction and the Colonial Experience,* says that Kurtz should be associated with Rimbaud, who wrote home from Abyssinia in 1888 in exasperation against the natives he had to deal with. "Obliged to chatter their jibberish, to eat their filthy messes, to endure a thousand and one annoyances that come from their idleness, their treachery, and their stupidity." Meyers makes no suggestion that Conrad was thinking of Rimbaud, only that both men were at the same moment passing through the same experience—one of the many deaths of the nineteenth-century liberal imagination. Certainly, given the imaginative ascendancy achieved by both Kurtz and Rimbaud in the 1920s and 1930s, in England at least, it behooves us to keep them bracketed in our minds.

6. For instance, in 1898 he wrote about Marryat, the sea-novelist he was emulating, "To his young heroes the beginning of life is a splendid and warlike lark, ending at last in inheritance and marriage . . ." (Notes on *Life and Letters,* p. 53). Marryat wrote when the century was young, and Conrad was conscious of writing when it was old. He was also conscious of being an artist, a sophisticated Romantic artist, as Marryat was not. "There is an air of fable about it . . . [Marryat's world] . . . It is the beginning and the embodiment of an inspiring tradition . . . His figures move about between water and sky, and the water and the sky are there only to frame the deeds of the Service" (p. 54). Conrad of course paid great attention to the water and the sky in themselves. Marryat's heroes "do not belong to life; they belong exclusively to the service. And yet they live; there is a truth in them, the truth of their time; a headlong, reckless audacity, an intimacy with violence, an unthinking fearlessness, and an exuberance of vitality, which only years of war and victories can give" (p. 54). Marryat's books, as well as his heroes, drew vitality from those years of war and victories. But the truth of Conrad's times is very different, he implies.

Conrad feels himself further from such figures, and his own heroes, than Kipling does from his subalterns, but it is not a distance of unfamiliarity. Conrad has known the sailors he writes about. It is a distance of alienation—while Kipling embraced his heroes, Conrad felt his inner self very remote from his. His Captain Beards and Captain MacWhirrs are incredible, incomprehensible, phenomenal. He compared Marryat with Cooper and noted that the latter was more concerned—like himself—with Nature and with Art. Conrad, of course, felt himself much more the artist and the metaphysician than either.

However, Cooper and Marryat also served their countries' navies, and Conrad no

# Notes

doubt saw himself as like them in that. At least he often endorsed that service of theirs. "Perhaps no two authors influenced so many lives and gave so many the initial impulse towards a glorious or a useful career." And he was something of a recruiting agent himself. In *A Mirror of the Sea* (1905) he said, "The British navy may well have ceased to count its victories. It is rich beyond the wildest dreams of success and fame. . . . It is too great for mere pride" (p. 185). Of course, his fiction is more ambivalent.

7. *Nostromo* is of particular interest because, according to Jerry Allen in *The Sea Years of Joseph Conrad*, the setting Conrad had in mind was Colombia, a setting that combines memories of Raleigh's search for gold in the sixteenth century with a reference to Theodore Roosevelt's 1903 promotion of the secession of the province of Panama, in order that America might dig the Panama Canal. Thus the story links sixteenth-century El Dorado with twentieth-century technology. For instance, the San Thome mine which Gould works had been abandoned by the Indians; just as the mine at San Thome mine which Raleigh sought was filled in by the Indians, to save themselves from rapacious adventurers. Costaguana is Raleigh's Coast of Guinea.

In 1876, when he was eighteen, Conrad had sailed from Marseilles to Martinique and on to Colombia, and his ship was carrying a cargo of arms to help the conservative side in the revolution then taking place, just like the one he described in *Nostromo*. The story of El Dorado could not fail to have excited his imagination, then or whenever he heard it. In fact the legends are told by Santiago Perez Triana in one of his books, and Triana was the Panamanian Minister to London and the man Conrad drew as the character Don José in *Nostromo*. Triana tells how de Quesada led seven hundred Spanish soldiers in search of the gold in 1536, and how Raleigh followed de Quesada. It is one of the great stories of the second half of the sixteenth century, and of modern imperialist adventure.

8. This is very half-hearted. Charles Gould, the representative Englishman of *Nostromo* is made out to betray his wife, by caring more about his mine; but this, like Jim's betrayal of Jewel, is little more than a rhetorical device in Conrad. Perhaps because Conrad had blended the material of the serious novel with that of adventure, he quite often makes such a point against his adventurers; a diagnosis of just the kind that D. H. Lawrence was to make the starting point of his philosophy of eroticism (see Lydia's account of her Polish husband in *The Rainbow*). But Conrad clearly has no sense of eroticism as a serious idea by which to live. He merely makes a point against his adventure heroes, because he is uneasy with their heroism.

## Chapter XI

1. Morris's *The Well at the World's End* (1898) is an extraordinary evocation of stripling eroticism, which was very popular with the whole generation before 1914, according to Paul Fussell, in *The Great War and Modern Memory*. Here the adventure component in romance is quite melted out by the heat of sexual fantasy. The young hero is loved by everyone, typically older women, who hold his hands, kiss his lips, weep to look upon him—he lets one cut a lock from his thatch of golden curls. The monk of Higham laughs to see him sleepy and naked in the morning, and the carline of the Castle of Abundance says, "Far would many a Maiden run to kiss thy mouth, fair lad," —whereupon he "laughed gaily" and went into the hall with her. The adventures are nothing but hazy episodes in the heat of erotic excitement. Nothing could be further from Defoe's kind of story. Its relevance to our interest is just that it shows the tribute that Edwardian culture paid to the young man figure. But it is notable also that the

story's various representatives of the commercial impulse—called "chapmen"—are all scorned. The story is clearly romance, but of the sexual-fantasy kind.

2. He thought of his father as having been lord-like in Ireland, in his first marriage —before being carried off and subdued by Lawrence's Puritan mother. As an old woman, the latter went out to China as a medical missionary, with her older son, Robert—at a time when T. E. Lawrence was serving in the Air Force in India. Thus there was a caste drama in the family, like a *Pamela* in which Mr. B. escaped literal marriage (but underwent everything else); the mother, lower class, Puritan, and dominant; the father, upper class, amoral, and subdued. Naturally, this affected the way Lawrence saw himself. He described himself in a letter to Mrs. G. B. Shaw in 1925 as being two people: "Naturally the very strong one, Say 'No,' the Puritan, is in firm charge, and the other poor little vicious fellow can't get a word in, for fear of him" (John E. Mack's *A Prince of our Disorder*, p. 403). This suggests why Lawrence chose the chivalric style so decidedly.

3. Among American books on similar topics, one might cite John Seelye's *Prophetic Waters* as having a similar character. Seelye for instance calls the explorer, La Salle, an American Kurtz; he describes how in 1680 La Salle found the fort he had established (Fort Frontenac) deserted by the men he had left in it; while the boat which was to have carried him down the Mississippi had a "Conradian graffito" scrawled across it: *"Nous sommes tous sauvages."*

# Bibliography

The primary purpose of this bibliography is to name the editions I used, so that the reader can find my page references. Secondly, I want to identify more fully books cited only glancingly. And finally, I name some books just because I am so indebted to them. But this principle has not been followed consistently, because of the counter-principle —that a full list of everything I'd used would be too long.

Allen, Jerry. *The Sea Years of Joseph Conrad.* New York, 1965.
Arendt, Hannah. *The Origins of Totalitarianism.* New York, 1966.
Bakeless, John. *Daniel Boone.* New York, 1939.
Bercovitch, Sacvan. *The Puritan Origins of the American Self.* New Haven, Conn., 1975.
Biglow, Poultney. *White Man's Africa.* New York, 1898.
Billington, James. *The Icon and the Axe.* New York, 1966.
Bird, R. M. *Nick of the Woods.* New Haven, Conn.: Yale University Press, 1967.
Birukoff, Paul. *Leo Tolstoy, His Life and Works.* New York, 1906.
Bodelson, C. A. *Studies in Mid-Victorian Imperialism.* London, 1924.
Bonner, William. *Captain William Dampier.* Stanford, Calif., 1934.
Borrow, George. *The Bible in Spain.* London, 1906.
 *Lavengro.* London, 1906.
Bosworth-Smith, R. *Life of Lord Lawrence.* New York, 1885.
Bowle, John. *The Imperial Achievement.* New York, 1975.
Braudel, Fernand. *Capitalism and Material Life 1400–1800.* London, 1974.
 *The Mediterranean.* London, 1972.
Buchan, John. *African Colony.* Edinburgh, 1903.
 *Prester John.* Popular Library, New York, 1973.
 *Salute to Adventurers.* London, 1915.
Burrow, J. W. *Evolution and Society.* London, 1966.
Burton, Richard. *Narrative of a Pilgrimage to Mecca and Al-Medinah.* London, 1879.
Butterfield, Herbert. *The Whig Interpretation of History.* New York, 1951.
Cammaerts, Emile. *Discoveries in England.* London, 1930.
Campbell, Lily B. "English History in the 16th Century," in *Shakespeare's Histories: 20th Century Views,* ed. Waith.
Carrington, C. E. *The British Overseas.* London, 1968.
 *The Life of Rudyard Kipling.* New York, 1956.
Cawley, R. R. *The Voyagers and Elizabethan Drama.* Boston, 1938.
Chesneaux, Jean. *Une Lecture Politique de Jules Verne.* Paris, 1971.
Christian, R. F. *Tolstoy's War and Peace.* Oxford, 1962.
Christie, J. A. *Thoreau as World Traveller.* New York, 1965.
Conrad, Joseph. *Almayer's Folly.* Kent Edition, New York, 1925.
 *Heart of Darkness, Typhoon,* and *Youth,* in *Three Short Novels.* New York, 1960.
 *Lord Jim.* New York, 1968.
 *Mirror of the Sea.* Kent edition. New York, 1925.
 *Nigger of the Narcissus.* Kent edition. New York, 1925.
 *Nostromo.* Signet Classic, New York, 1960.
 *Notes on Life and Letters.* London, 1925.
 *Outcast of the Islands.* Kent edition. New York, 1925.

    *The Rescue.* Kent edition. New York, 1925.

    *Victory.* Kent edition. New York, 1925.

Cooper, James Fenimore. the Leatherstocking Tales in the Iroquois edition, New York, 1906, except for those listed below.

    *The Chainbearer.* New York, 1856.

    *The Crater.* Cambridge, Mass., 1962.

    *The Deerslayer.* New York, 1963.

    *Notions of the Americans.* New York, 1913.

    *The Pilot.* New York, 1859.

    *The Pioneers.* New York, 1959.

    *The Prairie.* New York, 1964.

    *Satanstoe.* New York, 1859.

    *The Sea-Lions.* New York, 1856.

    *Wyandotte.* New York, 1856.

Crockett, Davy. *Davy Crockett's own story as written by himself.* New York, 1955.

Dana, R. H. *Two Years Before the Mast.* New York, 1909.

Dangerfield, George. *The Damnable Question.* New York, 1976.

Darling, Richard L. *A History of Children's Book Reviewing in America.* New York, 1968.

Defoe, Daniel. "Appeal to Honour and Justice," in *The Shortest Way With Dissenters and Other Pamphlets.* Oxford, England, 1928.

    *The Complete English Gentleman.* London, 1890.

    *The Complete English Tradesman.* London, 1841.

    *Captain Singleton.* London, 1973.

    *The Chimera.* London, 1720.

    *Conjugal Lewdness.* Gainesville, Fla., 1967.

    *An Essay Upon Projects.* London, 1697.

    *The Family Instructor.* London, 1841.

    *The Four Year Voyage of Captain Roberts.* London, 1726.

    *The Farther Adventures of Robinson Crusoe.* London, 1925.

    *A General History of the Pyrates.* Columbia, S. Car., 1972.

    *A History of the Principal Discoveries and Improvements in the Several Arts and Sciences.* London, 1727.

    *Impartial History of the Life and Achievements of Peter Alexandrovitz.* London, 1723.

    *The Letters,* G. H. Healey (Ed.). London, 1955.

    *Madagascar.* London, 1890.

    *Memoirs of a Cavalier.* London, 1972.

    *New Voyage Round the World,* in *Duncan Campbell.* London, 1725.

    *A Plan of the English Commerce.* London, 1728.

    *The Poor Man's Plea.* London, 1698.

    *Religious Courtship.* Edinburgh, 1803.

    *The Review.* ed. A. W. Secord. New York, 1938.

    *Robinson Crusoe.* London, 1963.

    *A Tour of the Whole Island of Great Britain.* London, 1928.

Dekker, George, and J. P. McWilliams. *Fenimore Cooper: the Critical Heritage.* London, 1973.

Devanesan, C.D.S. *The Making of the Mahatma.* New Delhi, 1969.

Dinesen, Isak. *Out of Africa.* New York, 1938.

    *Shadows on the Grass.* New York, 1960.

Dottin, Paul. *The Life and Strange and Surprising Adventures of Daniel Defoe.* New York, 1929.

Earle, Peter. *The World of Defoe.* New York, 1977.

Edwardes (Lady). *Memorials of Herbert B. Edwardes.* London, 1886.

Elliott, J. H. *The Old World and the New 1492–1650,* Cambridge, 1970.

Ellis, John. *The Social History of the Machine Gun.* New York, 1975.

Emerson, R. W. *English Traits.* Boston, 1856.

Farwell, Byron. *The Man Who Presumed.* London, 1958.

Fenn, G. Manville. *G. A. Henty.* London, 1907.

Feuer, K. B. The Genesis of War and Peace. New York, 1965.

Feuer, Lewis. *The Scientific Intellectual.* New York, 1963.

Fleishman, Avrom. *The English Historical Novel.* Baltimore, Md., 1971.

Froude, J. A. *Oceana.* London, 1886.

Fussell, Paul. *The Great War and Modern Memory.* New York, 1975.

Giergielewicz, M. *Henryk Sienkiewicz.* New York, 1968.

Gleason, Abbott. *European and Muscovite.* Harvard University Press, Cambridge, Mass., 1972.

Gossett, T. F. *Race: the history of an idea in America.* Dallas, 1963.

Grieve, C. M. *Lucky Poet.* London, 1943.

Gross, Felix. *Rhodes of Africa.* London, 1956.

Guillen, Claude. *Literature as a System.* Princeton, New Jersey, 1971.

Haggard, H. Rider. *Allan Quatermaine, King Solomon's Mines, Nada the Lily.* Macdonald Illustrated Edition. London, 1949.

Hakluyt, Richard. *Voyages and Discoveries.* London, 1598.

Hall, James. *Letters from the West.* London, 1828.

Hall, R. *Stanley; an Adventurer Explored.* Boston, 1975.

Harcave, Sidney. *Years of the Golden Cockerel.* New York, 1968.

Hart, B. Liddell. *T.E. Lawrence, in Arabia and after.* London, 1934.

Hayden, John O. *Scott: the Critical Heritage.* New York, 1970.

Henkin, Leo J. *Darwinism and the English Novel.* New York, 1940.

Herzen, Alexander. *My Past and Thoughts.* New York, 1968.

Hill, H. *Mark Twain: God's Fool.* New York, 1973.

Hirst, F. W. *The Political Economy of the War.* London, 1915.

Hodgson, Margaret T. *Early Anthropology in the 16th and 17th Centuries.* Philadelphia, 1964.

Howard, Michael. *War in European History.* London, 1976.

Huet, Marie-Hélène. *Histoire des Aventures Extraordinaires.* Paris, 1973.

Hunt, J. W. *Forms of Glory.* Carbondale, Ill., 1973.

Huttenback, R. A. *The British Imperial Achievement.* New York, 1966.

Huxley, Aldous. *Grey Eminence.* New York, 1941.

Jackson, Henry W. *Robinson Crusoe—Social Engineer.* New York, 1922.

Johnson, W.R. *Darkness Visible.* Berkeley, Calif., 1976.

Joyce, James. *Daniel Defoe.* Buffalo, N.Y., 1964.

Kaplan, Justin. *Mark Twain and His World.* New York, 1974.
　　*Mr. Clemens and Mark Twain.* New York, 1966.

Kingsley, Charles. *The Heroes.* London, 1868.
　　*The Roman and the Teuton.* New York, 1891.
　　*Westward Ho!.* New York, 1934.

Kipling, Rudyard. "An English School," in *Land and Sea Tales.* London, 1923.
　　*Book of Words,* Burwash edition. Garden City, N.Y., 1941.

# Bibliography

    *From Sea to Sea.* Burwash edition. Garden City, N.Y., 1941.
    *Kim.* New York, 1959.
    *A Kipling Pageant,* Garden City, N.Y., 1935.
    *Letters on Leave,* in *Uncollected Prose.* New York, 1941.
    *Letters of Travel.* New York, 1941.
    *Many Inventions.* Burwash edition. Garden City, N.Y., 1941.
    *The Naulakha.* New York, 1891.
    *Something of Myself.* Burwash edition. Garden City, N.Y., 1941.
    *Stalky and Co.,* New York, 1959.
    *The War and the Fleet in Being.* Burwash edition. Garden City, N.Y., 1941.
Kisch, H. M. *A Young Victorian in India,* E. A. W. Cohen (Ed.). London, 1957.
Kliushevsky, V.O. *Peter the Great.* London, 1958.
Koebner, Richard. *Empire.* London, 1961.
    with H.D. Schmidt. *Imperialism.* London, 1964.
Krause, Sidney J. *Mark Twain as Critic.* Baltimore, Md., 1967.
Lane, Michael. *Introduction to Structuralism.* New York, 1970.
Laqueur, Walter. *Guerilla.* Boston, 1976.
Leach, Edmund. "The Legitimacy of Solomon," in Lane, *Introduction to Structuralism.*
Lensen, G.A. *Russia's Eastward Expansion.* New Jersey, 1964.
Lévi-Strauss, Claude. *Tristes Tropiques.* New York, 1977.
Levin, David. *History as Romantic Art.* Stanford, Calif., 1959.
Longworth, Philip. *The Cossacks.* New York, 1969.
Lord, John. *Duty, Honor, Empire.* New York, 1970.
McWilliams, J. P. *Political Justice in a Republic,* Berkeley, Calif., 1972.
Macaulay, T.B. "Lord Clive" and "Warren Hastings" in *Essays.* London, 1907.
Mack, John E. *A Prince of Our Disorder.* Boston, 1976.
MacShane, Frank. *The Life of Raymond Chandler.* New York, 1976.
Marryat, F. *Masterman Ready.* London, 1937.
Mason, Philip. *Kipling.* New York, 1975.
    *A Matter of Honour.* London, 1974.
    *Prospero's Magic.* London, 1962.
Maurois, André. *The Titans.* New York, 1957.
Meigs, Cornelia, Eaton, Anne, and Viguers, Ruth Hill. *A Critical History of Children's Literature.* New York, 1953.
Meyers, Jeffrey. *Fiction and the Colonial Experience.* Rowman and Littlefield, Totawa, N.J., 1973.
Millin, S.G. *Rhodes.* London, 1933.
Moon, Parker T. *Imperialism and World Politics.* New York, 1928.
Moore, Arthur K. *The Frontier Mind.* Lexington, Ky. 1957.
Morgan, Edward S. *The Puritan Family.* New York, 1966.
Morris, James. *Heaven's Command.* New York, 1968.
    *Pax Britannica.* New York, 1973.
Moskowitz, Sam. *Explorers of the Infinite.* New York, 1973.
Mott, Frank L. *Golden Multitudes.* New York, 1947.
Mudrick, Marvin. ed. *Conrad: 20th Century Views.* New Jersey, 1966.
Mumford, Lewis. *Technics and Civilization.* New York, 1934.
Naipaul, V.S. *The Loss of El Dorado.* New York, 1969.
Nef, John U. *War and Human Progress.* Cambridge, Mass., 1950.
Novak, Max. *Defoe and the Nature of Man.* New York, 1963.

O'Connor, John J. "Amadis de Gaul" and Its Influence on Elizabethan Literature. New Brunswick, N.J., 1970.
Orwell, George. "Such, Such, Were the Joys," in A Collection of Essays. New York, 1970.
Pace, Antonio. Benjamin Franklin and Italy. Philadelphia, 1958.
Parker, Alexander A. Literature and the Delinquent. Edinburgh, 1967.
Parkman, F. The Oregon Trail. Madison, Wis., 1969.
Parry, J. H. The Age of Reconnaissance. Cleveland, 1963.
        Trade and Dominion. New York, 1971.
Paton, James. The Story of John G. Paton. New York, 1896.
Payne, Robert. The White Rajahs of Sarawak. London, 1960.
Petit, Paul. Pax Romana. Berkeley, Calif., 1967.
Philbrick, Thomas. James Fenimore Cooper and the Development of American Sea Fiction. Cambridge, Mass., 1961.
Plum, H.G. Restoration Puritanism. Chapel Hill, N. Car., 1943.
Prescott, W.H. The Conquest of Mexico. New York, 1913.
Raeff, Marc. Michael Speransky. The Hague, 1969.
        Peter the Great. Boston, 1963.
Rayfield, Donald. The Dream of Lhasa. Athens, Ohio, 1977.
Reynolds, Reginald. White Sahibs in India. London, 1946.
Ridley, Hugh. "Germany in the Mirror of Its Colonial Literature," German Life and Letters. July 1975.
Robinson M.B. "The House of the Mighty Warrior . . . ?" in Lane Introduction to Structuralism.
Rogers, Pat. Grub Street. London, 1972.
Rogin, M.P. Fathers and Children. New York, 1975.
Ross, John F. Swift and Defoe. Los Angeles, 1941.
Runciman, Steven. The White Rajahs of Sarawak. London, 1960.
Salmon, Edward, and Longden, Major A. A. The Literature and Art of the Empire. London, 1924.
Schmitt B.F. (Ed.) Poland. Berkeley, California, 1945.
Scholes, Robert. Structuralism and Literature. New Haven, Conn., 1974.
Schücking, Levin L. The Puritan Family. New York, 1970.
Scott, Walter. The Fair Maid of Perth. Sterling Edition, Boston, 1892.
        The Journal, W.E.K. Anderson, (Ed.). London, 1972.
        The Legend of Montrose. Sterling Edition, Boston, 1892.
        The Pirate. Sterling Edition, Boston, 1892.
        Quentin Durward. Sterling Edition, Boston, 1892.
        Rob Roy. Century Edition, Edinburgh, 1870.
        The Surgeon's Daughter. in A Legend of Montrose.
        Waverley. New York, 1969.
Seeley, J.R. The Expansion of England. Chicago, 1971.
Seelye, John. Prophetic Waters. New York, 1977.
        "Some Green Thoughts on a Green Theme," Tri-Quarterly, 1972.
Semmel, Bernard. Imperialism and Social Reform. Cambridge, Mass., 1960.
Simmons, E.J. Tolstoy. Boston, 1946.
Slotkin, R. Regeneration Through Violence, Middletown, Conn., 1973.
Smiles, Samuel. Character. London, 1878.
        Lives of the Engineers. London 1874.
        Self-Help. London, 1958.
        George Stephenson. Boston, 1858.

# Bibliography

Smith, H.N. *Mark Twain: the development of a writer*. Cambridge, Mass., 1962.
  *Mark Twain: 20th Century Views*. Englewood Cliffs, N.J., 1963.
  *Virgin Land*. Cambridge, Mass., 1950.
Sombart, W. *Luxury and Capitalism*. Ann Arbor, Mich., 1967.
Spiller, R.E. *Fenimore Cooper*. New York, 1931.
Stevenson, R.L. *From Scotland to Silverado*. Cambridge, Mass., 1966.
Strachey, J. *The End of Empire*. New York, 1960.
Street, Brian V. *The Savage in Literature*. London, 1975.
Sumner, B.H. *Peter the Great*. London, 1950.
  *Survey of Russian History*. London, 1944.
Swift, J. *Gulliver's Travels*, in *Works*, ed. W. Scott, vol. XII.
Thaden, E.C. *Conservative Nationalism in 19th Century Russia*. Seattle, Wash., 64.
Thomas, Henry. *Spanish and Portuguese Romances of Chivalry*. London, 1920.
Thompson, J.W. *A History of Historical Writing*. New York, 1942.
Tolstoy, Alexandra. *Tolstoy: A Life of My Father*. New York, 1953.
Tolstoy, L.N. *The Cossacks and the Raid*. New York, 1961.
  *Hadji Murad*, in *Posthumous Works*, Vol. I, New York, 1920.
  *War and Peace*. New York, 1966.
Tolstoy, Sonia. *The Diary of Tolstoy's Wife*. London, 1928.
Traversi, Derek. *Shakespeare: The Roman Plays*. Stanford, Calif., 1963.
Trelawny, E.J. *Adventures of a Younger Son*. New York, 1974.
Turner F.J. *The Frontier in American History*. New York, 1953.
Twain, Mark. *Connecticut Yankee*. New York, 1963.
  *Following the Equator*. Author's National Edition, New York, vol. XV.
  *Life on the Mississippi*. Stormfield Edition, New York, *Letters*, Stormfield.
    New York
  *Mark Twain-Howells Letters*. Cambridge, Mass., 1960.
  *Notebooks and Journals*. Berkeley, 1975.
  *Roughing It*. Stormfield Edition, New York,
Van Dijk, Tenn A. *Some Aspects of Text Grammars*. The Hague, 1972.
Veblen, Thorstein. *Imperial Germany and the Industrial Revolution*. New York, 1915.
  *The Viking Veblen*, Max Lerner (Ed.). New York, 1948.
Vorpahl, B.M. *My Dear Wister -*. Palo Alto, Calif., 1973.
Waith, Eugene M., ed. *Shakespeare's Histories: 20th Century Views*. Englewood
  Cliffs, New Jersey, 1965.
Watts, C.Y., ed. *Joseph Conrad's Letters to R. B. Cunninghame Graham*. Cambridge,
  1969.
Wallerstein, Immanuel. *The Modern World System*. New York, 1974.
Ward, J.H. *Andrew Jackson*. New York, 1955.
Watson, Colin. *Snobbery with Violence*. London, 1971.
Watt, Ian. *The Rise of the Novel*. Berkeley, Calif., 1957.
Webb, W.J. *The Great Frontier*. Boston, 1952.
Weil, Simone. *The Iliad; or the Poem of Force*. Pendle Hill, 1956.
White, J.M. *Cortes and the Downfall of the Aztec Empire*. New York, 1971.
Wolff, Tatiana. *Pushkin on Literature*. London, 1971.
Woolf, Leonard. *Growing*. London, 1961.
Ziff, Larzer. *Puritanism in America*, New York, 1973.
Zweig, Paul. *The Adventurer*, New York, 1974.

# Index

# Index

# Index

# Index

# Index

# Index

# Index

Mille, Pierre, 397, 398
Millin, Sarah G., 287, 398
Milner, Alfred, 285
Milton, John, 40, 64, 156, 209, 352, 355
*Mind at the End of Its Tether* (Wells), 336
*Mine Own People* (Kipling), 278
Mir Jaffir (Indian prince), 32
*Mirror of the Sea, A* (Conrad), 402
Mirsky, D. S., 181
Mitford, Nancy, 369
*Moby Dick* (Melville), 87, 140
Modern empire, 3–36; Arendt on, 400; capitalist adventure and, 20–27; caste and (*see* Caste); Cooper and, 129–32; dating, 5–7; energizing myth of, 3–4, 7, 345; Belgian, 239, 258–63, 303, 387–88; French, 397–98; German, 167, 168, 239–40, 256–57, 397–98; historical adventurers of, 27–36 *(see also specific historical adventurers);* Kipling and, 285–89, 389–400; modern world system and, 7–14, 345; resistance to, 338–44; Russian (*see* Tolstoy, Lev); Scott and, 118–20
"Modest Proposal, A" (Swift), 90
Modjeska, Helena, 301
Moffat, Robert, 120
*Moll Flanders* (Defoe), 51, 70, 73
Moltke, Count Helmuth von, 378
*Monikins, The* (Cooper), 156
*Montalbodo, Francanzano, 38*
*Montcalm and Wolfe* (Parkman), 153, 376
Montesquieu, Baron de la Brède et de, 122
Montezuma, 27, 29, 30, 32, 88
Montgomerie, Capt. T. G., 270
Moon, Parker T., 342
Moore, Arthur K., 159, 373
Moore, George, 125
Moore, Tom, 112
More, Hannah, 352–53, 371
Morgan, Edmund S., 353
Morris, Christopher, 356
Morris, James, 114, 218, 232, 276, 277, 290, 326
Morris, William, 276, 277, 402
Morse, Samuel, 239

Moses, Claude, 325
"Mother-Hive, The" (Kipling), 350
Motley, John Lathrop, 31, 153–55, 376, 377–78
Mott, F. L., 245
*Mr. Midshipman Easy* (Marryat), 214–15
*Mrs. Dalloway* (Woolf), 296
Mudrick, Marvin, 316
Mullah, Kazi, 194
Müller, Max, 384
Mumford, Lewis, 12, 345–46, 362
*Music of Time, The* (Powell), 336
*My Dear Wister* (Vorpahl), 254
*My Kalulu: Prince, King and Slave* (Stanley), 261
*My Past and Thoughts* (Herzen), 178
Myth: energizing, 3–4, 7, 345; structuralist approach to, 55–57; *see also* Adventure narratives; *and specific titles*

Nabokov, Vladimir, 175
Nader (Félix Tournachon), 227
*Nada the Lily* (Haggard), 231–32
Naipaul, V. S., 332, 335
Napier, Sir Charles, 120, 208
Napoleon I, 7, 152, 299, 355; as historical hero, 25, 27, 35–36; in popular literature, 231; Rhodes and, 287; Scott and, 101, 111, 361; Tolstoy and, 169, 176, 196
Napoleon III, 192, 225
*Narrative of a Pilgrimage to Meccah and Medinah* (Burton), 291
Narvaez, Pánfilo de, 348
*Naulahka, The* (Kipling), 393–94
Nechaev, Sergei, 180, 196
Nef, John U., 11
Nelson, Horatio, 152, 322, 355
Nevins, Allan, 153
Newbolt, Henry, 222, 223, 321
*New Family Instructor, The* (Defoe), 70
*New Machiavelli, The* (Wells), 279
Newman, Cardinal, 110
Newton, Sir Isaac, 205, 356
Newton, John, 371
*New Voyage Round the World, A* (Defoe), 71–74, 85
Nicholas I, Czar, 165, 178

# Index

# Index

# Index

78734

PN
3448
A3
G7

GREEN, MARTIN
    DREAMS OF ADVENTURE, DEEDS OF

| DATE DUE | |
|---|---|
| DEC 2 0 1996 | |
| | |
| | |
| | |
| | |
| | |
| | |
| | |
| | |
| | |
| | |
| | |
| | |
| | |

Fernald Library
Colby-Sawyer College
New London, New Hampshire

GAYLORD                                    PRINTED IN U.S.A.